Doing Right and Being Good
Catholic and Protestant Readings in Christian Ethics

Introduced with Essays and Edited by

David Oki Ahearn

and

Peter R. Gathje

A Michael Glazier Book

LITURGICAL PRESS
Collegeville, Minnesota

www.litpress.org

Cover design by Joachim Rhoades, O.S.B. Cover photo courtesy of Getty Images.

Essays by the editors include references to the "The Catholic Edition of the New Revised Standard Version of the Bible (NRSV), copyright 1965, 1966 by the Division of Christian Education of the National Council of the Churches of Christ in the United States of America. Used by permission. All rights reserved.

Where noted, the NRSV and RSV translations were used to adapt quoted excerpts to modern standards of inclusive language. NRSV is copyrighted as above. Revised Standard Version of the Bible, copyright 1952 [2nd edition, 1971] by the Division of Christian Education of the National Council of the Churches of Christ in the United States of America. Used by permission. All rights reserved.

In all other instances, quoted excerpts were sometimes adapted by the editors themselves for inclusive language, otherwise excerpts are quoted as from the source.

A Michael Glazier Book published by the Liturgical Press

1   2   3   4   5   6   7   8

Library of Congress Cataloging-in-Publication Data

Doing right and being good : Catholic and Protestant readings in Christian ethics / introduced with essays and edited by David Oki Ahearn and Peter R. Gathje.
    p. cm.
    Summary: "Introduces the reader to the sources of Christian ethics and to critical reflection on moral issues, including interpretations of love, justice, and the formation of a virtuous character. Selected readings discuss issues of family and sexuality, violence and peace, economic justice, abortion, and euthanasia"—Provided by publisher.
    Includes bibliographical references and index.
    ISBN 13: 978-0-8146-5179-7 (pbk. : alk. paper)
    ISBN 10: 0-8146-5179-8 (pbk. : alk. paper)
    1. Christian ethics.   I. Ahearn, David Oki. II. Gathje, Peter R.

BJ1251.D65 2005
241—dc22   2004022421

CONTENTS

Chapter Seven: Christian Love at the Margins of Life

ACKNOWLEDGMENTS

I am grateful to my coauthor, Peter R. Gathje, for his dedicated work on this project. I can only hope that the readers of this book will learn half as much from it as I have from him. I also wish to thank the administration of LaGrange College for granting me a sabbatical leave so that I could finish the book. I also wish to express my gratitude to the students in my Christian ethics classes who endured an unfinished version of this text and offered many helpful suggestions about how it could be improved. You all taught me how to teach! I am especially appreciative of the editorial staff at the Liturgical Press, who were the very model of encouragement and support throughout this endeavor. Finally, I am as always indebted to my wife, Minako Oki Ahearn, who would not let me abandon this project during its many years of gestation.

David Oki Ahearn

I am grateful to David Ahearn for suggesting that we work together on this book and for all of the hard work he has done to bring this project to completion. Further, I want to express my gratitude to the Open Door Community of Atlanta and how they have been my teacher in the practice of Christian ethics. I would also like to thank my students at Christian Brothers University and in the Adult Theology Program in the Diocese of Little Rock for their willingness to engage in serious moral discussion in light of their Christian faith. Finally, I am continuously graced by the good moral sense, intellectual insight, and love of my wife, Jennifer Case.

Peter R. Gathje

INTRODUCTION

The title of this book is *Doing Right and Being Good: Protestant and Catholic Readings in Christian Ethics.* As the title indicates, this book falls within the discipline of ethics. And what is *ethics?* In brief, ethics is critical reflection on morality. *Morality,* in turn, is the construction of values, beliefs and practices that order our life in society. It concerns our sense of how we should behave and how others should behave toward us. Our morality is the values we hold so deeply that they are visible to us only in the breach. Like the blue sky and green grass, morality recedes into the background of our expectations. For example, we do not get up in the morning and ruminate about whether we should wear clothing that day. We would be aware that this is a deeply held value only if one our colleagues marched into class naked!

Most of our lives, then, are governed by morality and not ethics. In fact, our morality is most powerful when we don't think about it at all. In static, isolated societies, the hegemony of morality is complete. These societies are guided unerringly by custom and the received wisdom of the past. Life *is* as it *should be* and *should be* as it *is*.

What, then, is the point of ethics? If morality is most powerful when it is invisible, why should we want to reflect critically on it? In the modern world, we actually have little choice in the matter. First, we cannot simply take our moral universe for granted in our pluralistic world. We are aware that our ethos is just one of many, so we have no choice but to justify it through some sort of critical reasoning. Second, our moral universe often gives us conflicting guidance. We are taught, for example, *both* to be loyal children to our parents *and* to be autonomous, self-directed persons. It is not always clear which of these mandates applies when. Figuring out such questions is a task of ethics. Third, in our world we have to adapt to continual change. The breathtaking development of technology in the modern world has gone hand in hand with an equally breathtaking restructuring of our social institutions. Consider, for example, how even a single new technology like the automobile or telephone has utterly changed family life, work patterns, travel, and even the basic architecture of cities. It is not always clear what ancient wisdom can say to us now. The discipline of ethics helps us sort through what must endure and what must adapt.

This book is a work in *Christian* ethics. All normative ethics is particular. Each system has a modifier, either explicit or implicit. We might have, then, *Buddhist* ethics or *Thomistic* ethics or *postmodern* ethics, but never ethics *simpliciter*. In this book, we will examine the singular way that *Christians* do ethics. Christian ethics has emerged from an unbroken conversation that has endured across generations. This conversation employs a common moral language that is shared by conversation partners. We will wrestle in this study with some key moral terms like love and justice that have particular meanings in the Christian moral tradition. We will return again and again to the Christian *Scriptures*, which are foundational for the Church's moral vision. We'll also seek guidance from some figures in Christian history whose ethical reflections have been especially important in the development of this conversation.

The dialogue must continue with you, the reader. The contributors to this book endeavor to engage you in conversation about what it means to live a good life. You have no choice but to start this conversation from your particular place, as the person who has been formed by a specific moral and religious community. If you have been shaped by the Christian tradition, you might engage these writers with hopes of gaining *normative* guidance for your life—that is, providing insights about how you should live. Those who have been shaped by other traditions may see the book as a work in *descriptive* ethics—that is, an opportunity to gain some insights into how those people called Christians think that *they* should live. In any case, the authors of this book hope that it provokes constructive reflection and dialogue for *all* of its readers, regardless of their backgrounds and identities. We all are human beings, after all, with at least some enduring needs and wants. There is considerable overlap between cultures and religions in what is considered "right conduct" or "a good life." Thus, while all ethics is *particular,* none can be *exclusive. Christian* ethics is a particular manifestation of the common enterprise of *human* ethics.

In this book we will examine two broad ways of thinking about ethics: one that asks what it means *to do right* and another that asks what it *means to be good*.[1] The first type of ethics is interested primarily in determining the rightness or wrongness of specific acts and our duties toward them. Moral philosophers call this type of ethics "deontology" (literally, "the science of duty") or simply "the ethics of obligation." In Christian ethics, this type of ethics has been concerned to comprehend and follow God's commands. The second type of ethics is concerned more with character traits than specific actions, more with

---

[1] H. Richard Niebuhr argued persuasively that these two types of ethics should be supplemented by a third: an ethics of "responsibility" that seeks to act appropriately to God's action on us. Niebuhr developed this third way through his concept of covenant. We have not treated the ethics of responsibility as a third type in this book, but rather see it as a perspective that is woven through the other two perspectives. See H. Richard Niebuhr, "The Meaning of Responsibility" in The Responsible Self: An Essay in Christian Moral Philosophy (New York: Harper & Row, 1963) 47–68.

being than doing. Its central task is to delineate the virtues that form a well-lived life. Moral philosophers call this type of ethics "virtue ethics."

These two paths are by no means exclusive, however. It is impossible to separate duty and character, even on the theoretical level. Good persons do good acts and good acts build good character. Every moral obligation (for example, "love your neighbor as yourself" (Matt 19:19) has a corresponding virtue (e.g., Christian love, or *agape*). To reflect this congruency, our title places the conjunction "and" between "Doing Right" and "Being Good."

The book's subtitle refers to two broad Christian ethical traditions: Catholic and Protestant. These two traditions have taken divergent paths at critical junctures. At times the debate between them has been quite contentious. The inclusion of readings from both Catholic and Protestant traditions thus means that no reader will agree with all of the positions that are represented. In fact, some readings may even produce outright consternation! Nevertheless, it is always a useful enterprise to study the viewpoints of others, if for no other reason than to reaffirm one's own tradition on a deeper level. However, the authors of this text also share the conviction that respectful dialogue between traditions can produce a deeper appreciation for the traditions of the others. The first ground of our hope is our common heritage. Protestants and Catholics share an allegiance to the teachings and example of Jesus. We are guided by common Scriptures. We affirm the same ecumenical creeds. Until the sixteenth century, we also were shaped by the same "giants" in Christian history. Among the authors studied in this book, both Catholics and Protestants look to Tertullian, Thomas Aquinas, Bernard of Clairvaux, and Augustine as belonging to "their story."

A second ground of hope is the ecumenical dialogue that has taken place between the two traditions in recent decades. Protestant and Catholic ethicists have been engaged in deep, respectful dialogue with one another and have learned a great deal from the other's tradition. Many Protestant ethicists are working out new understandings of virtue and are endeavoring to ground Christian ethics in common human experience. Many Catholics, for their part, are turning to traditional Protestant emphases like grace and freedom. The result has been a simultaneous diversification within traditions and convergence between them. As James Gustafson writes, "some Roman Catholics have more in common in theological ethics with some Protestants than they do with other Catholics; some Protestants have more in common with some Roman Catholics than they do other Protestants."[2] In any case, neither Protestants nor Catholics can do Christian ethics in isolation from each other. We all have a great deal that we can and must learn from one another. Thus, this book is a study of Protestant and Catholic Christian ethics, both classical and contemporary, that explore what it means to "do right" and "be good."

---

[2] James M. Gustafson, Protestant and Roman Catholic Ethics: Prospects for Rapprochement (Chicago: University of Chicago Press, 1978) 156.

The first three chapters of the book will explore questions of ethical methodology: (1) an understanding of the moral person; (2) the use of sources—Scripture, tradition, reason, and experience—in Christian ethics; and (3) an exploration of the central moral norms of love and justice in Christian ethics. After addressing these methodological matters, the remainder of the book will explore some issues that are especially contentious in Christian ethics today: (4) marriage, family, and sexuality; (5) war and violence; (6) stewardship of the economy and environment; and (7) our obligations to those at the margins; that is, those not yet born and those soon to die.

Chapter One

The Moral Person

What is the relation between who we are and what we do? How do we become good persons who consistently know and do what is right? In the history of Christian ethics these questions have been typically addressed under two broad areas of analysis: moral character and conscience.

Moral Character

The analysis of moral character is concerned with the processes, both internal (spiritual and psychological) and external (the influence of other persons and institutions), by which we become good persons. There has been a long and intense debate about how to delineate those processes and define what is meant by "good person." Within Christian ethics Thomas Aquinas' work from the thirteenth century remains central to this debate (reading 2). His understanding of the characteristics of human persons and his discussion of the processes of the formation of persons as good drew upon both classical Greek philosophy, especially Aristotle, and biblical understandings.

For Aquinas, the human person has specific characteristics endowed by God through creation, and with the aid of human society and grace (mediated by the church) those characteristics are developed toward the goal of union with God. We are created for union with God and the good human person is on that journey toward God. The good human person thus develops moral virtues and is endowed by grace with theological virtues that empower the person to consistently and rightly practice the human capabilities necessary for moral excellence.

Aquinas drew on classical philosophy to discuss the four cardinal moral virtues of courage (or fortitude), prudence, temperance, and justice—and their connection with specific capabilities in human life. He drew upon the Bible and the Christian tradition to discuss the theological virtues of faith, hope, and love and to show how each of them addresses aspects of our being human. Aquinas argued that as each of these virtues flourish in our lives, our various

1

capabilities of being human are coordinated and perfected in accord with the true end of human life, namely, union with God.

Aquinas' discussion of what it means to be a good human being and the processes by which we become good has remained crucial in the ongoing debate about moral character. In particular two large issues continue to focus the debate. The first is the relationship between human effort and grace in the development of the good human life. The second is the grounding of the understanding of what it means to be a good person in some vision of human nature or understanding of human capabilities.

What Is the Relation of Grace with Human Effort in the Life of Virtue?

Discussion of the relationship between grace and human effort within the process of moral formation traditionally reflected a theological split between Catholicism and Protestantism. The former emphasized the complementarity of grace with human effort since the human effort itself was seen as made possible by God's creation of humans with certain capacities. The latter position is exemplified by Martin's Luther's treatise, *Concerning Christian Liberty* (reading 3). Luther believed that human effort was so tainted by sin as to be worthless in terms of moving toward union with God. Against the historic Catholic emphasis on complementarity of divine grace and human works, Luther emphasized free, unmerited grace, believing that a focus on human effort would lead to works righteousness. Luther's position can be summed up in the Protestant slogan: *sola fide* (faith alone), *sola gratia* (grace alone), and *sola scriptura* (Scripture alone).

There has been significant theological development within both Catholic and Protestant circles to resolve this split, so that today a consensus of sorts has been emerging. This is evident in the renewed emphasis in Catholic ethics upon grace and the centrality of Christ for the Christian moral life, while in Protestant ethics there is a renewed attention to the development of moral character. Peter R. Gathje reflects the former convergence. His essay on moral personhood (reading 4) reflects his Roman Catholic roots by drawing on phenomenological observation, but it also includes the traditionally Protestant emphasis on our relationship with God, sin, and grace as dimensions of human existence revealed in the Bible. We can see the latter convergence in Stanley Hauerwas' work (reading 5) on virtue ethics. Writing from the Methodist tradition, Hauerwas not only has played an important role in revitalizing attention to moral character not only in Protestant ethics, but in contemporary Catholic ethics as well. In particular, Hauerwas argues for a mediation of God's grace through story and the church community.

What Is a Good Human Being?

When we turn to the second issue, that of the ground for our understanding of what it means to be a good person in some vision of human nature, there is much contemporary debate. For Aquinas the understanding of what it meant to be a good human person was metaphysically grounded. Aquinas argued that God creates humans in a certain way, and this divine structuring of human life is knowable by reason with the help, when necessary, of revelation. Today there is significantly less confidence in our reason's ability to know universal and timeless characteristics of being human. One factor in this development has been the growing recognition of the historically and culturally conditioned quality of human thought. Additionally, there is also the recognition that attempts to define what is "human" are fraught with the danger of defining some *out* of the human community since they do not conform to a particular definition. This has happened historically in the case of slaves, women, and various indigenous peoples. It is also evident in current debates about moral personhood in regard to abortion, euthanasia, and cloning.

There are currently two major competitors for replacing a metaphysically grounded conception of the good human person. The first focuses on the psychological dynamics of moral development. This approach attempts to provide a universal grounding for an understanding of what it means to be a good human person, but it is psychology instead of metaphysics that provides the grounding. The work of developmental psychologists, such as Jean Piaget, Lawrence Kohlberg, and Erik Erikson—and especially the contemporary theologian James Fowler—has been crucial in this field. Each of these, in various ways, gives stages of moral development through which, it is argued, human beings must pass to reach moral maturity. At each stage, cognitive, moral affective, and faith dimensions of life are interlinked. Critics of such theories seek to show how the purported stages reflect biases of gender, social class, or institutional structures that are characteristic of only some societies. For example, Carol Gilligan has criticized the work of Lawrence Kohlberg, arguing that women's moral experience is ignored in his particular conception of moral development.

The second competitor for replacing a metaphysically grounded conception of the good human person draws upon more "external" sources. These can take the form of the narrative and/or the social construction of human identity or phenomenology. Narrative theory emphasizes the role of story in the forming of understandings of not only the individual self but also entire communities. We make sense of our lives through narrative structures that order our experiences into coherent stories that have recognizable beginnings and movement toward certain ends. Alasdair McIntyre's work in philosophical ethics has been crucial in advancing this narrative view. In theological ethics the work of Stanley Hauerwas has been central, and we can see in his essay how he attends to both story and the church as the major sources for the formation of moral character.

Though not focused exclusively on narrative, social construction theory examines how human understandings of "reality," including what it means to be a good human being, emerge through the complex interplay of our social relationships, including institutional arrangements in particular societies. Berger and Luckmann's *The Social Construction of Reality* remains the foundational work in this area. Close to this sociologically grounded approach is that of phenomenology. A phenomenological approach to the issue of what it means to be a human person relies upon observation of human life over time. It may thus draw upon both narrative and understandings drawn from social and institutional dynamics of human life. Gathje's essay draws on phenomenological observations of human life, supplemented by the biblical narrative and its insights into the human condition.

All three of these approaches share the conviction that our understandings of what it means to be human are socially conditioned. Critics of them point to the danger of cultural relativism, since too heavy of an emphasis upon the social and historical construction of our understanding can lead to the view that there are no moral standards that transcend particular cultures. There thus remains a significant challenge for moral development theories along with narrative, social construction, and phenomenological theories. How might we develop understandings of the good human person sufficiently chastened by recognition of the historical and cultural limitations of our understandings that still have some degree of cross-cultural commonality? Without that commonality it is difficult to see how an understanding of the good human person would be able to serve as the basis for evaluation of our moral development, both as individuals and societies. And without such a basis we do not have merely cultural pluralism, but cultural relativism.

READINGS

---

1. Biblical Foundations

A. JEREMIAH 31:29-34

The prophet Jeremiah wrote during the sixth century B.C.E., the time of the destruction of Judah and the exile of its inhabitants to Babylon. These disastrous events seemed to toll the death knells of the Jewish people and its faith. Nevertheless, Jeremiah speaks words of hope. He looks forward to a new age in which faithful Jews will no longer follow the law as an external authority. Rather, he sees a "new covenant" in which the law will be written on the heart.

B. Galatians 3:19-29; 5:1-26

In this early letter, Paul struggles to relate the old path of righteousness set forth in the Hebrew scriptures with a new life of faith that is characterized by freedom in Christ. Paul sets aside the many commandments of his Jewish past for one new standard: faith working through love. The Christian life is for Paul a radical freedom ruled only by the demands of love. Paul is sensitive to the human tendency to abuse this freedom, however. He sets forth some vices that indicate "works of the flesh" and some virtues that indicate "fruit of the Spirit."

C. Colossians 3:1-17

The authorship and context of this letter, once attributed to Paul, is now a matter of debate among New Testament scholars. The author urges his audience to "put to death" their old earthly natures and take on a new nature modeled after the image of the Creator. This new life in Christ gives flower to a whole new set of virtues: "compassion, kindness, humility, meekness, patience," love and forgiveness.

2. Thomas Aquinas, Selections from the *Summa Theologiae*

Thomas Aquinas (1225–1274) wrote the Summa Theologiae[1] *as a manual of Christian theology for the use of students. Aquinas systematically works through the major theological issues of his day. Each section is comprised of a question, a brief list of objections to his position, a citation of an authority, Aquinas' own position on the question, and finally a reply to the objections. (We have included only the question and Aquinas' response when quoting from the* Summa *in this book.) The selections in this chapter are from the section of the* Summa *called the "Treatise on Habits." Here Aquinas builds on Aristotle's philosophy of virtue, adding to it the theological virtues, which are rooted in revelation and aim toward the ultimate good of the love of God. Note that this translation uses the traditional word "charity" for Christian love.*

WHETHER HABITS ARE DIVIDED INTO GOOD AND BAD

I answer that, as stated above, habits are specifically distinct not only in respect of their objects and active principles, but also in their relation to nature. Now, this happens in two ways. First, by reason of their suitableness or

---

[1] Thomas Aquinas, *Summa Theologiae,* translated by the Fathers of the English Dominican Province under the title *Summa Theologica* (New York: Benzinger Brothers, 1948). Readings are selections from the First Part of the Second Part (*Prima Secundae Partis* = I-II), questions 54, article 3 (= 54.3); 55.1; 58.3; 61.2; 62.1–4; 63.1–2; 64.1 and 64.4; 65.2–3.

unsuitableness to nature. In this way a good habit is specifically distinct from a bad habit: since a good habit is one which disposes to an act suitable to the agent's nature, while an evil habit is one which disposes to an act unsuitable to nature. Thus, acts of virtue are suitable to human nature, since they are according to reason, whereas acts of vice are discordant from human nature, since they are against reason. Hence it is clear that habits are distinguished specifically by the difference of good and bad.

Secondly, habits are distinguished in relation to nature, from the fact that one habit disposes to an act that is suitable to a lower nature, while another habit disposes to an act befitting a higher nature. And thus human virtue, which disposes to an act befitting human nature, is distinct from godlike or heroic virtue, which disposes to an act befitting some higher nature.

WHETHER HUMAN VIRTUE IS A HABIT

I answer that, [v]irtue denotes a certain perfection of a power. Now a thing's perfection is considered chiefly in regard to its end. But the end of power is act. Wherefore power is said to be perfect, according as it is determinate to its act.

Now there are some powers which of themselves are determinate to their acts; for instance, the active natural powers. And therefore these natural powers are in themselves called virtues. But the rational powers, which are proper to humans,[2] are not determinate to one particular action, but are inclined indifferently to many: and they are determinate to acts by means of habits, as is clear from what we have said above. Therefore human virtues are habits.

WHETHER VIRTUE IS ADEQUATELY DIVIDED INTO MORAL AND INTELLECTUAL

I answer that, human virtue is a habit perfecting human beings in view of their doing good deeds. Now, in humans there are but two principles of human actions, viz. the intellect or reason and the appetite: for these are the two principles of movement in humans as stated in *De Anima* iii, text. 48. Consequently every human virtue must needs be a perfection of one of these principles. Accordingly if it perfects human speculative or practical intellect in order that one's deed may be good, it will be an intellectual virtue: whereas if it perfects one's appetite, it will be a moral virtue. It follows therefore that every human virtue is either intellectual or moral.

WHETHER THERE ARE FOUR CARDINAL VIRTUES

I answer that, things may be numbered either in respect of their formal principles, or according to the subjects in which they are: and either way we find that there are four cardinal virtues.

---

[2] The readings in this book have been adapted to present standards of sensitivity and inclusivity in regard to gender.

For the formal principle of the virtue of which we speak now is good as defined by reason; which good is considered in two ways. First, as existing in the very act of reason: and thus we have one principal virtue, called "Prudence." Secondly, according as the reason puts its order into something else; either into operations, and then we have "Justice"; or into passions, and then we need two virtues. For the need of putting the order of reason into the passions is due to their thwarting reason: and this occurs in two ways. First, by the passions inciting to something against reason, and then the passions need a curb, which we call "Temperance." Secondly, by the passions withdrawing us from following the dictate of reason, e.g. through fear of danger or toil: and then we need to be strengthened for that which reason dictates, lest we turn back; and to this end there is "Fortitude."

In like manner, we find the same number if we consider the subjects of virtue. For there are four subjects of the virtue we speak of now: viz. the power which is rational in its essence, and this is perfected by "Prudence"; and that which is rational by participation, and is threefold, the will, subject of "Justice," the concupiscible faculty, subject of "Temperance," and the irascible faculty, subject of "Fortitude."

WHETHER THERE ARE ANY THEOLOGICAL VIRTUES

I answer that, humans are perfected by virtue, for those actions whereby we are directed to happiness, as was explained above. Now human happiness is twofold, as was also stated above. One is proportionate to human nature, a happiness, to wit, which we can obtain by means of our natural principles. The other is a happiness surpassing human nature, and which we can obtain by the power of God alone, by a kind of participation of the Godhead, about which it is written (2 Pet 1:4) that by Christ we are made "partakers of the Divine nature." And because such happiness surpasses the capacity of human nature, our natural principles which enable us to act well according to our capacity, do not suffice to direct us to this same happiness. Hence it is necessary for us to receive from God some additional principles, whereby we may be directed to supernatural happiness, even as we are directed to our connatural end, by means of our natural principles, albeit not without Divine assistance. Such like principles are called "theological virtues": first, because their object is God, inasmuch as they direct us aright to God: secondly, because they are infused in us by God alone: thirdly, because these virtues are not made known to us, save by Divine revelation, contained in Holy Writ.

WHETHER THE THEOLOGICAL VIRTUES ARE DISTINCT FROM THE INTELLECTUAL AND MORAL VIRTUES

I answer that, as stated above, habits are specifically distinct from one another in respect of the formal difference of their objects. Now the object of the theological virtues is God, Who is the last end of all, as surpassing the knowledge of our reason. On the other hand, the object of the intellectual and moral virtues is something comprehensible to human reason. Wherefore the theological virtues are specifically distinct from the moral and intellectual virtues.

WHETHER FAITH, HOPE, AND CHARITY ARE FITTINGLY RECKONED AS THEOLOGICAL VIRTUES

I answer that, as stated above, the theological virtues direct humans to supernatural happiness in the same way as by the natural inclination we are directed to our connatural end. Now the latter happens in respect of two things. First, in respect of the reason or intellect, in so far as it contains the first universal principles which are known to us by the natural light of the intellect, and which are reason's starting-point, both in speculative and in practical matters. Secondly, through the rectitude of the will which tends naturally to good as defined by reason.

But these two fall short of the order of supernatural happiness, according to 1 Cor 2:9: "The eye hath not seen, nor ear heard, neither hath it entered into the human heart, what things God hath prepared for us that love God." Consequently in respect of both the above things we needed to receive in addition something supernatural to direct us to a supernatural end. First, as regards the intellect, we receive certain supernatural principles, which are held by means of a Divine light: these are the articles of faith, about which is *faith*. Secondly, the will is directed to this end, both as to that end as something attainable—and this pertains to *hope*—and as to a certain spiritual union, whereby the will is, so to speak, transformed into that end—and this belongs to *charity*. For the appetite of a thing is moved and tends towards its connatural end naturally; and this movement is due to a certain conformity of the thing with its end.

WHETHER FAITH PRECEDES HOPE, AND HOPE CHARITY

I answer that, order is twofold: order of generation, and order of perfection. By order of generation, in respect of which matter precedes form, and the imperfect precedes the perfect, in one same subject faith precedes hope, and hope charity, as to their acts: because habits are all infused together. For the movement of the appetite cannot tend to anything, either by hoping or loving, unless that thing be apprehended by the sense or by the intellect. Now it is by faith that the intellect apprehends the object of hope and love. Hence in the order of generation, faith precedes hope and charity. In like manner we love a thing because we apprehend it as our good. Now from the very fact that we hope to be able to obtain some good through someone, we look on the one in whom we hope as a good of our own. Hence for the very reason that we hope in someone, we proceed to love that one: so that in the order of generation, hope precedes charity as regards their respective acts.

But in the order of perfection, charity precedes faith and hope: because both faith and hope are quickened by charity, and receive from charity their full complement as virtues. For thus charity is the mother and the root of all the virtues, inasmuch as it is the form of them all, as we shall state further on.

WHETHER VIRTUE IS IN US BY NATURE

. . . To make this clear, it must be observed that there are two ways in which something is said to be natural to human beings; one is according to our specific nature, the other according to our individual nature. And, since each thing derives its species from its form, and its individuation from matter, and, again, since the form of human beings is our rational soul, while our matter as human beings is our body, whatever belongs to us in respect of our rational soul, is natural to us in respect of our specific nature; while whatever belongs to us in respect of the particular temperament of each of our bodies, is natural to us in respect of our individual nature. For whatever is natural to us in respect of our bodies, considered as part of our species, is to be referred, in a way, to the soul, in so far as this particular body is adapted to this particular soul.

In both these ways virtue is natural to us as humans inchoatively. This is so in respect of the specific nature, in so far as in human reason are to be found instilled by nature certain naturally known principles of both knowledge and action, which are the nurseries of intellectual and moral virtues, and in so far as there is in the will a natural appetite for good in accordance with reason. Again, this is so in respect of the individual nature, in so far as by reason of a disposition in the body, some are disposed either well or ill to certain virtues: because, to wit, certain sensitive powers are acts of certain parts of the body, according to the disposition of which these powers are helped or hindered in the exercise of their acts, and, in consequence, the rational powers also, which the aforesaid sensitive powers assist. In this way one person has a natural aptitude for science, another for fortitude, another for temperance: and in these ways, both intellectual and moral virtues are in us by way of a natural aptitude, inchoatively, but not perfectly, since nature is determined to one, while the perfection of these virtues does not depend on one particular mode of action, but on various modes, in respect of the various matters, which constitute the sphere of virtue's action, and according to various circumstances.

It is therefore evident that all virtues are in us by nature, according to aptitude and inchoation, but not according to perfection, except the theological virtues, which are entirely from without.

WHETHER ANY VIRTUE IS CAUSED IN US BY HABITUATION

I answer that, we have spoken above in a general way about the production of habits from acts; and speaking now in a special way of this matter in relation to virtue, we must take note that, as stated above, human virtue perfects us in relation to good. . . And since Divine Law is the higher rule, it extends to more things, so that whatever is ruled by human reason, is ruled by the Divine Law too; but the converse does not hold.

It follows that human virtue directed to the good which is defined according to the rule of human reason can be caused by human acts: inasmuch as such acts proceed from reason, by whose power and rule the aforesaid good is established. On the other hand, virtue which directs humans to good as defined by the Divine Law, and not by human reason, cannot be caused by human acts, the principle of which is reason, but is produced in us by the Divine operation alone. Hence Augustine in giving the definition of the latter virtue inserts the words, "which God works in us without us" (*Super Ps* 118, Serm. 26).

WHETHER MORAL VIRTUES CAN BE WITHOUT CHARITY

I answer that, as stated above, it is possible by means of human works to acquire moral virtues, in so far as they produce good works that are directed to an end not surpassing the natural power of humans: and when they are acquired thus, they can be without charity, even as they were in many of the Gentiles. But in so far as they produce good works in proportion to a supernatural last end, thus they have the character of virtue, truly and perfectly; and cannot be acquired by human acts, but are infused by God. Such like moral virtues cannot be without charity. For it has been stated above (I 58.4–5) that the other moral virtues cannot be without prudence; and that prudence cannot be without the moral virtues, because these latter make humans well disposed to certain ends, which are the starting-point of the procedure of prudence. Now for prudence to proceed aright, it is much more necessary that we be well disposed towards our ultimate end, which is the effect of charity, than that we be well disposed in respect of other ends, which is the effect of moral virtue: just as in speculative matters right reason has greatest need of the first indemonstrable principle, that "contradictories cannot both be true at the same time." It is therefore evident that neither can infused prudence be without charity; nor, consequently, the other moral virtues, since they cannot be without prudence.

It is therefore clear from what has been said that only the infused virtues are perfect, and deserve to be called virtues simply: since they direct humans well to the ultimate end. But the other virtues, those, namely, that are acquired, are virtues in a restricted sense, but not simply: for they direct humans well in respect of the last end in some particular genus of action, but not in respect of the last end simply. Hence a gloss of Augustine (cf. *Lib. Sentent.* Prosperi, 106) on the words, "All that is not of faith is sin" (Rom 14:23), says: "Those that fail to acknowledge the truth, have no true virtue, even if their conduct be good."

WHETHER CHARITY CAN BE WITHOUT MORAL VIRTUE

On the contrary, the whole Law is fulfilled through charity, for it is written (Rom 13:8): "Those that loveth their neighbor, hath fulfilled the Law." Now it is not possible to fulfil the whole Law, without having all the moral virtues: since the law contains precepts about all acts of virtue, as stated in *Ethic.* v, 1, 2. Therefore those that have charity, have all the moral virtues. Moreover, Augustine says in a letter (Epis. 167) that charity contains all the cardinal virtues.

I answer that, all the moral virtues are infused together with charity. The reason for this is that God operates no less perfectly in works of grace than in works of nature. Now, in the works of nature, we find that whenever a thing contains a principle of certain works, it has also whatever is necessary for their execution: thus animals are provided with organs whereby to perform the actions that their souls empower them to do. Now it is evident that charity, inasmuch as it directs humans to their last end, is the principle of all the good works that are referable to their last end. Wherefore all the moral virtues must needs be infused together with charity, since it is through them that humans perform each different kind of good work.

It is therefore clear that the infused moral virtues are connected, not only through prudence, but also on account of charity: and, again, that whoever loses charity through mortal sin, forfeits all the infused moral virtues.

3. Martin Luther, *Concerning Christian Liberty*

Martin Luther (1483–1546) was one of the leaders of the Reformation of the sixteenth century in Germany. In criticizing the Catholicism of his time, he emphasized three central tenants: salvation by faith alone (sola fide), *which is given by God as an act of unmerited grace* (sola gratia), *and is communicated to the believer directly through the witness of Scripture* (sola scriptura). *Luther centers Christian morality in a personal relationship with God in Christ rather than in the law and "works." Luther's teachings remain core doctrines for Protestants of all denominations.*

I.   Now,[3] though I cannot boast of my abundance, and though I know how poorly I am furnished, yet I hope that, after having been vexed by various temptations, I have attained some little drop of faith, and that I can speak of this matter, if not with more elegance, certainly with more solidity, than those literal and too subtle disputants who have hitherto discoursed upon it without understanding their own words. That I may open then an easier way for the ignorant—for these alone I am trying to serve—I first lay down these two propositions, concerning spiritual liberty and servitude:

> A Christian person is the most free lord of all, and subject to none; a Christian person is the most dutiful servant of all, and subject to every one.

[3] Martin Luther, *Concerning Christian Liberty* (1520), trans. R. S. Gringnon (Boston: P. F. Collier, 1910) selections.

Although these statements appear contradictory, yet, when they are found to agree together, they will make excellently for my purpose. They are both the statements of Paul himself, who says, "Though I be free from all people, yet have I made myself servant unto all" (1 Cor 9:19), and "Owe no one anything, but to love one another" (Rom 8:8). Now love is by its own nature dutiful and obedient to the beloved object. Thus even Christ, though Lord of all things, was yet made of a woman; made under the law; at once free and a servant; at once in the form of God and in the form of a servant.

Let us examine the subject on a deeper and less simple principle. Human beings are composed of a twofold nature, a spiritual and a bodily. As regards the spiritual nature, which they name the soul, we are called the spiritual, inward, new human; as regards the bodily nature, which they name the flesh, we are called the fleshly, outward, old human. The Apostle speaks of this: "Though our outward humanity perish, yet the inward humanity is renewed day by day" (2 Cor 4:16). The result of this diversity is that in the Scriptures opposing statements are made concerning the same humanity, the fact being that in the same human these two aspects of being human are opposed to one another; the flesh lusting against the spirit, and the spirit against the flesh (Gal 5:17).

II.   We first approach the subject of the inward person, that we may see by what means a human being becomes justified, free, and a true Christian; that is, a spiritual, new, and inward person. It is certain that absolutely none among outward things, under whatever name they may be reckoned, has any influence in producing Christian righteousness or liberty, nor, on the other hand, unrighteousness or slavery. This can be shown by an easy argument.

What can it profit the soul that the body should be in good condition, free, and full of life; that it should eat, drink, and act according to its pleasure; when even the most impious slaves of every kind of vice are prosperous in these matters? Again, what harm can ill-health, bondage, hunger, thirst, or any other outward evil, do to the soul, when even the most pious of persons and the freest in the purity of their conscience, are harassed by these things? Neither of these states of things has to do with the liberty or the slavery of the soul.

And so it will profit nothing that the body should be adorned with sacred vestments, or dwell in holy places, or be occupied in sacred offices, or pray, fast, and abstain from certain meats, or do whatever works can be done through the body and in the body. Something widely different will be necessary for the justification and liberty of the soul, since the things I have spoken of can be done by any impious person, and only hypocrites are produced by devotion to these things . . . And, to cast everything aside, even speculation, meditations, and whatever things can be performed by the exertions of the soul itself, are of no profit. One thing, and one alone, is necessary for life, justification, and Christian liberty; and that is the most holy word of God, the Gospel of Christ, as He says, "I am the resurrection and the life; those that believeth in Me shall not die eternally" (John 6:25). . .

Since then this faith can reign only in the inward person, as it is said, "With the heart we believeth unto righteousness" (Rom 10:10); and since it alone justifies, it is evident that by no outward work or labor can the inward person be at all justified, made free, and saved; and that no works whatever have any relation to that one. And so, on the other hand, it is solely by impiety and incredulity of heart that one becomes guilty and a slave of sin, deserving condemnation, not by any outward sin or work. Therefore the first care of every Christian ought to be to lay aside all reliance on works, and strengthen their faith alone more and more, and by it grow in the knowledge, not of works, but of Christ Jesus, who has suffered and risen again for him, as Peter teaches (1 Pet 5) when he makes no other work to be a Christian one . . .

Meanwhile it is to be noted that the whole Scripture of God is divided into two parts: precepts and promises. The precepts certainly teach us what is good, but what they teach is not forthwith done. For they show us what we ought to do, but do not give us the power to do it. They were ordained, however, for the purpose of showing us to ourselves, that through them we may learn our own impotence for good and may despair of our own strength. For this reason they are called the Old Testament, and are so.

For example, "Thou shalt not covet," is a precept by which we are all convicted of sin, since nobody can help coveting, whatever efforts to the contrary we may make. In order therefore that we may fulfil the precept, and not covet, we are constrained to despair of ourselves and to seek elsewhere and through another the help which we cannot find in ourselves; as it is said, "O Israel, thou hast destroyed thyself; but in Me is thine help" (Hos 8:9). Now what is done by this one precept is done by all; for all are equally impossible of fulfillment by us.

Now when we have through the precepts been taught our own impotence, and become anxious by what means we may satisfy the law—for the law must be satisfied, so that no jot or tittle of it may pass away, otherwise we must be hopelessly condemned—then, being truly humbled and brought to nothing in our own eyes, we find in ourselves no resource for justification and salvation.

Then comes in that other part of Scripture, the promises of God, which declare the glory of God, and say, "If you wish to fulfill the law, and, as the law requires, not to covet, lo! believe in Christ, in whom are promised to you grace, justification, peace, and liberty." All these things you shall have, if you believe, and shall be without them if you do not believe. For what is impossible for you by all the works of the law, which are many and yet useless, you shall fulfill in an easy and summary way through faith, because God the Father has made everything to depend on faith, so that whosoever has it has all things, and he who has it not has nothing. . .

From all this you will again understand why so much importance is attributed to faith, so that it alone can fulfill the law and justify without any works. For you see that the First Commandment, which says, "Thou shalt worship one God only," is fulfilled by faith alone. If you were nothing but good works from the soles of your feet to the crown of your head, you would not be worshipping God, nor fulfilling the First Commandment, since it is impossible to worship God without ascribing to God the glory of truth and of universal goodness, as it ought in truth to be ascribed. Now this is not done by works, but only by faith of heart. It is not by working, but by believing, that we glorify God, and confess God to be true. On this ground faith alone is the righteousness of a Christian person, and the fulfilling of all the commandments. For to those who fulfil the first, the task of fulfilling all the rest is easy.

Works, since they are irrational things, cannot glorify God, although they may be done to the glory of God, if faith be present. But at present we are inquiring, not into the quality of the works done, but into those who do them, who glorifies God, and brings forth good works. This is faith of heart, the head and the substance of all our righteousness. Hence that is a blind and perilous doctrine which teaches that the commandments are fulfilled by works. The commandments must have been fulfilled previous to any good works, and good works follow their fulfillment, as we shall see . . .

Let it suffice to say this concerning the inner person and its liberty, and concerning that righteousness of faith which needs neither laws nor good works; nay, they are even hurtful to it, if any one pretends to be justified by them.

III.   And now let us turn to the other part: to the outward person. Here we shall give an answer to all those who, taking offence at the word of faith and at what I have asserted, say, "If faith does everything, and by itself suffices for justification, why then are good works commanded? Are we then to take our ease and do no works, content with faith?" Not so, impious people, I reply; not so. That would indeed really be the case, if we were thoroughly and completely inner and spiritual persons; but that will not happen until the last day, when the dead shall be raised. As long as we live in the flesh, we are but beginning and making advances in that which shall be completed in a future life.

Although, as I have said, inwardly, and according to the spirit, we are amply enough justified by faith, having all that we require to have, except that this very faith and abundance ought to increase from day to day, even till the future life, still we remain in this mortal life upon earth, in which it is necessary that we should rule our own bodies and have relations with others. Here then works begin; here we must not take our ease; here we must give heed to exercise our bodies by fastings, watchings, labor, and other regular discipline, so that it may be subdued to the spirit, and obey and conform itself to the inner human and faith, and not rebel against them nor hinder them, as is its nature to do if it is not kept under . . .

These works, however, must not be done with any notion that by them we can be justified before God—for faith, which alone is righteousness before God, will not bear with this false notion—but solely with this purpose: that the body may be brought into subjection, and be purified from its evil lusts, so that our eyes may be turned only to purging away those lusts. For when the soul has been cleansed by faith and made to love God, it would have all things to be cleansed in like manner, and especially its own body, so that all things might unite with it in the love and praise of God. Thus it comes that, from the requirements of our own bodies, we cannot take our ease, but we are compelled on our own account to do many good works, that we may bring it into subjection. Yet these works are not the means of our justification before God; we do them out of disinterested love to the service of God; looking to no other end than to do what is well-pleasing to God whom we desire to obey most dutifully in all things . . .

To make what we have said more easily understood, let us set it forth under a figure. The works of a Christian, who is justified and saved by faith out of the pure and unbought mercy of God, ought to be regarded in the same light as would have been those of Adam and Eve in paradise and of all their posterity if they had not sinned. Of them it is said, "The Lord God took human beings and put them into the garden of Eden to dress it and to keep it" (Gen 2:15). Now Adam had been created by God just and righteous, so that he could not have needed to be justified and made righteous by keeping the garden and working in it; but, that he might not be unemployed, God gave him the business of keeping and cultivating paradise. These would have indeed been works of perfect freedom, being done for no object but that of pleasing God, and not in order to obtain justification, which he already had to the full, and which would have been innate in us all.

So it is with the works of believers. Being by our faith replaced afresh in paradise and created anew, we do not need works for our justification, but that we may not be idle, but may exercise our own bodies and preserve them. Our works are to be done freely, with the sole object of pleasing God. Only we are not yet fully created anew in perfect faith and love; these require to be increased, not, however, through works, but through themselves . . .

True, then, are these two sayings: "Good works do not make a good human, but a good human does good works"; "Bad works do not make a bad person, but a bad person does bad works." Thus it is always necessary that the substance or person should be good before any good works can be done, and that good works should follow and proceed from a good person. As Christ says, "A good tree cannot bring forth evil fruit, neither can a corrupt tree bring forth good fruit" (Matt 7:18). Now it is clear that the fruit does not bear the tree, nor does the tree grow on the fruit; but, on the contrary, the trees bear the fruit, and the fruit grows on the trees . . .

Lastly, we will speak also of those works which we perform towards our neighbor. For we do not live for ourselves alone in this mortal body, in order to work on its account, but also for all people on earth; nay, we live only for others, and not for ourselves. For it is to this end that we bring our own bodies into subjection, that we may be able to serve others more sincerely and more freely, as Paul says, "None of us liveth to ourselves, and no one dieth to oneself. For whether we live, we live unto the Lord; and whether we die, we die unto the Lord" (Rom 14:7, 8). Thus it is impossible that we should take our ease in this life, and not work for the good of our neighbors, since we must needs speak, act, and converse among other people, just as Christ was made in human likeness and found in fashion as a human, and had His conversation among people.

Yet Christians have need of none of these things for justification and salvation, but in all our works we ought to entertain this view and look only to this object—that we may serve and be useful to others in all that we do; having nothing before our eyes but the necessities and the advantage of our neighbor. Thus the Apostle commands us to work with our own hands, that we may have to give to those that need. He might have said, that we may support ourselves; but he tells us to give to those that need. It is the part of Christian life to take care of our own body for the very purpose that, by its soundness and well-being, we may be enabled to labor, and to acquire and preserve property, for the aid of those who are in want, that thus the stronger member may serve the weaker member, and we may be children of God, thoughtful and busy one for another, bearing one another's burdens, and so fulfilling the law of Christ.

In this we see clearly that the Apostle lays down this rule for a Christian life: that all our works should be directed to the advantage of others, since every Christian has such abundance through our faith that all our other works and our whole life remain over and above wherewith to serve and benefit our neighbor of spontaneous goodwill.

To this end he brings forward Christ as an example, saying, "Let this mind be in you, which was also in Christ Jesus, who, being in the form of God, thought it not robbery to be equal with God, but made Himself of no reputation, and took upon Him the form of a servant, and was made in the likeness of men; and being found in fashion as a man, He humbled Himself, and became obedient unto death" (Phil 2:5-8) . . . Paul's meaning is this: Christ, when He was full of the form of God and abounded in all good things, so that He had no need of works or sufferings to be just and saved—for all these things He had from the very beginning—yet was not puffed up with these things, and did not raise Himself above us and arrogate to Himself power over us, though He might lawfully have done so, but, on the contrary, so acted in laboring, working, suffering, and dying, as to be like the rest of humanity, and no otherwise than a human in fashion and in conduct, as if He were in want of all things and had nothing of the form of God; and yet all this He did for our sakes, that He might serve us, and that all the works He should do under that form of a servant might become ours.

Thus Christians, like Christ their Head, being full and in abundance through their faith, ought to be content with this form of God, obtained by faith; except that, as I have said, we ought to increase this faith till it be perfected . . . Though we are thus free from all works, yet we ought to empty ourselves of this liberty, take on ourselves the form of a servant, be made in the likeness of humanity, be found in fashion as human beings, serve, help, and in every way act towards our neighbor as we see that God through Christ has acted and is acting towards us. All this we should do freely, and with regard to nothing but the good pleasure of God, and we should reason thus:

Lo! my God, without merit on my part, of God's pure and free mercy, has given to me, an unworthy, condemned, and contemptible creature all the riches of justification and salvation in Christ, so that I no longer am in want of anything, except of faith to believe that this is so. For such a Father, then, who has overwhelmed me with these inestimable riches of God's, why should I not freely, cheerfully, and with my whole heart, and from voluntary zeal, do all that I know will be pleasing to God and acceptable in God's sight? I will therefore give myself as a sort of Christ, to my neighbor, as Christ has given Himself to me; and will do nothing in this life except what I see will be needful, advantageous, and wholesome for my neighbor, since by faith I abound in all good things in Christ.

Thus from faith flow forth love and joy in the Lord, and from love a cheerful, willing, free spirit, disposed to serve our neighbor voluntarily, without taking any account of gratitude or ingratitude, praise or blame, gain or loss. Its object is not to lay others under obligations, nor does it distinguish between friends and enemies, or look to gratitude or ingratitude, but most freely and willingly spends itself and its goods, whether it loses them through ingratitude, or gains goodwill. For thus did its Father, distributing all things to all people abundantly and freely, making God's sun to rise upon the just and the unjust. Thus, too, the child does and endures nothing except from the free joy with which it delights through Christ in God, the Giver of such great gifts . . .

We give this rule: the good things which we have from God ought to flow from one to another and become common to all, so that every one of us may, as it were, put on our neighbor, and so behave towards them as if we were ourselves in their place. They flowed and do flow from Christ to us; He put us on, and acted for us as if He Himself were what we are. From us they flow to those who have need of them; so that my faith and righteousness ought to be laid down before God as a covering and intercession for the sins of my neighbor, which I am to take on myself, and so labor and endure servitude in them, as if they were my own; for thus has Christ done for us. This is true love and the genuine truth of Christian life. But only there is it true and genuine where there is true and genuine faith. Hence the Apostle attributes to charity this quality: that she seeketh not her own. . .

4. Peter R. Gathje, "A Christian Vision of Life"
Seeing With a Moral Vision Informed by the Christian Story

To develop as Christian persons we need a vision of human life "in Christ" so that we have a moral vision consistent with union with God. The starting point of such a vision is Jesus' call to follow his true way that leads to life. We are called and empowered by Christ to be his disciples—to share in the work of building the kingdom of God. We read in the First Letter of John that the story or word of our lives is to tell the story or word of Jesus: "whoever obeys his [Jesus'] word, truly in this person the love of God has reached perfection. By this we may be sure that we are in him: whoever says, 'I abide in him,' ought to walk just as he walked." (1 John 2:5-6). Jesus in his life and teachings gives us the truth about what we are as human beings, and how we are to live as human beings in relation to God, to each other, and to all of God's creation. In living the way of Jesus, in living the truth of Jesus, we live in Christ, and we come to share in the fullness of life that God intends for us as children of God. This vision of Gospel truth, and therefore of what it means for us to live good human lives, provides the foundation for evaluating our lives and the basic standards to which we will hold each other accountable.

In this vision we seek to discern certain focal points for reflecting upon what it means to be human and to live well in light of the truth of Christ for human life. The hope is that highlighting such focal points will help us on our journey toward God. These focal points should not be used as a checklist for determining who is or is not "fully human." Rather they are to help us examine how we might seek to promote in our lives, and in the lives of others, certain aspects of being human basic for human flourishing consistent with God's will for human life seen in the Gospel. Attention to these focal points will give us some shared sense of what we need to be aware of in our lives and the lives of others if we are seeking to be in right relationship with God, that is, if we are seeking to live the kingdom of God as proclaimed and lived by Jesus.

Seven Focal Points in a Christian Vision of Human Life

FIRST FOCAL POINT: WE ARE IN RELATIONSHIP WITH GOD

A Christian vision of life first of all sees that God has initiated and continues a life-giving relationship with us. It is for this reason that our flourishing as human beings depends upon our being in relationship with God our Creator and our Redeemer. Christian faith sees that God is the source and goal of our existence. Thus, as human beings we are not sovereign over human life (whether our own or the lives of others), and we are not sufficient unto ourselves.

In seeing that we are made from and for God we also see that through our relationship with God as Creator we are related to God's creation. Through God we are joined to all persons as brothers and sisters, and to the whole of the universe, and this earth. In the Genesis accounts of creation, the original goodness and harmony of the creation are emphasized. God as good brings into existence a world that is good. Likewise in John's Gospel, the redemptive Word made flesh in Christ is revealed to be that of the creative Word of God present in God's creative activity. Redemption is to renew all of creation, including us, by our coming once again into right relationship with God. A Christian vision of life emphasizes that God creates us out of love and acts in redemption to restore creation to its original goodness so that creation and our lives as part of God's creation will reflect God's love.

Faith empowers us to see our lives in relationship with God. Faith thus leads to hope by which "we desire the kingdom of heaven and eternal life as our happiness, placing our trust in Christ's promises and relying not on our own strength, but on the help of the grace of the Holy Spirit."[4] This desire for the kingdom is enacted in our lives through love by which we work for the redemptive restoration of right relationships. In love we practice respect for the dignity of all human persons as created and redeemed by God. Love helps us to see each other as fellow children of God, whom God has freely liberated from sin in Christ, and to live with regard for the well being of others.

In our relations with the whole of creation, our basic moral stance is similar. We will live with a respect for creation as God's handiwork. We will practice love insofar as we are concerned for the flourishing of others, including the creation. Love empowers us to love God above all else, and it is through our love for God that we come to rightly love all else. As we are graciously formed in love we come to love others as God loves us. This love is thus not a matter of mere human will or feeling, but it is rather grounded in the grace of God. God's grace empowers us to love those who are humanly unlovable.

SECOND FOCAL POINT: WE ARE PERSONS

A second focal point in a Christian vision of human life is that God creates us as human persons. As persons we are subjects, not objects; each of us is a unique "I" and not merely a thing or an "it." As persons we are created in relationship with God. We are persons first of all because we are made in the image of God and thus in relation with God. Our human personhood is not dependent upon our achievement or fulfilling of certain capabilities. Being a person is rather integral to our being humans created by God. Each of us, as unique persons created in the image of God, is to be treated with the appropriate dignity. Respect for this human dignity is the basic measure of every social institution, culture, and human action.[5]

---

[4] Ibid., 1817.

[5] See the National Conference of Catholic Bishops, *Economic Justice for All: Pastoral Letter on Catholic Social Teaching and the U.S. Economy* (Washington, D.C.: United States Catholic Conference, 1986) §25.

Within the Christian tradition our being created in the image of God has often been spoken of in terms of our having the powers of freedom and reason. Our living out of our capabilities for freedom and reason are ways in which we may come to reflect the creative and reflective power of God in our lives. In a Christian vision of life these are two of the many ways in which God graciously endows human life. Further, in addition to creating us as free and reflective beings, God acts in history to bring human beings from oppression to freedom, and God acts in history so that human beings may live truthfully, that is, rightfully with each other.

To deny these powers in our own lives, or to enslave others by denying them a free and reasoned living of their lives consistent with the truth, are clearly rejections of God's intentions for human life as we know those intentions through the Gospel story. When we live and act in ways that are contrary to reason and freedom, we fail to be excellent as human beings because we are failing to live out our being human as created in the image of God.

Each of us as persons is called to uniquely enact our freedom and our abilities to know truth in our lives in relationship with God, each other, and the creation. Our bonding in relationships, our ability to make commitments and to be faithful are important aspects of our being persons with each other. As unique persons made in the image of God we are called to resist being reduced or reducing others to objects, to things. Such a reduction is the ultimate expression of injustice. As the Bible indicates, God calls each of us for a unique purpose in this life. God speaks to each of us in the interior reaches of our being. We are to respect the mystery of each of us as God's unique creatures through our mutual respect for each other's freedom, for conscience, and the interiority we each have.

This respect entails our refusal to use another person as an object for our own gain or for our own plans. Our holding of each other morally accountable is a crucial statement of respect for each other as human beings. We do not hold rocks or birds morally accountable. We do not hold the wind and the sea morally accountable. We do hold each other morally accountable as human persons capable of shaping our lives and making choices in light of moral deliberation that is, among other things, rational and concerned for the truth. It therefore makes sense to say that to be good as human beings we should live in such a way that we promote human freedom and we respect our capacities for reason.

THIRD FOCAL POINT: WE ARE EMBODIED

A third focal point in a Christian vision of life is that we are embodied, and as embodied we are in relation to the material world. The second creation account shows God shaping our existence out of the earth (Gen 2:4-7). The meaning of "Adam" is literally "earth creature." We are creatures of this earth.

Our relationship with God is an "earthy" relationship. God's breath gives us life as physical human beings. We are spirit-body as human beings. In creating us as embodied spirit-persons, God sees the creation in all of its materiality, including our bodies, as good.

Further underscoring the importance of bodily life, God acts in history to save us from both spiritual and physical evil. The Exodus story is about God freeing people from slavery—not simply a spiritual slavery but also a physical slavery. Central to the Gospel story is the Incarnation in which God enters into human existence even more intimately and physically than in creation. God becomes incarnate in Jesus—a fellow human being as the Word made flesh (see John 1). Jesus' resurrection, in which the whole bodily person Jesus rises from the dead, shows that salvation is not simply spiritual but includes our physical nature. The stories of Creation, Exodus, Incarnation, and Resurrection within the Christian story imply that in our moral lives we ought to recognize and respect our materiality; we exist as embodied creatures.

Consistent with our recognition of our embodiedness we will reject a dualistic separation of body and soul as contrary to a Christian vision of human life given in the stories of Creation and Redemption. How we treat our own bodies, and the bodies of others, indicates the quality of our relationship with God, who creates us as embodied. Not only are we created as material beings, but as we have noted, the Christian belief in the Resurrection also reveals that we are saved as embodied human persons. Christian salvation includes the whole human person and not the soul alone. Our very bodily relations with each other are tied into our salvation as the Hebrew prophets and Jesus make clear. Jesus tells us that feeding the hungry, giving the thirsty something to drink, welcoming strangers, clothing the naked, caring for the sick, visiting those in prison, provide the basis for judgment (Matt 25:31-40). To ignore or denigrate the physical needs of human beings is to deny our relationship to God as Creator and Redeemer of physical—embodied—human beings.

Our physical nature is not only crucial in our relationship with each other. It is also the basis for our relationship with the whole of God's creation. Respect for our embodiedness requires respect for the creation. We are created so that we cannot flourish as human beings and at the same time destroy the world of which we are a part.

The notion that we stand independent from the rest of creation is unbiblical. We are not only created from the earth, but God also entrusts us with the special responsibility of stewardship for the creation (Gen 1:28, 2:15). Likewise, the story of redemption reveals that the creation itself is the subject of redemption "groaning" until it too is completely freed from the powers of sin and death (Rom 8:19-23).

The biblical insistence on stewardship acknowledges the gift of creation and recognizes that the creation does not simply exist for us. Stewardship emphasizes that God's creation exists for future generations. But stewardship also sees that the creation exists as a manifestation of God's goodness and beauty, and a sign of this is that not all of creation is for human use. We may think here of the tree in the Garden of Eden that was reserved to God and was to be left untouched by human hands. A Christian vision of life must take seriously that God creates us to be in good relation with the whole of God's creation.

FOURTH FOCAL POINT: WE ARE SOCIAL

A fourth focal point in a Christian vision of life is that we are social. We stand in relationship with each other as human persons. The Genesis account, in stating that, "It is not good that the man should be alone" (Gen 2:18), not only indicates the importance of the partnership between man and woman, but it also indicates how we are created for human relationship. Likewise Paul's metaphor of the "body of Christ" (for example, Eph 4) stresses that our salvation does not take place apart from our union with others in Christ. In order to flourish as human beings we need social interaction, we need loving and caring human relationships. We do not fully develop as individuals except through our relations with others through which we become unique persons. We learn how to love, and God's love for us is mediated to us through the love and care of family, friends, church members, and fellow workers. The traditional African Ubuntu philosophy puts it this way, "a person is a person by and because of other people."[6]

This social nature of human life is underscored by the biblical stories that emphasize that God's redemptive work is always through a community. God works first through Israel and then through the church—the body of Christ. The vision of the end of salvation history is of the "holy city, the new Jerusalem, coming down out of heaven from God" (Rev 21:2). God gathers people together; sin drives people apart. This social nature of human life means that an important standard for the quality of Christian moral life is how we stand in solidarity with each other and seek the common good rather than our own private individual gain, or the gain of our particular group or nation. Salvation is personal but never without community. The biblical vision of the new creation given to us in the Book of Revelation states that God dwells "with mortals" (Rev 21:3) that is, with *us* and not "with me."

FIFTH FOCAL POINT: WE ARE HISTORICAL

Fifth, a Christian vision of life sees that as embodied and social we are also historical creatures. When God reveals Godself to Moses, God states, "I am

---

[6] Quoted in T. Richard Synder, *The Protestant Ethic and the Spirit of Punishment* (Grand Rapids: Eerdmans, 2001) 106.

the God of your father, the God of Abraham, the God of Isaac, and the God of Jacob" (Exod 3:6). We know of God and of ourselves through our historical relations. We stand in time and have relationships with each other within particular historical contexts. We make commitments to each other that involve our lives as time-bound. We also stand within relationships that we did not create but in which we live, whether we like it or not. None of us is self-made, either in terms of our basic existence or who we are in this world. Our lives as human beings are built on a past and oriented to a future. We do not simply begin anew, but we stand on the shoulders of those who came before us. We both gain from the accomplishments of those in the past, and we shoulder the burdens left by the failings of those who went before us. This is true in our family histories, our community histories, our national histories, our world histories and our church histories. How we tell the stories of the past, and how we envision the possible futures will greatly influence how we shape our lives with each other and what we will hope to accomplish within our own lives.

As historical creatures we are responsible for correcting the injustices of the past that still affect human life and the world in the present. The biblical conviction that the sins of the ancestors negatively affect their children and their children's children (Exod 20:5-6; 34:6-7) gets at the truth of the matter. To ignore the sins of those who went before us is to ignore how those sins still shape our lives together now. We cannot undo the past, but as part of God's redemptive work we are called to redemptively address the consequences of past actions in ways that will create a better present and future.

We learn how to do this work by recognizing how God acts for our redemption. The grip of sin on human history, on human life, is not simply ignored. Rather God enters into human history through Jesus to confront the power of sin and death. Jesus' death on the cross and his resurrection defeats sin's hold on those who had already died and also opens the possibility of salvation for us who have since entered into the world. We are saved through a historical action, and we too are called to respond to sin in history by how we live now and with an eye toward the future God is creating. Thus we are called through God's love to practice love by seeking justice—right relationship in all dimensions of human life.

The denial of our connections with others (and thus our responsibilities), and the denial of our limitations both reflect the denial of our historicity. Individualism wrongly asserts that we have no responsibility in relation to the sins of the past and that each of us is self-made. Both of these assertions ignore the many ways our personal and communal identities are shaped by history. Where we live and how we live reflect a history (or more accurately, histories), whether this be on the small scale of our family or on a larger scale, such as our nation. Faith gives us the courage to engage in this evaluation as we know that ultimately we are children of God, that our actions do not need to be determined by the past even as we acknowledge the past. Hope empowers us to see that though we are shaped by history we are not determined by it. As free human beings we can move in love to redemptively address the past. We do this by responsibly recognizing how the past has shaped the present as we seek to transform this present in accord with God's design for human life.

SIXTH FOCAL POINT: WE ARE SINNERS

A sixth focal point in a Christian vision of life is that we are broken and sinful. The Genesis story of the Fall indicates that we are all capable of evil, and in fact, we all lead lives that are marked by sin. We were created for loving union with God, and through union with God, for harmony with one another and creation. Yet our lives reflect our break from God, and thus an inner disharmony manifests itself in our internal struggles for moral integrity and in the damaged relationships, cultures, institutions, and world in which we live. Our lives, instead of being consistently directed toward God and thus toward human good and the good of all of God's creation, become disordered and we become death-dealing in our relationships. When we sin we separate ourselves from God, and this leads us to seek ways to dominate others in order to secure ourselves, and we even become willing to destroy others in this desperate attempt to live without relationship with God. A Christian vision of human life must recognize the power of sin in our lives and the many ways in which sin deadens our relationships and destroys our lives.

SEVENTH FOCAL POINT: WE ARE GRACED BY GOD

A Christian vision of life urges a seventh focal point that our Christian realism about sin must also recognize, namely, the graciously transforming and redemptive power of Christ in Christian discipleship. Sent into the world, we are to be as Christ said, "wise as serpents and innocent as doves" (Matt 10:16). Our awareness of sin in our own lives and the lives of others (and in our cultures and social institutions) should make us wary and encourage careful planning, but it should not paralyze us or prevent us from reaching out in love and working for justice. The truth of our gracious redemption in Jesus Christ and the in-breaking of the kingdom of God are realities that trump sin in human life. Thus this seventh aspect of our being human is the "Good News" that we are offered God's gracious transforming presence in our lives through Jesus Christ. Joined in the death of Christ in baptism we are to consider ourselves "dead to sin and alive to God in Christ Jesus" (Rom 6:11). Our faith in this redemption will give us the hope necessary to live consistent with the kingdom of God and thus to practice love in our relations with others.

The Seven Focal Points of a Christian Vision of Human Life
and Our Moral Character

These basic points of focus in a Christian vision of life—being in relation to God, being embodied, social, and historical persons who are broken and sinful, yet also graced by God, help us to see what important aspects of our lives we need to attend to if we are to develop as good human beings consistent with our relationship with God. These focal points sharpen the vision by which we live so that we may move toward moral excellence. Each of us, in seeking to live in union with Christ, is called to acknowledge these aspects of human existence, both individually and communally. Each of us is called to hold ourselves accountable with the help of a Christian vision of life and to responsibly face what these focal points indicate for how we need to live. In this way we will resist the power of sin in human life with its deadly consequences. Instead of living under the threat of death, we will live with the hope of resurrection, of being made fully human, of being in union with God.

5. Stanley Hauerwas, "Peacemaking: the Virtue of the Church"

Dr. Stanley Hauerwas is the Gilbert T. Rowe Professor of Theological Ethics at Duke Divinity School. He is perhaps the most publicly recognizable Christian ethicist working today. Dr. Hauerwas was named "America's Best Theologian" by Time *in 2001 and delivered the prestigious Gifford Lectureship at the University of St. Andrews that same year. His most influential work is* A Community of Character: Toward a Constructive Christian Social Ethic. *A central task of Hauerwas' work is the recovery of virtue as a central category for Protestant ethics. This essay also manifests two additional themes characteristic of his work: that virtue must be understood communitarianly as well as individually, and that non-violence is a constitutive characteristic of Christian love.*

If[7] another member of the church sins against you, go and tell that person of the fault when the two of you are alone. If the member listens to you, you have regained that one. But if you are not listened to, take one or two others along with you, that every word may be confirmed by the evidence of two or three witnesses. If the member refuses to listen to them, tell it to the church; and if the offender refuses to listen even to the church, let that one be to you as a Gentile and a tax collector. Truly I tell you, whatever you bind on earth shall be bound in heaven, and whatever you loose on earth shall be loosed in heaven. Again I say to you, if two of you agree on earth about anything they ask, it will be done for them by my Father in heaven. For where two or three are gathered in my name, there am I in the midst of them. Then Peter came up and said to him,

---

[7] Stanley Hauerwas, "Peacemaking: the Virtue of the Church," Originally published in *The Furrow* 36 (1985) 605–614. Used by permission.

"Lord, if another member of the church sins against me, how often shall I forgive? As many as seven times?" Jesus said to him, "Not seven times, but I tell you, seventy-seven times." (Matt 18:15-22)[8]

This is surely a strange text to begin an article on peacemaking as a virtue. The text does not seem to be about peacemaking but about conflict making. It does not say if you have a grievance you might think about confronting the one you believe has wronged you. The text is much stronger than that. It says if you have a grievance you must, you are obligated to, confront the one you believe has sinned against you. You cannot overlook a fault on the presumption that it is better not to disturb the peace. Rather, you must risk stirring the waters, causing disorder, rather than overlook the sin.

But on what possible grounds could Christians, people supposedly of peace, be urged actively to confront one another? It seems out of character for Jesus to urge us to do so, and out of character for the Christian community to follow such an admonition. Yet I want to suggest that we will understand peacemaking as a virtue only when we see that such confrontation is at the heart of what it means to be a peacemaker. Even more important, however, I think that by attending to this passage we will be able to see how peacemaking, as well as any virtue, is correlative to a community's practices.

This is a crucial issue if we are to appreciate peacemaking as a virtue. It is interesting to note how seldom peacemaking is treated as a virtue. Courage, temperance, and even humility are usually acknowledged as virtues much more readily than is peacemaking. For many, peacemaking may sound like a "good thing," but they would be hesitant to call it a virtue. Peacemaking is usually seen more as a matter of political strategy than a disposition forming the self. Some people may even be peaceful, but that hardly seems a virtue.

Why do we seem reticent to think of peacemaking as a virtue? I suspect it is because we think of virtue as personal characteristics that everyone should possess irrespective of their membership in any specific community. But, as I hope to show, such an understanding of virtue is far too limited, if not an outright mistake. For as Aristotle argues, some virtues, such as justice and friendship, are correlative to certain kinds of relations and cannot exist without those relations being valued by a community. Peacemaking is that sort of virtue insofar as the church believes that peace (and a very particular kind of peace at that) is an essential characteristic of its nature.

As important as understanding why we rightly consider peacemaking a virtue is how we understand what kind of activity it is. It is in this context the passage from Matthew is so important for helping us understand peacemaking as a virtue. Normally we tend to think of peacemaking as the resolution of conflict rather than the encouragement of conflict. That such is the case, I sus-

---

[8] This Scripture passage has been adapted to conform to the Revised Standard Version of the Bible.

pect, is also one of the reasons that peacemaking, even if it is understood as a virtue, is not really all that appealing. Have you ever known anyone, yourself included, who would rush out to see a movie or play about peace? . . .

We simply have to admit that for most of us peace is boring. Of course, in the midst of terrible turmoil we may well think we could stand a bit of boredom, but it is interesting how often people look back on past "troubles" nostalgically. Life needs movement, which most of us believe, rightly or wrongly, entails conflict. Therefore, peacemaking for most of us appears a bit like Bernard Shaw's view of heaven—namely, that on reflection he thought he preferred hell, since at least hell promised to contain some interesting people.

But this text from Matthew puts the issue of peacemaking in quite a different light. As I noted above, Jesus does not suggest that if you have a grievance against someone in the community it might be a good idea for you to "try to work it out." Rather, he says that you must go and speak to the one whom you believe has sinned against you. Such a speaking, of course, may well involve nothing less than confrontation. You must do it first alone, but if reconciliation does not take place then you must "go public," taking witnesses with you. If that still is not sufficient, you must take the matter before the whole church.

Our first reaction to this text is to think that surely this procedure is far too extreme for most of our petty conflicts. I may get angry at someone, but if I wait I discover that I will get over it. Moreover, who wants to appear like someone who is too easily offended? No one likes people who tend to make mountains out of molehills, especially when they claim to be doing so only because of the "principle involved." Even more important, most of us learn that time heals all wounds, and thus we are better off waiting for some conflicts to die through the passage of time.

Yet Jesus seems to have been working with a completely different set of presuppositions about what is necessary to be a community of peace and peacemaking. It seems that peace is not the name of the absence of conflict, but rather, peacemaking is that quality of life and practices engendered by a community that knows it lives as a forgiven people. Such a community cannot afford to "overlook" one another's sins because they have learned that such sins are a threat to being a community of peace.

The essential presupposition of peacemaking as an activity among Christians is our common belief that we have been made part of a community in which people no longer regard their lives as their own. We are not permitted to harbor our grievances as "ours." When we think our brother or sister has sinned against us, such an affront is not just against us but against the whole community. A community established as peaceful cannot afford to let us relish our sense of being wronged without exposing that wrong in the hopes of reconciliation. We must learn to see wrongs as "personal" because we are part of a community where the "personal" is crucial to the common good.

It is an unpleasant fact, however, that most of our lives are governed more by our hates and dislikes than by our loves. I seldom know what I really want, but I know what or whom I deeply dislike and even hate. It may be painful to be wronged, but at least such wrongs give me a history of resentments that, in fact, constitute who I am. How would I know who I am if I did not have my enemies?

It seems our enemies are exactly who Jesus is forcing us to confront. For he tells us that we cannot cherish our wrongs. Rather, we are commanded to engage in the difficult task of confronting those whom we believe have sinned against us. Such confrontation is indeed hard because it makes us as vulnerable as the one we confront. The process of confrontation means that we may well discover that we have been mistaken about our being wronged. Still more troubling, it means that even if we have been wronged, by confronting our brother or sister we will have to envision the possibility that, like Jonah, he or she may repent and we will therefore have to be reconciled. We will be forced to lose the subject of our hatred.

From this perspective peacemaking is anything but boring. Rather, it is the most demanding of tasks. One of the interesting aspects of this passage in Matthew is it assumes that the Christian community will involve conflict and wrongs. The question is not whether such conflict can be eliminated but rather how we are to deal with the conflict. Conflict is not to be ignored or denied, but rather conflict, which may involve sins, is to be forced into the open. That we are to do so must surely be because the peace that Jesus brings is not a peace of rest but rather a peace of truth. Just as love without truth cannot help but be accursed, so peace without truthfulness cannot help but be deadly. In short, peacekeeping is that virtue of the Christian community that is required if the church is to be a community of people at peace with one another in truth.

The truth seems to be about the last thing we want to know about ourselves. We may say that the truth saves, but in fact we know that any truth worth knowing is as disturbing as it is fulfilling. Surely that is why Jesus is so insistent that those who would follow him cannot simply let sins go unchallenged. For when we fail to challenge sinners, we in fact abandon them to their sin. We show we care little for them by our unwillingness to engage in the hard work of establishing a truthful peace.

That the church is such a community of truthful peace depends on its being a community of the forgiven. As the text from Matthew notes, Peter realized that Jesus' command that we confront the sinner is not an easy one. For such confrontation is based on the presupposition that forgiveness is also to be offered. But how often, Peter asks, can forgiveness be offered—seven times? We cannot help but be sympathetic with Peter's question, for it just seems to be against good sense to be ready to offer forgiveness. What kind of community would ever be sustained on the presupposition that forgiveness is always available?

Yet there seems to be no limit to forgiveness, as Jesus elaborates his response to Peter by telling the story of the servant who, having been forgiven his debt, refuses to forgive a fellow servant his debt. The lord of the unforgiving servant, on being told of his servant's behavior, threw him in jail until he paid his debt. And so, we are told, our "heavenly Father will also do to every one of you, if you do not forgive your brother or your sister from your heart" (Matt 18:35; NRSV through this essay). What it seems we must remember, if we are to be peacemakers capable of confronting one another with our sins, is that we are forgiven and we are part of a community of the forgiven. Our ability to be truthful peacemakers depends on our learning that we owe our lives to God's unrelenting forgiveness.

The forgiveness that makes peacemaking possible, moreover, does not mean that judgment is withheld. The question is not whether we should hold one another accountable but what is the basis for doing so and how is it to be done. To be sinned against or to know we have sinned requires that we have a language and correlative habit that makes it possible to know what it is to be a sinner. Only on such a basis do we have the capacity to avoid arbitrariness of judgment as we learn to see our relations with one another as part of a continuing tradition of discourse that helps us serve a common good. That good, at least among Christians, is to be a community of the forgiven empowered to witness to God's kingdom of peace wrought through Jesus of Nazareth.

We therefore do not confront one another from a position of self-righteousness; we must come to the other as one who has been forgiven. Such a perspective, I think, throws quite a different light on this passage from that which is often given it. Too often it is assumed that this text legitimates our confrontation with the brother or sister on the assumption that we have power over the other because we have been wronged and thus can decide to forgive. Forgiveness from such a position is but another form of power, since it assumes that one is in a superior position. But the whole point of this text is that we confront one another not as forgivers, not as those who use forgiveness as power, but first and foremost as people who have learned the truth about ourselves—namely, that we are all people who need to be and have been forgiven.

That is why we must and can confront one another as sinners, because we understand ourselves to share with the other our having been forgiven. We thus share a common history of forgiveness and repentance that makes our willingness to confront one another a process of peace rather than simply another way to continue conflict. That is why those who refuse to listen must be treated as a Gentile or tax collector, for they are acting like those who have not learned that they have been forgiven. To act like one is not needing forgiveness is to act against the very basis of this community as a community of peacemaking. That is why they must be excluded: they must learn that they are not peacemakers insofar as they refuse to live as the forgiven. From such a perspective there is no more violent act than the unwillingness to accept reconciliation freely and honestly offered. But the truth is that few of us are willing to be so reconciled.

From this perspective, we should not be surprised if peacemakers and peacemaking appear anything but peaceful. Moreover, if the church is to be a community of peace in a world at war, it cannot help but be a community that confronts the world in uncompromising manner. The task of peacemaking cannot ignore real wrongs, past or present. The peace that the world knows too often is but order built on forgetfulness, but that is not the peace of the church, which is built on forgiveness. No genuine peace can come from simply forgetting past wrongs, but rather must come by encompassing those wrongs in a history of forgiveness. Those peacemakers, however, who insist on reminding us of our past sins cannot help but often appear as troublemakers.

This is particularly true when so often the wrongs that we must remember are those that no amount of effort or goodwill can make right. No matter how hard Christians work against anti-Semitism, there is finally nothing that can be done to make "right" the terror of the Holocaust. If there is to be a reconciliation between Christians and Jews, it cannot come through forgetting such a terrible wrong but by learning to face that history as a forgiven people.

This is but to remind us that peacemaking as a virtue has a peculiar stake in the temporal. Peace, as well as forgiveness, must take place in time. Disembodied beings cannot know peace; only beings who know themselves as truthful are capable of being at peace. As we are told in Ephesians, the relation between Israel and the Gentiles has not been resolved by some temporal decree, but rather, "now in Christ Jesus you who once were far off have been brought near by the blood of Christ. For he is our peace, who has made us both one, and has broken down the dividing wall, that is, the hostility between us, by abolishing in his flesh the law with its commandments and ordinances, that he might create in himself one new humanity in the place of the two, thus making peace, and might reconcile both groups to God in one body through the cross, thus putting to death that hostility through it. So he came and proclaimed peace to you who were far off and peace to those who were near; for through him both of us have access in one Spirit to the Father" (Eph 2:13-18).

Peacemaking among Christians, therefore, is not simply one activity among others but rather is the very form of the church insofar as the church is the form of the one who "is our peace." Peacemaking is the form of our relations in the church as we seek to be in unity with one another, which at least means that we begin to share a common history. Such unity is not that built on shallow optimism that we can get along if we respect one another's differences. Rather, it is a unity that profoundly acknowledges our differences because we have learned that those differences are not accidental to our being a truthful people—even when they require us to confront one another as those who have wronged us.

If peacemaking as a virtue is intrinsic to the nature of the church, what are we to say about those without the church? First, I think we must say that it is the task of the church to confront and challenge the false peace of the world which is too often built more on power than truth. To challenge the world's sense of peace may well be dangerous, because often when sham peace is exposed it threatens to become violent. The church, however, cannot be less truthful with the world than it is expected to be with itself. If we are less truthful we have no peace to offer to the world.

Second, Christians are prohibited from ever despairing of the peace possible in the world. We know that as God's creatures we are not naturally violent nor are our institutions unavoidably violent. As God's people we have been created for peace. Rather, what we must do is to help the world find the habits of peace whose absence so often makes violence seem like the only alternative.

Peacemaking as a virtue is an act of imagination built on long habits of the resolution of differences. The great problem in the world is that our imagination has been stilled, since it has not made a practice of confronting wrongs so that violence might be avoided. In truth, we must say that the church has too often failed the world by its failure to witness in our own life the kind of conflict necessary to be a community of peace. Without an example of a peacemaking community, the world has no alternative but to use violence as the means to settle disputes.

I have tried to show how peacekeeping as a virtue is community-specific— that is, how it is an activity intrinsic to the nature of the church. Yet the fact that peacekeeping is community-specific does not mean it ought to be community-restrictive. The sinning person referred to in Matthew is no doubt a member of the Christian community, but the Matthean community is also one that understood it was to go among the nations to witness to God's peace. Therefore, the habits of peacekeeping acquired in the church are no less relevant when the church confronts those not part of our community and who may even threaten or wrong our community. For it is our belief that God is no less present in our enemy calling us to find the means of reconciliation.

If the tack I have taken is close to being right, then it puts pacifism in singular perspective. For pacifism is often associated with being passive in the face of wrong. As a result, some even suggest that pacifism is immoral insofar as the pacifist suffers wrong and as a result fails to fulfill the obligation to the brother by resisting his injustice. But peacemaking is not a passive response; rather, it is an active way to resist injustice by confronting the wrongdoer with the offer of reconciliation. Such reconciliation is not cheap, however, since no reconciliation is possible unless the wrong is confronted and acknowledged.

Contrary to usual stereotypes, this means that peacekeepers, rather than withdraw from politics, must be the most political of animals. Peacekeeping requires the development of the processes and institutions that make possible confrontation and resolution of differences so that violence can be avoided. The problem with politics, at least as politics is currently understood, is not that it involves compromises but that it so little believes in truth. As a result, it becomes but a form of coercion without due acknowledgment that it is so. In such a situation the church can be a peacemaker by being the most political of institutions.

No doubt peacemaking, as I have tried to depict it, is a demanding business. I think it is impossible to sustain it if it is thought to be a virtue of heroic individuals. Rather, peacemaking must be a virtue of a whole community, so that the kind of support and care necessary to sustain peacemaking as an ongoing task will be forthcoming. As Christians, however, we cannot help but rejoice that God has called us to be peacemakers, for what could possibly be a more joyful and exciting task than to be a part of God's peace?

Chapter Two

Sources of Christian Ethics

Life often presents us with difficult choices. How do I respond to a close friend who has revealed to me that he or she is homosexual? What sort of career reflects my personal sense of vocation? Should I support a political candidate who rejects capital punishment? As we saw in the last chapter, we do not approach such questions from a blank slate. Rather, each of us makes our life choices as a person whose character has been formed within a particular moral tradition. At each point, we ask ourselves if a proposed action best reflects who we truly are. This textbook invites its readers to reflect on what is most "fitting" or "appropriate" for those who are shaped by the Christian vision of the moral life. Still, some choices are particularly perplexing and it is not always clear to us what choice we should make, even if our characters are well-formed. At this point, we need to consult the various sources that together form the Christian moral tradition.

And what are these sources? Albert Outler observed in 1966 that John Wesley, the eighteenth-century founder of the Methodist movement, drew on a "quadrilateral" of sources for his theology: Scripture, tradition, reason, and experience.[1] The *United Methodist Book of Discipline* describes the Wesleyan quadrilateral this way: "Wesley believed that the living core of the Christian faith was revealed in Scripture, illumined by tradition, vivified in personal experience, and confirmed by reason."[2] In the intervening years, this way of understanding the relationship of sources has entered into the common vocabulary of Christian theological ethics. All Christian denominations and theorists draw from all four of these sources, though they differ in how each is understood and the relative weight given to a particular source.

---

[1] Albert Outler, "The Wesleyan Quadrilateral—in John Wesley," in *Doctrine and Theology in the United Methodist Church*, ed. Thomas Langford (Nashville: Abingdon Press, 1991).

[2] *The Book of Discipline of the United Methodist Church, 1996* (Nashville: United Methodist Publishing House, 1996) 74. See §63.4, "Our Theological Task" for a full analysis of the use of the four sources in Christian theological reflection.

1. Scripture

Among these four sources, *Scripture* plays a foundational role. The term "Scripture" denotes writings that are regarded as especially sacred by a religious tradition. Christians and Jews regard the fifty-four books that compose the Hebrew Bible as Scripture. Christians also have a special reverence for the twenty-seven *canonical* writings that compose the New Testament. "The canon" (from the Greek, *kanon*, "rule") is the collective term for those books that are commonly recognized as authoritative by official church decision. In the West, the canon was set by the Synod of Rome in 382 and ratified by the councils of Hippo (393) and Carthage (397).[3]

Christians have seen Scripture as the foundation of their faith from the very beginning. When the writer of 2 Timothy claims that "All Scripture is inspired by God and is useful for teaching, for reproof, for correction, and for training in righteousness" (2 Tim 3:16), he means, of course, the Hebrew Scriptures. Jesus, as a pious Jew, knew the Hebrew Scriptures intimately and no doubt had committed large sections of it to memory. Jesus is clear that the God he knows as "Father" is identical with the God who called Abraham to leave Mesopotamia, freed the Hebrews from slavery in Egypt, and was glorified in the Psalms. The early Christians, too, turned to the Hebrew Scriptures to interpret the meaning of Jesus' teachings, death, and resurrection. Matthew, for example, pictures Jesus as the new Moses, proclaiming the new law of the kingdom from the top of a mountain. Luke sees Jesus as the one who will fulfill the promise of Isaiah: "he has sent me to proclaim release to the captives, and recovery of sight to the blind, to set at liberty those who are oppressed, to proclaim the acceptable year of the Lord" (Isa 61:1-2). Matthew and Mark interpret Jesus' death as the "God-forsakenness" described in the poetry of Psalm 22. Paul interprets the death and resurrection of Jesus as bringing to fruition a hope for human faith and redemption promised to Abraham.

Scripture thus remains the fountainhead of the Christian faith and the final arbiter of Christian moral debate. When we actually turn to the Bible for guidance on perplexing moral issues, however, we often find that it does not give clear, unambiguous guidance. One difficulty is that the Christian Scriptures are a much more complex body of work than, for example, the Koran. Muslims believe that the Koran has one author; the Bible has many. Muhammad's revelations were limited only to a few short decades; the Christian Scriptures

---

[3] These councils for the most part gave official seal to a general consensus about the canon that gradually emerged in the church after centuries of reflection and debate. The four gospels and the writings of Paul were regarded as authoritative from the first century forward. The books of Hebrews, James, 2 Peter and Revelation were disputed even in the fourth century, but finally included. Other books were regarded as authoritative in some traditions (additional gospels, the *Didache, The Shepherd of Hermas,* and *1 Clement,* for example) but finally were denied inclusion in the canon. In addition, we now know of many extra-canonical gospels that seem to have fallen into disfavor by the mainstream church sometime in the second century.

were formed over thousands of years. Allah characteristically gives direct, unambiguous commands in the Koran; in the Bible, God's will is often gleaned through the open-ended interpretation of story, poetry, historical event, and parable. Allah is believed to literally speak Arabic in the Koran; in the Christian Scriptures the revelation is mediated through the human languages of Hebrew, Aramaic, and Greek. Another difficulty is that the world of the Bible is very much removed from our own. We will find nothing in the Bible that speaks directly to modern technological problems like euthanasia or industrial pollution. Even enduring features of human existence, such as family and the political community, are very different institutions in the world of ancient Israel or the Greco-Roman Mediterranean civilization.

In our second reading, the Old Testament scholar Walter Brueggemann addresses some of these difficulties. He sees the Bible as "inherently the live word of God" but also acknowledges that it is authored by "circumstance-situated men and women of faith." Discovering what the Bible *means* for us now in our context means that we must first discover what it *meant* in a very different one. "The Bible requires and insists upon human interpretation," Brueggemann argues, "which is inescapably subjective, necessarily provisional and inevitably disputatious."

2. Tradition

A second source of Christian ethics is *tradition*. A tradition is the story of faith that is passed down from generation to generation. The Christian moral tradition includes *official* elements, such as creeds, authoritative church teachings, and formal statements of councils. For example, the Vatican II document, the Pastoral Constitution on the Church in the Modern World, which we will encounter in chapter 6, belongs to this category. The Christian moral tradition also includes *unofficial* elements, such as the meanings given to words in common usage, liturgy, prayer, hymns and spirituals, and customary moral practices. An example is Martin Luther King's challenge to the official segregation of southern churches by appealing to a richer Christian understanding of love and justice. We will find throughout this text that the Catholic Church characteristically guides its moral reflection through official teachings to a greater degree than Protestant bodies, and consequently tends to be more coherent, unified, and systematic—but also more hierarchical—in its moral thought.

In living, growing religions, tradition has simultaneously conservative and dynamic functions. If a religion can be compared to a conversation, then its tradition is the grammar of shared meanings that allows communication to take place. Without a common understanding of basic terms and commitment to some ethical first principles, we would have only babbling nonsense. Similarly, if a religion can be compared to a river, then its tradition is the two banks that hold the river on its course, pushing it forward through time. Without the restraint of a lively tradition, the moral tradition would become a diffuse and stagnant swamp.

This tension about tradition has been a hallmark of Christianity from the beginning. On the one hand, Jesus never repudiated his identity as a Jew. His radical conception of the coming kingdom was deeply informed by the great prophets of old. He learned and taught in the synagogue, read the Scriptures, and for the most part kept the Torah. On the other hand, Jesus very clearly attacked the oppressive, life-draining effects of a moral tradition. Some of his acts seem deliberately provocative—even iconoclastic. In order to "make ready" for the coming kingdom of God, Jesus and his followers worked and healed on the Sabbath, deliberately violated laws of ritual cleanliness as they ate with Gentiles and sinners, and seemed shockingly oblivious to the social mores regarding the proper place of women.

Jesus' ministry is a warning about the tendency for religious traditions to become ideologies. The control over official traditions, like the telling of history itself, belongs to the victors. The voices of those without power—women, minorities, the poor—are hushed or ignored. The passage of time and the weight of authority can give even oppressive practices the air of legitimacy. The reading by Rosemary Radford Ruether in this chapter takes on this issue. She insists that those who are oppressed must critique inherited traditions against their own life experience.

3. Reason

A third source of Christian ethics is *reason*. As conscious, reflective beings, human beings must make sense of life. We ask questions about our faith. We read and interpret Scripture. We sift out the various strands of tradition that we have inherited so that it will "make sense" in our world. We order religious beliefs into a coherent whole and relate it to the other beliefs we have about the world and our place in it. The reasoning capacity is simply part of what it means to be a human. Moreover, in this age of religious terrorism and strange utopian sects, we have an especially clear duty to reflect critically on religious claims.

The intellectual discipline charged with the systematic "making sense" of life is philosophy. Since the beginning, the connections between the Christian moral tradition and philosophy have been extensive and deep. Paul writes in Romans that the invisible truth of God is "plain" and can be clearly "understood and seen through the things [God] has made" (Rom 1:19-20). For Paul the truths of Christianity revealed in the Scriptures mirrors the truth that is written into the fabric of the cosmos. These brief musings of Paul provided the basis for a linkage between the Jewish Jesus and the rich intellectual culture of the Greco-Roman world. Christians encountered and ultimately integrated into Christianity the systems of philosophy they found there. Augustine, who we will encounter throughout this book, built his theological system on the intellectual foundation of Neoplatonism. This system endured until the Middle Ages, when Thomas Aquinas reinterpreted Christian doctrine in the light of the newly discovered writings of Aristotle. The selections from Thomas' *Summa theologiae* included in this chapter set forth the foundations of natural law, which have remained one of the most characteristic features of Catholic ethics. The basic assumption here is that human reason still preserves the divine image, though it is limited in its scope and clarity by human finitude and sinfulness.

Protestants historically have been less enthusiastic about the synergy of faith and philosophy. Martin Luther believed that human sinfulness has so distorted the human will that it does not allow us to reason rightly. The captive mind sees what it wants to see. We should keep in mind that Luther's suspicions of philosophy did not extend to all academic disciplines, however. Luther himself held a doctorate in theology and was a highly skilled philologist of biblical languages. Luther would have no truck with the anti-intellectualism we see in some extreme forms of fundamentalism today.

In the modern West, the work of reason is dominated by the empirical sciences. While the church has not always embraced the fruits of science (the trial of Galileo comes to mind!), just about all contemporary Christian ethicists believe that their work must take science into account. Christian bioethicists, for example, are expected to know something about medicine and clinical practice. Ethicists of marriage and sexuality believe that their work should be informed by scientific understandings of human sexuality, sexual orientation, and family systems.

Just how to relate faith and the empirical sciences, however, is not altogether clear. To what degree should moral reflection be guided by scientific information? Can science itself produce moral values? Is the scientific world view compatible with the world view of religious faith? Does science itself produce new moral problems? John Habgood explores all of these issues in a reading that has been excerpted from *The Westminster Dictionary of Christian Ethics*.

4. Experience

A final source of Christian ethics is *experience*. We have seen already that liberation theologians place heavy emphasis on experience as an antidote to oppressive tradition. They mean experience in the most expanded sense: It includes not only our personal experiences, but also careful, imaginative listening to the experiences of those from different social locations than our own. It means not only individual experiences but also those shared by a class, gender, or racial group. Experience includes not only social structural experiences, such as political oppression and poverty, but also spiritual experiences, such as humiliation, degradation, and hopelessness. Finally, as a religion of hope and salvation, Christian experience must account for experiences of liberation, both those experienced socially as political and economic restructuring and spiritually as grace, forgiveness, and reconciliation.

Jesus, too, continually directs his hearers to reflect on their own life experiences. His teachings and parables are full of lessons drawn from family life, from work, from household chores. For example, Jesus invites his hearers to reflect on their own experience of parenting in order to gain insights into the character of God. "Who among you," he asks, "would give your child a rock when he asks for bread? Who would give your child a snake when he asks for some fish?" (Matt 7:9-10, paraphrase). On a more profound level, the community of disciples that formed the first church were brought into being and shaped by the experience of resurrection. The Gospel writers make plain that none of the disciples understood Jesus at all while he walked among them. It is only through their shattering experience of Jesus' crucifixion and his wholly unexpected resurrection that they reinterpreted those memories into a coherent narrative.

The appeal to experience sometimes brings the charge of subjectivity. Are all life experiences equally valid? If my experiences engender different ethical conclusions than yours, who is to say which of us is right? Rosemary Ruether responds to this charge in the included reading. She argues that *all* theological reflection is rooted in experience. This can remain partiality hidden, however, when a theological position simply reflects our assumptions. Moreover, Ruether argues that the relationship between Scripture and experience is profoundly circular: the New Testament shapes and interprets the experience of Christians, but the experience of the first Christians produced the New Testament.

Conclusion

Thus theological ethics draws from four sources: Scripture, tradition, reason, and experience. One of the first tasks of Christian ethics is to make explicit the sources that guide us and how each of these sources informs the others. We need especially to be on the lookout for unacknowledged sources lurking in the background. An approach to ethics that claims to come purely from the New Testament, for example, inescapably interprets the New Testament through the work of reason, shaped by one or more traditions of interpretations, and viewed through the lens of experience from a specific social location.

All of the readings included in this chapter help us understand these basic sources of Christian ethics and their relationship to one another. Readers also may wish to consult in this regard Martin Luther King's "Letter from Birmingham City Jail" in chapter 5. King makes a sophisticated use all four sources as he constructs his famous Christian critique against segregation.

READINGS

1. Biblical Foundations

A. 2 TIMOTHY 3:10-17

This letter, probably written by an anonymous writer in the Pauline tradition, is couched as a final testament of Paul to his followers. He urges his followers to maintain the faith that they have received from him, especially by holding steadfast to a good moral character. He directs his followers to the Scriptures (here the Hebrew Scriptures) as an inspired guide for a holy life.

B. ROMANS 1:18-23

This letter probably is the last written by the apostle Paul. The Letter to the Romans demonstrates the work of a mature theological mind and is the most systematic of all Paul's works. Paul, a Jew, had achieved outstanding success in founding churches in the Gentile Mediterranean world. However, along with that success came increasing tensions between the Jewish and Gentile churches. In this letter, Paul endeavors to set forth a basis for a truly universal Christianity, which is rooted in the common human failure to live up to God's righteousness. In this article, he shows that the righteousness of God should be plain even to those who have not read the Jewish Scriptures because it is observable in the created order. This passage provided the basis for a linkage between the Jewish Scriptures and Greco-Roman philosophy, and it is the foundation for natural law theory in Christian theology.

2. Walter Brueggemann, "Biblical Authority"

Walter Brueggemann is professor emeritus of Old Testament at Columbia Theological Seminary, a seminary related to the Presbyterian Church (U.S.A.) in Atlanta, Georgia. He is a prolific writer on the interpretation of the Old Testament. Among his many publications is the highly regarded Theology of the Old Testament. *In this article, Brueggemann explores how we might interpret Scripture with an awareness that we always approach it from our own context, yet we recognize that Scripture always remains "intrinsically unfamiliar" and "strange and new."*

The[4] authority of the Bible is a perennial and urgent issue for those of us who stake our lives on its testimony. This issue, however, is bound to remain

[4] Walter Brueggemann, "Biblical Authority,"*Christian Century,* January 3–10, 2001. Subscriptions: $49/year from P.O. Box 378, Mt. Morris, IL 61054. Ph.: 1–800–208–4097. Copyright 2001 Christian Century. Reprinted with permission.

unsettled and therefore perpetually disputatious. It cannot be otherwise, since the biblical text is endlessly "strange and new." It always and inescapably out-distances our categories of understanding and explanation, of interpretation and control. Because the Bible is "the live word of the living God," it will not compliantly submit to the accounts we prefer to give of it. There is something intrinsically unfamiliar about the book; and when we seek to override that un-familiarity, we are on the hazardous ground of idolatry. Rather than proclaiming loud, dogmatic slogans about the Bible, we might do better to consider the odd and intimate ways in which we have each been led to where we are in our relationship with the Scriptures. How each of us reads the Bible is partly the result of family, neighbors and friends (a socialization process), and partly the God-given accident of long-term development in faith. Consequently, the real issues of biblical authority and interpretation are not likely to be settled by cognitive formulations or by appeals to classic confessions. These issues live in often unrecognized, uncriticized and deeply powerful ways—especially if they are rooted (as they may be for most of us) in hurt, anger or anxiety.

Decisions about biblical meanings are not made on the spot, but result from the growth of habits and convictions. And if that is so, then the disputes over meaning require not frontal arguments but long-term pastoral attentiveness to one another in good faith.

A church in dispute will require great self-knowing candor and a generous openness among its members. Such attentiveness may lead us to recognize that the story of someone else's nurture in the faith could be a transformative gift that allows us to read the text in a new way. My own story leads me to identify six facets of biblical interpretation that I believe are likely to be op-erative among us all.

INHERENCY

The Bible is inherently the live word of God, revealing the character and will of God and empowering us for an alternative life in the world. While I be-lieve in the indeterminacy of the text to some large extent, I know that finally the Bible is forceful and consistent in its main theological claim. It expresses the conviction that the God who created the world in love redeems the world in suffering and will consummate the world in joyous well-being. That flow of conviction about God's self-disclosure in the Bible is surely the main claim of the apostolic faith, a claim upon which the church fundamentally agrees. That fundamental agreement is, of course, the beginning of the conversation and not its conclusion; but it is a deep and important starting point. From that inherent claim certain things follow:

First, all of us in the church are bound together by this foundation of ap-ostolic faith. As my tradition affirms, "in essentials unity." It also means, moreover, that in disputes about biblical authority nobody has the high ground morally or hermeneutically. Our common commitment to the truth of the book makes us equal before the book, as it does around the table.

Second, since the inherency of evangelical truth in the book is focused on its main claims, it follows that there is much in the text that is "lesser," not a main claim, but probes and attempts over the generations to carry the main claims to specificity. These attempts are characteristically informed by particular circumstance and are open to variation, nuance and even contradiction. It is a primal Reformation principle that our faith is evangelical, linked to the good news and not to biblicism. The potential distinction between good news and lesser claims can lead to much dispute.

Third, the inherent word of God in the biblical text is refracted through many authors who were not disembodied voices of revealed truth but circumstance-situated men and women of faith (as are we all) who said what their circumstances permitted and required them to say of that which is truly inherent. It is this human refraction that makes the hard work of critical study inescapable, so that every text is given a suspicious scrutiny whereby we may consider the ways in which bodied humanness has succeeded or not succeeded in bearing truthful and faithful witness.

Fourth, given both inherency and circumstance-situated human refraction, the Bible is so endlessly a surprise beyond us that Karl Barth famously and rightly termed it "strange and new." The Bible is not a fixed, frozen, readily exhausted read; it is, rather, a "script," always reread, through which the Spirit makes all things new. When the church adjudicates between the inherent and the circumstance-situated, it is sorely tempted to settle, close and idolize. Therefore, inherency of an evangelical kind demands a constant resistance to familiarity. Nobody's reading is final or inerrant, precisely because the key Character in the book who creates, redeems and consummates is always beyond us in holy hiddenness. When we push boldly through the hiddenness, wanting to know more clearly, what we thought was holy ground turns out to be a playground for idolatry. Our reading, then, is inescapably provisional. It is rightly done with the modesty of those who are always to be surprised again by what is "strange and new."

INTERPRETATION

Recognizing the claim of biblical authority is not difficult as it pertains to the main affirmations of apostolic faith. But from that base line, the hard, disputatious work of interpretation needs to be recognized precisely for what it is: nothing more than interpretation. As our mothers and fathers have always known, the Bible is not self-evident and self-interpreting, and the Reformers did not mean to say that it was so when they escaped the church's magisterium. Rather the Bible requires and insists upon human interpretation, which is inescapably subjective, necessarily provisional and inevitably disputatious. I propose as an interpretive rule that all of our interpretations need to be regarded, at the most, as having only tentative authority. This will enable us to make our best, most insistent claims, but then regularly relinquish our pet interpretations and, together with our partners in dispute, fall back in joy into the inherent apostolic claims that outdistance all of our too familiar and too partisan interpretations. We may learn from the rabbis the marvelous rhythm of deep interpretive dispute and profound common yielding in joy and affectionate well-being. The characteristic and sometimes demonic mode of Reformed interpretation is not tentativeness and relinquishment, but tentativeness hardening into absoluteness. It often becomes a sleight-of-hand act, substituting our interpretive preference for the inherency of apostolic claims.

The process of interpretation which precludes final settlement on almost all questions is evident in the Bible itself. A stunning case in point is the Mosaic teaching in Deuteronomy 23:1-8 that bans from the community all those with distorted sexuality and all those who are foreigners. In Isaiah 56:3-8 this Mosaic teaching is overturned in the Bible itself, offering what Herbert Donner terms an intentional "abrogation" of Mosaic law through new teaching. The old, no doubt circumstance-driven exclusion is answered by a circumstance-driven inclusiveness.

In Deuteronomy 24:1, moreover, Moses teaches that marriages broken in infidelity cannot be restored, even if both parties want to get back together. But in Jeremiah 3, in a shocking reversal given in a pathos-filled poem, God's own voice indicates a readiness to violate that Torah teaching for the sake of restored marriage to Israel. The old teaching is seen to be problematic even for God. The latter text shows God prepared to move beyond the old prohibition of Torah in order that the inherent evangelical claims of God's graciousness may be fully available even to a recalcitrant Israel. In embarrassment and perhaps even in humiliation, the God of Jeremiah's poem willfully overrides the old text. It becomes clear that the interpretive project that constitutes the final form of the text is itself profoundly polyvalent, yielding no single exegetical outcome, but allowing layers and layers of fresh reading in which God's own life and character are deeply engaged and put at risk.

IMAGINATION

Responsible interpretation requires imagination. I understand that imagination makes serious Calvinists nervous because it smacks of the subjective freedom to carry the text in undeveloped directions and to engage in fantasy. But I would insist that imagination is in any case inevitable in any interpretive process that is more than simple reiteration, and that faithful imagination is characteristically not autonomous fantasy but good-faith extrapolation. I understand imagination, no doubt a complex epistemological process, to be the capacity to entertain images of meaning and reality that are beyond the givens of observable experience. That is, imagination is the hosting of "otherwise," and I submit that every serious teacher or preacher invites people to an "otherwise" beyond the evident. Without that we have nothing to say. We must take risks and act daringly to push beyond what is known to that which is hoped for and trusted but not yet in hand.

Interpretation is not the reiteration of the text but, rather, the movement of the text beyond itself in fresh, often formerly unuttered ways. Jesus' parables are a prime example. They open the listening community to possible futures. Beyond parabolic teaching, however, there was in ancient Israel and in the early church an observant wonder. As eyewitnesses created texts out of observed and remembered miracles, texted miracles in turn become materials for imagination that pushed well beyond what was given or intended even in the text. This is an inescapable process for those of us who insist that the Bible is a contemporary word to us. We transport ourselves out of the 21st century back to the ancient world of the text or, conversely, we transpose ancient voices into contemporary voices of authority.

Those of us who think critically do not believe that the Old Testament was talking about Jesus, and yet we make the linkages. Surely Paul was not thinking of the crisis over 16th-century indulgences when he wrote about "faith alone." Surely Isaiah was not thinking of Martin Luther King's dream of a new earth. Yet we make such leaps all the time. What a huge leap to imagine that the primal commission to "till and keep the earth" (Gen 2:15) is really about environmental issues and the chemicals used by Iowa farmers. Yet we make it. What a huge leap to imagine that the ancient provision for Jubilee in Leviticus 25 has anything to do the cancellation of Third World debt or with an implied critique of global capitalism. Yet we make it. What a huge leap to imagine that an ancient purity code in Leviticus 18 bears upon consenting gays and lesbians in the 21st century and has anything to do with ordination. Yet we make it.

We are all committed to the high practice of subjective extrapolations because we have figured out that a cold, reiterative objectivity has no missional energy or moral force. We do it, and will not stop doing it. It is, however, surely healing and humbling for us to have enough self-knowledge to concede that what we are doing will not carry the freight of absoluteness.

Imagination can indeed be a gift of the Spirit, but it is a gift used with immense subjective freedom. Therefore, after our imaginative interpretations are made with vigor in dispute with others in the church, we must regularly, gracefully and with modesty fall back from our best extrapolations to the sure apostolic claims that lie behind our extremities of imagination, liberal or conservative.

IDEOLOGY

A consideration of ideology is difficult for us because we American churchpeople are largely innocent about our own interpretive work. We are seldom aware of or honest about the ways in which our work is shot through with distorting vested interests. But it is so, whether we know it or not. There is no interpretation of Scripture (nor of anything else) that is unaffected by the passions, convictions and perceptions of the interpreter. Ideology is the self-deceiving practice of taking a part for the whole, of taking "my truth" for the truth, of palming off the particular as a universal. It is so already in the text of Scripture itself, as current scholarship makes clear, because the spirit-given text is given us by and through human authors. It is so because spirit-filled interpretation is given us by and through bodied authors who must make their way in the world—and in making our way, we humans do not see so clearly or love so dearly or follow so nearly as we might imagine.

There are endless examples of ideology at work in interpretation. Historical criticism is no innocent practice, for it intends to fend off church authority and protect the freedom of the autonomous interpreter. Canonical criticism is no innocent practice, for it intends to maintain old coherences against the perceived threat of more recent fragmentation. High moralism is no innocent practice, even if it sounds disciplined and noble, for much of it grows out of fear and is a strategy to fend off anxiety. Communitarian inclusiveness is no innocent practice, because it reflects a reaction against exclusivism and so is readily given to a kind of reactive carelessness.

There is enough truth in every such interpretive posture and strategy—and a hundred others we might name—to make it credible and to gather a constituency for it. But it is not ideologically innocent, and therefore has no absolute claim.

In a disputatious church, a healthy practice might be to reflect upon the ideological passion not of others, but of one's self and one's cohorts. I believe that such reflection would invariably indicate that every passionate interpretive voice is shot through with vested interest, sometimes barely hidden. It is completely predictable that interpreters who are restrictive about gays and lesbians will characteristically advocate high capitalism and a strong national defense. Conversely, those who are "open and affirming" will characteristically maintain a critique of consumer capitalism, and consensus on a whole cluster of other issues. One can argue that such a package only indicates a theological-ethical coherence. Perhaps, but in no case is the package innocent, since we incline to make our decisions without any critical reflection, but only in order to sustain the package.

Every passionate vested interest has working in it a high measure of anxiety about deep threats, perhaps perceived, perhaps imagined. And anxiety has a force that permits us to deal in wholesale categories without the nuance of the particular. A judgment grounded in anxiety, anywhere on the theological spectrum, does not want to be disturbed or informed by facts on the ground. Every vested interest shaped by anxiety has near its source old fears that are deep and hidden, but for all of that, authoritative. Every one has at its very bottom hurt—old hurt, new hurt, hurt for ourselves, for those we remember, for those we love. The lingering, unhealed pain becomes a hermeneutical principle out of which we will not be talked.

Every ideological passion, liberal or conservative, may be encased in Scripture itself or enshrined in longstanding interpretation until it is regarded as absolute and trusted as decisive authority. And where an ideology becomes loud and destructive in the interpretive community, we may be sure that the doses of anxiety, fear and hurt within it are huge and finally irrepressible.

I do not for an instant suggest that no distinctions can be made, nor that it is so dark that all cats are gray. And certainly, given our ideological passions, we must go on and interpret in any case. But I do say that in our best judgments concerning Scripture, we might be aware enough of our propensity to distort in the service of vested interests, anxiety, fear and hurt that we recognize that our best interpretation might be not only a vehicle for but also a block to and distortion of the crucified truth of the gospel.

I have come belatedly to see, in my own case, that my hermeneutical passion is largely propelled by the fact that my father was a pastor who was economically abused by the church he served, abused as a means of control. I cannot measure the ways in which that felt awareness determines how I work, how I interpret, who[m] I read, whom I trust as a reliable voice. The wound is deep enough to pervade everything; I suspect, moreover, that I am not the only one for whom this is true. It could be that we turn our anxieties, fears and hurts to good advantage as vehicles for obedience. But even in so doing, we are put on notice. We cannot escape from such passions; but we can submit them to brothers and sisters whose own history of distortion is very different from ours and as powerful in its defining force.

INSPIRATION

It is traditional to speak of Scripture as "inspired." There is a long history of unhelpful formulations of what that notion might mean. Without appealing to classical formulations that characteristically have more to do with "testing" the spirit (1 John 4:1) than with "not quenching" the spirit (1 Thess 5:19), we may affirm that the force of God's purpose, will and capacity for liberation, reconciliation and new life is everywhere in the biblical text. In such an affirmation, of course, we say more than we can understand, for the claim is precisely an acknowledgment that in and through this text, God's wind blows through and past all our critical and confessional categories of reading and understanding. That powerful and enlivening force, moreover, pertains not simply to the ordaining of the text but to its transmission and interpretation among us.

The spirit will not be regimented [see John 3:8 and 2 Tim 2:9], and therefore none of our reading is guaranteed to be inspired. But it does happen on occasion. It does happen that in and through the text we are blown beyond ourselves. It does happen that the spirit teaches, guides and heals through the text, so that the text yields something other than an echo of ourselves. It does happen that in prayer and study believers are led to what is "strange and new." It does happen that preachers are led to utterances beyond what they set out to make. It does happen that churches, in councils, sessions and other courts, are led beyond themselves, powered beyond prejudice, liberated beyond convention, overwhelmed by the capacity for new risks.

IMPORTANCE

Biblical interpretation, done with imagination willing to risk ideological distortion, open to the inspiring spirit, is important. But it is important not because it might allow some to seize control of the church, but because it gives the world access to the good truth of the God who creates, redeems and consummates. That missional intention is urgent in every circumstance and season. The church at its most faithful has always understood that we read Scripture for the sake of the church's missional testimony.

But the reading of the Bible is now especially urgent because our society is sorely tempted to reduce the human project to commodity. In its devotion to the making of money it reduces persons to objects and thins human communications to electronic icons. Technique in all its military modes and derivatively in every other mode threatens us. Technique is aimed at control, the fencing out of death, the fencing out of gift and, eventually, the fencing out of humanness.

Nonetheless, we in the church dare affirm that the lively word of Scripture is the primal antidote to technique, the primal news that fends off trivialization. Thinning to control and trivializing to evade ambiguity are the major goals of our culture. The church in its disputatious anxiety is tempted to join the move to technique, to thin the Bible and make it one-dimensional, deeply tempted to trivialize the Bible by acting as though it is important because it may solve some disruptive social inconvenience. The dispute tends to reduce what is rich and dangerous in the book to knowable technique, and what is urgent and immense to exhaustible trivia.

The Bible is too important to be reduced in this way because the dangers of the world are too great and the expectations of God are too large. What if liberals and conservatives in the church, for all their disagreement, would together put their energies to upholding the main truth against the main threat? The issues before God's creation (of which we are stewards) are immense; those issues shame us when our energy is deployed only to settle our anxieties. The biblical script insists that the world is not without God, not without the holy gift of life rooted in love. And yet we twitter! The Bible is a lamp and light to fend off the darkness [see Ps 119:105]. The darkness is real, and the light is for walking boldly, faithfully in a darkness we do not and cannot control. In this crisis, the church must consider what is entrusted peculiarly to us in this book.

Recently an Israeli journalist in Jerusalem commented on the fracturing dispute in Israel over who constitutes a real Jew, orthodox, conservative or reform. And he said about the dispute, "If any Jew wins, all Jews lose." Think about it: "If anyone wins, everyone loses."

3. Thomas Aquinas, Selections from the *Summa Theologiae* "Treatise on Law"

Thomas Aquinas (1225–1274) wrote the Summa Theologica *as a manual of Christian theology for the use of students. The selections in this chapter are from the section of the* Summa *called the "Treatise on Law." Here Aquinas builds on Aristotle's (to whom he refers simply as "the Philosopher") conception of natural law, which is instructed and completed by a revealed divine law.*

WHETHER LAW IS SOMETHING PERTAINING TO REASON

Law[5] is a rule and measure of acts, whereby a person is induced to act or is restrained from acting: for *lex* [law] is derived from *ligare* [to bind], because it binds one to act. Now the rule and measure of human acts is the reason, which is the first principle of human acts, as is evident from what has been stated above; since it belongs to the reason to direct to the end, which is the first principle in all matters of action, according to the Philosopher (*Phys.* 2). Now that which is the principle in any genus, is the rule and measure of that genus: for instance, unity in the genus of numbers, and the first movement in the genus of movements. Consequently it follows that law is something pertaining to reason.

WHETHER THE LAW IS ALWAYS SOMETHING DIRECTED TO THE COMMON GOOD

As stated above, the law belongs to that which is a principle of human acts, because it is their rule and measure. Now as reason is a principle of human acts, so in reason itself there is something which is the principle in respect of all the rest: wherefore to this principle chiefly and mainly law must needs be referred. Now the first principle in practical matters, which are the object of the practical reason, is the last end: and the last end of human life is bliss or

---

[5] Thomas Aquinas, *Summa Theologiae,* translated by the Fathers of the English Dominican Province under the title *Summa Theologica* (New York: Benzinger Brothers, 1948) adapted. See note 1 in chapter 1 of this book; these selections are from I-II 90.1–2; 91.1–4, 6; 93.3; 94.2; 95.2; 97.1–2.

happiness, as stated above. Consequently the law must needs regard principally the relationship to happiness. Moreover, since every part is ordained to the whole, as imperfect to perfect; and since one person is a part of the perfect community, the law must needs regard properly the relationship to universal happiness. Wherefore the Philosopher, in the above definition of legal matters mentions both happiness and the body politic: for he says (*Ethic.* 5.1) that we call those legal matters "just, which are adapted to produce and preserve happiness and its parts for the body politic": since the state is a perfect community, as he says in *Polit.* 1.1.

Now in every genus, that which belongs to it chiefly is the principle of the others, and the others belong to that genus in subordination to that thing: thus fire, which is chief among hot things, is the cause of heat in mixed bodies, and these are said to be hot in so far as they have a share of fire. Consequently, since the law is chiefly ordained to the common good, any other precept in regard to some individual work, must needs be devoid of the nature of a law, save in so far as it regards the common good. Therefore every law is ordained to the common good.

WHETHER THERE IS AN ETERNAL LAW

As stated above, a law is nothing else but a dictate of practical reason emanating from the ruler who governs a perfect community. Now it is evident, granted that the world is ruled by Divine Providence, as was stated in . . . I.22.2 that the whole community of the universe is governed by Divine Reason. Wherefore the very Idea of the government of things in God the Ruler of the universe, has the nature of a law. And since the Divine Reason's conception of things is not subject to time but is eternal, according to Proverbs 8:23, therefore it is that this kind of law must be called eternal.

WHETHER THERE IS IN US A NATURAL LAW

As stated above, law, being a rule and measure, can be in a person in two ways: in one way, as in him that rules and measures; in another way, as in that which is ruled and measured, since a thing is ruled and measured, in so far as it partakes of the rule or measure. Wherefore, since all things subject to Divine providence are ruled and measured by the eternal law, as was stated above; it is evident that all things partake somewhat of the eternal law, in so far as, namely, from its being imprinted on them, they derive their respective inclinations to their proper acts and ends. Now among all others, the rational creature is subject to Divine providence in the most excellent way, in so far as it partakes of a share of providence, by being provident both for itself and for others. Wherefore it has a share of the Eternal Reason, whereby it has a natural inclination to its proper act and end: and this participation of the eternal law in the rational creature is called the natural law. Hence the Psalmist after saying (Ps 4:6): "Offer up the sacrifice of justice," as though someone asked what the works of justice are, adds: "Many say, Who showeth us good things?" in answer to which question he says: "The light of Thy countenance, O Lord, is signed upon us": thus implying that the light of natural reason, whereby we discern what is good and what is evil, which is the function of the natural law, is nothing else than an imprint on us of the Divine light. It is therefore evident that the natural law is nothing else than the rational creature's participation of the eternal law.

WHETHER THERE IS A HUMAN LAW

As stated above, a law is a dictate of the practical reason. Now it is to be observed that the same procedure takes place in the practical and in the speculative reason: for each proceeds from principles to conclusions, as stated above. Accordingly we conclude that just as, in the speculative reason, from naturally known indemonstrable principles, we draw the conclusions of the various sciences, the knowledge of which is not imparted to us by nature, but acquired by the efforts of reason, so too it is from the precepts of the natural law, as from general and indemonstrable principles, that the human reason needs to proceed to the more particular determination of certain matters. These particular determinations, devised by human reason, are called human laws, provided the other essential conditions of law be observed, as stated above.

WHETHER THERE WAS ANY NEED FOR A DIVINE LAW

Besides the natural and the human law it was necessary for the directing of human conduct to have a Divine law. And this for four reasons: First, because it is by law that human beings are directed how to perform their proper acts in view of their last end. And indeed if human beings were ordained to no other end than that which is proportionate to their natural faculties, there would be no need for them to have any further direction of the part of their reason, besides the natural law and human law which is derived from it. But since human beings are ordained to an end of eternal happiness which is inproportionate to their natural faculties, as stated above, therefore it was necessary that, besides the natural and the human law, human beings should be directed to their end by a law given by God.

Secondly, because, on account of the uncertainty of human judgment, especially on contingent and particular matters, different people form different judgments on human acts; whence also different and contrary laws result. In order, therefore, that human beings may know without any doubt what they ought to do and what they ought to avoid, it was necessary for them to be directed in their proper acts by a law given by God, for it is certain that such a law cannot err.

Thirdly, because humans can make laws in those matters of which they are competent to judge. But human beings are not competent to judge of interior movements, that are hidden, but only of exterior acts which appear: and yet for the perfection of virtue it is necessary for human beings to conduct themselves aright in both kinds of acts. Consequently human law could not sufficiently curb and direct interior acts; and it was necessary for this purpose that a Divine law should supervene.

Fourthly, because, as Augustine says, human law cannot punish or forbid all evil deeds: since while aiming at doing away with all evils, it would do away with many good things, and would hinder the advance of the common good, which is necessary for human intercourse. In order, therefore, that no evil might remain unforbidden and unpunished, it was necessary for the Divine law to supervene, whereby all sins are forbidden.

And these four causes are touched upon in Psalm 19:7, where it is said: "The law of the Lord is perfect," i.e. allowing no foulness of sin; "reviving the soul," because it directs not only exterior, but also interior acts; "the decrees of the Lord are sure," because of the certainty of what is true and right; "making wise the simple," by directing human beings to an end supernatural and Divine.[6]

WHETHER THERE IS A LAW IN THE FOMES OF SIN

. . . Accordingly under the Divine Lawgiver various creatures have various natural inclinations, so that what is, as it were, a law for one, is against the law for another: thus I might say that fierceness is, in a way, the law of a dog, but against the law of a sheep or another meek animal. And so the law of human beings, which, by the Divine ordinance, is allotted to them, according to their proper natural condition, is that they should act in accordance with reason: and this law was so effective in the primitive state, that nothing either beside or against reason could take a person unawares. But when human beings turned their backs on God, they fell under the influence of their sensual impulses: in fact this happens to each one individually, the more a person deviates from the path of reason, so that, after a fashion, he or she is likened to the beasts that are led by the impulse of sensuality, according to Psalm 49:20: "Mortals cannot abide in their pomp; they are like the animals that perish."

So, then, this very inclination of sensuality which is called the "fomes," in other animals has simply the nature of a law (yet only in so far as a law may be said to be in such things), by reason of a direct inclination. But in human beings, it has not the nature of law in this way, rather is it a deviation from the law of reason. But since, by the just sentence of God, humans are destitute of

---

[6] The notation and wording of this biblical quotation has been revised to conform to the Revised Standard Version.

original justice, and their reason bereft of its vigor, this impulse of sensuality, whereby they are led, in so far as it is a penalty following from the Divine law depriving human beings of their proper dignity, has the nature of a law.

WHETHER EVERY LAW IS DERIVED FROM THE ETERNAL LAW

As stated above, the law denotes a kind of plan directing acts towards an end. Now wherever there are movers ordained to one another, the power of the second mover must needs be derived from the power of the first mover; since the second mover does not move except in so far as it is moved by the first. Wherefore we observe the same in all those who govern, so that the plan of government is derived by secondary governors from the governor in chief; thus the plan of what is to be done in a state flows from the king's command to his inferior administrators: and again in things of art the plan of whatever is to be done by art flows from the chief craftsworker to the under-workers, who work with their hands. Since then the eternal law is the plan of government in the Chief Governor, all the plans of government in the inferior governors must be derived from the eternal law. But these plans of inferior governors are all other laws besides the eternal law. Therefore all laws, in so far as they partake of right reason, are derived from the eternal law. Hence Augustine says (*De lib. arb.* 1.6) that "in temporal law there is nothing just and lawful, but what humans have drawn from the eternal law."

WHETHER THE NATURAL LAW CONTAINS SEVERAL PRECEPTS, OR ONLY ONE

. . . Now a certain order is to be found in those things that are apprehended universally. For that which, before aught else, falls under apprehension, is "being," the notion of which is included in all things whatsoever a person apprehends. Wherefore the first indemonstrable principle is that "the same thing cannot be affirmed and denied at the same time," which is based on the notion of "being" and "not-being": and on this principle all others are based, as is stated in *Metaph.* 4, text. 9. Now as "being" is the first thing that falls under the apprehension simply, so "good" is the first thing that falls under the apprehension of the practical reason, which is directed to action: since every agent acts for an end under the aspect of good. Consequently the first principle of practical reason is one founded on the notion of good, viz. that "good is that which all things seek after." Hence this is the first precept of law, that "good is to be done and pursued, and evil is to be avoided." All other precepts of the natural law are based upon this: so that whatever the practical reason naturally apprehends as human good (or evil) belongs to the precepts of the natural law as something to be done or avoided.

Since, however, good has the nature of an end, and evil, the nature of a contrary, hence it is that all those things to which a person has a natural inclination, are naturally apprehended by reason as being good, and consequently as objects of pursuit, and their contraries as evil, and objects of avoidance. Wherefore according to the order of natural inclinations, is the order of the precepts of the natural law. Because in human beings there is first of all an inclination to good in accordance with the nature which they have in common with all substances: inasmuch as every substance seeks the preservation of its own being, according to its nature: and by reason of this inclination, whatever is a means of preserving human life, and of warding off its obstacles, belongs to the natural law. Secondly, there is in human beings an inclination to things that pertain to them more specially, according to that nature which they have in common with other animals: and in virtue of this inclination, those things are said to belong to the natural law, "which nature has taught to all animals" (*Pandect.*, Just., 1, t. 1), such as sexual intercourse, education of offspring and so forth. Thirdly, there is in human beings an inclination to good, according to the nature of his reason, which nature is proper to them: thus humans have a natural inclination to know the truth about God, and to live in society: and in this respect, whatever pertains to this inclination belongs to the natural law; for instance, to shun ignorance, to avoid offending those among whom one has to live, and other such things regarding the above inclination.

WHETHER EVERY HUMAN LAW IS DERIVED FROM THE NATURAL LAW

As Augustine says (*De lib. arb.* 1.5) "that which is not just seems to be no law at all": wherefore the force of a law depends on the extent of its justice. Now in human affairs a thing is said to be just, from being right, according to the rule of reason. But the first rule of reason is the law of nature, as is clear from what has been stated above. Consequently every human law has just so much of the nature of law, as it is derived from the law of nature. But if in any point it deflects from the law of nature, it is no longer a law but a perversion of law.

But it must be noted that something may be derived from the natural law in two ways: first, as a conclusion from premises, secondly, by way of determination of certain generalities. The first way is like to that by which, in sciences, demonstrated conclusions are drawn from the principles: while the second mode is likened to that whereby, in the arts, general forms are particularized as to details: thus the craftsman needs to determine the general form of a house to some particular shape. Some things are therefore derived from the general principles of the natural law, by way of conclusions; e.g. that "one must not kill" may be derived as a conclusion from the principle that "one should do harm to no person": while some are derived therefrom by way of determination; e.g. the law of nature has it that evil-doers should be punished; but that they be punished in this or that way, is a determination of the law of nature.

Accordingly both modes of derivation are found in the human law. But those things which are derived in the first way, are contained in human law not as emanating therefrom exclusively, but have some force from the natural law also. But those things which are derived in the second way, have no other force than that of human law.

WHETHER HUMAN LAW SHOULD BE CHANGED IN ANY WAY

As stated above, human law is a dictate of reason, whereby human acts are directed. Thus there may be two causes for the just change of human law: one on the part of reason; the other on the part of human beings whose acts are regulated by law. The cause on the part of reason is that it seems natural to human reason to advance gradually from the imperfect to the perfect. Hence, in speculative sciences, we see that the teaching of the early philosophers was imperfect, and that it was afterwards perfected by those who succeeded them. So also in practical matters: for those who first endeavored to discover something useful for the human community, not being able by themselves to take everything into consideration, set up certain institutions which were deficient in many ways; and these were changed by subsequent lawgivers who made institutions that might prove less frequently deficient in respect of the common weal.

On the part of human beings, whose acts are regulated by law, the law can be rightly changed on account of the changed condition of human beings, to whom different things are expedient according to the difference of their condition. An example is proposed by Augustine (*De lib. arb.* 1.6): "If the people have a sense of moderation and responsibility, and are most careful guardians of the common weal, it is right to enact a law allowing such a people to choose their own magistrates for the government of the commonwealth. But if, as time goes on, the same people become so corrupt as to sell their votes, and entrust the government to scoundrels and criminals; then the right of appointing their public officials is rightly forfeit to such a people, and the choice devolves to a few good persons."

WHETHER HUMAN LAW SHOULD ALWAYS BE CHANGED,
WHENEVER SOMETHING BETTER OCCURS

As stated above, human law is rightly changed, in so far as such change is conducive to the common weal. But, to a certain extent, the mere change of law is of itself prejudicial to the common good: because custom avails much for the observance of laws, seeing that what is done contrary to general custom, even in slight matters, is looked upon as grave. Consequently, when a law is changed, the binding power of the law is diminished, in so far as custom is abolished. Wherefore human law should never be changed, unless, in some way or other, the common weal be compensated according to the extent of the harm done in this respect. Such compensation may arise either from some very great and very evident benefit conferred by the new enactment; or from the extreme urgency of the case, due to the fact that either the existing law is clearly unjust, or its observance extremely harmful. Wherefore the jurist says (*Pandect.,* Justin., 1ff., t. 4, "De Constit. Princip.") that "in establishing new laws, there should be evidence of the benefit to be derived, before departing from a law which has long been considered just."

4. Lord John Habgood, "Science and Ethics"

John Habgood is an authoritative voice in England on the relationship of science and religion. His career is rich and varied: demonstrator in pharmacology at Cambridge University, university president, priest and rector, Archbishop of York in the Church of England, and member of the House of Lords. Presently he does his work at the Ian Ramsey Centre for the Interdisciplinary Study of Religious Beliefs in Relation to the Sciences and Medicine at Oxford University. This article, written for The Westminster Dictionary of Christian Ethics, *sets forth the basic questions raised by the relationship of science and the Christian faith.*

The[7] word "science" covers a wide range of meanings: (1) a system of knowledge, split up into a number of distinct "sciences," which together constitute a more or less coherent scientific world view; (2) a method of investigation characterized by a rational empirical, objective, and critical approach to natural phenomena; (3) applied science (technology)—the ability to manipulate the natural world predictably. "Science" in all these senses is of concern to ethics, though in different ways that need to be carefully distinguished.

1. SCIENCE AS A SOURCE OF FACTUAL INFORMATION

Moral judgments are not made *in vacuo,* but require a knowledge of facts and an ability to predict the probable consequences of actions. Scientists are concerned with both. The general scientific understanding of the world is therefore an important part of the background of moral choice, and many traditional moral issues have been seen in a different light as scientific knowledge has increased. Sexual morality, for example, has been affected by advances in physiology and psychology, even among those who would claim that there has been no change in the fundamental principles that should govern sexual behavior. Homosexuality remains for many an area of moral uncertainty, partly for the reason that there is not as yet any scientific agreement about its causes. A soundly based concern about the moral dimensions of animal welfare needs to pay proper attention to biology. Sociologists offer interpretations of human behavior that, by revealing the character and extent of

---

[7] John Habgood, "Science and Ethics" in *The Westminster Dictionary of Christian Ethics,* ed. James F. Childress and John Macquarrie (Philadelphia: Westminster Press, 1986) 563–66.

social constraints, can enlarge the area of choice. To know that one is conforming to type is to be given the freedom not to do so. Psychology can create similar areas of freedom, as well as enlarge perceptions of the consequences of behavior on other people.

In addition to these countless general ways in which scientific knowledge has ethical implications, there are also examples of particular discoveries that relate to particular moral choices. The link between cigarette smoking and lung cancer has created new moral problems for smokers and tobacco manufacturers. Work on the deleterious effects of bottle-feeding infants in Third World countries has opened up a new moral dimension in the promotion and export of dried milk. Once again, the list is endless.

There are also less direct ways in which scientific information has influenced ethical thinking. Anthropology has weakened the appeal of authoritarian ethical systems by its disclosure of the enormous variety of social patterns and of the extent to which morality is socially conditioned. The moral sense itself has become an object of scientific study. Research on the social behavior of animals, developmental psychology, and the evolutionary origins of altruism have led some scientists to conclude that there are certain moral norms or tendencies, discoverable by science, built into human nature. The new, and controversial, science of sociobiology attempts to explore this field from an evolutionary perspective.

2. SCIENCE AS A SOURCE OF VALUES

Since G. E. Moore's description of the naturalistic fallacy, it has been customary to hold that statements of value cannot be derived exclusively from statements of fact; in other words, science by itself cannot prescribe what is right or wrong. In most practical contexts this is obviously true. Sound factual information is a necessary but not a sufficient basis for moral choice. Judgment about the facts goes beyond the facts themselves.

This neat distinction, however, ignores the extent to which facts and values are interrelated. It can be questioned whether any facts are totally value-free. Thus it is possible for moral judgments to appear to be made on strictly factual grounds by overlooking the element of evaluation already built into them.

The various systems of evolutionary ethics, of which T. H. Huxley, Julian Huxley, and, from a Christian perspective, Walter Rauschenbusch were notable exponents, made use of the idea of evolutionary "progress" as a moral guide, as if it could somehow be read directly from the biological facts themselves. Sociobiology provides the most modern attempt to perform the same operation, but has difficulty in producing convincing evidence of evolutionary traits in human nature strong enough to be treated as ethically normative. Psychology has been a fruitful source of hidden norms, as expressed in such concepts as abnormality or maturity, both of which are extremely hard to detach from their cultural contexts.

The most powerful claim that science provides a source of values is made, not on the basis of any particular discoveries or theories, but by extrapolation from the scientific method itself. Science "works," runs this claim, and intrinsic to it are certain values and attitudes that are validated by this success. Jacques Monod[8] proposed what he called "an ethic of knowledge" in which the main value is objective knowledge itself.

Monod's proposal was criticized for its arbitrariness and restrictiveness. There is, however, a more general and acceptable sense in which the values inherent in scientific activity spill over into ordinary life. Scientists form a community with its own professional code concerned with such matters as honesty in reporting facts, the publication of unfavorable as well as favorable evidence, the acknowledgment of sources and the safeguarding of original discoveries, and cooperation with colleagues irrespective of nationality. In addition the successful scientist depends on personal moral qualities such as open-mindedness, a readiness to accept criticism, patience, persistence, love of the truth for its own sake, even an element of passion. Some have described science as an adventure of faith. Scientific progress would not be possible unless by and large scientists could trust one another, and this is why in professional terms the penalties for fraud are high.

In its beginnings modern science depended on the moral and philosophical assumptions of Christian Europe. Nowadays, in the light of its practical achievements, the values that sustain it have come to be regarded by many as self-authenticating. Science is its own justification, and what makes for good science must itself be good. Misplaced trust is eventually exposed, and the overwhelming weight of scientific opinion acts to reinforce the values of the scientific community. In this very general sense, therefore, it can be argued that science operates as a moral force. Critics of this argument point out that in practice the main characteristic of science is power rather than disinterested knowledge. And scientific power can suffer the same corruptions as any other kind of power.

3. SCIENCE AS A SOURCE OF NEW ETHICAL PROBLEMS

Applied science has given humanity increasing power to control and adapt its environment, and to manipulate some of the most fundamental characteristics of human life and society. New powers always create ethical problems of peculiar difficulty, since there are no precedents to act as guides. Nevertheless certain general principles seem to apply. Broadly speaking, answers to questions about the use of new powers reflect differing views about the place of human beings in nature. At one extreme are those who stress the "givenness"

---

[8] Jacques Monod, *Chance and Necessity: An Essay on the Natural Philosophy of Modern Biology,* trans. Austryn Wainhouse (New York: Vintage Books; London: Collins, 1972).

of the natural world and the dangers of upsetting the existing order of things. At the other extreme are those who doubt whether "givenness" means much in an evolving universe, and who see every new advance as increasing the range of human choice, and hence the possibilities of human freedom and personal fulfillment. Both extremes are found among Christians, some emphasizing human creatureliness and others human creativeness. The weight of Christian opinion, however, has generally been on the side of conservatism, and there is a long history of opposition to new techniques, not least in medicine.

Technical power tends to be morally ambiguous. The new freedoms it brings often have hidden costs. The automobile is a classic example of a technological advance that has enormously increased the range of human experience, but has also created new forms of enslavement as well as huge environmental damage. Nuclear energy contains both a promise and a threat. New understandings of human psychology open the way to new forms of human manipulation. Perhaps the biggest source of moral ambiguity today is the extent to which almost any discovery can be made to serve military purposes.

Advances in the biological sciences closely affecting human life itself already pose some intractable problems that are likely to become even more difficult as research continues. The ethics of research on human embryos, for example, must depend in part on the length of time for which it is possible to keep an isolated embryo alive; and all the evidence suggests that this is likely to increase. The possibilities of genetic manipulation pose in an especially acute form questions about the extent to which the "givenness" of human nature should be regarded as inviolable. Even such a relatively simple operation as choosing the sex of one's children has deep personal and social implications.

The abuse of psychiatry for penal purposes in the [former] U.S.S.R. is a particularly striking example of the way therapeutic insights can be used to serve evil ends. Fears that some genetic studies might act as a basis for racial discrimination have led to acrimonious controversy both in Britain and in the U.S.A. And at the more trivial end of the scale, there are those who regard public opinion polls, a very modest instance of scientific data collection, as a threat to electoral integrity.

"Big science," of a size that has to be funded directly by government or some major industry, presents special problems of control and assessment, not least when most of the available expertise is engaged in, and therefore has a vested interest in, the particular project in question. The preliminary work on atomic energy suffered this kind of isolation, with the result that its moral and political implications came to the surface too late to influence the course of research.

It is an open question whether some research may or may not be inherently immoral. Clearly there are, or ought to be, moral limits to the methods used in research, especially insofar as these apply to human beings or animals. But are there some things that it is better not to know? Most scientists would deny this, even though Pandora's box once opened proves impossible to close.

5. Rosemary Radford Ruether,
"Women's Experience and Historical Tradition"

Rosemary Radford Ruether is Carpenter Professor of Feminist Theology at the Pacific School of Religion. This selection is excerpted from her landmark work, Sexism and God-Talk: Toward a Feminist Theology, *first published in 1983. In this selection, Ruether defends the experiential basis of liberation theology. She counters that experience is the basis of all theological reflection, including those that claim to be founded in other, more "objective" sources. Readers should pay special attention to her discussion of the "hermeneutical circle" and her careful analysis of the circular relationship of experience, Scripture, and tradition. Ruether's later work has been seminal in the development of Christian ecofeminism. She is a contributor to chapter 6 of this book, which addresses issues of stewardship and the environment.*

It[9] has frequently been said that feminist theology draws on women's experience as a basic source of content as well as a criterion of truth. There has been a tendency to treat this principle of "experience" as unique to feminist theology (or, perhaps, to liberation theologies) and to see it as distant from "objective" sources of truth of classical theologies. This seems to be a misunderstanding of the experimental base of all theological reflection. What have been called the objective sources of theology; Scripture and tradition, are themselves codified collective human experience.

Human experience is the starting point and the ending point of the hermeneutical circle. Codified tradition both reaches back to roots in experience and is constantly renewed or discarded through the test of experience. Experience includes experience of the divine, experience of oneself, and experience of the community and the world, in an interacting dialectic. Received symbols, formulas, and laws are either authenticated or not through their ability to illuminate and interpret experience. Systems of authority try to reverse this relation and make received symbols dictate what can be experienced as well as the interpretation of that which is experienced. In reality, the relation is the opposite. If a symbol does not speak authentically to experience, it becomes dead or must be altered to provide a new meaning.

The uniqueness of feminist theology lies not in its use of the criteria of experience but rather in its use of women's experience, which has been almost entirely shut out of theological reflection in the past. The use of women's experience in feminist theology, therefore, explodes as a critical force exposing classical theology, including its codified traditions, as based on male experience rather than on universal human experience. Feminist theology makes the sociology of theological knowledge visible, no longer hidden behind mystifications of objectified divine and universal authority.

---

[9] Rosemary Radford Ruether, *Sexism and God-Talk: Toward a Feminist Theology,* 10th ed. (Boston: Beacon Press, 1993) 12–20.

The Hermeneutical Circle of Past and Present Experience

A simplified model of the Western theological tradition can illustrate this hermeneutical circle of past and present experience. We must postulate that every great religious idea begins in the revelatory experience. By revelatory we mean breakthrough experiences beyond ordinary fragmented consciousness that provide interpretive symbols illuminating the means of the *whole* of life. Since consciousness is ultimately individual, we postulate that revelation always starts with an individual. In earlier societies in which there was much less sense of individualism, this breakthrough experience may have been so immediately mediated through a group of interpreters to the social collective that the name of the individual is lost. Later, the creative individual stands out as Prophet, Teacher Revealer, Savior, or Founder of the religious tradition

However much the individual teacher is magnified, in fact, the revelatory experience becomes socially meaningful only when translated into communal consciousness. This means, first, that the revelatory experience must be collectively appropriated by a formative group, which in turn promulgates and teaches a historical community. Second, the formative group mediates what is unique in the revelatory experience through past cultural symbols and, traditions. As far back as human memory stretches, and certainly within the history of [b]iblical traditions, no new prophetic tradition ever is interpreted in a cultural vacuum. However startling and original the vision, it must always be communicated and made meaningful through some transformation of ideas and symbols already current. The hand of the divine does not write on a cultural *tabula rasa* [i.e., blank slate]. Thus the Hebrew prophets interpreted in new ways symbols from Canaanite and Near Eastern religions. Christianity, in successive stages, appropriated a great variety of both Jewish and Hellenistic religious symbols to interpret Jesus. The uniqueness of the vision is expressed by its ability to combine and transform earlier symbolic patterns to illuminate and disclose meaning in new, unexpected ways that speak to new experiential needs as the old patterns ceased to do.

The formative community that has appropriated the revelatory experience in turn gathers a historical community around its interpretation of the vision. This process goes through various stages during which oral and written teachings are developed. At a certain point a group consisting of teacher and leaders emerges that seeks to channel and control the process, to weed out what it regards as deviant communities and interpretations, and to impose a series of criteria to determine the correct interpretive line. The group can do this by defining an authoritative body of writings that is then canonized as the correct interpretation of the original divine revelation and distinguished from other writings, which are regarded either as heretical or of secondary authority. In the process the controlling group marginalizes and suppresses other branches of the community, with their own texts and lines of interpretation. The winning group declares itself the privileged line of true (orthodox) interpretation. Thus a canon of Scripture is established.

Once a canon of Scripture is defined, one can then regard subsequent tradition as reflection upon Scripture and always corrected by Scripture as the controlling authority. In Catholicism and Orthodoxy the notion of the other equally authoritative "apostolic" traditions flowing from early times and existing alongside canonical Scripture does not quite disappear. Creeds, liturgical customs, and oral tradition passed down through apostolic sees also provide access to the original faith of the "primitive community." However much the [members of the] community, both leaders and led, seek to clothe themselves in past codified tradition that provides secure access to divinely revealed truth, in reality the experience of the present community cannot be ignored.

This contemporary community may consist of many different layers, from the "maximal" leaders to the "ordinary believer." Even an Athanasius or a Leo I,[10] who claim to be merely teaching what has always been taught, are in fact engaged in a constant process of revision of the symbolic pattern in a way that reflects their experience. Received ideas are tested by what "feels right," that is, illuminates the logic of the symbolic pattern in a way that speaks most satisfyingly to their own experience of redemption. It is true that theology can evolve into a secondary and tertiary reflection on the logic of ideas themselves. It continues its vital development only to the extent that such thinking remains in touch with depth experience.

The ordinary believers now have increasingly complex formulas of faith, customs, rituals, and writings proposed to them as the basis for appropriating the original revelatory paradigm as personal redeeming experience. These individuals, in their local communities of faith, are always engaged in making their own selection from the patterns of received tradition that fit or make sense in their lives. There is always an interaction between the patterns of faith proposed by teachers to individuals and the individuals' own appropriation of these patterns as interpretations of experience. But these differences remain unarticulated, held within the dominant consensus about what the revelatory pattern "means."

A religious tradition remains vital so long as its revelatory pattern can be reproduced generation after generation and continues to speak to individuals in the community and provide for them the redemptive meaning of individual and collective experience. Such has been the Exodus-Passover pattern for Jews and the death-resurrection paradigm of personal conversion for Christians. The circle from experience to experience, mediated through instruments of tradition, is thus completed when the contemporary community appropriates the foundational paradigm as the continuing story of its own redemption in relation to God, self, and one another.

---

[10] Editors' note: Athanasius (296–373), Bishop of Alexandria, and Pope Leo I (400–461) worked forcefully to establish orthodox positions on the nature of Christ.

Crises of Tradition

Religious traditions fall into crisis when the received interpretation of the redemptive paradigms contradict experience in significant ways. The crisis may be perceived at various levels of radicalness. Exegetical criticism of received theological and Scriptural traditions can bring forth new interpretations that speak to new experiences. This kind of reform goes on in minor and major ways all the time, from individuals making their own private adaptations to teachers founding new schools of interpretation. So long as this is accommodated within the community's methods of transmitting tradition, no major break occurs.

A more radical break takes place when the institutional structures that transmit tradition are perceived to have become corrupt. They are perceived not as teaching truth but as teaching falsehood dictated by their own self-interest and will to power. The revelatory paradigms, the original founder and even the early stages of the formulation of tradition are still seen as authentic. It seems necessary to go behind later historical tradition and institutionalized authorities and "return to" the original revelation. In the literal sense of the word there is no possibility of return to some period of the tradition that predates the intervening history. So the myth of return to origins is a way of making a more radical interpretation of the revelatory paradigm to encompass contemporary experiences, while discarding institutions and traditions that contradict meaningful, just, and truthful life. Usable interpretative patterns are taken from Scripture and early community documents to set the original tradition against its later corruption. The original revelation itself, and the foundational stages of its formulation, are not challenged but held as all the more authoritative to set them as normative against later traditions. The Reformation followed this pattern of change.

A still more radical crisis of tradition occurs when the total religious heritage appears to be corrupt. This kind of radical questioning of the meaningfulness of the Christian religion began to occur in Western Europe during the Enlightenment. Marxism carried the Enlightenment critique of religion still further. Marxism teaches that all religion is an instrument the ruling class uses to justify its own power and to pacify the oppressed. This makes religion not the means of redemption but the means of enslavement. The very nature of religious knowledge is seen as promoting alienation rather than integration of the human person. This kind of ideological critique throws the truth content of religion into radical ethical disrepute . . .

Ideological criticism of the truthfulness of the religion may still allow for some residue of genuine insight into the original religious experiences and foundational teachers. The prophets of Jesus may be said to have had truthful insights into just and meaningful life, but this became corrupted and turned into its opposite by later teachers, even within Scripture. Discarding even the truthfulness of foundational teachers, the critic may turn to alternative sources of truth: to recent critical schools of thought against the religious traditions, to suppressed traditions condemned as heretical by the dominant tradition, or to pre-Christian patterns of thought. Modern rationalist, Marxist, and romantic criticism of religion have followed such alternatives in the last two hundred years.

Why seek alternative traditions at all? Why not just start with contemporary experience? Doesn't the very search for foundational tradition reveal a need for authority outside contemporary experience? It is true that the received patterns of authority create a strong need, even in those seeking radical change, to find an authoritative base of revealed truth "in the beginning"[11] as well as a need to justify the new by reference to recognized authority. These needs reveal a still deeper need: to situate oneself meaningfully in history.

The effort to express contemporary experience in a cultural and historical vacuum is both self-deluding and unsatisfying. It is self-deluding because to communicate at all to oneself and others, one makes use of patterns of thought, however transformed by new experience, that have a history. It is unsatisfying because, however much one discards large historical periods of dominant traditions, one still seeks to encompass this "fallen history" within a larger context of authentic and truthful life. To look back to some original base of meaning and truth before corruption is to know that truth is more basic than falsehood and hence able, ultimately, to root out falsehood in a new future that is dawning in contemporary experience. To find glimmers of this truth in submerged and alternative traditions through history is to assure oneself that one is not mad or duped. Only by finding an alternative historical community and tradition more deeply rooted than those that have become corrupted can one feel sure that in criticizing the dominant tradition one is not just subjectively criticizing the dominant tradition but is, rather, touching a deeper bedrock of authentic Being upon which to ground the self. One cannot wield the lever of criticism without a place to stand.

The Critical Principle of Feminist Theology

The critical principle of feminist theology is the promotion of the full humanity of women. Whatever denies, diminishes, or distorts the full humanity of women is, therefore, appraised as not redemptive. Theologically speaking, whatever diminishes or denies the full humanity of women must be presumed not to reflect the divine or an authentic relation to the divine, or to reflect the authentic nature of things, or to be the message or work of an authentic redeemer or a community of redemption.

This negative principle also implies the positive principle: what does promote the full humanity of women is of the Holy, it does reflect true relation to

---

[11] Editors' note: notice the allusion to Genesis 1:1, the beginning of the Bible.

the divine, it is the true nature of things, the authentic message of redemption and the mission of redemptive community. But the meaning of this positive principle—namely, the full humanity of women—is not fully known. It has not existed in history. What we have known is the negative principle of the denigration and marginalization of women's humanity. Still, the humanity of women, although diminished, has not been destroyed. It has constantly affirmed itself, often in only limited and subversive ways, and it has been the touchstone against which we test and criticize all that diminishes us. In the process we experience our larger potential that allows us to begin to imagine a world without sexism.

This principle is hardly new. In fact, the correlation of original, authentic human nature (*imago dei*/Christ) and diminished, fallen humanity provided the basic structure of classical Christian theology. The uniqueness of feminist theology is not the critical principle, full humanity, but the fact that women claim this principle for themselves. Women name themselves as subjects of authentic and full humanity.

The use of this principle in male theology is perceived to have been corrupted by sexism. The naming of males as norms of authentic humanity has caused women to be scapegoated for sin and marginalized in both original and redeemed humanity. This distorts and contradicts the theological paradigm of *imago dei*/Christ. Defined as male humanity against or above women, as ruling-class humanity above servant classes, the *imago dei*/Christ paradigm becomes an instrument of sin rather than a disclosure of the divine and an instrument of grace.

This also implies that women cannot simply reverse the sin of sexism. Women cannot simply scapegoat males for historical evil in a way that makes themselves only innocent victims. Women cannot affirm themselves as *imago dei* and subjects of full human potential in a way that diminishes male humanity. Women, as the denigrated half of the human species, must reach for a continually expanding definition of inclusive humanity—inclusive of both genders, inclusive of all social groups and races. Any principle of religion or society that marginalizes one group of persons as less than fully human diminishes us all. In rejecting androcentrism (males as norms of humanity), women must also criticize all other forms of chauvinism: making white Westerners the norm of humanity, making Christians the norm of humanity, making privileged classes the norm of humanity. Women must also criticize humanocentrism; that is, making humans the norm and crown of creation in a way that diminishes the other beings in the community of creation. This is not a question of sameness but of recognition of value, which at the same time affirms genuine variety and particularity. It reaches for a new mode of relationship, neither a hierarchical model that diminishes the potential of the "other" nor an "equality" defined by a ruling norm drawn from the dominant group; rather a mutuality that allows us to affirm different ways of being.

Chapter Three

Interpretations of Love and Justice

Few would question the centrality of love in Christian life. Jesus' life and death on the cross are clear examples of his love for fallen humanity. In John's Gospel, Jesus calls his followers to love as he has loved: "I give you a new commandment, that you love one another. Just as I have loved you, you also should love one another" (John 13:34). Yet, Christians have struggled to discern what it means to love as Jesus loved, and to relate the Christian practice of love with another central biblical concern, namely, justice.[1] Much of the struggle appears to center around how love and justice are defined. In the New Testament, the Greek word translated as love is *agape*. Agape is one of three Greek words for love; the other two are *eros* and *philia*. Eros is love marked by desire or attraction to another, including but not limited to sexual desire. Philia is the love known in friendship between equals.

In the selection from Augustine we see an early attempt to understand Christian love as grounded not in the natural desires either of eros or philia but in the love of God. Augustine's position has helped to support a view of Christian love as self-sacrificial or unconditional—the giving of self for the good of others without any regard for their good in relation to us. We love others, Augustine says, for the sake of God.[2] This tradition has especially emphasized that Jesus is the model of this self-sacrificial love, with his cross as the supreme symbol of such love.

The "Christian realist" position of Reinhold Niebuhr is deeply influenced by Augustine's conception of agapic love. Niebuhr understands agape as essentially self-sacrifice, which stands in sharp contrast to justice as the balance of power between individuals and groups. Love is self-emptying, but justice is bound by the limits of giving to each person what they are due. In Christian re-

---

[1] The centrality of justice to biblical life is evident in that justice or righteousness is mentioned some 1,060 times in the Bible.

[2] The classic statement of such a position is Anders Nygren, *Agape and Eros,* trans. Philip S. Watson (New York: Harper and Row, 1969).

alism, the full expression of love is thus limited to the sphere of one's personal life. Christian love as self-sacrificial provides no direct guide for such areas of life as economics, politics, and international relations. These spheres are measured against the more limited norm of justice. Niebuhr writes, "The kingdom of God is always a possibility in history, because its heights of pure love are organically related to the experience of love in all human life, but it is also an impossibility in history and always beyond every historical achievement. Humans living in nature and in the body will never be capable of the sublimation of egoism and the attainment of the sacrificial passion, the complete disinterestedness which the ethic of Jesus demands. The social justice which Amos demanded represented a possible ideal for society."[3] Love's role in social institutions is to function as "impossible possibility" that reveals the limited nature of justice and motivates us to overcome injustice. For Niebuhr the concepts of love and justice thus remain sharply distinct from, or even in tension with, one another.

But is this too sharp of a line between love and justice? Without justice, can there be a loving personal relationship? What sense would it make for a husband to say to his wife, "I love you" and yet treat her unjustly? What sense would it make to say, "We love the poor," yet not seek economic justice that addresses the root causes of poverty? What about justice in relation to love? Would we seek justice for others without also loving them—without deeply caring for their good? Is love necessary so that justice will be structured not as a mere balance of power but as concern for the most vulnerable as well as accountability open to reconciliation and restoration of relationship?

Recent biblical scholarship and theological reflection sees a close connection between love and justice. Such studies are evident in the selections from Christine Gudorf and Lewis B. Smedes in this chapter, both of whom see love and justice acting together, as essentially two sides of one coin. Both of these build from a possible *second meaning* or *dimension to love* in the New Testament and thus also in Christian ethics. In this second meaning of love, *agape* includes self-sacrifice or self-giving, but such self-giving love is for the sake of mutuality, the creation and sustaining of right relationship.

A biblical basis for their positions emerges from a consideration of Old and New Testament depictions of love and love's relation to justice. In the Old Testament there are two different Hebrew words that refer to God's love. The first, *ahabah,* indicates God's love as creating God's covenant relationship with the people of Israel. This is God's free and loving choice of Israel as the chosen people. Biblical scholar Norman Snaith calls this form of love, *election-love*—the love by which God "elects" to make Israel God's chosen people.[4] This love can be seen as analogous to self-giving love. The second term,

---

[3] Reinhold Niebuhr, *An Interpretation of Christian Ethics* (New York: Seabury Press, 1979) 19, revised.

[4] Norman H. Snaith, *The Distinctive Ideas of the Old Testament* (London: Epworth Press, 1944) 103.

hesed, speaks to God's faithful love within God's covenant with Israel. Snaith identifies this as *covenant love.* This love can be seen as grounding and shaping the covenant relationship between God and God's people that includes justice expectations. Thus, as we see in the prophets such as Jeremiah (2:2, 15:16), Isaiah (54:5-8), and Hosea (4:1-10) that God calls Israel to be faithful to justice obligations in the covenant, and Israel, in turn, hopes in God because God is faithful.

When we turn to the New Testament we see that Jesus gives of himself in healing and feeding others for the purpose of restoration of community, that is, for creation of right or just relations. Further, the joining of love to justice is evident if we see that Jesus' death on the cross is redemptive because it leads to resurrection, the restoration of life, both for him and for all who believe. Jesus' self-sacrificial love is not an end in itself; rather it is for the sake of redemption, restoring right relationship with God and thus with others. Likewise, Paul in his letters stresses self-giving love as the power that shapes and enables right relations within the church. It is love that builds and sustains the righteous living that we are called to in Christian community, the body of Christ (Rom12:1-21; 1 Cor 12–13; Gal 5:16-26; Eph 4:1-16; Col 3). Consistent with the New Testament, agape may thus be more fully understood as self-giving for the sake of human flourishing and such flourishing requires mutuality.

The close relation of love and justice becomes even more evident when we turn to consider biblical understandings of justice. Two words in Hebrew, *mishpat* and *sedakah* are translated as justice or righteousness. *Mishpat* refers to right rule in the sense of the particular duties and responsibilities that structure our lives in community with each other under God. (See for example Deut 10:17-18, Ps 10:18, Jer 5:28, Amos 5:15). Sedakah refers to righteousness and also expresses deliverance, uprightness, right, and even prosperity.[5] Justice here is a characteristic of God's being, as when we say, "God is just." Love is often closely associated with these forms of biblical justice in that both mishpat and sedakah express God's *hesed* or steadfast love. In Jeremiah, for example, we read, "I am the LORD; I act with steadfast love, justice, and righteousness in the earth, for in these things I delight" (Jer 9:24).

The Exodus story grounds the biblical view that our practice of love and justice is to reflect God's love and justice. God, in loving Israel, seeks justice for Israel. Thus God judges Pharaoh and slavery as unjust and sets the Israelites free from injustice—from slavery, oppression, and death, and so the Israelites are to live in a way consistent with how God acted with them. We are to do unto others as God has done unto us (Exod 22:21; 23:9; Deut 6:20-25; 10:19).

God's loving redemptive work as an expression of God's justice has two major qualities. First, God is lovingly faithful to God's covenant with the Is-

[5] Bruce Birch, *Let Justice Roll Down: The Old Testament, Ethics, and Christian Life* (Louisville, Ky.: Westminster/John Knox, 1991) 153.

raelites. God's faithfulness to the covenant grounds God's work for justice. The Israelites did not earn or "merit" God's love; rather God initiated the covenant and continues to be lovingly faithful to the covenant even when the Israelites are unfaithful. Likewise, just persons are to manifest loving faithfulness through fidelity to right relationship with God and others.

Second, God practices a special concern for the poor and vulnerable. The Exodus story reveals the Israelites in severe need, crying out for justice. God responds to the cry of the Israelites, and God's response sets the pattern for God's continuing work for justice for all who are oppressed (see Ps 103). Biblical law, as an expression of God's justice, does not treat everyone "equally" nor does it favor those judged by a society to be superior in some way. Rather, God's justice shows a special concern for the most vulnerable members of the society, the poor, widows and orphans, and the stranger. Thus God's special concern for the poor is built into covenant law—the structure of society. The leftovers of the harvest are to go to the poor (Lev 19:9-10, Deut 24:19-22). The charging of interest is limited to protect the poor (Exod 22:25; Lev 25:35-37; Deut 23:20-21). A cloak taken in pledge for a loan must be returned before nightfall (Exod 22:26-27).[6] Abuse of the poor is a basis for judgment (Isa 3:14-15; Pss 82, 146, 149; Ezek l 22:29). God identifies with the poor, "Those who mock the poor insult their Maker" (Prov 17:5). The poor are always to be cared for, "Give liberally and be ungrudging when you do so. . . Since there will never cease to be some in need on the earth, I therefore command you, 'Open your hand to the poor and needy neighbor in your land'" (Deut 15:10-11).[7] God's pattern of loving justice is also evident in the Sabbath and related Jubilee legislation in Leviticus 25 and Deuteronomy 15, and their relation to the Exodus story of the manna in the desert (Exod 16) and the Sabbath of God in Genesis (2:2).

In relation to women, though Israel was a patriarchal society, the law protected women from types of exploitation that took further advantage of their subordinate position (Exod 21 and 22). In terms of strangers, the covenant law was tied into Israel's remembrance of their previous status within Egypt and what God had done for them. Exodus states, "You shall not oppress a resident alien; you know how an alien feels, for you were aliens in the land of Egypt" (Exod 23:9; see also 22:21; Deut 10:19, 24:17 and Ps 146:9).

---

[6] This law is perhaps at the background of the teaching of Jesus regarding "if anyone wants to sue you and take your coat, give your cloak as well" (Matt 6:4). Jesus is instructing persons in nonviolent resistance to those who would unjustly sue for one's outer garment in a court of law. In response, one should strip naked to reveal the injustice of this lawsuit. See Walter Wink, "Neither Passivity nor Violence: Jesus' Third Way, (Matt 5:38-42 par.)" in Willard M Swartley, ed., *The Love of Enemy and Nonretaliation in the New Testament,* (Louisville, Ky.: Westminster/John Knox Press, 1992) 102–125.

[7] This passage from Deuteronomy stands behind Jesus' saying, "you always have the poor with you" (Matt 26:11) Jesus, of course, is not urging passivity in the face of this reality, as some readers of the New Testament have wrongly argued.

The prophets returned again and again to the theme that God calls Israel to practice justice, and justice requires social structures that attend to the well being of the most vulnerable in the society.[8]

In the New Testament, the Old Testament view of justice is continued and expanded. Taking up the themes of special concern for the poor and prophetic critique of injustice, Jesus begins his public ministry in Luke's gospel with an announcement of good news to the poor and a jubilee year (Luke 4:16-19). In his acts of healing the sick and the blind and feeding the crowds Jesus points to the restoration of human life consistent with the kingdom.

With regard to the poor, Jesus echoes the Old Testament prophets with his parable of judgment in Matthew 25:31-46, which indicates that we will be judged on our treatment of "the least of these," with whom Christ identifies himself. Luke's Gospel gives many indications of the special standing of the poor in the eyes of God (Luke 12:13-34; 16:13; 18:18-30; 19:1-10; 21:1-4). Jesus' statement that "you always have the poor with you" (Matt 26:11) is a direct reference to Deut. 15:4-11 in which the continuing presence of the poor is a call to serve the poor. It is not the poor man Lazarus—who lays at the door of the rich man and begs—who is damned, but rather the rich man, who did not help Lazarus (Luke 16:19-31).

With regard to the stranger and the marginal, Jesus' teaching is embodied in his actions toward lepers, the blind and the lame, and is perhaps best summarized in the story of the Good Samaritan (Luke 10:25-37). The special place of women in the life and ministry of Jesus reveals a concern for the good of women which goes beyond the Old Testament. Women are the first preachers of the resurrection (Luke 21:1-12; Mark 16:9-10; John 20:17-18). Jesus turns in a special way to heal or address a request for healing from women on a number of occasions (Luke 7:36-50; 13:10-17). Jesus heals the woman with the flow of blood. Instead of rejecting her as she feared, given the standards of the day, Jesus welcomed her back into full life within the community, and praising her faith (Matt 9:20-22; Mark 5:25-34; Luke 8:43-48). In Jesus' encounter with the Samaritan woman at the well, Jesus not only violates the expectation that no Jew would speak with a Samaritan stranger, but he also violates the expectation that no Jewish man would deign to speak with a woman stranger. Jesus not only speaks with her; he transforms her life so that she becomes a preacher of the Gospel, a full member of the community of faith (John 4:1-42).

In Paul the action of God is also the basis for love and justice. Paul tells the church in Rome to "Welcome those who are weak in faith . . . for God has welcomed them" (Rom 14:1, 3) and "Welcome one another . . . just as Christ has welcomed you" (Rom 15:7). Paul grounds his concern for right relationships in community in living in the loving Spirit of Christ.[9]

---

[8] See Isa 1:10-17; 3:13-15; 10:1-4; 11:4; 22:13-14; 32:7; 58:6-7; Jer 2:34-35; 7:5-7; 22:13-16; Ezek 16:49; 18:10-13; 22:29-31; Amos 2:4-7; 5:11-24; 8:4-8, 10; Zech 7:8-12.

[9] See Gal 5:22-26; Phil 2:1-5; Col 3:12-17; 1 Thess 5:12-15; Eph 5:1-2.

For Paul, the justice of God is seen in the life, death, and resurrection of Christ. Jesus reveals in word and deed the Good News of the redemptive, healing, nature of God's justice, which has the loving purpose of restoring us to life. Paul writes, "[God] who did not withhold God's own Son, but gave him up for all of us, will God not with him also give us everything else? Who will bring any charge against God's elect? It is God who justifies. Who is to condemn?" (Rom 8:32-33).

Paul urges that the church attend to needs of the vulnerable, the poor, women, and the stranger. When Paul seeks a just distribution of economic goods, he grounds that concern for the poor in the work of God in Christ (2 Cor 8:9-15; 9:7-8). Paul employs the metaphor of the body of Christ to underline the importance of structuring our lives together so that the most weak and vulnerable members of the community be treated with dignity and justice (1 Cor 12 and Rom 12). Like the prophets of the Old Testament, Paul criticizes those who separate worship from economic justice. He rebukes the church at Corinth for turning the Lord's Supper into a time of reinforcing economic and social differences (1 Cor 11:17-34). In the structures of its life, the church is to be the body of Christ—in which the least are honored, not shamed (1 Cor 12:12-27).

With regard to the stranger, Paul is careful to list "hospitality to strangers" as one of the practices in which the church in Rome should engage (Rom 12:13). He also, as we have noted, emphasized the necessity to welcome others as God has welcomed us (Rom 14:1, 3; 15:7). In Paul's view, the saving work of Christ breaks down barriers between persons, including reconciliation with those who had been enemies (Gal 3:28; 2 Cor 5:15-21; Eph 2:11-22).

In turning to women in relation to Paul's understanding of justice, we enter into controversial ground. Statements in some letters attributed to Paul have been used and continue to be used to justify the domination of women by men. This argument cannot be fully joined here. However, there have been serious questions raised as to his authorship of Ephesians, along with First Timothy and Titus where the most "sexist" statements are found. Further, there have been questions raised about the authenticity of Colossians 3:18 and 1 Corinthians 14:34-36, that command submissiveness for women. Are these passages evidence that the early church fell back into more patriarchal gender relations after a brief period in which there was a redemptive mutuality between men and women? Paul's statement that "there is no longer male and female; for all of you are one in Christ Jesus" (Gal 3:28) and his advice about marriage may reflect this earlier period (1 Cor 7:3-5, 12-16). So, too, would Paul's own relations with women as fellow ministers of the Gospel (Acts 18:1-4, 24-26; Rom 16:1-7).

As we turn to the articles in this chapter we will need to pay attention to how love and justice are described in relationship with each other. The Bible sees each as distinct yet as closely related to each other. The command to love one another will involve justice in some way. But what that relationship will be will depend upon how we understand love and justice. And, as Douglass

Sturm's article shows, understandings of justice vary, and which understanding we adopt will shape how we construct and/or support certain institutional arrangements. Which understanding of justice might best reflect our love for others, and our love-shaped concern for justice?

READINGS

1. Biblical Foundations

Love and justice are two of the great motifs of scripture that we encounter continually from Genesis to Revelation. These selected texts can only indicate a broad outline of these pivotal terms.

A. Exodus 6:1-13; 14:30-31; 20:1-21; 23:6-13

These texts introduce God's covenant of liberation with the Hebrew peoples—which in turn requires them to learn in liberating covenant relationships with one another. A people freed from oppression are to fight oppression themselves. Note that the covenant requires special care for the weak and powerless in Israel.

B. Amos 5:18-24; Isaiah 58

The great prophets held Israel accountable to uphold their covenant with God, which included both faithfulness of worship and political justice. Here we encounter prophets who represent two different contexts in this enduring prophetic tradition. Amos, a poor agricultural worker who lived in Judah in the eighth century B.C.E., is historically the first of the great prophets. He journeyed to the northern kingdom of Samaria to announce their coming destruction as punishment for failing to keep the covenant. The precise context for our second selection is of some debate. Many scholars believe that the setting of Isaiah 56–66 is around 520–515 B.C.E., after the Jews have returned to Judah from captivity in Babylon. Life there was very harsh, which tempted them both to engage in economic exploitation to take up some of the pagan religious practices of the region. Isaiah urges his hearers to maintain covenant loyalty, waiting a deliverance that surely will come soon.

C. Leviticus 19:18; Matthew 22:34-40; Mark 12:28-34; Luke 10:25-28; John 13:31-35

Scribes in Jesus' day often debated the grounding for the Mosaic Law. Jesus' formulation of a "love command" is repeated, with some variations, in each of the Synoptic Gospels and is suggested in John. Jesus' quotation of the charge in Leviticus that we should love our neighbors as ourselves is not in itself remarkable. The formulation begs the questions "who is my neighbor?" (Luke 10:29) and "What does it mean to love neighbors?" These questions are answered in Jesus' teaching and example.

D. MATTHEW 5

This chapter belongs to the "Sermon on the Mount" (Matt 5–7). This "sermon" probably is a collection of Jesus' sayings, gathered into one place. The Sermon on the Mount is the first of five great teaching sections in this Gospel, suggesting, perhaps, that Matthew sees Jesus as the "new Moses," promulgating a new law from atop a mountain. As the first block of teaching, the Sermon sets forth the charter for the kingdom of heaven.

E. ROMANS 12, 1 CORINTHIANS 12-13

The early church struggled with what it meant to be a true community that practiced Jesus' teachings about love. The first reading is the advice of the apostle Paul to the church in Rome. He urges the believers there to live a truly transformed life of humility, love, and peace. The second selection comes from one of Paul's letters to the church in Corinth, which seems to have been fractured by internal dissent. He asks the Corinthians to think of themselves as members of a single body, each with different gifts. Chapter 13 of this letter is a lilting, poetic hymn to love that is one of the most loved and most quoted passages in the New Testament.

2. Augustine of Hippo (354–430), *On Christian Doctrine*

Augustine, bishop of Hippo in North Africa, undoubtedly ranks as one of the most influential theologians in the history of the church. Born only a generation after the Edict of Milan granted Christians legal toleration in the Roman Empire, Augustine developed the first great synthesis of the biblical and classical world views. Augustine's compelling vision established the basic framework of Christian theology for the next thousand years.

These selections on love are from Book I of On Christian Doctrine,[10] *a manual written by Augustine to assist Christians in the proper interpretation of scripture. In this volume Augustine sets forth a general overview of the subjects*

---

[10] Augustine of Hippo, *Christian Doctrine* in *Augustin: City of God; Christian Doctrine*, A Select Library of the Christian Church, Nicene and Post-Nicene Fathers, first series, vol. 2, ed. Philip Schaff, American edition (Buffalo, N.Y.: Christian Literature Publishing Company, 1887) 519–57, revised.

treated in scripture. He divides all things into three classes: those that are to be enjoyed, those that are to be used, and those that are to be both used and enjoyed. Since all things but God are to be used and not enjoyed in themselves, only God alone can be truly loved. All things and all persons, then, are to be loved only in relation to God. He concludes the volume by reasoning that the love of God and love of all things in God is the fulfillment of all scripture.

3.   There are some things, then, which are to be enjoyed, others which are to be used, others still which enjoy and use [sic]. Those things which are objects of enjoyment make us happy. Those things which are objects of use assist, and (so to speak) support us in our efforts after happiness, so that we can attain the things that make us happy and rest in them. We ourselves, again, who enjoy and use these things, being placed among both kinds of objects, if we set ourselves to enjoy those which we ought to use, are hindered in our course, and sometimes even led away from it; so that, getting entangled in the love of lower gratifications, we lag behind in, or even altogether turn back from, the pursuit of the real and proper objects of enjoyment.

4.   For to enjoy a thing is to rest with satisfaction in it for its own sake. To use, on the other hand, is to employ whatever means are at one's disposal to obtain what one desires, if it is a proper object of desire; for an unlawful use ought rather to be called an abuse. Suppose, then, we were wanderers in a strange country, and could not live happily away from our fatherland, and that we felt wretched in our wandering, and wishing to put an end to our misery, determined to return home. We find, however, that we must make use of some mode of conveyance, either by land or water, in order to reach that fatherland where our enjoyment is to commence. But the beauty of the country through which we pass, and the very pleasure of the motion, charm our hearts, and turning these things which we ought to use into objects of enjoyment, we become unwilling to hasten the end of our journey; and becoming engrossed in a factitious delight, our thoughts are diverted from that home whose delights would make us truly happy. Such is a picture of our condition in this life of mortality. We have wandered far from God; and if we wish to return to our Father's home, this world must be used, not enjoyed, that so the invisible things of God may be clearly seen, being understood by the things that are made (Rom 1:20)—that is, that by means of what is material and temporary we may lay hold upon that which is spiritual and eternal.

22.   Among all these things, then, those only are the true objects of enjoyment which we have spoken of as eternal and unchangeable. The rest are for use, that we may be able to arrive at the full enjoyment of the former.

We, however, who enjoy and use other things are things ourselves. For a great thing truly are human beings, made after the image and similitude of God, not as respects the mortal body in which we are clothed, but as respects the rational soul by which we are exalted in honor above the beasts. And so it becomes an important question, whether humans ought to enjoy, or to use, themselves, or to do both. For we are commanded to love one another: but it is a question whether a human is to be loved by another human for his or her own sake, or for the sake of something else. If it is for his or her own sake, we enjoy that person; if it is for the sake of something else, we use that person. . . For if a thing is to be loved for its own sake, then in the enjoyment of it consists a happy life, the hope of which at least, if not yet the reality, is our comfort in the present time. But a curse is pronounced on those who place their hope in humankind.

Neither ought any one to have joy in one's self, if you look at the matter clearly, because no one ought to love even one's self for one's own sake, but for the sake of God who is the true object of enjoyment. For a person is never in so good a state as when the person's whole life is a journey towards the unchangeable life, and the person's affections are entirely fixed upon that. If, however, we love ourselves for our own sake, we do not look at ourselves in relation to God, but turn our minds in upon ourselves, and so we are not occupied with anything that is unchangeable. And thus we do not enjoy ourselves at our best, because we are better when our mind is fully fixed upon, and our affections wrapped up in, the unchangeable good, than when we turn from that to enjoy even ourselves. Wherefore if you ought not to love even yourself for your own sake, but for God in whom your love finds its most worthy object, no other person has a right to be angry if you love him or her too for God's sake. For this is the law of love that has been laid down by Divine authority: "Thou shall love thy neighbor as thyself"; but, "Thou shall love God with all thy heart, and with all thy soul, and with all thy mind" (Matt 22:37-39; cf. Lev 19:18; Deut 6:5) : so that you are to concentrate all your thoughts, your whole life and your whole intelligence upon God from whom you derive all that you bring. For when God says, "With all thy heart, and with all thy soul, and with all thy mind," God means that no part of our life is to be unoccupied, and to afford room, as it were, for the wish to enjoy some other object, but that whatever else may suggest itself to us as an object worthy of love is to be borne into the same channel in which the whole current of our affections flows. Whoever, then, loves their neighbor aright, ought to urge upon them that they too should love God with their whole heart, and soul, and mind. For in this way, loving one's neighbor as one's self, we turn the whole current of our love both for ourselves and our neighbor into the channel of the love of God, which suffers no stream to be drawn off from itself by whose diversion its own volume would be diminished.

23.   Those things which are objects of use are not all, however, to be loved, but those only which are either united with us in a common relation to God, such as another person or an angel, or are so related to us as to need the goodness of God through our instrumentality, such as the body. For assuredly the martyrs did not love the wickedness of their persecutors, although they used it to attain the favor of God. As, then, there are four kinds of things that

are to be loved—first, that which is above us; second, ourselves; third, that which is on a level with us; fourth, that which is beneath us—no precepts need be given about the second and fourth of these. For, however far we may fall away from the truth, we still continue to love ourselves, and to love our own body. The soul which flies away from the unchangeable Light, the Ruler of all things, does so that it may rule over itself and over its own body; and so it cannot but love both itself and its own body.

Moreover, it thinks it has attained something very great if it is able to lord it over its companions, that is, other persons. For it is inherent in the sinful soul to desire above all things, and to claim as due to itself, that which is properly due to God only. Now such love of itself is more correctly called hate. For it is not just that it should desire what is beneath it to be obedient to it while itself will not obey its own superior; and most justly has it been said, "One who loveth iniquity hateth one's own soul" (Ps 10:5 in the Septuagint [LXX]; cf. NRSV 11:5). And accordingly the soul becomes weak, and endures much suffering about the mortal body. For, of course, it must love the body, and be grieved at its corruption; and the immortality and incorruptibility of the body spring out of the health of the soul. Now the health of the soul is to cling steadfastly to the better part, that is, to the unchangeable God. But when it aspires to lord it even over those who are by nature its equals—that is, its fellow humans—this is a reach of arrogance utterly intolerable.

25.   Humans, therefore, ought to be taught the due measure of loving, that is, in what measure we may love ourselves so as to be of service to oneself. For that we do love ourselves, and do desire to do good to ourselves, nobody but a fool would doubt. We are to be taught, too, in what measure to love our own body, so as to care for it wisely and within due limits. For it is equally manifest that we love our own body also, and desire to keep it safe and sound. And yet we may have something that we love better than the safety and soundness of our own body. For many have been found voluntarily to suffer both pains and amputations of some of their limbs that they might obtain other objects which they valued more highly. But no one is to be told not to desire the safety and health of one's body because there is something one desires more. For misers, though they love money, buy bread for themselves—that is, they give away money that they are very fond of and desire to heap up—but it is because they value more highly the bodily health which the bread sustains. It is superfluous to argue longer on a point so very plain, but this is just what the error of wicked people often compels us to do.

26.   Seeing, then, that there is no need of a command that every person should love one's self and one's own body—seeing, that is, that we love ourselves, and what is beneath us but connected with us, through a law of nature which has never been violated, and which is common to us with the beasts (for even the beasts love themselves and their own bodies)—it only remained necessary to lay

injunctions upon us in regard to God above us, and our neighbor beside us. "Thou shalt love," God says, "the Lord thy God with all thy heart, and with all thy soul, and with all thy mind; and thou shalt love thy neighbor as thyself. On these two commandments hang all the law and the prophets" (Matt 22:37-40). Thus the end of the commandment is love, and that twofold, the love of God and the love of our neighbor. Now, if you take yourself in your entirety—that is, soul and body together—and your neighbors in their entirety, soul and body together (for humans are made up of soul and body), you will find that none of the classes of things that are to be loved is overlooked in these two commandments. For though, when the love of God comes first, and the measure of our love for God is prescribed in such terms that it is evident all other things are to find their center in God, nothing seems to be said about our love for ourselves; yet when it is said, "Thou shall love thy neighbor as thyself," it at once becomes evident that our love for ourselves has not been overlooked.

27.   Now one is a person of just and holy life who forms an unprejudiced estimate of things, and keeps one's affections also under strict control, so that one neither loves what one ought not to love, nor fails to love what one ought to love, nor loves that more which ought to be loved less, nor loves that equally which ought to be loved either less or more, nor loves that less or more which ought to be loved equally. No sinner is to be loved as a sinner; and every person is to be loved as a person for God's sake; but God is to be loved for God's own sake. And if God is to be loved more than any person, each person ought to love God more than one's self. Likewise we ought to love another person better than our own body, because all things are to be loved in reference to God, and another person can have fellowship with us in the enjoyment of God, whereas our body cannot; for the body only lives through the soul, and it is by the soul that we enjoy God.

28.   Further, all persons are to be loved equally. But since you cannot do good to all, you are to pay special regard to those who, by the accidents of time, or place, or circumstance, are brought into closer connection with you. For, suppose that you had a great deal of some commodity, and felt bound to give it away to somebody who had none, and that it could not be given to more than one person; if two persons presented themselves, neither of whom had either from need or relationship a greater claim upon you than the other, you could do nothing fairer than choose by lot to which you would give what could not be given to both. Just so among people: since you cannot consult for the good of them all, you must take the matter as decided for you by a sort of lot, according as each person happens for the time being to be more closely connected with you.

29.   Now of all who can with us enjoy God, we love partly those to whom we render services, partly those who render services to us, partly those who both help us in our need and in turn are helped by us, partly those upon whom we

confer no advantage and from whom we look for none. We ought to desire, however, that they should all join with us in loving God, and all the assistance that we either give them or accept from them should tend to that one end. For in the theatres, dens of iniquity though they be, if we are fond of a particular actor, and we enjoy that actor's art as a great or even as the very greatest good, we are fond of all who join us in admiration of our favorite, not for their own sakes, but for the sake of the actor whom we admire in common; and the more fervent we are in this admiration, the more we work in every way to secure new admirers for the actor, and the more anxious we become to show the actor to others; and if we find any one comparatively indifferent, we do all that can be done to excite the other's interest by urging our favorite actor's merits: if, however, we meet with any one who opposes the actor, we are exceedingly displeased by such a person's contempt of our favorite, and we strive in every way we can to remove it. Now, if this be so, what does it become us to do who live in the fellowship of the love of God, the enjoyment of whom is true happiness of life, to whom all who love God owe both their own existence and the love they bear God, concerning whom we have no fear that any one who comes to know God will be disappointed in God, and who desires our love, not for any gain to God, but that those who love God may obtain an eternal reward, even Godself whom they love? And hence it is that we love even our enemies. For we do not fear them, seeing they cannot take away from us what we love; but we pity them rather, because the more they hate us the more are they separated from God whom we love. For if they would turn to God, they must of necessity love God as the supreme good, and love us too as partakers with them in so great a blessing.

31.   And on this ground, when we say that we enjoy only that which we love for its own sake, and that nothing is a true object of enjoyment except that which makes us happy, and that all other things are for use, there seems still to be something that requires explanation. For God loves us, and Holy Scripture frequently sets before us the love God has towards us. In what way then does God love us? As objects of use or as objects of enjoyment? If God enjoys us, God must be in need of good from us, and no sane person will say that; for all the good we enjoy is either Godself, or what comes from God. And no one can be ignorant or in doubt as to the fact that the light stands in no need of the glitter of the things it has itself lit up. The Psalmist says most plainly, "I said to the Lord, Thou art my God, for Thou needest not my goodness" (Ps 16:2, LXX). God does not enjoy us then, but makes use of us. For if God neither enjoys nor uses us, I am at a loss to discover in what way God can love us.

32.   But neither does God use after our fashion of using. For when we use objects, we do so with a view to the full enjoyment of the goodness of God. God, however, in God's use of us, has reference to God's own goodness. For it is because God is good we exist; and so far as we truly exist we are good. And, further, because God is also just, we cannot with impunity be evil; and

so far as we are evil, so far is our existence less complete. Now God is the first and supreme existence, who is altogether unchangeable, and who could say in the fullest sense of the words, "I AM THAT I AM," and "Thou shalt say to them, I AM hath sent me unto you"; (Exod 3:14) so that all other things that exist, both owe their existence entirely to God, and are good only so far as God has given it to them to be so. That use, then, which God is said to make of us has no reference to God's own advantage, but to ours only; and, so far as God is concerned, has reference only to God's goodness. When we take pity upon a another and care for that person, it is for that person's advantage we do so; but somehow or other our own advantage follows by a sort of natural consequence, for God does not leave the mercy we show to that person who needs it to go without reward. Now this is our highest reward, that we should fully enjoy God, and that all who enjoy God should enjoy one another in God.

33.   For if we find our happiness complete in one another, we stop short upon the road, and place our hope of happiness in humans or angels. Now the proud person and the proud angel arrogate this to themselves, and are glad to have the hope of others fixed upon them. But, on the contrary, the holy person and the holy angel, even when we are weary and anxious to stay with them and rest in them, set themselves to recruit our energies with the provision which they have received of God for us or for themselves; and then urge us thus refreshed to go on our way towards God, in the enjoyment of whom we find our common happiness. For even the apostle exclaims, "Was Paul crucified for you? or were ye baptized in the name of Paul?" (1 Cor 1:13) and again: "Neither is he that planteth anything, neither he that watereth; but God that giveth the increase" (1 Cor 3:7). And the angel admonisheth the person who is about to worship him, that the person should rather worship God who is the person's Master, and under whom the angel is a fellow-servant.

36.   Whoever, then, thinks that they understand the Holy Scriptures, or any part of them, but puts such an interpretation upon them as does not tend to build up this twofold love of God and our neighbor, does not yet understand them as they ought. If, on the other hand, we draw a meaning from them that may be used for the building up of love, even though we do not happen upon the precise meaning which the author whom we read intended to express in that place, our error is not pernicious, and we are wholly clear from the charge of deception. For there is involved in deception the intention to say what is false; and we find plenty of people who intend to deceive, but nobody who wishes to be deceived . . .

Whoever takes another meaning out of Scripture than the writer intended, goes astray, but not through any falsehood in Scripture. Nevertheless, as I was going to say, if our mistaken interpretation tends to build up love, which is the end of the commandment, we go astray in much the same way as a person who by mistake quits the high road, but yet reaches through the fields the same place to which the road leads. That person is to be corrected, however, and to be shown how much better it is not to quit the straight road, lest, if the person get into a habit of going astray, the person may sometimes take cross roads, or even go in the wrong direction altogether.

39.   And thus a person who is resting upon faith, hope and love, and who keeps a firm hold upon these, does not need the Scriptures except for the purpose of instructing others. Accordingly, many live without copies of the Scriptures, even in solitude, on the strength of these three graces. So that in their case, I think, the saying is already fulfilled: "Whether there be prophecies, they shall fail; whether there be tongues, they shall cease; whether there be knowledge, it shall vanish away" (1 Cor 13:8). Yet by means of these instruments (as they may be called), so great an edifice of faith and love has been built up in them, that, holding to what is perfect, they do not seek for what is only in part perfect—of course, I mean, so far as is possible in this life; for, in comparison with the future life, the life of no just and holy person is perfect here. Therefore the apostle says: "Now abideth faith, hope, charity, these three; but the greatest of these is charity" (1 Cor 13:13): because, when a person shall have reached the eternal world, while the other two graces will fail, love will remain greater and more assured.

3. Christine E. Gudorf, "Parenting, Mutual Love, and Sacrifice"

A Catholic ethicist, Christine Gudorf is professor of comparative religions at Miami International University. She writes in sexual ethics, comparative religious ethics, and feminist theology. In this essay she reflects on Christian love from her experience as a parent. In addition to one natural child, she and her husband adopted two children with severe disabilities. Parenting is a traditional metaphor for disinterested, sacrificial love. Gudorf reveals, however, that such assessments of parenting are not honest. Rather, her relationship with her children was not simply sacrificial, but aimed toward the mutual giving and reception of love. She urges a transformation of traditional understandings of agapic love in Christian ethics from one-sided sacrifice to mutual love in community.

Agape: Disinterested and Sacrificial

Much[11] treatment of individual relations assumes that this is the realm of disinterested sacrificial love, of agape. Now this is strange, since the strongest individual relation would seem to be the marriage tie, which is by modern definition one of eros, or mutual love. Moreover, it is this tie which structures

---

[11] Barbara Hilkert Andolsen, Christine E. Gudorf, and Mary D. Pellauer, eds., *Women's Consciousness, Women's Conscience* (San Francisco: Harper and Row, 1985) 175–91.

the social unit in and from which other relationships take place: the family. It has always seemed to me that only if one dealt solely with individual acts, refusing to link them in relationships, could one understand the family as the center of disinterested love. For the family is really the center of give and take, as the historical specialized division of labor within it makes clear.

With our own children we realized very clearly that though much of the early giving seemed to be solely ours, this was not disinterested, because the children were considered extensions of us, such that our efforts for them rebounded to our credit. Failure to provide for them would have discredited us. And we had expectations that the giving would become more mutual.

This led to the most revealing lesson the children taught us: that complete agape as either intention or result is impossible. Love can never be disinterested. It can be patient, but never disinterested. Christian preachers consistently point out, especially during Lent, that all actions are tainted with self-interest to some degree, if only by pride in one's own goodness. But a common understanding is that agape, disinterested, self-sacrificing love, is the ideal which always stands over against our actions as the standard impossible of achievement.[12] It is the standard because it exemplifies the love of God as expressed in Jesus Christ.

I have come to criticize this understanding. This conception of agape does not prove adequate in its application, which must be the final test of adequacy. Nor does it correspond to the historical event from which it is supposedly deduced, i.e., Jesus Christ. Christian love should not be construed as disinterested or set apart from other love as essentially self-sacrificing. All love both involves sacrifice and aims at mutuality. We need to rework the understanding of Christian love. What Christianity does for "natural" love, as for human nature in general, is to articulate forcefully its end and meaning.

[12] Many major Christian figures have not been explicit on this point. The real question is whether Christ-like love consists primarily in the sacrifice of self, or in devotion to the other, as well as whether any degree of self-interest invalidates Christian love. Luther clearly thought it did; Nygren reports that Luther called self-love "vicious," and held that love of one's neighbor has the task of completely dispossessing and annihilating self-love (*Agape and Eros* [New York: Harper and Row, 1969] 712–13). Kierkegaard agreed (*Works of Love,* trans. Howard and Edna Hong [New York: Harper and Row, 1964] 68, 133–34). The Christian tradition before Luther did not exclude the self so rigorously—major figures of the patristic period described Christian love in terms of eros, or mutual love, as Nygren reports. Thomas argued that the proper objects of love are both those having a more excellent good, and those to which we are more closely united (*Summa Theologica,* II-II 26.9–12). Neither way of speaking about love excludes the self; rather the reverse. In this he follows Aristotle, who understands love and friendship in terms of mutuality: "And in loving a friend men love what is best for themselves; for the good man in becoming a friend becomes a good to his friend. Each, then, both loves what is good for himself, and makes an equal return in goodwill and in pleasantness, for friendship is said to be equality, and both of these are found most in the friendship of the good" (*Nicomachean Ethics,* Bk. 8, 1157b). However clear this split may be in the theological traditions, I do not think that it is reflected in popular piety. The Lutheran Protestant view is almost universal in the churches. I suspect that the strong influence yet today of medieval passion mysticism is responsible for the present state of affairs in Catholicism.

Of agape as essentially self-sacrificial, others have also been critical. Gene Outka writes out of an extended discussion of Christian writers on this theme: "Generally, therefore, I am inclined to think that instead of appraising self-sacrifice as the purest and most perfect manifestation of agape, the difficulties I have considered are avoided if one allows it only instrumental warrant. Self-sacrifice must always be purposive in promoting the welfare of others and never simply expressive of something resident in the agent."[13]

To understand self-sacrificing love in any other way is to condone and even encourage the worst abuses of human dignity. As for agape as disinterested love, not only is this incapable of achievement, but its idealization as the Christian love destroys human relationships and distorts the God/human relationship. While we should realize that we constantly fail to achieve the best of which we are capable it is wrong to identify this failure with a lack of total disinterestedness. To make this identification is to refuse to see how interdependent we are, to insist instead on our radical separation, to encourage masochism and domination, as well as to fail to understand the kingdom of God which Jesus preached.

The problems we faced with these children revolved around making the children able to participate in normal society. There was no way to do that without also gratifying our own self-interest, in that when they learned to walk, talk, eat, use the toilet, attend school, and form other relationships not only would their horizons expand, but ours also. As with all children, every achievement of the child is both a source of pride and a freeing of the parent from responsibility for the child. This sounds very simple. But in the case of our children, the medical, psychological, physical therapy, and other specialists counseled against thwarting the children's wishes, against letting them cry, against pushing them to achieve with other children their age. In the case of the elder child, we were accused of selfishness for not accepting the medical judgment that the child was terminal within two years; we should "let the poor child die in peace in a family" rather than put him through more doctors and hospitals. Yet our efforts in finding experimental surgery have paid off in eleven normal years of school, camp, swimming, and bikes thus far. In the case of our youngest son, a diagnosis of brain damage from temporary heart failure led many "experts" to counsel us to expect nothing of Mike, though he continues to progress. One's self-interest is often, but not always, also the interest of the other. When we assume that to do the hard, self-sacrificing thing is to do the loving thing, we have, in fact, defined the interest of the other in terms of ourselves, and not in terms of the person and conditions of the other.

Even more, in the original decision to adopt these children, we found that apparently selfless love is not so. There is, as C. S. Lewis observed, not only

---

[13] Gene H. Outka, *Agape: An Ethical Analysis,* Yale Publications in Religion, 17 (New Haven, Conn.: Yale University Press, 1972) 278.

Gift-love, but also Need-love.[14] We adopted a hard-to-place child, we said, because such children needed homes, and because we felt they had a right to parents. But in living with the decision, we saw that two people from large families living eight hundred miles from our homes in a large, strange city were lonely, and wanted a child to make them a family. But not a baby, for that would interfere with plans for graduate school for both of us. The wait was shortest for hard-to-place children.

In the second adoption, we wanted a girl, because we had two boys. We asked for a healthy, two-year-old, biracial girl. We were offered Mike, a two-year-old biracial boy with the same medical condition as our elder son. We cringed—if the elder son died could we go on, waiting for Mike to be stricken? But the agency used real moral pressure: since there were no other adoptive or foster homes open and the hospital would no longer keep him, Mike would be placed in a nursing home for the elderly. Our sons settled the question, the elder asking "Are you sorry you took me?" No matter how it seemed, our adoption of Mike was not a case of simple self-sacrificing love of another. I do not know how we would have responded if no one else had known of the offer made us, if our moral pride were not on the line.

When we overemphasize the Gift-love in our loving and de-emphasize the need-love, we end up disguising our needs by calling them gifts for others. This can seriously damage the other, distorting his/her real needs and desires. A well-meaning woman (a social worker!) once told our eldest son that he should be grateful every day of his life that we had adopted him. Only because we had come to see the two-sidedness of both our intention and the result of that adoption was I able to respond furiously that no child should have to be grateful for parents, *especially* one who had been through so much and waited so long for them.

Much love is mutual; all is directed at mutuality. It could not be any other way, for we find love rewarding. If we love the other, we want him/her to experience that reward to the utmost, and that includes loving us. In a more impersonal sense, we may do a deed for another we do not know well—but in the action is the hope that the deed opens the other to love, if not specifically to us as individuals, then at least to the humanity which includes us. This is why Aquinas says, ". . . hope precedes love at first; though afterwards hope is increased by love. Because from the fact that a man thinks that he can obtain a good from someone, he begins to love him; and from the fact that he loves him, he then hopes all the more in him."[15]

This is true of the divine love for us. It is true in the life of Jesus. Jesus did not come to earth to give himself disinterestedly to save us. Jesus was motivated by a mutual love with "Abba." Love expands; Jesus felt impelled not only to

[14] C. S. Lewis, *The Four Loves* (New York: Harcourt, Brace, Jovanovich, 1960) 11.
[15] *Summa Theologica,* II-II 64.4 ad 3.

love others, but to bring others into the relationship he shared with "Abba," to share himself and "Abba" with others and to show these others to share themselves with each other, with himself, and with "Abba." This sharing was the kingdom he announced; in the kingdom all relationships, individual and social, would be restructured to reflect this mutual love.

This mutuality is true of God's love also. If God is love, then he/she needs an object for his/her love; he/she needs us. The community within the Trinity was not alone sufficient, for one person of the Trinity, the Son, presupposes in his historical function our existence, and the third member of the Trinity, the Spirit, presupposes in her historical function both the Son and us. Moreover, the history of our interaction with God has been one of God's making known to us his/her desire for a relationship of mutual love. The moments of self-sacrifice, such as we find in the crucifixion of Jesus, are just that—moments in a process designed to end in mutual love.

Advantages of Love and Mutuality in Social Relations

Understanding Christian love as essentially self-sacrifice has contributed to the common view that Christian love is inappropriate in social decision making. To move to an understanding of Christian love as intending mutuality could alter this view. Social decisions are not made by the whole, but by representatives pledged to act in the best interests of the group. Since self-sacrifice is not considered in the best interest of the group, the present, essentially sacrificial understanding of Christian love prevents representatives from heeding the demands of love, or at least limits them to those loving acts which have clear mandates and/or minimum impact.

With love understood as intending mutuality, instead of rejecting actions which call for some degree of sacrifice from the group in question, leaders might be led to consider the long-term situation and the possibilities for mutual benefit. In social relations, as in individual relations, all units are related. It is never the case that a group's action stands alone. It affects other groups which react to it. The group which dominates other groups must constantly stay vigilant to prevent their combination and rebellion, and must maintain the muscle necessary to subdue others. This does not leave the dominant group free to do other things—it has exacted a cost. No situation is without cost, though we tend to be blinded to the cost of dominance. One of the most common errors in policy making is to reject plans which do not maintain the advantages the group presently enjoys (which sacrifice its dominance). But we need to ask: does the plan eliminate the present cost? Does it benefit the group in the long run? Can the present advantage be maintained indefinitely without additional cost?

The failure to take into consideration the long term is common not only in decisions to reject alternatives to the present, but also in decisions deemed of mutual benefit. The U.S. Food for Peace Program has been a good example of this. Without even considering the mechanisms of the bill which made the immediate benefit to hungry nations less than optimal, critics could ask whether it benefits hungry nations to indefinitely depend on another country for their food. Does it detract from the independence of that country's decisions and leave them open to manipulation? Does it encourage self-sufficiency? How does it affect their economy? (The program has, in fact, been amended to attempt to deal with many of the problems.) In being very critical concerning the formulation of the interests of both sides, we must be careful to cast these formulations in terms of the long run.

When we consider the long run, what appears to be sacrifice now can be in our best interest as the Marshall Plan to rebuild Europe after World War II intended and demonstrated. Many decisions involving sacrifice now—foreign aid plans, affirmative action plans, job training programs, ecology plans—can also be considered just smart, self-interested long-term planning.

Jesus on Sacrifice and Reward

This seems strange and repugnant to many of us who have interpreted Jesus to demand disinterested, sacrificial love for neighbor. But I believe that the message of Jesus is more ambiguous than that. He did not only say, "But . . . Love your enemies," and "do good," and "lend, expecting nothing in return" (Luke 6:27, 33, 35). He also gave us the second great commandment, "love your neighbor as yourself" Matt 19:19).[16] Not more than yourself, but as yourself. This should give us pause, for the golden rule is the basis of natural law ethics; it assumes that mutual peace and cooperation—the end—is obtained through treating the neighbor as oneself.

Yet Jesus did constantly urge action usually regarded as sacrificial—giving possessions to the needy, leaving relatives and friends, undergoing persecution. These actions were not, however, disinterested, for he continually added that the reward or punishment for the response to this demand would be great in the kingdom now on the horizon. In these circumstances he often stressed that to follow him was not only righteous, it was shrewd, a looking to one's own best interest. The parable of the dishonest steward is a good example of this, as are the verses of Luke 12 ending: "Instead, seek God's kingdom, and these things shall be yours as well" (v. 31, RSV alternate).[17] Throughout the Gospels Jesus told those who follow him, "Ask and it will be given you; seek, and you will find; knock, and it will be opened to you" (Luke 11:9).

---

[16] This sentence, and the previous, have been adjusted from the original publication to correspond with the Revised Standard Version of the Bible. Similar adjustments through this article.

[17] The New Testament: Luke 16:19; 12:31; also, John 16:23-24; 5:24; Matt 25:34-36, 6:1-33; 24:45-51; 5:11-12; 21:22; 19:21; 7:78; Mark 9:41; 10:21, 29-31, 43-44; and Luke 13:22-30; 14:7-14; 18:29-30.

Jesus connected his demand for sacrifice with the promise of reward, making sacrificial actions not one-sided, but mutually beneficial. I am not claiming that Scripture inspired the conception of Christian love as mutual. Only because I see this in my own experience did I look for it in Scripture. The scriptural issue is not whether Jesus promised reward for loving—that much is clear. The issue is whether the reward is the natural result of the love, or whether it is an addition, a gift from God extrinsic to the love of neighbor. Was Jesus telling us to open ourselves to a dynamic process of love in which we experience God's promise of fulfillment, or was he urging us to deny ourselves in the present so as to receive promised fulfillment in the future? When is the kingdom? I believe the kingdom has begun, that Jesus opened us to an ongoing process of kingdom, and I hope that the fullness of this kingdom is to come. We experience the kingdom in partial ways, within the struggle against injustice and indignity.

It is better to derive one's strength and hope from the partial experience of kingdom than solely from the belief in ultimate reward in the culmination of kingdom. Kingdom is not a bifurcated entity in which our efforts toward kingdom in the present incur only misery and occur in pitch darkness, with the joyful realization postponed to an indefinite future. We have partial realizations of kingdom, and not to be fed on these, not to rely on the energy and hope they generate, but to keep our eyes fixed only on the far-off future, is to refuse God's gift, to risk burnout in one's work of resisting evil and suffering. What is it that keeps people going through years of working to alleviate starvation, persecution, or epidemic disease amidst overwhelming odds? It is the small moments of victory, the moments where people really touched each other, where the barriers of evil and suffering were broken in a brief moment of resurrection. If not for such moments, how could we positively envision the meaning of kingdom?

These partial realizations are, I think, what Jesus referred to in the parables of the kingdom. The unexpected surprise, the wondrous discovered amongst the ordinary—these partial realizations of kingdom are experiences of love returned. Love is not always returned as we had hoped, or when we would have wished; it often engulfs us far more radically than we had envisaged and stretches us beyond what we had understood as our limits. Love is not happy, so much as it is joyful, in the way that resurrection is not a moment of carefree happiness, but a moment of deep joy. The impetus to love is the experience of kingdom. Love is an act of hope, and experiences of kingdom feed that hope, allowing us to sacrifice in love. Our experiences of mutual love, of love returned, love victorious, are the concretization of Jesus' promise of reward.

Mutuality Not Immediate

One way in which the preaching of love as disinterested and self-sacrificial has been useful is in depressing expectations of the immediate return of love.

This is good in that mutual love seldom begins mutually. Certainly God's love is prior; he/she initiates the relationship with us beginning with our creation. Often persons who have been deprived of love require much love and reassurance before they become confident enough to make themselves vulnerable to love. To expect immediate return of love from these is naive. Love is a process. Sometimes one's gifts are greater and one's needs lesser in the beginning of relationships, but the balance often shifts. Sometimes time runs out before the balance shifts. But the intention is always that it shall.

Nevertheless, the preaching of selfless love has had some disastrous consequences in the history of Christianity. It has sometimes distorted the understanding of Jesus, presenting him as a masochist, searching for a way to suffer and die. It has also distorted some people's understanding of God, suggesting a depiction of God as a vengeful Lord demanding the slaughter of his/her Son. The insistence on Christian love as selfless has created tremendous guilt in people who constantly find that they cannot forget themselves completely in their loving as they feel they should. The experience of having their love rewarded, returning fourfold, frustrates many who come to assume that Christian love must be only for the saints, not for ordinary people. Even worse, the understanding of Christian love as self-sacrificing has pushed some to mistake destructive acts of self-sacrifice as Christian love precisely because there is no return of their love. Counselors who deal with battered women hear often that women recovering from beatings intend to return to abusive spouses, expecting further abuse, because that is what Jesus did: "he took what they did to him, and turned the other cheek" (see Matt 5:39 and the Passion narratives). This notion of love as selfless, says John Cobb, "has promoted a 'love' that is devoid of genuine sensitivity to the deepest needs of the loved ones."[18]

This is not to argue against the need for sacrifice. Sacrifice is essential in the furthering of the kingdom. But we need to be very clear that self-sacrificing love is always aimed at the establishment of mutual love. An act is only a loving act if it has the potential to provoke loving response, however far in the future. Acts of no matter how much self-sacrifice, which support or encourage unloving actions or attitudes, are not acts of love. Agape is valuable in the service of eros and does not exist otherwise.[19]

---

[18] John B. Cobb Jr. and David Ray Griffin, *Process Theology: An Introductory Exposition* (Philadelphia: Westminster, 1976) 46.

[19] This is, I think, the corrective to the situation pointed out by Saiving in the article discussed above. [Valerie Saiving Goldstein, "The Human Situation: A Feminine View," *Journal of Religion* 40 (1960) 100–12.] Saiving pointed out that in the Christian tradition sin has been defined in terms of the self-sacrifice missing in male conditioning. Agape, the corrective to sin is, however, not a corrective to the sinful tendency in the socialization of women, which is passivity and diffusion. Rather, agape confirms women's sinful tendency. I would say that the function of agapeistic teaching for men has been to increase their capacity and tendency for mutuality; for females it has served to reduce possibilities for mutuality. Women are already over-socialized to

In conclusion, I propose that we have been led to emphasize dissimilarities between individuals and groups by idealizations of individual relations and mistaken notions about Christian love. Love in both individual and social relations involves the intention of mutuality and the probability of self-sacrifice to establish the interdependence of all which dictates that our ultimate self-interest demands sacrifice in the interest of the disadvantaged other.

4. Lewis B. Smedes (1921–2002), "How Do Love and Justice Work Together?"

Lewis Smedes taught for twenty-five years at Fuller Theological Seminary, a leading evangelical seminary. Smedes' theological identity is in the Christian Reformed Church, a denomination with historic ties to Dutch Calvinism. He is known as a mediating figure, able to build bridges between evangelical theology and other theological traditions. The following excerpt is taken from his Mere Morality,[20] *a systematic overview of ethics written for laypeople. Smedes' position on the close interrelationship of love and justice reflects his Reformed roots. This tradition historically has emphasized covenant community as the embodiment of love.*

The two absolute mandates that pervade all our human relationships are love and justice. How do these touch on each other? Does love tell us anything about the duties of justice or justice about the duties of love?

Some would say that love and justice have nothing to do with each other. They speak different languages and work on different premises. Love is practiced person-to-person; justice is practiced through institutions like government and courts. Love is spontaneous and generous; justice carefully calculates the merits of competing claims. Love goes out to people regardless of their undeserving; justice deals only with what people merit. Love gives without counting costs; justice counts the cost to the penny. Love and justice are like oil and water; each has its place, but each loses its own usefulness if you try to mix them.

---

give (see Margaret Adams' "The Compassion Trap," in *Women in a Sexist Society,* ed. Vivian Gornick and Barbara Moran (New York: Basic Books, 1971), but have often not learned to recognize their own needs. Agape teaching prevents them from recognizing their own needs and directs them to serve others' needs. In this process, ironically, women become less able to give towards the real needs of others. That is, women are encouraged to ignore self needs and to fulfill those of others, although recognizing the needs of others is best done by those who recognize their own. At the same time, women's self needs go unmet because unrecognized, resulting in a frustration which manifests itself either in feelings of self-pitying worthlessness, or in demands for gratitude for their services, and often in both. Women can both give too much (they surrender the possibility of real personhood) and too little (for often they do not give what others really need).

[20] Lewis B. Smedes, *Mere Morality: What God Expects from Ordinary People* (Grand Rapids: Wm. B. Eerdmans, 1983) 54–57, revised.

Quite the contrary, others would retort. Love and justice are the same: justice is the tough side of love. Or, to change the image, love is the motor, justice is the rudder. Love has the vision, justice the direction. If there are two wounded men on the road to Jericho, justice is only love deciding which one to help first. And when we are asking what a decent wage should be or who should bear the brunt of the fight against inflation, justice is love's tough mind working out the painful compromise.

The discussion of how love and justice are related tends to become a matter of definitions, and we find our attention straying from life to ideas. If we do focus on life, however, I think we sense that love and justice are two different dimensions of reality that belong together. There are several ways in which love and justice need each other, and if they are kept together they help us to know what God expects us to do.

1. LOVE DEMANDS THAT WE DO JUSTICE

Justice is love's minimum demand. Since the law of love commands us to help our neighbor (see the story of the Good Samaritan, Luke 10:25-37, for example), it requires us at least to help him get or keep what is coming to him. Although love does not tell us what our neighbors have a right to have, it does require that we support them in their right, whatever it is. Love always seeks at least justice because people are deeply hurt when they are denied their rights.

But love is never satisfied with justice. If people received only what was theirs by right and gave others only what they had coming to them, we would all be shorn of love's beautiful extravagance. No woman would ever pour expensive ointment on a Savior's head (see Matt 26:6-13; Mark 14:3-9; Luke 7:36-50). Nobody would know what it was like to receive a gift and bless the giver. Love adds heart to the hands of justice. But we who love may never ignore the cool claims of justice in the name of love's warmer gifts. If love does not work for justice, it probably does nothing at all.

2. LOVE ENLARGES THE SCOPE OF JUSTICE

Usually we do well first to care for people close to us. A father owes it to his own children to care for their survival before he tends to the claims of strangers' children. A city owes its own needy residents special care. If 30% of the heads of households in a poverty-stricken town in Appalachia have no jobs, is it reasonable to expect them to invite refugees from Cambodia or Haiti to settle in their town?[21] Love does not deny such special bonds of family and country, but it keeps our eyes open to the just claims of strangers as well. It

---

[21] Cf. [John] Calvin: "I do not deny that the more closely any person is united to us, the greater claim he has to the assistance of our kind offices" (*Institutes*, 2.8.55) in John T. McNeill, ed., *Calvin: Institutes of the Christian Religion* (Philadelphia: Westminster Press, 1960).

nudges our concerns for justice beyond those who are close to us. It helps us see that hungry children far away are not getting their rights to live and that we can best help our own children if we help other people's children too.

3. LOVE ENRICHES JUSTICE

Love keeps pushing the common sense of justice beyond itself into the righteousness of the kingdom of God. The temptation to be satisfied too quickly with legal justice is a strong one: if others are getting what the laws of their society allow them, we too easily assume, justice is being done. But no society of sinful people achieves even the bare bones of a structure of justice through its legal system. Without generous love to move its people to a richer sense of justice, a society tends to be satisfied with the minimum.

The first way love enriches justice is by injecting mercy into law. Portia's word to Shylock reflects the spark of agape that still burns in the heart of everyone: "Earthly power doth then show likest God's when mercy seasons justice" (William Shakespeare [Merchant of Venice, Act 4, Scene 1]).[22] Love enables us to push justice beyond legal codes to actual human needs, to accommodate the letter of the law to the special needs of real people.

Love also enriches justice by keeping the biblical vision of righteousness and *shalom* alive. Love wants more for people than what they have coming to them within a secular social order. Love envisions a community in which people care for one another and help each other find joy in life. Love seeks a society in which people flourish together as children of God. Under the sway of love's law, the believer will keep alive a vision of the City of God: "Behold the dwelling of God is with [people]. [God] will dwell with them, and they shall be God's people . . . and God will wipe every tear from their eyes, and death shall be no more, neither shall there be mourning nor crying nor pain any more" (Rev 21:3-4).[23]

4. LOVE GETS DIRECTION FROM JUSTICE

There is seldom only one wounded person on the road to Jericho. And most Good Samaritans have a limited budget. Whenever we have resources for only one needy person and meet two, the calculations of justice must direct the work of love. If there are two wounded persons, we need to ask which of them needs help most. Will one survive if he or she waits for the next Samaritan to come along? Is one more deserving than the other, more useful, more needed? Is one more likely to die no matter what we do for him or her? These are not questions love is able to cope with; they call for the headwork of justice.

Justice also respects the responsibilities of the needy person. Justice says that a person who chooses to be poor should be allowed to have what he

---

[22] William Shakespeare, *The Merchant of Venice*, David Bevington, ed. (New York: Bantam Books, 1988) 72–73.

[23] The Revised Standard Version of the Bible has been adapted from the original.

chooses. Nor will justice allow us—for love's sake—to assume responsibility for other people's mistakes. If my neighbor goes deeply into debt for luxuries he bought with his credit card, and then habitually expects me to pay his heating bill, justice holds back the hand of love. If my neighbor's business is on the verge of ruin because he is incompetent and lazy, justice may require love to let his business fail, and then help him find another line of work.

5. Douglas Sturm, "On Meanings of Justice"

Douglas Sturm, professor emeritus at Bucknell University, held joint appointments in the Department of Religion and Philosophy, and the Department of Political Science. This unusual arrangement indicates the highly synthetic nature of his work. It is not uncommon for Sturm to integrate biblical exegesis, theological ethics, modern legal theory, political philosophy, and philosophy in a single essay. Although he has made important contributions in all of these areas, his overall project is a progressive reinterpretation of the covenantal theological tradition by placing it in dialogue with process philosophy. This particular essay is a synthesis of contemporary theories of justice in political philosophy, showing how each school of thought has deep connections with theological and biblical themes.

According[24] to John Rawls, a central focus, if not the central focus, of political reason is justice. Rawls suspects we share a common intuition, namely, that "justice is the first virtue of social institutions, as truth is of systems of thought. A theory however elegant and economical must be rejected or revised if it is untrue; likewise laws and institutions no matter how efficient and well-arranged must be reformed or abolished if they are unjust." If that be the case, justice may constitute a fruitful point of connection between religious thought and political theory, for, at least within the Western religious tradition, justice has been a central concern. Amos's thundering judgment, "let justice roll down like water, and righteousness like a mighty stream,"[25] (5:24) has been a constant theme in Hebraic and Christian communities.

But while the social problem, the "sense of injustice," may be in particular instances startlingly vivid, its reverse image, the sense of justice, may be woefully lacking in sharp edges. To alter the metaphor, justice, in current debates among political theorists, shows itself as many colors, some of which shade off into others, but not all of which seem consistent with each other. Justice appears as through a prism. . . As the prism metaphor applies to morality in

---

[24] Douglas Sturm, "On Meanings of Justice" in *Community and Alienation: Essays on Process Thought and Public Life* (Notre Dame, Ind.: University of Notre Dame Press, 1988) 94–111, revised.

[25] Translations as provided by author, resembling (but not identical to) several at http://www.biblegateway.com.

general, so it applies to political morality and to the principle of justice. There is a plurality of meanings of justice by which the social problem might be viewed. But a plurality is not necessarily pluralistic. At least on a formal level, these meanings of justice are related, for each is a particularization of the generic definition of justice phrased in the Justinian code—the constant and continuous intention to give everyone one's due—*suum cuique.*

There are four meanings of justice I shall entertain. The first is found in Robert Nozick and Richard Flathman: justice as liberty, the principle of classical liberalism. The second is present in A. M. Honorè and John Rawls: justice as equality, the principle of reformism. The third is argued by Carol Gould and Robert Johann: justice as community, which to Gould is the principle of socialism. The fourth is articulated by Leo Strauss and Eric Voegelin: justice as wisdom, the principle of aristocratic conservatism. With each of these meanings, there is a correlative way of categorizing the social problem. Thus authoritarianism is the bane of liberalism. Inequity is the enemy of reformism. Alienation is the *bête noire* of communalism. And provincialism, or in Voegelin's lexicon, gnosticism, is the antagonist of aristocratic conservatism. I would propose that each of these theories of justice and ways of giving formulation to the social problem has merit, although I would hold them all on my own terms.

1. Justice as Liberty

Justice as liberty: "God has sent me . . . to proclaim liberty to the captives" (Luke 4:18).[26] From Hegel's brilliant analysis of the dialectical intricacies of the master-slave relationship to Camus' interpretation of the meaning and implications of rebellion, we are reminded of the surging drive for liberty in the modern world. Those who are enslaved and oppressed reach a point at which they cry out for release, and release seems the only just thing to be done. Liberty from external constraint has been the inspiration of the liberal tradition and its principle of justice.

Liberalism in its modern form has been associated with the bourgeois revolutions of the seventeenth and eighteenth centuries. The bourgeois revolutions were an integral part of a radical transition from a mercantilist and monarchical order to a capitalist and constitutionalist system. Thus the bourgeois revolutions signaled a new epoch of economic and political liberty. Yet liberalism cannot be dismissed as merely a bourgeois ideology. Underlying the bourgeois ideology is a more profound principle which, to be sure, was not absent in the bourgeois revolutions but which was not fully captured in them and which, over the years, has been blunted by their consequences.

[26] Quoted from the English Standard Version as found at http:// www.biblegateway.com: The Holy Bible, English Standard Version © 2001 by Crossway Bibles, a division of Good News Publishers.

The more profound principle is captured in Simone Weil's declaration that "nothing on earth can stop us from feeling ourselves born for liberty. Never, whatever may happen, can we accept servitude; for we are thinking creatures. We have never ceased to dream of a boundless liberty whether as a past state of happiness of which a punishment has deprived us, or as a future state of happiness that is due to us by reason of a sort of pact with some mysterious providence."[27]

Despite the dream, boundless liberty is unattainable, even unimaginable. Yet liberty, if not boundless, does seem to belong to one. It is one's birthright. It is central to the meaning of human existence. But it is not simply a given. It must be intended even as it is a presupposition of all intentionality. This is the moral and political truth that underlies the liberal principle.

In Richard Flathman's defense of the "Great Rights" of liberal individualism—rights to freedom of speech and association, to habeas corpus and suffrage—he defines the liberal principle as meaning it is a good thing for individuals "to satisfy their desires, to serve their interests, and to achieve their purposes and objectives."[28] One must, that is, honor the subjective aim of individuals as something of intrinsic worth. The imposition of structures of action upon an individual without consent results in inevitable loss. The forced asylum, whether in the form of penitentiary, sanatorium, or bureaucracy, does violence to the human spirit. Indeed, the vitality of society depends on the strength of individuality. This is not to say that compulsion is always wrong or thoroughly unjust. But it is to say that resort to compulsion, even in the form of defensive counter-violence, cannot be accomplished without cost.

One of the historical roots of Western liberalism, according to William Ernest Hocking, is Christianity's stress on individual responsibility. In that root, of which modern liberalism is a mutation, the "essential freedom of the self" is "that it stands for a fateful moment outside of all belongings, and determines for itself alone whether its primary attachments shall be with actual earthly interests or with those of an ideal and potential 'Kingdom of God.' Individuality is . . . a continued living tension between various possibilities of belonging."[29] . . .

Yet the liberal principle of justice is not without its difficulties. Consider Robert Nozick's formulation of that principle: "From each according to what he chooses to do, to each according to what he makes for himself (perhaps with the contracted aid of others) and what others choose to do for him and choose to give to him of what they've been given previously (under the maxim) and haven't yet expended or transferred." More succinctly (though

[27] Simone Weil, *Oppression and Liberty,* trans. Arthur Wills and John Petrie (Amherst: University of Massachusetts Press, 1973) 83.

[28] Richard Flathman, *The Practice of Rights* (Cambridge: Cambridge University Press, 1976) 171.

[29] William Ernest Hocking, *The Lasting Elements of Individualism* (New Haven, Conn.: Yale University Press, 1937) 23.

ungrammatically): "From each as they choose, to each as they are chosen."[30] Nozick's formulation, which seems innocuous on the surface, is tied to an entitlement theory which, as it works out, is troubling. Given that theory, persons have a right to whatever holdings they have acquired or have been transferred to them in keeping with historically inherited legal principles. It would be utterly contrary to that theory to redistribute holdings according to some patterned or "end-state" principle (e.g., to each according to I. Q. or ethnic origin or need or strict equality). Nozick's entitlement theory means that however things work out in accordance with historically inherited legal principles is the way they ought to have worked out; only in that way can liberty be preserved.

The irony is that the liberal principle, so understood, subverts itself. In the economic realm, the liberal principle has led to massive concentrations of wealth; in the political realm, it has led to analogous concentrations of power; in the cultural realm, it has tended toward the strangulation of creativity and difference. The rhetoric of a free society is not matched by the reality of the social order. The name of liberty, once invoked to stall the forces of authoritarianism, has become an apology for inequity.

2. JUSTICE AS EQUALITY

And so I am led to justice as equality: "There is neither Jew nor Greek; there is neither slave nor free; there is neither male nor female; for you are all one in Christ Jesus" (Gal 3:28, RSV). Paul's message to the Galatians, declares Sanford Lakoff, "must surely have been received as a doctrine of equality."[31] Independently of the Mosaic [L]aw, Gentiles may become children of Abraham. The inheritance of the dignity of a child of God is open to all by faith regardless of ethnicity, social status, or sex. While Ernst Troeltsch insists that primitive Christianity was far from presenting a program of social reform, he noted that the "revolutionary power of the idea of equality" inherent in the primitive Christian message has not been without historical impact."[32]

The principle of justice as equality has been the basis of various types of reformism, all of which retain their appeal. The most modest type has been that of equality before the law. The impartiality of strict conformity to rule is, despite some criticisms to the contrary, more than a merely formal principle. Anyone who has been subjected to arbitrary or capricious action by parent or

---

[30] Robert Nozick, *Anarchy, State, and Utopia* (New York: Basic Books, 1974) 160.

[31] Sanford A. Lakoff, "Christianity and Equality," in *Equality,* ed. J. Roland Pennock and John W. Chapman (New York: Atherton Press, 1967) 117.

[32] Ernst Troeltsch, *Social Teaching of the Christian Churches,* trans. Olive Wyon (London: George Allen and Unwin, Ltd., 1931, originally published 1912) 77–78.

police, bureaucrat or boss knows of the importance of the principle. The files of Amnesty International are rife with cases where the principle has been violated with the ugliest of consequences. So elementary is the intuition of the principle of justice as impartiality, as treating like cases alike, that it finds spontaneous expression among young children in family and in school.

But the rule of law, despite its force as a principle of institutional justice, can not carry the full burden of the meaning of justice as equality. While in some cases, if applied seriously, it may mitigate the disadvantages of social division (even the indigent shall have their day in court), its general tendency is to reinforce any system that embodies that division. To treat a slave with impartiality, given the rules of the plantation system, is in itself just, but that does not mean the system as a whole is just.

Thus reformist movements have gone beyond appeal to justice as equality before law to justice as equality of opportunity, that is, equality in the distribution of things necessary and desirable for a humane life. . . Equality of opportunity may be understood narrowly as involving "equal chances to get ahead in a meritocratic rat-race" or broadly as "an equal claim on the earth's natural resources" or as "the same abilities and efforts should reap the same rewards."[33] These phrases are those of Brian Barry whose concern is to develop a conception of equality to deal sensibly with justice between richer and poorer nations and with justice across generations: "The planet is the common heritage of all people at all times and any appropriation of its resources must be subject to appraisal from the point of view of justice"[34] . . .

Underlying drives toward justice as equality before the law and as equality of opportunity is a profound sense of human dignity. Apart from whatever differences—physical, psychological, cultural, even moral—there are among persons, there is an irreducible quality that attaches to everyone simply as human and that must be honored and respected. In the formation of communities that quality must be factored in as central to the meaning of justice. A. M. Honorè captures this in his formulation of a principle of social justice: "All humans considered merely as human beings and apart from their conduct or choice have a claim to an equal share in all those things, here called advantages, which are generally desired and are in fact conducive to their well-being," that is, "conducive to human perfection and human happiness." "Advantages" include "such things as life, health, food, shelter, clothing, places to move in, opportunities for acquiring knowledge and skills, for sharing in the process of making decisions, for recreation, etc."[35]

---

[33] Brian Barry, "Justice as Reciprocity," in *Justice*, ed., Eugene Kamenka and Alice Erh-Soon Tay (New York: St. Martin's Press, 1980) 75–76.

[34] Ibid.

[35] A. M. Honore, "Social Justice," *Essays in Legal Philosophy*, ed. Robert S. Summers (Berkeley and Los Angeles: University of California Press, 1976) 62–63, 91 (italics removed).

Honorè admits, as a secondary principle, that there are exceptions given such considerations as choice, need, desert, special relations, but they are clearly exceptions. Furthermore, Honorè is aware of the radical implications of the principle. It mandates universal education, medical care for all, global redistribution of natural resources, indemnification of injured persons, etc. But the argument is that each and every person has a proper claim to those advantages needful or desirable for the fulfillment of human life. Nozick's principle of justice as liberty cannot accommodate this concern.

Yet principles of liberty and equality are both deficient. They are centrifugal in character. They separate. They individuate. At least within our current social setting, they set claim over against claim. They pull apart. As Wieslaw Lang argues in an especially focused critique of these principles, they "do not consider the fundamental problem of social justice, which is the problem of the control of the means of production by the working classes of society."[36]

3. JUSTICE AS COMMUNITY

I am drawn therefore to a third alternative, justice as community, a point at which considerations of justice and common good merge: "For just as the body is one and has many members, and all the members of the body, though many, are one body so it is with Christ. . . Now you are the body of Christ and individually members of it" (1 Cor 12:12, 27, RSV).

Atomism and organicism are polar metaphors employed in political theory. In their more simplified forms, they distort the full meaning of human interaction. Where atomism, with its analytic and individualistic orientation, neglects the participative dimension of interaction, organicism, with its systemic and functionalist approach, neglects the reality of the individual. Classical liberalism and reformism are reminders of the status of the individual in matters of justice, but they overlook the feature of solidarity in its ontological and ethical aspects.

The presence of solidarity assumes two forms in human experience: a negative form and a positive form. In its negative form, solidarity is alienation. In its positive form, it is community. Marxist socialism has been among the most influential movements in the modern world focused on the negative form of solidarity, that is, alienation. As Bertell Oilman summarizes the meaning of alienation under conditions of capitalism, it entails a fourfold separation of persons from their life-activity: they have no authority over their work; they have no control over the products of their work; they are set in competition with their fellow workers; in short, they are estranged from the context within which and through which their life is lived.[37] Alienation, from this perspective,

---

[36] Wieslaw Lang, "Marxism, Liberalism, and Justice," in *Justice,* ed. Eugene Kamenka and Alice Erh-Soon Tay, Ideas and Ideologies (New York: St. Martin's Press, 1980) 148.

[37] Bertell Ollman, *Alienation: Marx's Conception of Man in Capitalist Society* (Cambridge: Cambridge University Press, 1976) 133–34.

means more than physical or psychological separation between person and person. It is not merely the break in relations that often characterizes, say, parent and child, friend and friend, employer and employee, even nation and nation. It is, more significantly, a kind of relationship in which, curiously, persons act against themselves. It is a kind of institutional arrangement in which persons cannot help but participate, but when they do so, the consequences have a debilitating, deleterious effect on their lives. It is a quality of social life in which one's most creative endeavors contribute to a structure of domination from which one suffers and over which one lacks control. Within Marxist interpretation, the classic expression of alienation is the relation between capital and labor. In this case, to use Carol Gould's phrasing, "alienation does not simply refer to the separation of labor from its products and to labor's lack of control over its productive activity . . . beyond this, alienation underlies the whole production process by capitalism. In this systemic sense, alienation refers to the process by which labor produces capital and also constantly reproduces its relation to capital, in which it is dominated by capital."[38]

There is a reverse side to alienation which, in Carol Gould's innovative interpretation of Marx's social ontology, is a principle of justice. While Gould recognizes that Marx did not himself provide an explicit discussion of justice, she argues that he does provide a basis for the construction of such a conception. In its deepest sense, justice, within a Marxian framework, "consists . . . in mutuality in social relations"; it "designates social relations in which agents mutually enhance each other"; it "may be characterized as the most developed form of reciprocity." In short, a just society would be a communal society in which the primary form of relation between people would be not economic but social and in which "the activity of production itself becomes the activity of a community, as the differentiated, creative activity of its members in which they jointly determine the purposes of productive activity and the form of the distribution of its products."[39] Thus the principle of justice as community mandates the transformation of the social order in such a way that a people will gain control of its own life and will engage in continuously creative activity as a people . . .

Yet even justice as community is not without its potentially dark side. A community is too often an association that, while self-confident and comfortable, is smug, stagnant, and bent in upon itself. Within the framework of modern life, a commune has a strong appeal. But it may be an escape from the structural problems of the economic and political order. A commune easily becomes a new kind of tribalism. While it may be genuinely cooperative internally, it may also be a closed society whose horizons of thought and life are

---

[38] Carol C. Gould, *Marx's Social Ontology: Individuality and Community in Marx's Theory of Social Reality* (Cambridge, Mass.: MIT Press, 1978) 153.

[39] Ibid,, 173, 171, 175, and 177.

severely inflexible and limited. Moreover it may be, despite Marx's projection of a classless society, that the "dilemmas of communitarian politics," to use Roberto Unger's felicitous phrase, are ultimately insoluble.[40]

4. Justice as Wisdom

I am therefore led to a fourth prospect—justice as wisdom: "Do not be conformed to this world but be transformed by the renewal of your mind, that you may prove what is the will of God, what is good and acceptable and perfect" (Rom 12:2, RSV). Wisdom is an old-fashioned term that tends not to be used in modern essays on moral or political theory. The tendency not to use the term may be a mark of humility: Who is so impudent as to pretend to wisdom? It is also a mark of skepticism: Who is to say there is such a thing as wisdom? The corrosive acid of the modern skepticism has had a deep effect on our speaking and thinking about matters of truth, beauty, and goodness. And no wonder. All too often high sounding appeals have been used to cloak low level operations. All too often the invocation of principles of justice—as liberty, equality, or community—have served to rationalize self-interest. From widely divergent perspectives, Karl Marx, Sigmund Freud, and Reinhold Niebuhr have all taught us that elegant principles unmasked manifest inelegant—if not disreputable—motivations [dashes added]. There is, if I may put it this way, some wisdom in our skepticism about appeals to wisdom. But to put it this way is to begin to make the point I intend to make: The point is that what is just is what is wise, but knowing what is wise is no simple matter. Furthermore, while seeking to know what is wise may be of direct political pertinence, it may, paradoxically, lead one beyond the world of politics.

This is the complexion of justice that has been represented so powerfully in efforts by Leo Strauss and Eric Voegelin to recall us to the roots of political philosophy in classical antiquity.

Strauss argues, convincingly, that political thinking is fundamentally philosophical and essentially ethical. He insists that political action is aimed either to preserve or to change given circumstances. In the former case, one presumes to avoid what is worse. In the latter case, one seeks to achieve what is better. In both cases one is guided by some thought of what is good. The thought may be a matter of opinion. But, upon reflection, one might admit that one's opinion is questionable. If one admits that it is questionable, one is then directed toward the thought of a good that is not questionable even though one may not, at the moment, know what that good is. Nonetheless one is led to the idea of a good that is not a matter of opinion but a matter of knowledge.[41]

---

[40] Roberto Mangabeira Unger, *Knowledge & Politics* (New York: Free Press, 1975) 284–95.

[41] Leo Strauss, *What is Political Philosophy?; and Other Studies* (Westport, Conn.: Greenwood Press, 1973) 10.

In another version of the same reasoning, Strauss suggests that the concern of classical political thought is the regime, that is, the fundamental form of a society, its manner of life, its symbiotic structure, its quality as a whole. But regimes, each oriented toward some purpose as its good, vary; in their variance they clash and conflict with each other. Each regime is, by virtue of its being, a claim on behalf of its purpose and its way of life. But the conflicting claims give rise to the question of the best regime which is the definitive question of political philosophy.[42]

Political life thus involves conflicts among persons and groups asserting opposing claims in the name of justice. Such conflicts call for arbitration, "for an intelligent decision that will give each party what it truly deserves. . . The umpire par excellence is the political philosopher."[43] The point is that justice is giving to each one's due according to the nature of things; it means doing what is good for persons given what they are and who they are as humans within the order of the cosmos; but to know justice requires wisdom: "only the wise [person] truly knows what is good in each case for the soul. This being the case, there cannot be justice, i.e., giving to everyone what is by nature good for him, except in a society in which wise [persons] are in absolute control."[44] . . .

The curiosity is that political philosophy prods us toward philosophy proper. It presses us to transcend the political life for the contemplative life. It subordinates the realm of praxis for the realm of theory. It reminds us that in the quest for justice as wisdom we seek for a peace that goes beyond any possible creation of political peace. We are forced "to seek beyond the political sphere for perfect justice or, more generally, for the life that is truly according to nature."[45] To acknowledge justice as wisdom is, at least, to acknowledge the limitations of all structures of justice within the world of human interaction. It is to take seriously the finiteness of the human mind, the boundedness of our social orders, the circumscribed horizons of our common life. The principle of justice as wisdom enables us to lift our sights from the created good to the creative good and thus provokes openness to new possibilities of a cosmic justice in response to the calling of God.

Yet, the principle of justice as wisdom is not without its flaws. It can be and has been employed to justify the status quo as the best that can be accomplished under given conditions of political action. It can be and has been employed to promote escapism for, in its Straussian form, it favors philosophic contemplation over political action. It can be and has been employed to support elitism, for it suggests that those who are cultured, who are of a higher class, best rule over those not so advantaged. Taken as such, it is a doctrine of

---

[42] Ibid, 34.
[43] Ibid, 80–81.
[44] Ibid., *What is Political Philosophy?*, 11.
[45] Strauss, *Natural Right and History* (Chicago: University of Chicago Press, 1953) 151.

noblesse oblige. It assumes that those with knowledge of the whole best occupy positions of authority over those who are narrow minded and provincial.

5. JUSTICE AND HUMAN NATURE

In response to the social problem, four alternative principles of justice have been asserted—liberty, equality, community, wisdom. They seem incompatible with each other. How can one at the very same moment be a liberal, reformist, socialist, and aristocratic conservative?

Yet each principle seems to have some merit. Indeed I am convinced that hegemony, inequity, alienation, arid provinciality are all facets of the social problem that confronts us and are all properly condemned as unjust. Perhaps the four principles hang together as deriving from and referring to the same source, namely, our experience as humans and what we might reasonably take as the normative implication of that experience . . .

Without pretending to a complete doctrine of human nature, I would nonetheless suggest the following. Justice as liberty, the principle of classical liberalism, articulates the experience of self as individual, as a solitary one, as creative agent. Justice as equality, the principle of reformism, expresses the experience of self as relational, as engaged in a give-and-take with others, all of whom, as human, have the same right to the fulfillment of their humanity. Justice as community, the principle of socialism, is derived from the experience of self as communal, as belonging to and with others, as engaged in a shared existence from which one cannot in any simple or complete way be separated. Justice as wisdom, the principle of aristocratic conservatism, is rooted in the experience of self as transcendence, as openness to the beyond, as responsible to a higher order of goodness. Taken altogether, these four principles of justice constitute a sketch of "at any rate a vague mental picture of the sort of civilization one wishes humanity to reach."[46] The complexity of their relationship with each other is, most likely, a reflection of the complexity of the social problem. I would not want to give up any one of the principles totally, for each complements the others and is expressive of a vital dimension of moral experience.

The tragedy of the moral life in its political setting is that these principles clash at the point of decision and action. A policy to redistribute wealth through taxation might honor the principle of justice as equality, but it would violate Nozick's rendition of justice as liberty. The socialist principle—from each according to ability, to each according to need—might be expressive of community, but it transgresses considerations of simple equality.[47] An educational program directed by concern for the contemplative life and the search

---

[46] Weil, *Oppression and Liberty,* 103.

[47] Editors' note: Though this statement is often attributed to Karl Marx, Critique of the Gotha Program (1874), it is derived from the New Testament, Acts 2:45; 4:35.

for wisdom seems inconsistent with the view of education as a medium of social mobility and the equalization of social classes.

Yet tensions among these principles in political policy should not blind us to the prospect of synthesizing them in important ways in our political life. That is, if I am correct about their rootedness in our experience as human, they may hold together in the form of a moral possibility open to us if not burden upon us as individuals. They may, together, constitute the moral substance of what has traditionally been called civility, the personal counterpart of civilization. Justice is not only a virtue of social institutions, though it is that. It is as well a primary virtue of personal character. One may translate the four principles of justice into attributes of character.

Liberty means self-possession, independence of judgment and action, integrity, creativity in thought and conduct. Equality is manifest in respect for others, acknowledgment of their being as human, recognition of their potentialities and needs, and an active effort to enhance their lives. Community is evidenced in empathy in the strict sense of that word as "suffering in," that [is], the bodily apprehension of the feelings of others as if they were one's own. Wisdom is present in humility, receptivity, the continuous probing for deeper and wider understanding, and openness to new insight and responsiveness to new times.

These attributes—creativity, respect, empathy, humility—the attributes of civility, compose a way of being and acting in the world. Even as present in a single soul, they articulate a political statement. They exemplify the meaning of a genuinely human civilization. As attributes of character, they possess social significance, for they make a difference in whatever sphere of influence is open to one and they point a direction for the more encompassing public order . . .

Meanings of Justice: Summary of Types

	Individualistic		Holistic	
Political Ideology	classical liberalism	reformism	socialism	aristocratic conservatism
Central political category	justice as liberty	justice as equality	justice as community	justice as wisdom
Social-political problem	authoritarianism hegemony	inequity	alienation	provincialism gnosticism
Experience of self	self as individual, agent	self as relational	self as communal	self as transcendent, openness
Status of self	ego	ego-other	individuation-(societal) participation	individuation-(world) participation
Interpretive method	analytic, atomistic	analytic, relational	dialectic, societal	Dialectic,cosmic (hierarchical or progressive)
Scriptural Reference	Luke 4:18	Gal 3:28	1 Cor 12:12, 17	Rom 12:2
Representative political theorists	R. Nozick R. Flathman	A. M. Honorè S. Lakoff J. Rawls B. Barry	C. Gould R. Johann M. Sibley	L. Strauss E. Voegelin

Chapter Four

Marriage, Family, and Sexuality

Marriage and Family in the New Testament World

An appropriate place to begin our analysis of marriage, family, and sexuality in Christian life is by considering how our views of these areas of life contrast with those of the New Testament. When we hear the term "family," most of us immediately think about our nuclear families of parents and children who live independently from extended relatives. Most of us expect to make marriage decisions for ourselves as adults, form a partnership of equals with someone about our own age who shares our interests, and with whom we have "fallen in love." We anticipate that this bond will endure until death, which may be fifty years or more in the future. We expect to plan a limited number of children, whom we expect to live until adulthood. Increasingly, most of us expect egalitarian marriages in which both spouses may work outside the home and that both will share in the tasks of child-rearing. We expect that both spouses will remain sexually faithful to one another. Divorce, though tragic, will at least be conducted justly for both parties. Our society is beginning to recognize that there is such a thing as a sexual orientation and classifies homosexual and heterosexual acts by the gender of the persons who engage them.

Most of us assume that family life in the New Testament world was about like our own. When we encounter some familiar sounding words—man, woman, father, mother, child, marriage, family, homosexual, etc.—our first assumption is that these terms meant about the same thing then that they do now. However, sexuality and marriage practices in the ancient Mediterranean world[1] defy *all* of these assumptions listed in the paragraph above. To discover

[1] We should emphasize here that it is an over-simplification to speak of a single "New Testament world." Although there was, broadly speaking, a Mediterranean culture shared by most of the Roman Empire, there also was considerable variety in marriage and family life from region to region. For more on these differences see, Carolyn Osiek and David L. Balch, *Families in the New Testament World: Households and House Churches* (Louisville, Ky.: Westminster John Knox Press, 1997) and David L. Balch and Carolyn Osiek, eds., *Early Christian Families in Context: An Interdisciplinary Dialogue* (Grand Rapids, Mich.: William B. Eerdmans, 2003).

what the New Testament might mean for us today, then, we need to understand something about the context in which it was written.

Modern family life is shaped by our primary cultural values of *liberty,
equality,* and *fairness,* In contrast, ancient Mediterranean family life was
shaped by the values of *honor, hierarchy,* and *role differentiation.* The basic
social unit was a pyramidal extended family, headed by a male patriarch, or
paterfamilias. Under his authority were not only his wife and children, but
also a loose assemblage of step-children, adoptees, extended relations, slaves,
and dependent clients. The paterfamilias extended protection and economic
advantage to those in his care, while dependents owed him honor and service.
Within this larger pyramid were smaller family units, each headed by a male
"master of the household." Relations between members of the extended family were governed by their relative status within it. A family member's status
was clearest at the extremes. For example, the eldest adult son of the leading
family exercised authority over all but the paterfamilias himself, while slaves
lacked authority even over their own bodies. The status of those in the middle
shifted according to context. Gender trumped birth order and class standing
trumped everything. An adult daughter, for example, might find herself subject to the authority of a much younger adult brother, while she herself exercised authority over an older male slave.

Most ancients considered males and females to be radically different creatures, each with their appropriate virtues. Men should exemplify the virtue of
andreia, which called for assertiveness, authority, command of passions, and
judiciousness. Women, by contract, were thought to be held captive by their
passions, and thus required guidance or even overt control. Appropriate feminine character traits include pliability, receptivity, and warmth.

The ancient Mediterranean thus separated the world of men from that of
women to a degree that is almost inconceivable today. Women were confined
to the world of family relations and domestic production, while males also
were given access to the world of commerce and extra-familial relationships,
and those with property could participate in the public assembly. This ideal is
most apparent in prosperous families of the Greco-Roman world, whose
houses grouped private family functions to the protected rear of houses, out of
public sight. Poorer families did not have this luxury, though they aspired to
have it. The simple one or two room dwellings of the lower classes did not
allow segregation by gender, and the wives and daughters worked alongside
men in family businesses and agriculture. In the lower classes, then, gender
segregation was more social than physical. Men of *all* classes simply did not
enter into conversation with women who were not close relatives. Female
virtue was jealously projected by watchful fathers and brothers.

A woman in the ancient world could expect no real autonomy even as an
adult. First marriages were arranged by the young woman's father, who
sought an advantageous marriage for the family. Marriages were consum-

mated soon after the girl reached puberty. Her husband, on the other hand, customarily waited until his late twenties or early thirties to marry. At the time of the marriage the bride's father would transfer a dowry to the husband, who would administer it on behalf of the father. If the couple were divorced, the dowry would pass back to the woman's family of origin. Ancient laws and custom forbade women to make property decisions without the consent of a male guardian *(tutor)*.[2] Women thus found themselves economically dependent on men for their entire lives: to her father as a girl, to a husband twice her age after marriage, and to her eldest son or close relative as a widow.

Although we do have some historical evidence of real affection between spouses in the New Testament world, it was not considered essential to the marriage. The realities of family life tended to work against marital intimacy. The great disparity in ages between husband and wife and perceived differences between men and women made real friendship difficult. Since most adults did not live past their mid-forties, under the best of circumstances the couple might hope for a marriage of fifteen or twenty years.[3] In practice, however, many marriages were cut short by the dangers of childbearing, disease, and war. The short time remaining was focused on rearing children and running a household. Since only about two out of five children survived their tenth birthdays, each woman needed to accomplish five live births in order to replace the current generation. As a final impediment to marital intimacy, divorce seems to have been quite common throughout the Mediterranean world. A man or woman fortunate enough to live out a natural lifespan thus could anticipate multiple marriages. These transitions must have been especially taxing for women, who were required to uproot themselves and become part of their husbands' households.

The distinctions of licit and illicit sexual behavior in the first-century Greco-Roman world are often perplexing to the modern reader. It was much more severe in its protection of female virginity and chastity than our age, but curiously tolerant toward prostitution, unrestricted sexual activity with slaves, and pederasty, which are criminal offenses in our culture. The key to this seeming contradiction is the crucial place of male honor. Seduction of a young female virgin was seen as an assault on the dignity of her father, who is duty-bound to protect her. Similarly, adultery was an affront chiefly to the husband to whom one's paramour is married. In contrast, sexual relations with a prostitute were more tolerable because they do not violate any man's honor. Similarly, most ancients took it as a matter of course that slaves owed their masters unrestricted sexual access. While the master's wife might express feelings of jealousy, "the husband's action would be legally neutral, and for the majority

---

[2] See Osiek and Balch, *Families in the New Testament World,* 54–64.

[3] Second marriages may have provided more opportunity for intimacy between spouses. Here the woman often had more autonomy to make her decision about who to marry and the age disparity of husband and wife was often less.

of men, morally neutral."[4] Greco-Roman attitudes toward homosexuality also follow the standard of male honor. Homosexual acts are illicit when they place an adult, free male in a passive, feminine, role. Sexual relations between an adult male and a male slave or a young boy, even when coerced, avoid this difficulty and thus were widely tolerated.[5]

How does this brief sketch of marriage and family practices in the first-century Mediterranean world enlarge our understanding of these themes in the New Testament? Clearly, the New Testament directly challenges the Greco-Roman "family values" of honor, hierarchy, and role differentiation. Jesus turned the Roman world of status on its head. He taught, "Whoever want to be first must be last of all and servant of all" (Mark 9:35). Looking at the church he founded in Corinth, Paul remarked that not many in his congregation were considered wise, powerful, or noble by the standards of the Roman world: "But God chose what is foolish in the world to shame the wise; God chose what is weak in the world to shame the strong" (1 Cor 1:27). The early church defied the social mores of its day by opening leadership roles to women and welcoming both the free and slaves on equal footing. Paul wrote to his church in Galatians that in Christ "There is neither Jew or Greek, there is no longer slave or free, there is no longer male and female; for all of you are one in Christ" (Gal 3:28). Pagan observers of the church found this topsy-turvy world both perplexing and profoundly disturbing.

By the time Christianity became adopted by the Roman Empire in the fourth century, it had rounded the edges off its radical vision for the family and to some degree accommodated itself to its environment. But the church also profoundly changed the social environment of the Roman world and perhaps the family most of all.

Many scholars today believe that early Christianity invested a value in the conjugal family unit that was largely absent in the loose and shifting world of the Roman extended family.[6] Along with Christianity came a new emphasis on intimacy and love between husband and wife and greater fairness in their rights and duties. Christian families seem to have valued children more highly than their pagan counterparts, eschewing the Roman practice of abortion, exposure of newborns, and pederasty. Christian values of equality and respect forbade the sexual exploitation of slaves, and in time worked toward abolition

---

[4] Carolyn Osiek, "Female Slaves, *Porneia*, and the Limits of Obedience," in Balch and Osiek, *Early Christian Families in Context,* 264. Osiek points out another instance of the gendered double standard in the ancient Mediterranean: If a wife engaged in sexual acts with a male slave, she and the slave would be guilty of adultery against the master of the household. For additional information on sexuality and slaves, see also Christian Laes, "Desperately Different?: *Delicia* Children in the Roman Household," 298–324 in the same volume.

[5] We should note here that first-century Judaism did not share the toleration for homosexuality of the Greco-Roman world. These acts were considered to violate the Torah (see Lev 18:22; 20:13).

[6] Laes, "Desperately Different?" 323.

of slavery altogether. In constructing the new social institution of the church, it also created freedom for persons to stand apart from families, choosing vocations beyond progeny and household.

The New Testament thus sets forth a profoundly progressive agenda for marriage and family vis-à-vis the first-century Mediterranean world. What does it mean for us to be faithful to the New Testament's revolutionary moral vision? We will outline below some of the major issues that our readings will address in this chapter.

Should We Get Married at All?

The relative esteem given to marriage and celibacy has convoluted history in the church. Both the Greco-Roman and Jewish societies of the first century were built on the foundation of the family. To be cut off from family meant in a very real sense not to exist at all. In this world, Jesus' demands to "hate father and mother" (Luke 14:26) and leave behind household and family (Matt 10:16-23; Mark 10:23-31; Luke 8:19-21; Luke 9:57-62) forces a crisis of choice in his hearers. Similarly shocking is Paul's only grudging allowance for marriage to the Corinthian Christians as an accommodation to human weakness (1 Cor 7). We should be reminded here that the vision of both Jesus and Paul is profoundly eschatological: in the face of the immanent coming of the Kingdom, all of the institutions of this age seem to have but fleeting importance. Augustine's preference for the higher good of virginity underlined the preference in the early church for a celibate priesthood, which became the norm in the Middle Ages. Augustine rejected the path of radical asceticism, however, arguing that marriage is itself a good, albeit of a lower order than celibacy.

Protestantism inverted Augustine's appraisal of the relative goods of marriage and celibacy. Martin Luther objected to the narrow definition of vocation that confined the term to the ordained priesthood. He believed that lay occupations and marriage also can be vocations for people of faith, and as "callings" from God must be taken with great seriousness. In fact, he believed that very few persons are truly called to celibacy; for most it is an intolerable burden. Later Reformed Protestants extended their criticism of celibacy. They argued that marriage is the greatest symbol of the divine-human covenant that human beings can experience, offering to married persons an experience of grace unavailable to those who are not. Here we have come full circle from Augustine, with marriage and family considered the normal Christian path and vocational singleness viewed as a suspicious alternative.

Today Protestants and Catholics have much to gain through dialogue about each group's traditions on marriage and singleness. Although the Vatican staunchly maintains its commitment to a celibate, male clergy, some American Catholics are searching for a more inclusive model. Protestants, on the other hand, are realizing that they have not thought deeply enough about the real freedoms that singleness allows, and thus the possibility for a "calling" to a life of vocational singleness.

What Are the Characteristics of a Good Marriage?

We have seen above that Augustine counted marriage as a good—albeit of a lower order than the calling to clerical celibacy. But what, specifically, are the goods associated with marriage? Augustine identifies four:

1. THE PROCREATION OF CHILDREN

Like much of pagan philosophy, Augustine believes that family responsibilities are a distraction from more ultimate concerns but necessary for the continuation of the human race. Augustine anchors the good of procreation in first chapter of Genesis. In this story God gives human beings the task to be co-creators with God as they "fill the earth and subdue it" (Gen 1:28).

2. THE ASSOCIATION OF THE SEXES

By "association" Augustine means the intimate friendship that monogamous marriage provides. While Augustine himself does not make an explicit connection with Scripture in this writing, traditionally theologians have grounded the associative dimension of marriage in the deep, spiritual friendship between the first man and first woman in the second chapter of Genesis.[7]

3. THE RESTRAINT OF LUST

This good reflects Augustine's abhorrence for intemperate passions. Augustine is by no means alone here, for much of classical philosophy has the intent of rescuing persons from slavery to irrationality. Augustine also adds, for good measure, a healthy respect for the ravages of human sinfulness. He believed that sooner or later human beings will abuse whatever freedoms they are given. It is inevitable, then, that we pervert the goodness of sexuality. Augustine believed that human beings are in bondage to their own bad wills unless God grants them a grace that can transform them.

4. THE SACRAMENTAL SIGNIFICANCE OF MARRIAGE

As a remedy for sin that perverts the goodness of sexuality, God provides grace that is infused through the sacrament of marriage. Augustine believed

---

[7] Modern Catholics normally call this good the "unitive" dimension of marriage, while Protestants refer to it as "companionship" or simply "friendship." The difference in terminology reflects the more organic conception of marriage in the first group and the more voluntarist understanding in the second.

that those who look at marriage through the eyes of faith will see it as participation in a great, holy "mystery." It signifies the great unity between God and humankind and the coming unity of all citizens in the City of God. As a sacrament, the wedding service also transforms, enabling persons to live out the fidelity and Christ-like love that was intended in the beginning.

Augustine's formulation of the four goods of marriage became an important touchstone as the church developed its understanding of marriage throughout the ages.[8] Many contemporary Christian ethicists question some features of Augustine's teaching, however. A central question is whether we understand these goods as primarily descriptive or prescriptive. That is, is their primary intent to reveal a vision of the good life or to set forth unambiguous rules for licit and illicit sexual behaviors? Augustine's title for his treatise, *The Good of Marriage* (reading 2), certainly indicates that he intended to place his focus on the former. In practice, however, the church has tended to focus obsessively on individual sinful sexual acts and view sexuality as an impediment to holy living. James Nelson, a contemporary Christian ethicist who specialized in sexual ethics, has countered that the church must learn to see sex as fundamental to human life and thus an intrinsic part of the divine-human relationship. True salvation, he argues, must include sexual wholeness.[9]

In addition, many contemporary Christian ethicists believe that Augustine's treatment of the good of procreation requires some reformulation. Augustine made a direct link between the good of procreation and the prescription that all sexual acts must have a procreative intent. He regards as excessively lustful all sexual acts which do not specifically intend conception. It is curious, however, that Augustine never explored to any degree the link between sex and the good of association, which would have allowed him to welcome non-procreative sexuality that builds the companionship of the partners. In response, recent Catholic social teachings give equal weight to the unitive and procreative goods of marriage. Even official teachings allow natural family planning within marriage so that the couple can be free from worries about unwanted pregnancy and enjoy with regularity an act that builds intimacy.

What are Appropriate Gender Roles for Men and Women?

We saw above that the New Testament church challenged the Greco-Roman polarization of male and female and the exclusion of women from public life. The temptation toward patriarchy is a strong one, however, and the

---

[8] To be sure, the various denominations have interpreted these four goods differently. Protestants, for example, affirm that marriage is sacramental but deny that it is a sacrament. They acknowledge that it is like a sacrament because it can reveal much about the covenant love of God. Protestants reserve the formal title of sacrament for those rituals specifically instituted by Jesus in the New Testament: baptism and communion.

[9] See James Nelson, *Between Two Gardens* (New York: Pilgrim Press, 1983).

church struggles with this issue anew in each generation. The debate certainly includes debates within denominations about the role of women as religious leaders, but it is much wider than that. Contemporary Christian ethicists struggle to value men and women as equals while also recognizing the ways that they are different.[10]

Our readings in this chapter take two very different positions. The apostolic exhortation of Pope John Paul II, On the Role of the Christian Family in the Modern World (reading 3) begins with a recognition of the equal dignity of men and women as children of God. However, the document also argues that "clear recognition be given to the value of their maternal and family role, by comparison with all other public roles and all other professions" (3.1. 23). The document seeks to shore up the traditional roles of motherhood and father-hood as the best way to preserve the health of the family.

The essay by Sally Purvis (reading 4) takes a different tack. Her reflections on implications of Christian love for family life addresses the comparative ne-glect of the family in contemporary Christian feminist writing. She argues that defining *agape* as necessarily self-sacrificial undercuts the development of a healthy sense of self in mothers and even can support the worst forms of spousal abuse. She argues instead for an inclusive concept of Christian love that seeks to "enhance and expand the God-relation for all persons." Purvis believes that many non-traditional forms of family can exemplify such love, and not simply those headed by a "wage-earning male."

Sex Outside of Marriage?

The traditional understandings of the goods of marriage by definition limit sexual acts to marriage. So understood, only married sex intends procreation, is truly intimate, provides a structure that mitigates potential for harm, and com-municates sacramental grace. As we understand more about human sexuality, however, we have learned that sex is not simply about genital sexual intercourse. Sex embraces interior feelings, thoughts, and fantasies. In the realm of actions, sexuality covers a continuum from facial expressions, to holding hands, kissing, and so on to full genital intercourse. Karen Lebacqz (reading 6) reasons that re-sponsible sexual ethics is not simply a matter of "saying no," but knowing which of the many responses within the complex phenomenon of human sexuality is appropriate to a given context. Lebacqz by no means is arguing for pure per-missiveness. She is fully aware of the egregious ways that modern people can harm one another in the area of sexuality. Her essay is perhaps best understood as an attempt to affirm the church's concern for the consequences of human sin-fulness and need for fidelity without resorting to a rigid legalism.

---

[10] This struggle also is at the center of debates within feminism itself. See the exchange be-tween Beverly Harrison and Sidney Callahan to define what the liberation of women really means (chapter 7 of this volume).

How Should the Church Regard Homosexuality?

Perhaps no issue is more hotly debated in the church today than homosexuality. All mainline Protestant denominations are experiencing divisive battles over the appropriateness of homosexual unions, the ordination of homosexuals, and support of gay civil rights. The traditional definitions of the goods of marriage have categorically forbidden homosexual acts. Gay marriages, the argument goes, are not procreative, do not reflect the gender complementarity that true intimacy requires, condone rather than restrain sin, and cannot be sacramental because they violate church law. The majority of churches today recognize the reality of a sexual orientation that is difficult or impossible to change but recommend the path of celibacy for those unable to form heterosexual sexual relationships. The noted New Testament scholar Luke Timothy Johnson (reading 5) offers an alternative, albeit controversial, perspective. Harkening back to issues addressed in the second chapter of this book, Johnson cautions against a mechanical interpretation of Scripture. He believes that proper interpretation of Scripture requires deep sounding against our own experience. He also points out that Scripture itself attests to the unexpected works of God that at times challenge accepted wisdom. He also wonders if appropriate sexuality should be defined covenantally rather than biologically, opening up the possibility for homosexual relationships that embody covenantal love.

What is the Public Role of the Family?

The privatization of the family is a hallmark of modern liberal society. The industrial revolution moved workers away from home and farm to the factory and firm, splitting family life and work life into separate zones. As work became increasingly harsh and competitive, the family became the great refuge of love and comfort, valued precisely because it was wholly different than the world of work. Modern human beings often find it difficult to reconcile their public selves and private selves, family values and the realities of work life, intimate care for family members and the bureaucratic governance of mass society. This separation is only exacerbated by the tendency of modern Protestants to emphasize the associational goods of marriage above all the others. The apostolic exhortation, On the Role of the Christian Family in the Modern World (reading 3) is an attempt to reconnect the family with social and political life. It argues for political structures that support family life and urges its readers to become engaged as families in the political process. At the heart of the document is the principle of *subsidiarity,* the doctrine that we violate the integrity of small, personal, and local human associations when we take away from them their proper sphere of work and assign these tasks to larger institutions.

READINGS

1. Biblical Foundations

GENESIS 1:1–2:4A

Most scholars believe that this passage reflects the focus on order and stability of the Priestly tradition. This tradition is especially concerned to establish boundaries and distinctions that demarcate the clean from the unclean.
Here men and women are created collectively at the climax of creation in the
"image of God" (Gen 1:27). Procreation is commanded as an essential means
of governing the earth.

GENESIS 2:4B-3

This long narrative retells the story of human creation from the perspective
of a single man and woman. The narrative is rife with irony, emotion, and sudden reversal. In contrast to the first creation story, a single man is formed as the
first creature and then the garden, other animals, and finally the woman are created in order to meet his purposes. Here the relationship of the man and woman
has the purpose of companionship rather than procreation. Note, however, how
this original unity of the two is shattered by human sinfulness, but God inter-
venes to preserve the human family when the original paradise is lost.

MATTHEW 5:27-32; 19:1-12 (PARALLELS IN MARK 10:1-12; LUKE 16:18)

Referring to Genesis 2, Jesus teaches that the bond between a man and
woman in marriage is so deep that it is indissoluble. Divorce, which in Jesus'
day only could be initiated by the husband, exists only because of the "hard-
ness" of the human heart. Note that the Matthew passage adds the exception
of *porneia* (NRSV: "unchastity" v. 32) to the blanket condemnation of divorce
in Mark and Luke. The meaning of this term is uncertain. The term refers
broadly to some sort of illicit sex. In the Greek translation of the Hebrew
Scriptures, the term most commonly refers to adultery. The term also may
have some connection with relationships regarded as incestuous by Jewish
Law, for example, Paul's criticism of a man who took to himself his step-
mother (1 Cor 5:1).

MATTHEW 10:16-23, MARK 10:23-31, LUKE 8:19-21, LUKE 9:57-62

Included here are just a few passages in which Jesus questions the absolute
primacy given to family bonds in the ancient Mediterranean civilization.

Jesus' preaching creates a crisis in which his followers must make hard choices about their ultimate loyalties. Here the family has been supplanted by the new community of faithful disciples. Jesus holds up the itinerant preacher without family or property as the ideal.

1 CORINTHIANS 7

This chapter contains Paul's most extensive treatment of marriage and family. Paul's expectation of a speedy second coming of Christ and the harsh realities of persecution lead Paul to counsel single celibacy over the traditional roles of spouse and parent. Paul allows marriage only for those who cannot control their sexual drives.

PASSAGES THAT SPECIFICALLY ADDRESS THE ISSUE OF HOMOSEXUALITY: GENESIS 19:1-29; LEVITICUS 18:22; 20:13; 1 CORINTHIANS 6:9-11 (SIMILAR STATEMENT IN 1 TIMOTHY 1:10); ROMANS 1:16-32.

The above passages contain every reference to homosexual practice in the Bible. Clearly, the issue is not a central preoccupation of the biblical writers, though certainly it was a common practice in the Greco-Roman world. The Sodom story in Genesis 19 has long been referenced as a condemnation of homosexual sex acts in Christian history, though most modern interpreters now interpret the sin of Sodom as an extreme form of inhospitality to guests. The Leviticus passages include homosexuality along with other acts that lead to ritual pollution, such as incest and contact with menstruating women, reflecting the Priestly tradition's aversion to illicit boundary crossings. Homosexual acts are simply listed in the Corinthians and Timothy passages among a long list of condemned acts. More substantive is Paul's argument in Romans that homosexual acts are evidence of the effects of human sinfulness, which could lead us to reject our created nature.

2. Augustine, Bishop of Hippo (354–430), *The Good of Marriage*

It is impossible to overemphasize the influence of Augustine's The Good of Marriage *on the development of Christian conceptions of marriage and sexuality. While he exalts the special vocation of clerical celibacy, Augustine also affirms the essential goodness of human sexuality and the estate of marriage.*

1.   Every[11] human being is part of the human race, and human nature is a social reality and possesses a great and natural good, the power of friendship.

---

[11] Augustine of Hippo, *The Good of Marriage*, partially translated in *Marriage in the Early Church*, ed. and trans. David G. Hunter, Sources of Early Christian Thought, William G. Rusch, series ed. (Minneapolis: Fortress Press, 1992) 102, 104–14, 116–20. © 1992 Augsburg Fortress. Used by permission.

For this reason God wished to create all human beings from one, so that they would be held together in human society, not only by the similarity of race, but also by the bond of blood relationship. Therefore, the first natural union of human society is the husband and wife. God did not create even these as separate individuals and join them together as if they were alien to each other, but he created the one from the other. The power of the union was also signified in the side from which she was taken and formed, for they are joined to each other's side, when they walk together and together look where they are walking. The result is the bonding of society in children, who are the one honorable fruit, not of the union of male and female, but of sexual intercourse. For there could have been some kind of real and amiable union between the sexes even without sexual intercourse, a union in which the one rules and the other obeys.

3.   This is what we now say: according to that state of birth and death, which we experience and in which we were created, the union of male and female is something good. The divine Scripture commends this alliance to such an extent that a woman who is divorced by her husband is not allowed to marry another, while her husband is still alive; and a man who is divorced by his wife may not take another, unless the wife who has left him has died. It is right, therefore, to inquire why the good of marriage is a good, which even the Lord confirmed in the gospel, not only because he prohibited divorce, except in cases of fornication (cf. Matt 19:9), but also because when he was invited to the wedding, he attended (cf. John 2:1-11).

I do not believe that marriage is a good solely because of the procreation of children: there is also the natural association *(societas)* between the sexes. Otherwise, we would no longer speak of a marriage between elderly people, especially if they had lost or had never produced children. But now in a good marriage, even if it has lasted for many years and even if the youthful ardor between the male and female has faded, the order of charity between husband and wife still thrives. The earlier they begin to refrain from sexual intercourse, by mutual consent, the better they will be. This is not because they will eventually be unable to do what they wish, but because it is praiseworthy not to wish to do what they are able to do.

If, therefore, they keep faithful to the honor and the conjugal duties that each sex owes the other, even if both of their bodies grow weak and almost corpselike, yet the chastity of spirits joined in a proper marriage will endure; the more it is tested, the more genuine it will be; the more it is calmed, the more secure it will be. There is an additional good in marriage, namely the fact that carnal or youthful incontinence, even the most wicked, is directed toward the honorable task of procreating children. As a result, conjugal intercourse makes something good out of the evil of lust *libido,* since the concupiscence of the flesh, which parental affection moderates, is then suppressed and in a certain way burns more modestly. For a sort of dignity prevails over the fire of pleasure, when in the act of uniting as husband and wife the couple regard themselves as father and mother.

5.   It is often asked whether this situation should be called a marriage: when a man and a woman, neither of whom is married to another, have intercourse with each other, not in order to have children, but out of incontinence solely to have sex, and yet faithfully pledge not to do this with anyone else. Perhaps it would not be absurd to call this a marriage, if they made this agreement to last until the death of one of them, and if, although they have not come together for the sake of procreation, they at least do not avoid it, either by not wishing to have children or by acting in an evil way to prevent children from being born. But if one or both of these conditions are absent, I do not see how we could call this a marriage.

For if a man is living with a woman only until he finds someone else who is worthy either of his position or of his wealth, whom he can marry as an equal, in his heart he is an adulterer, not with the woman whom he would like to find, but with the woman with whom he is living but not in a marital union. The same applies to the woman, if she is aware of this and is still willing to have unchaste intercourse with a man, with whom she does not have a commitment as a wife. But if she preserves her fidelity to him as to a spouse after he has taken a wife, and if she refuses to marry and decides to remain completely continent, I would not find it easy to call her an adulteress. Yet who would not call it a sin, knowing that she had intercourse with a man who was not her husband?

6.   Furthermore, even when people make an excessive demand for the payment of the carnal debt—which the apostle did not give to them as a command but granted as a concession (cf. 1 Cor. 7:6)—so that they engage in intercourse even without the purpose of procreation; even if immoral conduct leads them to this sort of intercourse, nevertheless marriage protects them from adultery and fornication. It is not that this sort of behavior is permitted because of marriage; rather, it is forgiven because of marriage. Therefore, not only do married people owe each other the fidelity of sexual intercourse for the sake of procreation, which is the first association of the human race in this mortal life, but they also owe each other a sort of mutual service for the sustaining of each other's weakness, so that they may avoid illicit intercourse. As a result, even if one of them would prefer to adopt perpetual continence, it is not permitted without the consent of the partner. For in this matter "a wife does not have power over her body, but her husband does; likewise, a husband has no power over his body, but his wife does" (1 Cor 7:4).

Therefore, they should not deny one another that which the husband seeks from matrimony and that which the wife seeks from her husband [1 Cor 7:5], even if this proceeds not from a desire to have children but only from weakness and incontinence. This is to prevent them from falling into damnable seductions at the temptation of Satan because of the incontinence of one or both of them. Conjugal intercourse for the sake of procreation carries no fault; intercourse for the sake of satisfying lust, provided that it takes place with a spouse, carries a forgivable fault *(venialis culpa)* because of marital fidelity; but adultery or fornication carries a mortal fault. Therefore, abstention from all intercourse is better even than marital intercourse that takes place for the sake of procreation.

But while continence has greater merit, it is no sin to pay the conjugal debt; and although to demand it beyond the need for procreation is a forgivable fault, certainly fornication and adultery are crimes that must be punished. Therefore, the charity of marriage must be careful that, in seeking greater honor for itself, it does not create a situation in which a spouse incurs damnation. For whoever divorces his wife, except in the case of fornication, makes her commit adultery (Matt 5:32). Once the nuptial agreement has been made, it is a kind of sacrament to such an extent that it is not made void even by separation, since as long as the husband who left her still lives, she commits adultery if she marries someone else, and the husband who left her is the cause of this evil.

7.   Since it is permissible to divorce an adulterous wife, I wonder whether it is also permissible to marry again after the divorce. In this case Sacred Scripture creates a difficult problem, since the apostle cites a precept of the Lord saying that a woman ought not to leave her husband, but that if she leaves him, she should remain unmarried or be reconciled to her husband (cf. 1 Cor 7:10-11). She definitely should not withdraw and remain unmarried, except in the case of an adulterous husband, because by withdrawing from a husband who is not adulterous she may cause him to commit adultery. But, perhaps, she can be justly reconciled to her husband, either by tolerating him, if she is unable to restrain herself, or after he has been corrected. But I do not see how a man can be permitted to marry another woman when he leaves an adulterous wife, if a woman is not permitted to marry again when she leaves an adulterous husband. . .

8.   "Let marriage be held in honor by all and the marriage bed be undefiled" (Heb 13:4). We do not say that marriage is a good merely in comparison with fornication; in that case there would be two evils, one of which is worse. In that sense even fornication would be a good because adultery is worse—since to violate another person's marriage is worse than to have sex with a prostitute; and adultery would be a good because incest is worse—since it is worse to have intercourse with your mother than with another man's wife; and on it would go until you reach things which, as the apostle said, "it is disgraceful even to mention" (Eph 5:12). On this rendering all things would be good in comparison with something worse. But who has any doubts that this is false?

Marriage and fornication, therefore, are not two evils, one of which is worse, but marriage and continence are two goods, one of which is better.

Similarly, bodily health and sickness are not two evils, one of which is worse, but health and immortality are two goods, one of which is better. Likewise, knowledge and vanity are not two evils, of which vanity is the worse, but knowledge and love are two goods, of which love is the better. For "knowledge will be destroyed," the apostle says, and yet it is a necessity in the present life; but love will never fail (1 Cor 13:8). In the same way, the procreation of mortal bodies, which is the purpose of marriage, will be destroyed; but freedom from all sexual relations is a participation in the angelic life *(angelia meditation)* here and now, and it will remain so forever . . .

Therefore, just as Martha did something good when she ministered to the saints, but her sister Mary did something better when she sat at the Lord's feet and listened to his words (cf. Luke 10:38-42), so likewise we praise the good of Susanna in her conjugal chastity, and yet we rank more highly the good of the widow Anna, and much more highly the good of the virgin Mary. It was a good thing that they did, when they supplied Christ and his disciples with the necessities out of their own resources; but those who abandoned all their resources in order to follow the same Lord more readily did an even better thing. Yet, in both of these goods, whether that of Martha and Mary or that of the disciples, the better thing could not be done without bypassing or abandoning the lesser good.

9.   Surely, it must be acknowledged that God gave us some goods to be sought for their own sake, such as wisdom, good health, and friendship, and other goods that are necessary for the sake of something else, such as learning, food, drink, sleep, marriage, and sexual intercourse. Some of these goods are necessary for wisdom, such as learning; some are necessary for good health, such as food and drink and sleep; and some are necessary for friendship, such as marriage and sexual intercourse, for these lead to the propagation of the human race, in which a friendly association is a great good . . .

This leads me to conclude that in the earliest times of the human race the saints were required to make use of the good of marriage, not as something to be sought for its own sake, but as a good necessary for something else, namely the propagation of the people of God, through which the Prince and Savior of all peoples was both prophesied and born. But in the present, since there is abundant opportunity for spiritual kins to enter into holy and genuine associations everywhere and among all nations, even those people who wish to marry solely for the sake of procreation are urged to practice the better good of continence.

10.   But I know what they will murmur: "What if all people wish to abstain completely from sexual intercourse? How would the human race survive?" If only all people had this desire, as long as it proceeds from "a pure heart and a good conscience and a sincere faith" (1 Tim 1:5)! The City of God would be filled up much more quickly, and the end of time would be hastened. What

else does the apostle seem to encourage when he says; "I would like everyone to be as I am" (1 Cor 7:7)? Or, in another place:

> What I mean, my friends, is that the time is short. From now on even those who have wives should live as if they had none; those who mourn, as if they were not mourning; those who rejoice, as if they were not rejoicing; those who buy, as if they were not buying; and those who use this world, as if they were not using it. For the form of this world is passing away. I want you to be without care." Then he adds: "The man without a wife is concerned about the Lord's affairs, how to please the Lord. But the married man is concerned about the affairs of the world, how to please his wife, and he is divided. And the unmarried woman and virgin, she is concerned about the Lord's affairs, that she may be holy in body and spirit. But the married woman is concerned about the affairs of the world, how to please her husband. (1 Cor. 7:29-34)

For this reason, it seems to me that in the present time only those who do not restrain themselves should marry, in accord with that saying of the same apostle: "But if they cannot control themselves, they should marry, for it is better to marry than to burn" (1 Cor. 7:9).

12.   For when the natural use [of sexual relations] extends beyond the marriage pact (that is, beyond what is necessary for procreation), this is pardonable in a wife but damnable in a prostitute. Conversely, the use of sex beyond nature, which is abominable in a prostitute, becomes even more abominable in a wife. The ordinance of the Creator and the order of creation have such great force that an excessive use of something that is granted to be used is much more acceptable than even a single or rare excess in the use of something that has not been granted. That is why a spouse's immoderation must be tolerated when it is a question of licit sexual relations, so that lust will not erupt into illicit relations. This is also the reason why it is much less sinful to make constant demands of one's wife than to make even the rarest use of fornication.

But if a man wishes to use that part of his wife's body that has not been granted for this purpose, the wife is more shameful if she allows this to happen to herself than to another woman. The glory of marriage, therefore, is the chastity *(castitas)* of procreation and fidelity *(fides)* in rendering the duty of the flesh. This is the work of marriage, and this is what the apostle defends from all blame when he says: "If you have taken a wife, you have not sinned; and if a virgin marries, she does not sin" (1 Cor 7:28). And: "He may do whatever he wishes; be does not sin; let him marry" (1 Cor 7:36). Married persons are granted as a concession the right to demand from each other in a somewhat immoderate or excessive manner the payment of the conjugal debt, for the reasons that he gave above.

17.   Among the ancient fathers, of course, it was permissible to take another woman, with the permission of one's wife, and to produce children that were shared in common, the husband providing the seed and the intercourse, the wife

providing the right and authorization. Whether this is also permitted in our own day I would not be so rash as to say. For today there is not the same need of procreation that there was in the past. In those days it was even permissible for husbands who could have children to take other wives in order to produce more numerous progeny, which is something that is certainly not allowed today.

18.   For sexual intercourse is to the health of the human race what food is to the health of a human being, and neither exists without some carnal pleasure *(delectatio carnalis)*. When this pleasure is moderated and directed toward its natural use by the restraint of temperance, it cannot be lust *(libido)*. What illicit food is to the sustaining of life, however, that fornication or adulterous intercourse is to the desire for offspring. And what illicit food is in the indulgence of the stomach and the palate, that illicit intercourse is in the lust that does not seek children. And an immoderate desire for licit food is to some people what to spouses is the pardonable use of intercourse. Therefore, just as it is better to die of hunger than to eat food that has been sacrificed to idols [see 1 Cor 8], so it is better to die without children than to seek to have children by illicit intercourse. . .

19.   Married people today have something that is granted to them as a concession because of the honorable state of marriage, although this concession does not pertain to the essence of marriage itself; I am referring to the use of intercourse beyond the need of procreation, something that was not conceded to the ancients. Even if some married people today desire and seek in marriage only that for which marriage was instituted, even these spouses cannot be compared to the people of ancient times. For in people today the very desire for children is carnal, whereas in the ancients it was spiritual because it was in harmony with the sacred mystery *(sacramentum)* of the times. In fact, in our day no one who is perfect in piety seeks to have children except in a spiritual way, whereas in the past to have children in a carnal way was itself an act of piety, since the propagation of that people was a proclamation of future events and participated in the dispensation of prophecy.

20.   That is why a man was allowed to have several wives, while a woman was not allowed to have several husbands, not even for the sake of offspring, if perhaps she was able to bear children when her husband was not able to beget them. For according to the mysterious law of nature, things that serve as ruling principles love singularity. In fact, it is fitting that subordinate things should be subject not only as individuals to individual rulers, but also (if the natural and social conditions allow it) as a group to a single ruler. That is why one servant does not have several masters, whereas several servants do have one master.

In the same manner, nowhere do we read that any of the holy women served two or more living husbands. But we do read that one husband had several wives, when the social customs of that people permitted it and when the character of the times required it, since this does not contradict the nature of marriage itself. For several women can become pregnant by one man, but one woman cannot become pregnant by several men—this is the power of the ruling principle— just as it is right that many souls should be subject to one God. For this reason the only true God of souls is one: although one soul is able to commit fornication through many false gods, it cannot be made fruitful by them.

21.   For the very same reason, just as the several wives of the ancient fathers signified our churches that would come into being from the many nations and would be subject to the one man Christ, so our high priest, a man of one wife, signifies the unity that derives from the many nations and is subject to the one man Christ. This unity will be perfected in the future, when "he will reveal what is hidden in darkness and will make manifest the hidden motives of the heart, so that each will receive his praise from God" (1 Cor 4:5). In the present, however, there are disagreements, both manifest and hidden, even among those who, if charity is preserved, are to be one and in One. In the future these disagreements will be no more.

Therefore, just as in the past the sacrament of multiple marriages signified the multitude that would be subject to God in all the lands of the Gentiles, so in our time the sacrament of single marriages signifies the unity of all of us who will one day be subject to God in the heavenly City. Thus, just as servants do not serve two or more masters, so in the past it was forbidden (and is now forbidden and will always be forbidden) for a woman to marry another man while her husband is still alive. For it is always wrong to apostasize from the one God and to enter into the adulterous and superstitious worship of another god. Not even for the sake of more numerous offspring did our holy fathers do what the Roman Cato is said to have done, namely to have handed over his wife, while he was still alive, to fill the house of another man with children. Indeed, in the marriages of our women the holiness of the sacrament is more important than the fruitfulness of the womb.

3. Pope John Paul II, "Apostolic Exhortation on the Role of the Christian Family in the Modern World"

We noted in the introduction to this chapter that families are in the midst of a great transition. Over the last few decades, family relations increasingly reflect the values of autonomy, equality, and fairness. Pope John Paul II considers both the benefits and the dangers of this transformation. In sections of the exhortation not included in this excerpt, Pope John Paul II reaffirms many traditional Catholic themes on the family: the sacramentality and indissolubility of marriage, the blessing of children and rejection of contraception and abortion, and the importance of clerical celibacy. The selections included here discuss the dignity of mothers, fathers, and children within the communion of the family. Perhaps the richest sections of the document are its reflections on the family as "the first and irreplaceable school of social life." Pope John Paul II sets forth the responsibility of the family to support social justice but also the responsibility of the social order to support the family. These reflections add a social dimension to reflections on the family that is often absent in Protestant writings.

Part One: Bright Spots and Shadows for the Family Today

6. THE SITUATION OF THE FAMILY IN THE WORLD TODAY

The[12] situation in which the family finds itself presents positive and negative aspects: The first is a sign of the salvation of Christ operating in the world; the second, a sign of the refusal that man gives to the love of God.

On the one hand, in fact, there is a more lively awareness of personal freedom and greater attention to the quality of interpersonal relationships in marriage, in promoting the dignity of women, to responsible procreation, to the education of children. There is also an awareness of the need for the development of interfamily relationships, for reciprocal spiritual and material assistance, the rediscovery of the ecclesial mission proper to the family and its responsibility for the building of a more just society. On the other hand, however, signs are not lacking of a disturbing degradation of some fundamental values: a mistaken theoretical and practical concept of the independence of the spouses in relation to each other; serious misconceptions regarding the relationship of authority between parents and children; the concrete difficulties that the family itself experiences in the transmission of values; the growing number of divorces; the scourge of abortion; the ever more frequent recourse to sterilization; the appearance of a truly contraceptive mentality.

At the root of these negative phenomena there frequently lies a corruption of the idea and the experience of freedom, conceived not as a capacity for realizing the truth of God's plan for marriage and the family, but as an autonomous power of self-affirmation, often against others, for one's own selfish well-being.

Worthy of our attention also is the fact in the countries of the so-called Third World, families often lack both the means necessary for survival, such as food, work, housing and medicine, and the most elementary freedoms. In the richer countries, on the contrary, excessive prosperity and the consumer mentality, paradoxically joined to a certain anguish and uncertainty about the future, deprive married couples of the generosity and courage needed for raising

---

[12] Pope John Paul II, *Familiaris Consortio* (On the Role of the Christian Family in the Modern World), 1981. Excerpts are quoted as in the original source.

up new human life. Thus life is often perceived not as a blessing but as a danger from which to defend oneself.

Part Three: The Role of the Christian Family
I. Forming a Community of Persons

21. THE BROADER COMMUNION OF THE FAMILY

Conjugal communion constitutes the foundation on which is built the broader communion of family, of parents and children, of brothers and sisters with each other, of relatives and other members of the household.

This communion is rooted in the natural bonds of flesh and blood and grows to its specifically human perfection with the establishment and maturing of the still deeper and richer bonds of the spirit. The love that animates the interpersonal relationships of the different members of the family constitutes the interior strength that shapes and animates the family communion and community . . .

All members of the family, each according to his or her own gift, have the grace and responsibility of guiding day by day the communion of persons, making the family "a school of deeper humanity": [t]his happens where there is care and love for the little ones, the sick, the aged, where there is mutual service every day; when there is a sharing of goods, of joys and of sorrows . . .

Family communion can only be preserved and perfected through a great spirit of sacrifice. It requires, in fact, a ready and generous openness of each and all to understanding, to forbearance, to pardon, to reconciliation. There is no family that does not know how selfishness, discord, tension and conflict violently attack and at times mortally wound its own communion: [h]ence there arise the many and varied forms of division in family life. But, at the same time, every family is called by the God of peace to have the joyous and renewing experience of "reconciliation," that is, communion re-established, unity restored. In particular, participation in the Sacrament of Reconciliation and in the banquet of the one body of Christ offers to the Christian family the grace and the responsibility of overcoming every division and of moving toward the fullness of communion willed by God, responding in this way to the ardent desire of the Lord: "that they may be one" (John 17:21).

22. THE RIGHTS AND ROLE OF WOMEN

. . . In creating the human race "male and female" (Gen 1:27), God gives man and woman an equal personal dignity, endowing them the inalienable rights and responsibilities proper to the human person. God then manifests the dignity of women in the highest form possible, by assuming human flesh from the Virgin Mary, whom the Church honors as the mother of God, calling her the new Eve and presenting her as the model of redeemed woman. The sensitive respect of Jesus toward the women that he called to his following and his friendship, his appearing on Easter morning to a woman before the other disciples, the mission entrusted to women to carry the good news of the resurrection to the apostles—these are all signs that confirm the special esteem of the Lord Jesus for women. The apostle Paul will say: "In Christ Jesus you are all children of God through faith. . . There is neither slave nor free, there is neither male nor female; for you are all one in Christ Jesus" (Gal 3:26, 28).

23. WOMEN AND SOCIETY

There is no doubt that the equal dignity and responsibility of men and women fully justifies women's access to public functions. On the other hand the true advancement of women requires that clear recognition be given to the value of their maternal and family role, by comparison with all other public roles and all other professions. Furthermore, these roles and professions should be harmoniously combined if we wish the evolution of society and culture to be truly and fully human . . .

While it must be recognized that women have the same right as men to perform various public functions, society must be structured in such a way that wives and mothers are not in practice compelled to work outside the home, and that their families can live and prosper in a dignified way even when they themselves devote their full time to their own family.

Furthermore, the mentality which honors women more for their work outside the home than for their work within the family must be overcome. This requires that men should truly esteem and love women with total respect for their personal dignity, and that society should create and develop conditions favoring work in the home.

With due respect to the different vocations of men and women, the [C]hurch must in her own life promote as far as possible the equality of rights and dignity: and this for the good of all, the family, the Church, and society.

But clearly all of this does not mean for women a renunciation of their femininity or an imitation of the male role, but the fullness of true feminine humanity which should be expressed in their activity, whether in the family or outside it, without disregarding the differences of customs and cultures in this sphere.

24. OFFENSES AGAINST WOMEN'S DIGNITY

Unfortunately the Christian message about the dignity of women is contradicted by that persistent mentality which considers the human being not as a person but as a thing, as an object of trade, at the service of selfish interest and mere pleasure: The first victims of this mentality are women.

This mentality produces very bitter fruits, such as contempt for man *[sic]* and for women, slavery, oppression of the weak, pornography, prostitution—

especially in an organized form— and all those various forms of discrimination that exist in the fields of education, employment wages, etc.

Besides, many forms of degrading discrimination still persist today in a great part of our society that affect and seriously harm particular categories of women, as for example childless wives, widows, separated or divorced women, and unmarried mothers . . .

25. MEN AS HUSBANDS AND FATHERS

Within the conjugal and family communion-community, the man is called upon to live his gift and role as husband and father . . .

Authentic conjugal love presupposes and requires that man have a profound respect for the equal dignity of his wife: "You are not her master," writes St. Ambrose, "but her husband; she was not given to you to be your slave, but your wife. . . Reciprocate her attentiveness to you and be grateful to have her for her love."[13] With his wife a man should live "a very special form of personal friendship."[14] As for the Christian, he is called upon to develop a new attitude of love, manifesting toward his wife a charity that is both gentle and strong like that which Christ has for the Church (cf. Eph 5:25).

Love for his wife as mother of their children and love for the children themselves are for the man the natural way of understanding and fulfilling his own fatherhood. Above all where social and cultural conditions so easily encourage a father to be less concerned with his family or at any rate less involved in the work of education, efforts must be made to restore socially the conviction that the place and task of the father in and for the family is of unique and irreplaceable importance.[15] As experience teaches, the absence of a father causes psychological and moral imbalance and notable difficulties in family relationships, as does, in contrary circumstances, the oppressive presence of a father, especially where there still prevails the phenomenon of "machismo," or a wrong superiority of male prerogatives which humiliates women and inhibits the development of healthy family relationships.

26. THE RIGHTS OF CHILDREN

In the family, which is a community of persons, special attention must be devoted to the children by developing a profound esteem for their personal dignity and a great respect and generous concern for their rights. This is true of

[13] Ambrose, *Exameron [Hexameron],* 5.7.19: Corpus Scriptorum Ecclesiasticorum Latinorum,32.1.154.

[14] Paul VI, Encyclical *Humanae Vitae,* §9: *Acta Apostolicae Sedis,* 60 (1968) 486. The *Acta* is henceforth, *AAS.*

[15] Cf. John Paul II, Homily to the Faithful of Terni (March 19, 1981) 3–5: *AAS,* 73 (1981) 268–71, and John Paul II, Address to the General Assembly of the United Nations, October 2, 1979, §21: *AAS,* 71 (1979) 1159.

every child, but it becomes all the more urgent the smaller the child is and the more it is in need of everything, when it is sick, suffering or handicapped . . .

Acceptance[;] love[;] esteem[;] many-sided and united material, emotional, educational and spiritual concern for every child that comes into this world should always constitute a distinctive, essential characteristic of all Christians, in particular of the Christian family: [t]hus children while they are able to grow "in wisdom and in stature, and in favor with God and man" (Luke 2:52, RSV) offer their won precious contribution to building up the family community and even to the sanctification of their parents (cf. Luke 2:52).

III. Participating in the Development of Society

42. THE FAMILY AS THE FIRST AND VITAL CELL OF SOCIETY

. . . The family has vital and organic links with society since it is its foundation and nourishes it continually through its role of service to life: It is from the family that citizens come to birth and it is within the family that they find the first school of the social virtues that are the animating principle of the existence and development of society itself.

Thus, far from being closed in on itself, the family is by nature and vocation open to other families and to society and undertakes its social role.

43. FAMILY LIFE AS AN EXPERIENCE OF COMMUNION AND SHARING

The very experience of communion and sharing that should characterize the family's daily life represents its first and fundamental contribution to society . . .

The family is thus, as the synod fathers recalled, the place of origin and the most effective means for humanizing and personalizing society: It makes an original contribution in depth in building up the world, by making possible a life that is, properly speaking, human, in particular by guarding and transmitting virtues and "values." As the Second Vatican Council states, in the family "the various generations come together and help one another to grow wiser and to harmonize personal rights, with the other requirements of social living."[16]

Consequently, faced with a society that is running the risk of becoming more and more depersonalized and standardized and therefore inhuman and dehumanizing, with the negative results of many forms of escapism—such as alcoholism, drugs and even terrorism—the family possesses and continues still to release formidable energies capable of taking man out of his autonomy, keeping him conscious of his personal dignity, enriching him with deep humanity and actively placing him, in his uniqueness and unrepeatability, within the fabric of society.

---

[16] Second Vatican Council, Pastoral Constitution on the Church in the Modern World, §52.

44. THE SOCIAL AND POLITICAL ROLE

The social role of the family certainly cannot stop short at procreation and education even if this constitutes its primary and irreplaceable form of expression.

Families therefore, either singly or in association, can and should devote themselves to manifold social service activities, especially in favor of the poor or at any rate for the benefit of all people and situations that cannot be reached by the public authorities' welfare organization . . .

In particular, note must be taken of the ever greater importance in our society of hospitality in all its forms, from opening the door of one's home, and still more of one's heart, to the pleas of one's brothers and sisters, to concrete efforts to ensure that every family has its own home as the natural environment that preserves it and makes it grow. In a special way the Christian family is called upon to listen to the apostle's recommendation. "[P]ractice hospitality" (Rom 12:13, RSV) and therefore, imitating Christ's example and sharing in his love, welcome the brother or sister in need: "[W]hoever gives to one of these little ones even a cup of cold water because he is a disciple, truly, I say to you, he shall not lose his reward" (Matt 10:42, RSV)

The social role of families is called upon to find expression also in the form of political intervention: [f]amilies should be the first to take steps to see that the laws and institutions of the state not only do not offend, but support and positively defend the rights and duties of the family. Along these lines families should grow in awareness of being "protagonists" of what is know[n] as "family politics" and assume responsibility for transforming society; otherwise families will be the first victims of the evils that they have done no more than note with indifference. The Second Vatican Council's appeal to go beyond an individualistic ethic therefore holds good for the family as such.[17]

45. SOCIETY AT THE SERVICE OF THE FAMILY

Just as the intimate connection between the family and society demands that the family be open to and participate in society its development, so also it requires that society should never fail in its fundamental task of respecting and fostering the family.

The family and society have complementary functions in defending and fostering the good of each and every human being. But society—more specifically the state—must recognize that "the family is a society in its own original right,"[18] and so society is under a grave obligation in its relations with the family to adhere to the principle of subsidiarity. The public authorities should take care not to take from families the functions that they can just as well per-

---

[17] Ibid., §30.
[18] Second Vatican Council, Declaration on Religious Liberty, §5.

form on their own or in free associations; instead it must positively favor and encourage as far as possible responsible initiative by families. In the conviction that the good of the family is an indispensable and essential value of the civil community, the public authorities must do everything possible to ensure that families have all those aids—economic, social, educational, political and cultural assistance—that they need in order to face all their responsibilities in a human way.

46. THE CHARTER OF FAMILY RIGHTS

The ideal of mutual support and development between the family and society is often very seriously in conflict with the reality of their separation and even in opposition.

In fact, as was repeatedly denounced by the synod, the situation experienced by many families in various countries is highly problematical if not entirely negative: [i]nstitutions and laws unjustly ignore the inviolable rights of the family and of the human person; and society, far from putting itself at the service of the family[,] attacks it violently in its values and fundamental requirements. Thus the family, which in God's plan is the basic cell of society and subject of rights and duties before the state or any other community, finds itself the victim of society, of the delays and slowness with which it acts, and even of its blatant injustice.

For this reason the Church openly and strongly defends the rights of the family against the intolerable usurp[a]tions of society and the state. In particular the synod fathers mentioned the following rights of the family:

- The right to exist and progress as a family, that is to say, the right of every human being, even if he or she is poor, to found a family and to have adequate means to support it;
- The right to exercise its responsibility regarding the transmission of life and to educate children;
- The right to the stability of the bond and of the institution of marriage;
- The right to believe in and profess one's faith and to propagate it;
- The right to bring up children in accordance with the family's own traditions and religious and cultural values, with the necessary instruments, means and institutions;
- The right, especially of the poor and the sick, to obtain physical, social, political and economic security;
- The right to housing suitable for living family life in a proper way;
- The right to expression and representation, either directly or through associations, before the economic, social and cultural public authorities and lower authorities;
- The right to form associations with other families and institutions in order to fulfill the family's role suitably and expeditiously;

- The right to protect minors by adequate institutions and legislation from harmful drugs, pornography, alcoholism, etc;
- The right to wholesome recreation of a kind that also fosters family values;
- The right of the elderly to a worthy life and a worthy death;
- The right to emigrate as a family in search of a better life.[19]

Acceding to the synod's explicit request, the Holy See will give prompt attention to studying these suggestions in depth and to the preparation of a charter of rights of the family to be presented to the quarters and authorities concerned.

48. FOR A NEW INTERNATIONAL ORDER

In view of the worldwide dimension of various social questions nowadays, the family has seen its role with regard to the development of society extended in a completely new way: It now also involves cooperating for a new international order, since it is only in worldwide solidarity that the enormous and dramatic issues of world justice, the freedom of peoples[,] and the peace of humanity can be dealt with and solved.

The spiritual communion between Christian families, rooted in a common faith and hope and give life by love[,] constitutes an inner energy that generates, spreads and develops justice, reconciliation, fraternity and peace among human beings. Insofar as it is a "small scale church," the Christian family is called upon, like the "large-scale church," to be a sign of unity for the world and in this way to exercise its prophetic role by bearing witness to the kingdom and peace of Christ, toward which the whole world is journeying.

Christian families can do this through their educational activity—that is to say, by presenting to their children a model of life based on the values of truth, freedom, justice and love —both through active and responsible involvement in the authentically human growth of society and its institutions, and supporting in various ways the associations specifically devoted to international issues.

---

[19] *Propositio* 42. In paragraph 2, earlier (but not excerpted above) in this document, Pope John Paul II wrote:

A Sign of this profound interest of the Church in the family was the last Synod of Bishops, held in Rome from Sept. 26 to Oct. 25, 1980. This was a natural continuation of the two preceding synods[a] . . .

At the close of their assembly, the synod fathers presented me with a long list of proposals in which they had gathered the fruits of their reflections, which had matured over intense days of work, and they asked me unanimously to be a spokesman . . .

As I fulfill that mission with this exhortation, thus actuating in a particular matter the apostolic ministry with which I am entrusted, I wish to thank all the members of the synod for the very valuable contribution of teaching and experience that they made, especially through the *propositiones,* the text of which I am entrusting to the Pontifical Council for the Family with instructions to study it so as to bring out every aspect of its rich content.

[a] John Paul II, Homily for the Opening of the Sixth Synod of Bishops (Sept. 26, 1980) §2: *AAS* 72 (1980) 1008.

4. Sally B. Purvis, "A Common Love:
Christian Feminist Ethics and the Family"

Sally B. Purvis formerly taught Christian Ethics at Fairfield University and Candler School of Theology. Currently she serves as an ordained minister, affiliated with the United Church of Christ. She is the author of several books in Christian feminist ethics. In this essay, Purvis addresses the paucity of Christian feminist reflection on the family. The foundation of her ethical reflection is the dual love command of Jesus: "You shall love God with all your heart, and with all your soul, and with all your mind . . . And . . . your neighbor as yourself" (Matt 22:37-39). To discover what this means for family life, Purvis first explores the meaning of agape, picking up on the reflections of Christine Gudorf that we encountered in chapter 2 of this book. Purvis relates the particular love of the family to the "common love" that unites God and all of humanity.

As[20] a Christian feminist ethicist I was at first startled by a request to write about the family. I want to begin these reflections, then, by introducing some problems for a Christian feminist ethicist in working with the topic.

First, Christian feminist literature by and large does not address "the family" *per se.* Issues tend to be identified in more focused ways, as in the literature on motherhood, gender relations, reproductive issues, and so on. Or the issues are broader and deal with contextual questions of power relationships, economic factors and systems, sexual orientation, friendship, etc. Family relations have received normative attention in contemporary Christian ethics from ethicists such as James Gustafson, Gilbert Meilander, and Stanley Hauerwas, but their treatments do not take into account feminist perspectives in any direct way.[21] Conversely, Christian feminist ethics does not ordinarily deal with the family. In fact, the family sometimes seems to be the conceptual property of those who see feminists as the enemy of Christianity, and "family values" has become a slogan for such groups as the Christian Coalition. This phrase functions as a euphemism for a complex normative agenda embraced by the Coalition and other conservative Christian groups, including but not

---

[20] Sally B. Purvis, "A Common Love: Christian Feminist Ethics and the Family" in Anne Carr and Mary Stewart Van Leeuwen, eds., *Religion, Feminism, & the Family.* The Family, Religion and Culture series, Don S. Browning and Ian S. Evision, series eds. (Louisville, Ky.: Westminster/John Knox, 1996) 111–26. © Westminster Press, 1996. Used by permission of Westminter John Knox Press.

[21] See the second volume of James Gustafson's *Ethics From A Theocentric Perspective* (Chicago: University of Chicago Press, 1984), Gilbert Meilander's *The Limits of Love: Some Theological Explorations* (University Park, Pa.: The Pennsylvania State University Press, 1987), and Stanley Hauerwas' *A Community of Character: Toward a Constructive Christian Social Ethics* (Notre Dame, Ind.: University of Notre Dame Press, 1981). My point in listing these references is to note the widespread assumptions regarding the nature of the family that these authors share with the very conservative Christian groups, even though they may share very little else.

limited to their homophobic stance. Part of the reason that the family sometimes seems incompatible with feminism, then, is that the phrase *the family* as
it is commonly used trades on the assumption that there is one model, one normative shape for families. In fact, much of the traditional Christian teaching
about the family tends to support that assumption. The Christian family is a
constellation of related persons whose core is one or more heterosexual married couples, and there exists a nest of satellite assumptions and values and
norms that have to do with roles and relationships appropriate to various persons within that constellation. The family so understood has been one conceptual and institutional fortress of patriarchy, sexism, and heterosexism.

With so many of the traditional assumptions and teachings regarding
human sexuality and gender relations being challenged by Christian feminist
ethicists, it is tempting to say that the family is not a fertile place for our work.
It could be argued that we should simply jettison the term with its concomi-
tant assumptions, and talk instead about right relationships in all settings and
roles where they are found. Feminist ethics, however, is concerned with the
realities of women's lives, whatever official fictions may be told about those
lives. It continues to be the case that the family is central to the lives, loves,
work, and concern of many, many women, though perhaps not in the way the
traditional literature would suggest. Therefore it is appropriate that we reclaim
the territory from a feminist normative position.

I propose, then, to offer some thoughts regarding the family from a Christian feminist perspective. I will begin by stipulating the dual love command,
"You shall love God with all your heart and with all your soul and with all
your mind, and your neighbor as yourself," as the foundation for a constructive Christian feminist ethic. With that foundation, the basic building blocks
of my approach are the Christian feminist insight that persons are constitutively relational, and [share] the Christian communal values of diversity and
inclusivity. Some comments about those choices are in order. From the beginning of the recent wave of Christian feminist literature, feminists have rejected an anthropology that would characterize persons as fundamentally
separate individuals whose maturity is developed through, and rests on,
greater and greater degrees of separation and self-reliance. Rather, feminist
anthropology (or "gynepology") always insists on the deeply, formatively relational character of persons whose lives are interdependent in ways that are
sometimes obvious and sometimes very subtle.[22] Feminist anthropology does
not deny or denigrate individuality but affirms that individuality is itself constituted by its relationships, which for Christians includes the God-relation-
ship. I will couple this insight regarding the constitutively relational character
of human persons with the Christian values of diversity and inclusivity in our

---

[22] For a full and careful statement of a feminist anthropology, see Margaret Farley, "A Feminist Version of Respect for Persons," *The Journal of Feminist Studies in Religion,* 9 (1993) 183–98.

communities. I will claim the strand of the Christian tradition that understands membership in Christian community as radically independent of status in the wider society, and in some sense, at least, as subversive of "the divisions among us." This approach will offer a way to begin to develop new understandings of families that include the traditional understandings but that expose theological roots that support other types of clusters of persons as well.

I analyze the issue and choose the constructive concepts as one who has been shaped by and continues to confess a place on the liberal edge of "old line" Protestantism in North America. I am a white, middle-aged, privileged member of the United Church of Christ who taught in a mostly Methodist seminary in Atlanta, Georgia. These factors, as well as the particularities of my life experience, are my lenses. I trust that they will be transparent enough to provide some focus for these issues.

Some Notes on Christian Love

Anyone who posits the dual love command as foundational for Christian ethics has to wrestle, at least to some degree, with the question of the character of the love we are to hold and share. In fact, Christian love, *agape,* has a central place in the work of Christian ethicists both traditional and feminist. In his volume *Agape: An Ethical Analysis,* Gene Outka provides an overview of some of the key treatments of agape in the Christian tradition as well as offering his own constructive interpretation of the term.[23] In the traditional interpretation use of agape, both the qualities of self-sacrifice and of disinterest were thought to be constitutive. In one of the earliest feminist theological challenges to the tradition, Valerie Saiving deconstructed Reinhold Niebuhr's characterization of sin as "pride," and showed the male bias of his analysis. In that context, she also argued persuasively that the conceptualization of agape as necessarily self-sacrificial is "normative and redemptive precisely insofar as it answers to deepest need. If human nature and the human situation are not as described by [Niebuhr], then the assertion that self-giving love is the law of man's being is irrelevant and may even be untrue."[24] Thus her critique of Niebuhr's interpretation of agape as essentially self-sacrificial emanates from her general critique of his Christian anthropology and doctrine of sin, a critique rooted in the perspective of "female experience." Both the content and the analytical method of Saiving's article become classics in Christian feminist work and are richly suggestive for further developments by others.

Christine Gudorf has criticized a conception of agape as essentially sacrificial from a different perspective—her experience in parenting "medically

[23] Gene Outka, *Agape: An Ethical Analysis* (New Haven, Conn.: Yale University Press, 1972).
[24] Valerie Saiving Goldstein, "The Human Situation: A Feminine View," *Journal of Religion* 40 (1960) 100–12.

handicapped children."[25] She argues that while perhaps her behavior might want to describe it as self-sacrificial, her experience—or complex set of experiences—suggest that mutuality is the way to characterize the interactions of the persons involved. She is not primarily engaged in self-sacrifice, but rather in mutual development and transformation that involves all of the participants.

Valerie Saiving and Christine Gudorf both rebut, from women's experience, the traditional characterization of agape as *essentially* self-sacrificial. Self-sacrifice may be a temporary or tangential feature of what is involved when we love each other as Christians, but from the perspective of women, at least, and probably other socially disadvantaged groups as well, mutual relationship is closer to the heart of the experience.

The second aspect of traditional definitions of agape that has received challenges from Christian feminists is that of disinterestedness. It has been thought that "special relations" constitute a problem for agape in that agape is equal regard for all, thus special relations, like those of mother-child, friend-friend, and so on mean more regard for some than for others. One traditional solution to the "problem" is to prohibit "special relations"; the monastic tradition in Roman Catholicism and celibacy in general have represented attempts to address this "problem."

It is the case that special relations constitute a "problem" for agape if agape is thought to be disinterested love. Special relations are intensely interested, even passionate. Some Christian feminists have argued that the "problem" is not the presence of intense love but rather our suspicion of passion, which leads us to confine it so narrowly. The problem shifts, then, from that of renouncing passion in human relationships in favor of general disinterested regard on the one hand to that of a concern for the challenge of the inclusivity of passion itself on the other. If we expand our understanding of the energy and deep interestedness of passion, then the work of Christian agape is to make that passion more broadly available and more widely felt. The task is not to curb passion, but to nourish it and channel it . . .

I developed a somewhat different argument against characterizing agape as disinterested love by offering "mother-love" as a model for agape in light of an exegesis of Luke's story of the Good Samaritan.[26] This and other scriptural texts do not render an account of agape as disinterested but rather as extravagant outpourings of concern that are surprising only because they occur in relations with strangers as well as friends and family. Like mother-love, Lukan agape is intensely involved, other-regarding, and unconditional, and in his ac-

---

[25] Christine Gudorf, "Parenting, Mutual Love, and Sacrifice," in *Women's Consciousness, Women's Conscience,* ed. Barbara Hilkert Andolsen, Christine E. Gudorf, and Mary D. Pellauer (Minneapolis: Winston Press, 1985), 175–91. In that chapter, she uses the phrase "medically handicapped children," 176ff.

[26] Sally B. Purvis, "Mothers, Neighbors and Strangers: Another Look at Agape," *Journal of Feminist Studies in Religion* 7 (1991) 19–34.

count inclusive.[27] Again, the "problem" is not that we sometimes manage to love our children with this love, and perhaps other persons in our lives as well, but that we do not manage to love very many in such a way.

What does this discussion have to do with the family? In traditional interpretations of agape, the family has been part of the problem of special relations. That is, if Christian love is to be self-sacrificial and disinterested, then the special interests and loves and even obligations that a family entails are a threat to the Christian ideal.[28] There is a conflict on both the theoretical and experiential levels between agapic love (general, disinterested, self-sacrificial) on the one hand, and love of family (specific, passionate, perhaps even self-fulfilling) on the other.

With a feminist understanding of agape as mutual, passionate, deeply interested, and unconditional, the "problem of the family" shifts. The challenge is not the renunciation of affect and intensity but rather redevelopment of wider and wider circles of intense, passionate love. The traditional family, then, is rendered problematic not because of its "special relations" but only insofar as the family is defined as a unit of separation or division over against other relationships.

Christian love, agape, remains at the center of our normative analysis, but it is a very different model from that which the tradition has offered us. Christians are understood, as all persons are understood, to be deeply relational and constituted by the relationships in their lives, including their relationship with God. Love is the flow of that relationality when it is right relation: mutual, passionate, caring, and offered as widely as possible.

The Family in Christian Community

Just as agape is central to any Christian normative reflection, so such reflection must take place in terms of Christian community. Just as persons are radically relational, so Christian ethics is radically communal. I will make some general comments regarding the nature of the family and then place those observations within a Christian communal context.

I believe it is true to say that in all cultures through time "the family" constitutes some sort of biological relationship. The ordering of those relationships and facts about them vary widely, but biological connection is a part of what we mean when we speak generally about the family.

---

[27] As I argue more fully in my article (see note above), mother-love is only one aspect of the activities of mothering, and most of us do not manage in any sustained way the full embodiment of these qualities. They are, however, the essential features of mother-love when we are loving as we wish to do. The danger of using this model is that of idealizing mothering to the detriment of mothers. Its strength lies in its suggestive power with regard to agape.

[28] There are suggestions of this even in Paul, of course. See his discussion of marriage in 1 Corinthians.

But the family is also a sociological reality, often a complex one. Contemporary family systems theory addresses some of the sociological complexity within family units, however defined. Likewise, sociological theory addresses the family as a social institution, affecting and affected by other social institutions in which it is located. The feminist slogan "the personal is the political" captures some of the permeability of the boundaries between the family and those wider social forces that shape it and which it in turn helps to shape. Arguments about the institution of the family, about what does and does not count as family, about the advantages and sometimes disadvantages of being a family with regard to social services, and so forth, all suggest the fact and the complexity of the sociological reality of the family in our culture(s).[29]

What happens when we put the family as biological unit and the family as sociological unit in the context of Christian community? The record indicates that from the earliest times, both the biological reality and the sociological reality of the family were relativized by the theological reality of the family. Jesus' claim that those who do God's will were his mother and brothers and sisters (Mark 3:35; Matt. 12:50; Luke 8:21) is an explicit redefinition of "Christian family" in theological terms. The extensive use of familial language to refer to persons who were related only through Christian community and not through biological or sociological family units as well as Paul's explicit relativizing of family relations in the context of the coming *parousia* (1 Cor. 7), are other manifestations of the theological relativization of both the biological and sociological aspects of the Christian family. It is not the case, of course, that Christian community and the Christian family were hostile to or intentionally destructive of biological and sociological families. Jesus' relationship with his mother is a prominent feature of our foundational narratives. The sons of Zebedee and the siblings Mary, Martha. and Lazarus, among others, are comfortably incorporated into Christian community. Paul's letters teach us that sometimes whole Roman households, with their own complex mix of biological and sociological ties, were converted to this new movement, and "house churches" play a prominent role in his accounts. It is the case, however, that the Christian community itself is the normative context for assessing their value. If and when biological and/or sociological units threaten the community unit, the community takes normative precedence (e.g., words attributed to Jesus regarding the fundamental definition of his family noted above; Paul's advice in 1 Corinthians regarding "interfaith" marriages; and most significantly, the appropriation of familial language to characterize Christian relationships themselves).

It is probably stating the obvious to note that this theological relativization of biological and sociological families was both a function of and an incorpo-

---

[29] In conversation, Barbara Wheeler, president of Auburn Theological Seminary, used the phrase "culture soup." I find that a very helpful image. I put the "s" in parentheses because I am less convinced than Barbara Wheeler that there is a common cultural soup.

ration of the understanding that all love and all relationships are set within the context of love for God. When the God-relation is put in the center of life, whether individual or communal, and when that relationship is valued foundationally, then a certain teleology of loving begins to emerge, and all relationships are ordered in service of the central one. The measure, then, of the structure and the function of all human relationships becomes the degree to which they enhance and expand the God-relation for all persons. All other relationships—biological, sociological, or affective—are in service of a community that exists for the purpose of enabling and enhancing persons' relationship to the God known through Jesus Christ.

These norms, of course, function more as critical principles than as concrete realities, now and in the past. There is great danger in conflating the institution(s) of church, or communal claims to be God-centered, with a vision of Christian community that has at its heart the God-relation. Groups such as the Branch Davidians remind us of the possibility of relativizing the family in pernicious ways. The community as God-centered, however, is both the goal and the judge for all groups that call themselves Christian, and therefore the community as God-centered can be said to have concrete normative power even if it is not fully embodied, now or ever, by any actual community.

Christian community that has the God-relation at its core is a community formed around a common love, not a common enemy. Unlike most groups with which we are familiar, groups whose self-definition is over against something or someone else, Christian community exists in common attraction to a common love. Furthermore, this love is *all* that the members of the community are required to hold in common. The common love constitutes both the heart and the boundaries of community life, and in principle, therefore, is open to everyone without regard for other sorts of social connections or divisions that may exist.

All love, then—all relationships, including all family groups—are to be valued according to their relation to the common love. Insofar as a family enhances the God-relation of its members and the community, it is to be judged good. Insofar as it harms that relationship, it may be rearranged or abandoned in light of the deeper love for God, thus human relationships that enhance that love become the family.

We can see in the New Testament, and even more dramatically in the later history of the development of Christianity as a world religion, that the sociological reality of family—and to a lesser extent its biological reality, with its hierarchical structures and its economic and political import—became a growing concern for Christian normative teachings. I do not wish to ignore that history. Nor do I mean to deny the economic and political ramifications of rethinking the reality of family in theological terms. I am simply exposing and reclaiming an early—and I think normatively central—insight regarding the Christian family. Its fundamental reality is theological, and whatever else it may be it is to be formed by and measured by its fruitfulness for the common love of all Christian life.

Relationality, Diversity, and Inclusivity

"Whoever does the will of God is my brother and sister and mother" (Mark 3:35). These words, attributed to Jesus and clearly part of the self-conscious memory of early Christian groups, can serve as a kind of summary for the normative definition of the family toward which the section above has moved us. Without mounting an extensive exegetical defense, it is clear, I think, that doing "the will of God" is a fair characterization of the demands of agape. Christian love is never simply a question of attitude or affect; doing the will of God is never simply a matter of behavior somehow disconnected from character or motive. In direct contrast to, if not in conflict with, claims of those connected to him as biological and sociological family, Jesus, at least in the view of those who remembered him, offers a definition of the family that is theological and that takes priority over every other definition we can put forth.

Furthermore, this is not an isolated theme restricted to one passage in Mark (and its synoptic parallels). The question about who counts as family receives a reply that is consonant with Jesus' response to the question about who counts as neighbor. Both responses break out from common social definitions and understandings and emphasize the radical inclusivity and potential diversity of Christian community. *Family* is defined in terms of a common God-relation. *Neighbor* is defined in terms of the deeds of love. Relations among Christians are to be ordered by and determined only by a common love. No group or person is in principle ineligible for inclusion; the only commonality is love for God in Christ.

If we shape our question a bit differently in light of the argument above, we can inquire about who it is that is to be the beloved for a Christian. The answer, in principle, is "everyone." At the least, the answer would have to include "everyone with whom we come in contact."

Issues regarding the obligating scope of agape have occupied Christian theological ethicists throughout the tradition. Augustine, in fact offers a helpful analysis as he wrestles with questions regarding what limits on the duty to love a Christian can rightfully acknowledge. Without accepting his questionable duality of the earthly and heavenly realms, it is instructive to note that Augustine readily acknowledges the proximal limits of persons. He understands neighbor-love, or agape, primarily to consist of the honoring and nurturing of the neighbor's relation to God. He also understands, however, that there are limits on the degree to which this is possible, and on the number of persons it is possible for anyone to assist in this way. Thus he articulates the second part of the love command as "the observance of two rules:

first, to do no harm to anyone, and second, to help everyone whenever possible."[30] To use contemporary language, the principle of nonmaleficence is universally applicable without qualification. The principle of beneficence is subject to the limits of the mortality of the human person including the constraints of time, energy, opportunity, and so forth.

For Augustine, natural human limitations given in creation are not a problem for the understanding and implementation of the command to love our neighbor, since it is precisely to such limited creatures that the command was given. His treatment of the issue combines the theological rigor of the centrality of love of God with the exceptionless universality of the obligation of nonmaleficence, and a relaxed and common sense acceptance of human limitations.

Our world is dramatically different from Augustine's, so we must modify his helpful exposition of the proximal limits to agape in light of both the fact of and our awareness of implications of our actions, affections, and relationships for persons far beyond those with whom we actually come in contact. In light of the relational nature of human persons and the inclusivity and diversity, at least in principle, of the Christian family, we also need to add some remarks about how the social structures and policies within which we live have affected not only the theological but also the biological and sociological realities of families. It is clear at this point in our discussion that Christian concern for the family is informed by a concern for all persons based on our conviction that all persons are created by and beloved of God, and that all persons are essentially constituted by the centrality of their relationship to God. Agape has no boundaries in principle; the actual boundaries that Augustine articulated are themselves compromised by the fluidity of the boundaries between the personal and the political, in theory and in fact. Thus, any appeal to the well-being of the biological or sociological family at the expense of any person or group is, from a Christian point of view, an inversion of the priorities of Christian values. From the Christian perspective I have expressed, justice is the necessary context for normative claims about and evaluations of the Christian family, where justice is understood to be the instantiation of the theological reality of the common love at the heart of all Christian relationships, including the family.

Justice is the norm of right relations both within and outside of biological and sociological family units. Justice within the biological and sociological family unit would include a respect for diversity and the agapic obligation to nurture each person in his or her particularity. Intra-family relationships would

---

[30] Augustine, *City of God,* 19.14. See also *On Christian Doctrine*, 1.28–29.21. I am aware, of course, of the complex conversation in traditional theological ethics regarding the relationship between love and justice. Given the feminist critique and revision of traditional definitions of agape, however, and given the principles of inclusivity and diversity that emerge from considerations about the scope of agape, the possible conflict between love and justice is recast if not eliminated.

be characterized by the features of agape that were discussed above: mutuality, passionate concern, intense caring. Justice outside the family, too, would invite intense caring, passionate concern, mutuality, commitments to the betterment of persons' lives—with no limits in principle. The inclusivity of the Christian understanding of family means that the norm of right relation is always both theological and universal. There are no persons or groups who in principle are outside the scope of "our passion for justice," our commitment to the well-being of all. The stringent universality of the principle of nonmaleficence that Augustine's analysis recommends thus means that, in our world, we must take account of the effects of our behavior and our lives on persons whom we may never personally meet but who are affected by our choices.

Justice is the necessary context for Christian normative claims about and evaluations of the family. Justice in the family condemns the inequities and abuse that are so common within the biological and sociological units that are designated as families. It is also true that justice, as the social instantiation of the right relations required by our common love, must be the norm and guide for relationships within our Christian communities, the Christian families that are not necessarily family units in the ordinary sense.

If the Christian community is a foundational context for our ethical-reflection on the family, then we cannot assume that unjust church structures can support just biological/sociological family structures. We cannot ignore the inequalities, oppression, and even abuse that are all too frequent in our churches as we attempt to analyze and reform other social units. "The divisions among us" do move through the doors and walls of our churches; our common love is not necessarily the functional center of our communal lives. Without that center, the family will not thrive.

The Christian Family and a Common Love

When we set our reflections about the family within the theological context that I have outlined here, it becomes clear that family is an entity existing beyond biological definitions, while still encompassing them. What we mean first by family is Christian community, formed, shaped, and sustained by a common love of God. That was and is the context within which we understand and practice all human relationships. The biological family is not less valuable when viewed in this way, but it is accountable both to and for the norms of justice that are required by the common love of God. The sociological family as an economic and political unit likewise continues to exist and function, but the economic and political boundaries are understood to be more permeable than is sometimes acknowledged. Our relationships, behaviors, and choices about earning, saving, and spending—as well as our political choices—have implications far beyond the narrow scope of our daily lives, and those implications must become part of our daily choices.

If we understand all Christian life to be centered in and ordered around a common love of God, then there are in principle no limits to the scope of our family. Although the theological insights are specifically Christian, our common love of God means that our agapic concern and commitment is not confined to those who call themselves Christian. If we understand agape to be intense, caring, passionate, other-directed, and respectful of the specificity of the beloved, then we can envision the normative flow of our individual and communal lives as ever-widening circles of agape. If we take seriously the centrality of relationality as a feature of the human person and the centrality of community in our self-understanding and normative reflection, then our moral reflections on the Christian family move us far beyond any biological or sociological units that might obtain in a given society and into a consideration of the family as including all those whom God loves.

The "special relations" in our lives, the relationships in which we care most deeply and love most strongly, do not encompass the range of our obligation to love but rather serve as guides and models for the movement outward into concern for all human beings.

Struggles for the Future

This Christian feminist ethical discussion of the family has led us through and beyond the assumptions about the family that would understand it only or primarily in terms of biological and sociological units centered around a heterosexual union. The family, including, appropriate concern for families from a Christian theological ethical perspective, is understood to be the human family, including all those whom God loves. Insofar as we understand the goodness or health of families in relation to the presence of a wage-earning male, or in relation to any particular social form, we have lost our normative center. A Christian theological ethical understanding of the family encompasses and goes beyond all social arrangements of persons. The relevant questions have to do not with who is or is not a member but rather with how the members, whoever they are, are relating to one another and to the contexts of their lives. Our attention, then, shifts from familial constellations to concern for community, in whatever form, that exists in and around a common love of God.

Families, of whatever size and shape, must constitute places and spaces in which the common love of God is nurtured. In our world that means they must be communities of liberation and reconciliation, in that order.[31] As Rebecca

---

[31] Delores Williams, among other womanist writers, argues for the importance of kinship ties in the African-American community. The same importance holds for other groups as well. My argument is not an attempt to subsume or undermine the importance of kinship relations. Rather, I am insisting on the relativization and necessary normative scrutiny of any of their forms. See Williams's discussion in *Sisters in the Wilderness: The Challenge of Womanist God-Talk* (Maryknoll, N.Y.: Orbis Books, 1993).

Chopp has so eloquently argued, our communities must be vehicles for emancipation and transformation.[32] They must be vehicles for widening the circles of relationships formed around a common love.

We will not find good answers unless we ask good questions. I have challenged the sort of questions Christians commonly ask about the family and offered a different perspective and a different set of questions by which we should proceed. There are few answers here, because answers about how to love require the intersection of theory and concrete situations. We cannot always know in advance what love will require of us, but we can know that love's demands must shape our lives.

Insofar as the Christian family is defined as a biological and/or sociological reality apart from its theological center, it is an inadequate mechanism through which to consider its own problems. We must place it in the context of the relationality, inclusivity, and diversity of a community shaped around a common love. Only then can we accurately define its problems and begin to live toward solutions.

5. Luke Timothy Johnson, "Disputed Questions: Debate and Discernment, Scripture and the Spirit"

Luke Timothy Johnson is R.W. Woodruff Professor of New Testament and Christian Origins at Candler School of Theology of Emory University. He is the author of many commentaries, books, and articles that address broad themes in New Testament studies. Johnson's essay begins by reviewing the relationship between human experience and biblical interpretation that we explored in Chapter Two of this book. Johnson argues that God's inclusion of the Gentiles in Acts provides a fitting analogy for the problem of homosexuality in the church today. Reasoning from this analogy, Johnson argues that the church should accept homosexual relationships that reflect covenant love. Whether we finally accept Johnson's position or reject it, he is correct that the choice of a fitting analogy for homosexuality is critical to the debate. For example, viewing it as a willful act of sin (like adultery) or as a destructive predisposition (like alcoholism) lead to different conclusions than those Johnson draws.

Homosexuality[33] as an issue internal to the life of the church poses a fundamental challenge not only to moral discernment and pastoral care (the two aspects touched on in the recent *Catechism of the Catholic Church*) but to the self-understanding of the church as at once inclusive ("catholic") and separate

---

[32] Rebecca S. Chopp, *The Power to Speak: Feminism, Language, and God* (New York: Crossroad, 1989).

[33] Luke Timothy Johnson, "Disputed Questions: Debate and Discernment, Scripture and the Spirit," *Commonweal*, January 28, 1994. Copyright © 1994 Commonweal Foundation, reprinted by permission. For subscriptions call toll-free 1-888-495-6755.

("holy"). The question is not only how we feel or think or act concerning homosexuality, but also how those feelings, thoughts, and actions relate to the canonical texts which we take as normative for our lives together. Homosexuality in the church presents a hermeneutical problem.

The present essay has the modest goal of clearing some space for debate and discernment by setting out what seem to be appropriate boundary markers for what promises to be a long and difficult discussion. I proceed by staking out three basic premises concerning ecclesial hermeneutics, and then a number of theses pertinent to the issue of homosexuality.

I take it as a given, first, that any process of discernment within the church takes as its fundamental framework the Irenaean triad of ecclesial self-definition: the canon of Scripture, the rule of faith, and the teaching authority of bishops. To step outside this framework is to shift the debate to other grounds entirely. Conservatism in commitment to canon, creed, and council is paradoxically the necessary condition for genuine freedom in scriptural interpretation.

Second, I take it as basic that hermeneutics involves the complex task of negotiating normative texts and continuing human experiences. Within the faith community, this means an openness to the ways in which God's revelation continues in human experience as well as a deep commitment to the conviction that such revelation, while often, at first, perceived as dissonant with the symbols of Scripture, will, by God's grace directing human fidelity, be seen as consonant with those symbols and God's own fidelity. Essentially, however, the call of faith is to the living God whose revelation continues, rather than to *our previous understanding* of the texts. Faith in the living God seeks understanding; theological understanding does not define faith or the living God.

My third premise is that Scripture does not characteristically speak with a single voice. Rather, as an anthology of compositions it contains an irreducible and precious pluralism of "voices," shaped by literary genre, theme, and perspective. The *authority* of these texts, furthermore, is most properly distinguished in terms of their function. Their highest authority is found in their capacity to reliably "author" Christian identity. Almost as important is the way in which these texts "authorize" a certain freedom in interpretation, by presenting a model of how Torah was reinterpreted in the light of new experiences. A third sort of authority is important but not as fundamental. The Scripture contains a wide range of "authorities" in the sense of *auctoritates,* or "opinions," not on all the subjects we could desire, but on many of great significance. Responsible hermeneutics claims the "freedom of the children of God" authorized by the New Testament, and seeks to negotiate the various "voices/authorities" within the texts in an effort to conform to that "mind of Christ" (1 Cor 2:16) that is the authentic form of Christian identity which those texts are, through the power of the Holy Spirit, capable of "authoring."

I would like to think that these three premises, though perhaps nontraditional in formulation, are in essence profoundly Catholic, fairly and accurately representing not only the implications of the New Testament's own origin and canonization, but also of much loyal and creative interpretation within the tradition.

Before moving to the specific case of homosexuality, it might be helpful to amplify slightly two aspects of these premises which without explication might appear careless if not cavalier. The first concerns the experience of God in human lives. Nothing could be more offensive than to challenge tradition on the basis of casual or unexamined experience, as though God's revelation were obvious or easy, or reducible to popularity polls. The call to the discernment of human experience is not a call to carelessness, but its opposite; it is a call to the rigorous asceticism of attentiveness. I repeat: an appeal to some populist claim such as "everyone does it," or "surveys indicate" is theologically meaningless. What counts is whether *God* is up to something in human lives. Discernment of experience in this sense is for the detection of good news in surprising places, not for the disguising of old sins in novel faces.

Yet it is important to assert that God *does,* on the record, act in surprising and unanticipated ways, and upsets human perceptions of God's scriptural precedents. The most fundamental instance for the very existence of Christianity is the unexpected, crucified, and raised Messiah, Jesus. A considerable amount of what we call the New Testament derives from the attempt to resolve the cognitive dissonance between the experience of Jesus as the source of God's Holy Spirit, and the text of Torah that disqualifies him from that role, since, "cursed is every one that hangs upon a tree" (Deut 21:23; see Gal. 3:13).

Another example is the spread of the gospel to the Gentiles. It is easy for us at this distance, and with little understanding of the importance of the body language of table fellowship, to take for granted such a breaking of precedent that allowed Gentiles to share fully in the life of the Messianic community without being circumcised or practicing observance of Torah. Good for us, also, therefore, to read Acts 10–15 to see just how agonizing and difficult a task it was for that first generation of Christians to allow their perception of God's activity to change their perceptions, and use that new experience as the basis for reinterpreting Scripture.

The second aspect of the premises I want to amplify slightly is the requirement for responsible hermeneutics to take every voice of Scripture seriously. I spoke of the *auctoritates* as diverse and sometimes contradictory. But every ecclesial decision to live by one rather than another of these voices, to privilege one over another, to suppress one in order to live by another, must be willing to state the grounds of that decision, and demonstrate how the experience of God and the more fundamental principles of "the mind of Christ" (1 Cor 2:16) and "freedom of the children of God" [see 1 John 3] (principles also rooted in the authority of the text) legitimate the distance between ecclesial decision and a clear statement of Scripture. Do we allow divorce (even if we don't openly call it that) when Jesus forbade it? [see Mark 10:2-12]. We must be willing to support our decision by an appeal, not simply to changing circumstances, but to a deeper wisdom given by the Spirit into the meaning of human covenant, and therefore a better understanding of the sayings of Jesus. This is never easy. It is sometimes—as in the case of taking oaths and vows [see Matt 5:33-37]—not even possible. But it is the task of responsible ecclesial hermeneutics.

How does this approach provide a context for the hermeneutics of homosexuality? First, it cautions us against trying to suppress biblical texts which condemn homosexual behavior (Lev 18:22; Wis 14:26; Rom 1:26-7; 1 Cor 6:9) or to make them say something other than what they say. I think it fair to conclude that early Christianity knew about homosexuality as it was practiced in Greco-Roman culture, shared Judaism's association of it with the "abominations" of idolatry, and regarded it as incompatible with life in the Kingdom of God. These *auctoritates* emphatically define homosexuality as a vice, and they cannot simply be dismissed.

Second, however, Scripture itself "authorizes" us to exercise the freedom of the children of God in our interpretation of such passages. We are freed, for example, to evaluate the relative paucity of such condemnations. Compared to the extensive and detailed condemnation of economic oppression at virtually every level of tradition, the off-handed rejection of homosexuality appears instinctive and relatively unreflective. We are freed as well to assess the contexts of the condemnations: the rejection of homosexuality, as of other sexual sins, is connected to the incompatibility of *porneia* [see Matt 19:3-12, esp. v. 9] with life in the Kingdom. We can further observe that the flat rejection of *porneia* (any form of sexual immorality) is more frequent and general than any of its specific manifestations. We are freed, finally, to consider the grounds on which the texts seem to include homosexuality within *porneia,* namely that it is "against nature," an abomination offensive to God's created order.

Such considerations, in turn, provide an opening for a conversation between our human experience (including our religious experience) and the texts of our tradition. Does our experience now support or challenge the assumption that homosexuality is, simply and without exception, an "offense against nature"? Leviticus and Paul considered homosexuality a vice because they assumed it was a deliberate choice that "suppressed the truth about God." Is that a fair assessment of homosexuality as we have come to understand it? It is, of course grossly distorting to even talk about "homosexuality" as though one clearly definable thing were meant. But many of us who have gay and lesbian friends and relatives have arrived with them at the opposite conclusion: for many persons the acceptance of their homosexuality is an acceptance of creation as it applies to them. It is emphatically not a vice that is chosen. If this conclusion is correct, what is the hermeneutical implication?

Another order of questions concerns the connection of homosexuality to *porneia*. The church, it is clear, cannot accept *porneia*. But what is the essence of "sexual immorality"? Is the moral quality of sexual behavior defined biolog-ically in terms of the use of certain body parts, or is it defined in terms of per-sonal commitment and attitudes? Is not *porneia* essentially sexual activity that ruptures covenant, just as *castitas* is sexual virtue within or outside marriage be-cause it is sexuality in service to covenant?

If sexual virtue and vice are defined covenantally rather than biologically, then it is possible to place homosexual and heterosexual activity in the same context. Certainly, the church must reject the *porneia* which glorifies sex for its own sake, indulges in promiscuity, destroys the bonds of commitment, and seduces the innocent. Insofar as a "gay life style" has these connotations, the church must emphatically and always say "no" to it. But the church must say "no" with equal emphasis to the heterosexual "*Playboy/ Cosmo* lifestyle" ver-sion. In both cases, also, the church can acknowledge that human sexual ac-tivity, while of real and great significance, is not wholly determinative of human existence or worth, and can perhaps begin to ask whether the church's concentration on sexual behavior corresponds proportionally to the modest emphasis placed by Scripture.

The harder question, of course, is whether the church can recognize the pos-sibility of homosexual committed and covenantal love, in the way that it recog-nizes such sexual/personal love in the sacrament of marriage. This is a harder question because it pertains not simply to moral attitudes or pastoral care, but to the social symbolization of the community. The issue here is analogous to the one facing earliest Christianity after Gentiles started being converted. Granted that they had been given the Holy Spirit, could they be accepted into the people of God just as they were, or must they first "become Jewish" by being circum-cised and obeying all the ritual demands of Torah? [see, for example, Col, Gal, and Acts 10:44–11:18; 15] Remember, please, the stakes: the Gentiles were "by nature" unclean, and were "by practice" polluted by idolatry. We are obsessed by the sexual dimensions of the body. The first-century Mediterranean world was obsessed by the social implications of food and table-fellowship. The deci-sion to let the Gentiles in "as is" and to establish a more inclusive form of table-fellowship, we should note, came into direct conflict with the accepted interpretation of Torah and what God wanted of humans.

The decision, furthermore, was not easy to reach. Paul's Letter to the Gala-tians suggests some of the conflict it generated. Even the irenic Luke devotes five full chapters of Acts (10–15) to the account of how the community caught up with God's intentions, stumbling every step of the way through confusion, doubt, challenge, disagreements, divisions, and debate. Much suffering had to be endured before the implications of Peter's question, "If then God gave the same gift to them as he gave to us when we believed in the Lord Jesus Christ, who was I that could withstand God" (Acts 11:17, RSV), could be fully an-swered: "we believe that we [Jews] shall be saved through the grace of the Lord Jesus, just as they [Gentiles] will" (Acts 15:11, RSV).

The grounds of the church's decision then was the work that God was doing among the Gentiles, bringing them to salvation through faith. On the basis of this experience of God's work, the church made bold to reinterpret Torah, finding there unexpected legitimation for its fidelity to God's surprising ways (Acts 15:15-18). How was that work of God made known to the church? Through the narratives of faith related by Paul and Barnabas and Peter, their personal testimony of how "signs and wonders" had been worked among the Gentiles (Acts 15:4, 6-11, 12-13).

Such witness is what the church now needs from homosexual Christians. Are homosexuality and holiness of life compatible? Is homosexual covenantal love according to "the mind of Christ" (1 Cor 2:16) an authentic realization of that Christian identity authored by the Holy Spirit, and therefore "authored" as well by the Scripture despite the "authorities" speaking against it? The church can discern this only on the basis of faithful witness. The burden of proof required to overturn scriptural precedents is heavy, but it is a burden that has been borne before. The church cannot, should not, define itself in response to political pressure or popularity polls. But it is called to discern the work of God in human lives and adapt its self-understanding in response to the work of God. Inclusivity must follow from evidence of holiness; are there narratives of homosexual holiness to which we must begin to listen?

6. Karen Lebacqz, "Appropriate Vulnerability: A Sexual Ethic for Singles?"

Karen Lebacqz is the Robert Gordon Sproul Professor of Theological Ethics at Pacific School of Religion in Berkeley, California. She is a prolific scholar in the areas of professional ethics, bioethics, and ethical theory. Lebacqz also is ordained in the United Church of Christ. The Church's traditional teaching on sexuality is celibacy in singleness and fidelity in marriage. She argues not simply for a different conclusion about sexuality and singleness but for a different method for working through the question. (Readers may wish to consider where Lebacqz' proposed method reaffirms traditional Christian teachings on sexuality and where it supports innovation.)

All[34] of us spend our first years single. Most of us spend our last years single. As adults, many of us are single by circumstance or by deliberate choice. Given these simple facts, it is surprising how little attention and how precious little support the churches have given to singleness (except for the

[34] Karen Lebacqz, "Appropriate Vulnerability: A Sexual Ethic for Singles?" *The Christian Century*, May 6, 1987. Subscriptions: $49/year from P.O. Box 378, Mt. Morris, IL 61054. Ph.: 1–800–208–4097. Copyright 1987 Christian Century. Reprinted with permission.

monastic tradition, with its very particular demands and charisms). The scriptural witness on singleness is virtually ignored, despite the fact that Jesus never married and Paul preferred singleness. Throughout history, churches have simply assumed that marriage is the norm for Christians.

Single sexuality, when it is discussed at all, falls under the category of "premarital sex." Churches clearly expect that those who are single will get married and that those who have been married and are now single through divorce or widowhood will simply disappear into the closet until they marry again. The slogan recently adopted by the United Methodist Church might stand as a summary of the traditional Christian view of sexuality: "celibacy in singleness, fidelity in marriage."

A new ethic for single sexuality is needed, for the tradition that requires celibacy in singleness is not adequate. This situation does not mean that anything goes or that the church has nothing to offer by way of a positive ethic for single people. The task is to thread our way between two views of sexuality: the "old testament" or "thou shall not"[35] exemplified by much of church tradition, and the "new testament" or "thou shalt"[36] approach evident in much of our current culture.

The "old testament" or legalistic approach to single sexuality is well summed up in a delightful limerick by Joseph Fletcher:[37]

> There was a young lady named Wilde
> Who kept herself quite undefiled
> by thinking of Jesus
> and social diseases
> And the fear of having a child.

The "thou shalt not" ethic was characterized by fear—fear of pregnancy and venereal disease—and by a series of "don'ts": don't have sex, don't take pleasure in it: (at least, not if you are a woman) and don't talk about it. As the limerick suggests, sexual involvement was regarded as "defiling." "Bad girls" and "good girls" were defined according to their willingness to be sexual or not. There was no discussion of sexuality of divorced or widowed men and women, and gay men and lesbian women simply stayed in the closet.

With the advent of the so-called "sexual revolution" and the birth-control pill, fear of pregnancy was gone. After the "thou shalt not" of Christian tradition, we encountered the "thou shalt" of contemporary culture. Here, "love"

---

[35] Editors' note: The traditional wording as found in the King James Version (KJV) of the Bible, available at http://www.biblegateway.com (accessed September 18. 2004).

[36] Editors' note: See preceding note; in this case, for example, Matt 22:37 where Jesus is quoting Deut 6:5, but this author is also applying the traditional "thou shalt" as an expression of modern culture.

[37] Joseph Fletcher, *Moral Responsibility: Situation Ethics at Work* (Philadephia: Westminster, 1967) 88.

was all that counted. Women were "liberated" and virginity was redefined as "bad." Now people talked about sex all the time, with everyone. Far from being defiling, sexual involvement was regarded as mandatory. Sex was supposed to be pleasurable, and "how-to" manuals abounded. Finally, everyone knew how—but had forgotten why. In short, fear was replaced by pressure—pressure to engage in sex, to do it right, to enjoy it, and to let the world know how much and how well you were doing it.

. . . Neither the legalistic approach of earlier Christian morality nor the permissive approach of contemporary culture provides a satisfactory sexual ethic for singles. And without a good sexual ethic for singles, there cannot be a good sexual ethic for couples either.

Can we construct a positive, Christian sexual ethic for single people? I think so. Let us begin with Christian tradition, which affirms that sex is a gift from God. It is to be used within the boundaries of God's purposes. As part of God's creation, sex is good. Like all of creation, however, it is tainted by the fall, and therefore becomes distorted by human history. It needs redemption. Such redemption is achieved by using sexuality in accordance with God's purpose and through God's grace. The two redeeming purposes of sexuality have always been understood as procreation and union. With these purposes in mind, the Christian tradition maintained that marriage was the proper context for sex, since it was the proper context for raising children and for achieving a true union. Catholics have tended to stress procreation as the primary purpose while Protestants have stressed union, but both agree on the fundamental purposes of sexual expression.[38]

This tradition has had enormous practical implications for singles. The tradition condemns all genital sexual expression outside of marriage on the assumption that it violates the procreative and unitive purposes of sexuality. Nongenital sexual expression is also suspect, because it is thought to lead inexorably to genital expression. Given such a view of sexuality, it is difficult for single people to claim their sexuality or to develop a positive ethic for that sexuality.

Standards within both Catholic and Protestant traditions have recently loosened, but there has been no fundamental challenge to this basic paradigm. Today, some Catholics and most Protestants accept "pre-ceremonial" sex between responsible and committed adults.[39] Both traditions have moved toward affirming union as primary, while still upholding the importance of procreation. The meaning of the two fundamental purposes has been expanded by replacing the term "procreative" with "creative" and the term "unitive" with

[38] Editors' note: In recent decades Catholic teachings increasingly have stressed the unitive dimensions of sexuality, while many Protestant writers have placed renewed emphasis on parenting.

[39] Paul Ramsey argues that this is marriage in the moral sense. See his "On Taking Sexual Responsibility Seriously Enough," in Gibson Winter, ed., *Social Ethics* (San Francisco: Harper and Row, 1968) 45ff.

"integrative."[40] Thus, there is some acceptance of non-marital sexual expression, provided it is in the context of deep interpersonal commitment.

But however important such revisions may be, they do not really accept sexuality outside marriage. Single sexuality is still difficult to claim. Neither Catholic nor Protestant tradition provides a totally satisfactory explanation of why sexuality should be fully expressed only in marriage or in a "pre-ceremonial" relationship that will eventuate in marriage. Both traditions still uphold marriage as the ideal, but give no satisfactory reasons for that ideal.

I accept part of the method that has led to the traditional interpretation, but wish to offer an additional insight into the nature of sexuality that might provide a fuller appreciation of the ethical context in which sexuality is expressed. I agree with the traditional understanding that sex is a gift from God to be used within the confines of God's purposes. However, I would add to the traditional purposes of union and procreation another God-given purpose of sexuality that I believe opens up a different understanding of human sexuality and of a sexual ethic for singles (as well as couples).

Sexuality has to do with vulnerability. Eros, the desire for another, the passion that accompanies the wish for sexual expression, makes one vulnerable. It creates possibilities for great joy but also for great suffering. To desire another, to feel passion, is to be vulnerable, capable of being wounded.

There is evidence in Scripture for this view of sexuality. Consider the Song of Songs (the "holy of holies"), which displays in glowing detail the immense passion and vulnerability of lovers. This is not married or "pre-ceremonial" sexuality, nor are children the justification for the sexual encounter. It is passion pure and simple. And it is graphic sex. The Stoic fear of passion is not biblical. From the Song of Songs we can recover the importance of sexual desire as part of God's creation.

It is equally important to recover the creation stories in Genesis, which are often the grounds for our interpretation of what God intends human sexuality to be. It is from these stories that we take the phrase "be fruitful and multiply" (Gen 1:22, RSV) and turn it into a mandate for procreation. It is from these stories that we hear the deep call for union between sexual partners: "This at last is bone of my bones / and flesh of my flesh . . . and the two shall become one flesh" (Gen 2:23-24).[41]

Without denying the importance of these phrases and their traditional interpretation, I would stress another passage—one that has been ignored but is crucial for completing the picture. The very last line in the creation story in Genesis 2 reads: "And the man and his wife were both naked, and they felt no

---

[40] See Catholic Theological Society of America, *Human Sexuality: New Directions in American Catholic Thought* (New York: Paulist Press, 1977) 86.

[41] Editors' note: The first part of the quote is RSV, the last part is provided by the author but very similar to that of the New American Bible version, most recently updated in the 1991 copyrighted version.

shame" (Gen 2:25, RSV). In ancient Hebrew, "nakedness" was a metaphor for vulnerability, and "feeling no shame" was a metaphor for appropriateness. We can therefore retranslate the passage as follows: "And the man and his wife experienced appropriate vulnerability." As the summation and closure of the creation story, the verse tells us that the net result of sexual encounter—the purpose of the creation of man and woman as sexual beings who unite with one another to form "one flesh"—is that there be appropriate vulnerability.

Vulnerability may be the precondition for both union and procreation; without a willingness to be vulnerable, to be exposed, to be wounded, there can be no union. To be "known," as Scripture so often describes the sexual encounter,[42] is to be vulnerable, exposed, open. Sexuality is therefore a form of vulnerability and is to be valued as such. Sex, eros, passion are antidotes to the human sin of wanting to be in control or to have power over another. "Appropriate vulnerability" may describe the basic intention for human life—which may be experienced in part through the gift of sexuality.

If this is so, then a new approach to sexual ethics follows. If humans are intended to have appropriate vulnerability, then the desire to have power or control over another is a hardening of the heart against vulnerability. When Adam and Eve chose power, they lost their appropriate vulnerability and were set against each other in their sexuality. Loss of vulnerability is paradigmatic of the fall. Jesus shows us the way to redemption by choosing not power but vulnerability and relationship.

The implications for a sexual ethic are profound. Any exercise of sexuality that violates appropriate vulnerability is wrong. This includes violations of the partner's vulnerability and violations of one's own vulnerability. Rape is wrong not only because it violates the vulnerability of the one raped, but also because the rapist guards his own power and refuses to be vulnerable.

Similarly, seduction is wrong, for the seducer guards her or his own vulnerability and uses sex as a weapon to gain power over another. Any sexual encounter that hurts another, so that she or he either guards against vulnerability in the future or is unduly vulnerable in the future, violates the "appropriate vulnerability" which is part of the true meaning and purpose of our God-given sexuality. Prostitution and promiscuity are also generally wrong. In each there tends to be either a shutting down of eros or a form of masochism in which the vulnerability is not equal and therefore not appropriate. Sex is not "just for fun," for play, for physical release, for showing off or for any of the host of other human expressions that are often attached to sexuality. It is for the appropriate expression of vulnerability, and to the extent that that expression is missing, the sexual expression is not proper.

Nothing in what has been said so far suggests that the only appropriate expressions of vulnerability are in marriage. Premarital and post-marital sexuality

---

[42] Editors' note: See, for example, Gen 4:1.

might express appropriate vulnerability. Gay and lesbian unions, long condemned by the church because of their failure to be procreative, might also express appropriate vulnerability. At the same time, some sexual expressions within marriage might not be an appropriate expression of vulnerability—for example, spousal rape or unloving sexual encounter. We must beware of the deceptions through which we reduce or deny vulnerability in sexuality—both the "swinging singles" image and notions of sexual "duty" in marriage deny appropriate vulnerability.

But what about singleness specifically? Is there any need for a special sexual ethic for single people? Precisely because sexuality involves vulnerability it needs protective structures. A few years ago, the United Church of Christ proposed a "principle of proportionality" for single sexuality. According to this principle, the level of sexual expression should be commensurate with the level of commitment in the relationship. While I have some problems with this principle, it does have the merit of suggesting that the vulnerability involved in sexual encounter requires protection. The more sexual involvement there is to be, the more there needs to be a context that protects and safeguards that vulnerability. As Stanley Hauerwas puts it, "Genuine love is so capable of destruction that we need a structure to sustain us."[43]

Traditionally, monogamous marriage has been understood to provide that needed context. Whatever the pitfalls and failures of marriage in practice, certainly in theory the commitment of a stable and monogamous marriage provides a supportive context for vulnerable expressions of the self. Marriage at its best ensures that the vulnerability of sexuality is private and that our failures remain protected in a mutually vulnerable and committed relationship.

Singleness carries no such protections. It is an unsafe environment for the expression of vulnerability. No covenant of fidelity ensures that my vulnerability will not lead to my being hurt, foolish, exposed, wounded. In short, in singleness the vulnerability that naturally accompanies sexuality is also coupled with a vulnerability of context. Thus, singleness is a politically more explosive arena for the expression of vulnerability in sex because it lacks the protections of marriage. It heightens vulnerability.

An adequate sexual ethic for singles must therefore attend to what is needed for appropriate vulnerability in sexuality. Attention must be paid to the structural elements in the particular situation that heighten or protect vulnerability. For example, a sexual ethic for singles might take one form for those who are very young and another for those who are older. The protections of age and experience may make it sensible to permit sexual encounter for those who are older and single, while restricting it for the very young. Unequal vulnerability is not appropriate. Therefore, in a culture where men tend to have

---

[43] Stanley Hauerwas, *A Community of Character: Toward a Constructive Christian Social Ethic* (Notre Dame: University of Notre Dame Press, 1981) 181.

more power than women and women are more vulnerable to men, great care will be needed to provide an adequate context for the expression of sexuality.

We need a theology of vulnerability. Until such a theology is forthcoming we can only struggle toward a proper sexual ethic. Single people will have to explore their own vulnerability to find its appropriate expression in sexuality. Neither the "thou shalt not" of traditional prohibitions nor the "thou shalt" of contemporary culture provides an adequate sexual ethic for singles. "Celibacy in singleness" is not the answer. An appreciation of the link between sexuality and vulnerability is the precondition for an adequate sexual ethic.

Chapter Five

Political Life
and the Problem of Violence

Contemporary Americans typically approach the whole idea of Christian political ethics with some suspicion. If individual conscience is to be protected in the midst of great religious diversity, the argument goes, church and state must remain divided by a "wall of separation." To be sure, the United States Constitution *does* severely limit the formal entanglement of church and state. A separation of ecclesiastical and governmental institutions, however, does not require a corresponding separation of a person's religious faith and his or her political convictions. Life simply does not divide itself neatly into "religious" and "political" spheres. Rather, religious faith makes totalistic claims on the human person and so inevitably spills over into matters of social organization, public justice, law, and governance. It is imperative, then, that Christians think deeply about their engagement in the political world. Christians also must consider thoughtfully issues of coercion, violence, and war, since no state can sustain itself without some recourse to these means.

Indeed, Christians *have* thought deeply about their engagement with political life through the centuries. This is not to say that in Christian history we will find a single overarching vision of Christian political ethics—much less a systematic Christian philosophy of politics. We will find, however, some fairly consistent traditions of thought enduring over time that share common moral vocabularies and approaches to political life. We will find also that these traditions share a negative consensus; that is, they agree that at least some values and positions that must be *excluded* from any genuinely Christian approach to political life.

As we examine the various responses of the Christian moral tradition to issues of politics and violence in this chapter, it is imperative that we locate the readings in their historical and cultural contexts. Each writer operates within a particular political system—a tribal confederation, kingdom, empire, nation state, or liberal democracy, to name only a few examples. The writers also are influenced by their relative position vis-à-vis the power establishment of the day. Does he or she reflect a position of power or authority, for example, or the perspective of a persecuted minority? These contexts do not wholly determine the writer's vision, but they color the writer's vision of the world and shape his or her expectations about what is possible.

The readings selected for this chapter thus represent both the diversity and the coherence of Christian political ethics. We will set forth the major streams of thought, expose the reader to the most influential voices within those traditions, delineate issues debated between traditions, and indicate where they reach consensus. Throughout this survey, we will pay particular attention to the special problems of coercion, violence, and war. Before turning to the readings themselves, however, we will first make a broad historical survey of political ethics in Christian history.

The Ethics of Political Life and War in the Hebrew Scriptures

It is often said that history is a tale told by victors. The perspective of the Bible, however, is that of the perennial underdog and outsider. Throughout the two millennia of Israel's history during the biblical period, she experienced a series of internal political transformations and suffered unrelenting pressures from external threats. Israel's tragic history is in part a reflection of its geography. As the land bridge connecting Egypt, Mesopotamia, and Europe, Israel was at the strategic epicenter of the endless dynastic warfare between the great powers of the ancient Near East. But lacking arable land and seaports to sustain a great population, wealth, and armies, it was doomed to be a pawn in the hands of more powerful players.

During the conquest of the Promised Land, the tribes of Israel were united under the charismatic leadership of Moses and his successor Joshua. After settling in Palestine, what later became "Israel" was merely a loose confederation of tribes who cooperated only during periods of common emergency. Under pressures for political stability and military security, the tribes united under their first king, Saul. His successor, the great king David, succeeded in uniting all of the twelve tribes into a single kingdom. From this position of strength, David finally destroyed Israel's nemesis, Philistia. David's son, Solomon, subjugated Israel's neighbors to form an empire that stretched from Egypt to Mesopotamia.

These days of glory were short-lived, however. Solomon's sons were too weak to overcome the centripetal forces of the empire. The ten northern tribes split away from the two southern tribes, forming the much-weakened kingdoms of Israel and Judah. The subjugated neighboring kingdoms rebelled and broke away. After a brief period of relative prosperity, the northern kingdom of Israel was annihilated by a reinvigorated Assyria in 722 B.C.E. The remaining kingdom of Judah was conquered by the next world power, Babylon, in

586 B.C.E. and its political and religious leadership sent into exile. From this point forward, the little province of Judah remained a pawn in the hands of one conquering world power after the next: Babylon, Persia, the Hellenistic Seleucids, and finally Rome.

One wonders that Israel did not simply give in to despair or assimilate into the dominant cultures of the region like the other small kingdoms around her. Instead, Israel's telling and retelling of her history in its Scriptures is its attempt to wrest meaning from disaster. The most striking response is Israel's hope for a Messiah in the lineage of the great king David who would establish a kingdom that would surpass the glories of David's empire. But Israel's experience of political oppression also led it to develop a profound sensitivity to injustice against the weak and a deep suspicion of unrestrained political power. Israel's great prophets, such as Amos and Isaiah, were unrelenting critics of political oppression. This sensitivity is also embodied in Israel's law. The Deuteronomic Code, for example, commands the people of Israel to protect the vulnerable with a warning that repeats like a resounding gong throughout the book: "Remember that you were a slave in the land of Egypt" (Deut 15:15, for example).

A discerning reader of the Hebrew Scriptures notes that war is treated in two very different ways. The tradition of Deuteronomic history blames Israel's destruction on its failure to cleanse itself from the Canaanite peoples and their idolatry, and it often pictures God as commanding wars of "ethnic cleansing" aimed on complete extermination of Israel's enemies (see the reading from the book of Numbers below). This ethic is rooted in *henotheism,* or loyalty to a warlike tribal god who protects its people against other peoples and their gods. Quite a different view of war is taken by Israel's great prophets. Speaking from their direct experience of defeat and oppression, they viewed war as a terrible tragedy and yearned for a future kingdom in which justice and peace would reign. The greatest of these prophets developed a genuine *monotheism,* the belief that only one God exists and that God loves all humankind and not simply Israel alone. They bequeathed to the world a vision of a God who established universal standards of justice against which all nations must measure their actions.

The Ethics of Political Life and War in the New Testament

The New Testament builds on the foundations of the great prophets of the Hebrew Scriptures but adds its own special perspectives. The New Testament writers intensify and develop the prophetic and apocalyptic traditions of the Old Testament prophets. This perspective undoubtedly reflects the markedly changed socio-political perspective of the New Testament writers. In the Old Testament period the Jews could assume at least some measure of meaningful influence over their political destiny. During Jesus' day, however, Israel was ruled by a brutal occupying force unresponsive to local wishes. This rift between believers (both Jewish and "Christian"—keeping in mind that the division was not distinct for everyone) and empire was only deepened by Rome's annihilation of Israel as retribution for an uprising in the year 64 and by the imperial persecutions of Christians at the end of the New Testament era.

The new political perspective of the New Testament is more than simply a reflection of political context, however. At the moral center of the New Testament is Jesus' uncompromising, consistent nonviolence. Jesus not only taught love of enemies (see Matt 5:44; Luke 6:27), he also embodied his teachings by voluntarily giving himself up to trial and execution. Jesus' commitment seems to have been rooted in his hope for God's reign that he believed even now was breaking into human history to establish a divine kingdom. Theologians define this expectation as *eschatology,* or "teaching about the last things." Jesus calls on his hearers to prepare for the kingdom by embodying its vision into daily life here and now. For Jesus, the faithful must reject violence and coercion because they will have no place in the kingdom to come.

Jesus' rejection of violence made it problematic for Christians to serve in formal positions of state power, since states inevitably appeal to coercion and violence in order to sustain themselves. Moreover, the New Testament writers could only regard the empire with suspicion since Jesus himself was executed through the complicity of Pontius Pilate, the Roman governor of Palestine. These suspicions are taken to the extreme in the Book of Revelation (also called the Revelation of John, or the Apocalypse), which may have been written during a period of intense persecution of the church at the hands of the empire. The writer pictures the Roman state as an evil beast from the abyss under the control of Satan (Rev 13). On the other hand, the apostle Paul struggled to find some place for Roman rule in the great unfolding drama of divine providence. In the reading from the Letter to the Romans included in this chapter, Paul advises the church in Rome that Roman justice establishes at least a bare minimum of social order from which the church itself benefits while this world endures. The reader should keep in mind, however, that the political writings of the New Testament are profoundly contextual: they are responses to specific issues and do not intend to set forth a systematic theory. The church would have to take up that task in successive centuries.

The Ethics of Political Life and War in the Christian Church

The moral vision of the early church was profoundly shaped by the nonviolence of Jesus and by their periodic martyrdom at the hands of the Roman state. The church historian Roland Bainton believes that until approximately the years 170–80, military service by Christians is largely unknown. As the church grew in numbers and influence through the third century, however, it gradually came to include in its ranks some political leaders and even a great many soldiers. Still, most influential Christian writers from that period continued to reject violence and military service as appropriate expressions of Christian vocation (see, for example, the selection from Tertullian's *Apology,* included in this chapter.)

In the year 311, however, the Church experienced a watershed event: the Emperor Constantine's Edict of Toleration, which granted the church full legal recognition. By the year 380, Christianity was the official religion of the Roman Empire and became closely aligned with state power. Shortly thereafter the enormously influential theologian Augustine developed his theory of "two cities" (see his work *The City of God*) which attempted to reconcile the vision of heavenly peace with the realties of life in the present age. Augustine also developed the "just war doctrine," which accepted limited violence as legitimate Christian practice.

From the time of Augustine forward, theologians had to develop much more systematic statements about the relationship of the church to political life. Bainton groups these formulations into three basic types.[1] The first continued to emphasize the sharp differentiation of church and world. It recognized that political powers must employ coercion and violence but rejected these tactics as appropriate for Christians. Today this approach is most closely associated with the Anabaptist tradition and other "peace churches."

A second approach was taken by Martin Luther. He also believed that true Christians do not need a coercive state, for they are always looking for ways to serve others in ways that go far beyond what the law requires. Although the state departs from God's original "Order of Creation," God has graciously provided the state as an "Order of Preservation" that serves as a dam to restrain the raging flood of human sinfulness. Luther believed that Christians could take up the vocation of soldier and magistrate in good conscience if they were truly motivated to serve their neighbor in love. This position thus supports a minimalist state confined to the largely negative task of restraining evil.

Yet a third response is exemplified by the Catholic natural law tradition and also the Genevan reformer John Calvin. The position maintains that the state has a much more expansive vocation than simply the negative task of restraining evil. It purports that a well-ordered state can engender righteousness and holiness in its citizens. As it shapes human character, the law, then, has the "pedagogical" role of shaping human character.

Not only did the Church develop systematic statements about its relationship to the political realm, it also has had to take up explicitly the special problem of war and violence. In general terms, the Christian moral tradition thus has developed two separate tracks: a tradition of pacifism and a tradition of the just war. In addition, a third response to politics and war emerges in Christian history with distressing regularity: the ethics of a crusade or holy war.

---

[1] Roland H. Bainton, *Christian Attitudes toward War and Peace,* (New York: Abingdon Press, 1960) 59ff.

Most Christian ethicists believe that whereas pacifism and just war share a common commitment to the central Christian norms of love, justice, and peace, this last response rejects them. These typologies are examined in greater detail in the second reading of this chapter.

READINGS

1. Biblical Foundations

A. NUMBERS 25, 31:1-24

The events recounted in this passage take place in the land of Moab, just southwest of Israel. Besides Moabites, Midianites, a nomadic tribe, have taken up temporary residence there. The Hebrew slaves escaped slavery in Egypt a generation earlier and now are preparing to invade "the Promised Land" and wrest the land from the Canaanites, the land's native inhabitants. Like the Canaanites, the Moabites and Midianites are worshippers of Baal, a fertility god. As the narrative opens, a conflict erupts over intermarriage between the Hebrews and foreigners that threatens the ethnic and religious purity of the Hebrew people. Note that this story illustrates several features of the "crusade" mentality described above.

B. AMOS 1–2

Amos is the first of the great prophets of the eighth century B.C.E. By trade a shepherd and agricultural worker in the kingdom of Judah, he believed himself called to journey to the northern kingdom of Israel to indict the court of Jeroboam II (786–746 B.C.E.) for its injustices. His harsh words brought him into immediate conflict with the king and Temple authorities, and led to his immediate ejection from Israel. The book of Amos begins with a judgment against Israel's neighbors for war atrocities. Amos' prophecy reflects a fully developed *monotheism*. God is pictured as having complete authority over all of the nations in the region. According to Amos, God expects all nations—not just the Hebrew people—to uphold a common framework of justice in war. Note especially the profound self-criticism at the heart of Amos' prophecy. After first condemning Israel's neighbors, at the end of the reading he indicts Israel and Judah for idolatry and injustice.

C. ISAIAH 2:1-4; 11:1-9

The first thirty-nine chapters of Isaiah are generally regarded as the work of Isaiah of Jerusalem, who proclaimed his message from 742–687 B.C.E. In this catastrophic period the northern kingdom of Israel was destroyed by the Assyrian empire and the southern kingdom of Judah reduced to vassalage. Comparing Israel to a wanton woman, Isaiah, like Amos before him, places the blame squarely on Israel herself for this devastation: it is the just punishment for her idolatry and injustice. Yet, Isaiah tempers his message with profound hope for the future. He imagines a coming kingdom of peace and justice that will be ruled by an "anointed one," or Messiah, from the lineage of David.

D. MATTHEW 5:21-26, 38-48; 20:1-28; 22:15-22

The first selection from Matthew belongs to the well-known Sermon on the Mount that spans chapters 5–7 in this Gospel. In this collection of sayings, Jesus sets forth a charter for the coming kingdom of heaven. The radical vision expressed in these brief words has had an enormous impact in the history of Christian ethics of political life, violence, and war. This passage receives close treatment by all of the writers we will encounter throughout this chapter. In the second selection, Jesus contrasts a life based on power and might with his new ethic based on love and service. The last selection is Jesus' cryptic response to a question about the legitimacy of the Roman occupation in Palestine.

E. ROMANS 13:1-7

Paul was the first great missionary of the Christian faith as it spread out of Israel to the Gentile world. This selection, taken from Paul's letter to the church in Rome, probably was written at the height of Paul's career, between the years 54 and 58. Paul had a complex relationship with the Roman Empire. One the one hand, he appealed to his due process rights as a Roman citizen when arrested for preaching the Gospel in Jerusalem (see Acts 25–26). On the other hand, his eschatological perspective led him to see the Roman Empire as speeding toward destruction (see 1 Thess 5:1-11, 1 Cor 2:6-8). Paul's belief that "there is no authority except from God" (Rom 13:1) is oft-quoted in Christian history as a justification for the divine authority of the state and the humble obedience of Christian subjects. The reader should keep in mind, however, that Paul himself repeatedly disobeyed authorities who commanded him to cease his missionary activities, and he eventually was executed at the command of the emperor. Apparently, then, Paul himself did not believe that the authority of the governing powers is absolute.

F. REVELATION 13

The Book of Revelation originates from the reign of the emperor Domitian (81–96 C.E.), who sanctioned the first organized persecution of Christians. The author shaped the work in its present form while on the island of Patmos, where he had been exiled. The interpretation of John's cryptic vision has been a matter of much speculation in Christian history. Today, many scholars believe that this part of the vision signifies the actual or anticipated crisis of persecution that rent the church in John's day. The "beast rising out of the sea" (v. 1) represents the Roman Empire, which has taken on pretensions of divinity and has been incited by the dragon (Satan) to persecute the Church. The second beast, designated by the number of 666, is perhaps a veiled reference to the emperor Nero, who blamed the burning of Rome on the Christians. So understood, John's revelation is a carefully coded call to the church to remain faithful and resist the worship of the emperor and the Roman state.

2. David Oki Ahearn and Peter R. Gathje, "A Typology of Christian Responses to War and Violence: Pacifism, Just War, and the Crusade"

Throughout the ages, the mainstream of the Christian church has affirmed some responsibility to work for good in the political sphere. Its proper role most often has been measured against three central norms: love of neighbor, whose numbers include even one's enemies;[2] justice in the wider social order; and peace, both as a healing of temporal conflict and as the final goal of history. Various voices within the Christian moral tradition have defined love, justice, and peace differently and have placed the emphasis differently, stressing one of these norms over against the others. In general, the Christian moral tradition has split into two broad streams: the tradition of pacifism and the tradition of the just war. At times, the Christian church has also succumbed to calls for a holy war, though most Christian ethicists regard this last response more as a violation of the Christian vision for political life than as a legitimate application of love, justice, and peace.

1. The Tradition of Pacifism

After the emperor Constantine formed a close alliance between church and empire in the fourth century, nonviolence as a necessary feature of Christian discipleship quickly became a minority position, though it was never completely lost. Thomas Aquinas, for example, wrote in the thirteenth century that priests were not to shed blood because their ministry is to model the sacrifice of Christ for others as represented in the Eucharist.[3] It was not until the Reformation of the Anabaptists of the sixteenth century, however, that Christian nonviolence again became an explicit requirement of a church for laity as well as clerics. In general terms, the tradition of Christian pacifism may be seen as

---

[2] See Luke 10:25-37, the story of the Good Samaritan.
[3] *Summa Theologiae*, II-II 40.2. See the annotation to the *Summa* in chapter 1 of this volume.

consisting of three broad patterns: *classical Christian pacifism, liberal Christian pacifism,* and an emerging pattern of *nonviolent resistance.* Each of these responses emerged in the midst of different sorts of historical struggles and each reflects a distinctive interpretation of theological convictions.

Classical Christian pacifism rejects Christian participation in state violence (whether war or capital punishment) but does not seek a direct role in political change. In this type of pacifism, the Church stands apart from the sinful world in faithful witness to the life and teaching of Jesus, trusting in God's intervention in history to bring in the fullness of the kingdom. The role of the church is not to seek transformation of the world through participation in political life; rather it seeks transformation of the world through its witness and prayer, both of which rely upon God's grace. The Church and Christians are called to be faithful to God's way of life. Classical Christian pacifism thus recognizes that sin continues to lead to violent conflict and that states will use violence for the sake of political order. Nevertheless, this way of the world is not to be the way of Christians, even if that means the loss of their lives. Christians who follow the way of Jesus should not expect to be exempt from the cross. The selections from Tertullian and the Schleitheim Confession included in this chapter represent this type of pacifism. The latter influenced other reform movements within the Christian church, such as the Quakers, who, along with the Mennonites and the Church of the Brethren, became known as the "peace churches."

Liberal Christian pacifism rejects Christian participation in state violence but, unlike classical Christian pacifism, also seeks a direct role in fostering political change. This type of pacifism urges that the church has an important role in the world to bring peace through the nonviolent resolution of conflict. Unlike classical Christian pacifism, liberal pacifism has a great deal of confidence in the basic goodness of human beings and their rational capabilities to resolve disputes without violence. This type of pacifism emerged within Christianity in the late nineteenth and early twentieth centuries. At that point it reflected the confidence of an emergent modernity closely aligned with the dominance of mainline Protestant churches in the United States and the emergence of the Social Gospel movement that emphasized "the Fatherhood of God and the brotherhood of man."[4] Liberal pacifism sees an essential unity within humanity that only needs to be more consistently encouraged to come to fruition in a peaceful world order. Reasoned dialogue is the path to the resolution of all conflict.

Many theologians, most notably the Protestant theologian Reinhold Niebuhr, have harshly criticized this type of pacifism as unrealistic in its conception of sin and the role of power in struggles for justice. Two world wars, "the Cold War,"[5] and the persistence of war in the modern world have also undercut the

----

[4] This expression reflects the most common language terms of the time for God and humanity.

[5] The Cold War was a conflict between the United States and its allies and the Soviet Union and its allies that featured mutual hostility, tension, and intense nuclear arms race and military

viability of liberal pacifism. Still, its ideal of rational resolution of conflict has been institutionalized to some extent in the United Nations and the World Court. With some important qualifications, our included excerpts from the Pastoral Constitution on the Church in the Modern World issued by Vatican II reflects some of the sensibilities of liberal pacifism.

The emerging pattern of **nonviolent resistance** represents an attempt to incorporate the realism of classical Christian pacifism with the confidence in rational dialogue and political participation urged by liberal pacifism. This type of Christian pacifism—like liberal pacifism—sees Christian participation in the transformation of the world as consistent with Jesus' life and teachings directed toward bringing in the kingdom of God. At the same time, it shares with classical pacifism the realism that work for the kingdom in this sinful world involves the Cross-event as applicable to followers of Christ. Nonviolent struggles for justice and peace require a willingness to endure suffering or even death, combined with the confident hope that God's way ultimately will triumph. Many of the convictions and strategies in this type of pacifism have emerged from modern nonviolent movements for political change. Of particular importance have been the examples of Mahatma Gandhi's nonviolent movement for freedom from British rule in India; the Civil Rights movement in the United States, led in part by Dr. Martin Luther King Jr.; Dorothy Day's Catholic Worker movement; and the Solidarity movement in Poland that began the downfall of communism in Eastern bloc countries.

2. The Just War Tradition

The just ear tradition arose in response to the new position of responsibility in which the church found itself after Constantine. Just war theorists begin with the conviction that although it seems a direct contradiction of Jesus' teachings for Christians to engage in violent coercion and war, in some situations it may seem to be a greater evil *not* to do so. In a fallen world, innocents require protection and often peace cannot be established without coercion. (Many pacifists share this bleak assessment but believe that such responsibility is outside the proper role of Christians.) Ambrose of Milan first suggested the basic direction of the theory, and it was later developed by Augustine, though not in a systematic fashion. This task was taken up by Thomas Aquinas in the thirteenth century, and then later by the Jesuit theologians Francisco de Suarez and Francesco Vittorio, who endeavored to reign in the slaughter of native populations in the New World by the conquistadors in the sixteenth century. An important contemporary figure in the tradition is the

---

buildup, and conflict short of full-scale war. There were real wars—funded and sometimes participated in by the two major powers—but never directly between them. These so-called "proxy wars" included the Korean War, the Vietnam War, and the Soviet Union's war in Afghanistan.

Protestant ethicist Paul Ramsey, who addressed the massively destructive wars of the last century and the threat of nuclear annihilation. For Ramsey, the decision to go to war is not simply a matter of *justice,* but fundamentally a question of Christian *love*—love for defenseless innocents by defending them, and love for their attackers by limiting violence against them. Selections from Augustine and Ramsey are included in this chapter.

In its fully developed form,[6] the just war doctrine holds the Christian presumption against war, but recognizes it can be right to enter into war *(jus ad bellum)* only if it meets these criteria:

1. Just Cause. The war must confront a definite and real danger, such as to protect innocent human life against an aggressor or to defend a just political order.

2. Right Intention. The participants have the right intention of establishing peace with justice, and not simply to destroy or punish the opponent.

3. Last Resort. The violent act is undertaken only after all peaceful means of resolving the conflict have been exhausted.

4. Proportionality. The inevitable harm of the war must be less than the good that is sought through the war.

5. Legitimate Authority. The war must be sanctioned and carried out by those responsible for the common good, typically a legitimate governmental authority. This forbids private feuds and vigilante justice.

6. Comparative Justice. There must be the recognition that no party has absolute justice on its side.

7. Reasonable Likelihood of Success. There is a reasonable likelihood that the party can achieve its war aims, so that the suffering and destruction that war inevitably produces at least may bring about the good of protecting innocents and restraining aggressors.

If entrance into war or violence can be justified, the means used must themselves be just *(jus in bello)*. Traditionally, the just war theory measures acts of violence and war against these criteria:

1. Discrimination. Those carrying out the act of violence must discriminate between combatants and noncombatants, so that direct and intentional targeting of civilians is forbidden. Theologians in the Middle Ages developed the implications of the "principle of double effect," which recognizes that a single act may have multiple effects, some of which are intended, some of which are foreseen but unintended, and some of which are unforeseen. According to these theorists, some *limited* foreseen killing of innocents may be justifiable if they are an unintended consequence of targeting combatants.

---

[6] For a clear exposition of the just war criteria see, *The Challenge of Peace: God's Promise and Our Response, the U.S. Catholic Bishops Pastoral Letter on War and Peace,* National Conference of Catholic Bishops (Washington, D.C: 1983) 26–37.

2. Proportionality. The violent action must be proportionate to the desired end. A just response should use an economy of force, that is, limit destruction to the minimum amount needed to accomplish a just objective.

These criteria were intended both to place roadblocks in front of questionable wars and to limit the destruction of even those that are justified. Today Christian ethicists debate if this theory, which arose to deal with the hand-to-hand fighting of ancient and medieval warfare, is adequate in the face of nuclear weapons, totalistic wars of nation against nation, terrorism, popular revolutions, civil war, and wars of extermination.

Despite the very real issues of dispute between the pacifist and the just war perspectives, the two positions actually share a common commitment to love, justice, and peace. Pacifists are deeply committed to living out Jesus' command to *love* enemies, which categorically rules out attacking or killing them. Just war theorists, too, believe that their approach demonstrates Christian love both for innocents and for aggressors. Many pacifists are appreciative of the *peace* purchased by the state through the means of violence, although they consider such peace "outside the perfection of Christ." Just war theorists also remain committed to peace, both because violence is always a last resort and because a *just* peace is the final aim of war. Many pacifists also are actively engaged in the struggle for justice, though they eschew violent methods for achieving it. Thus, the point of contentions between pacifists and just war theorists is thus more narrow than it might first appear: pacifists believe that violence or war can *never* be justified while just war theorists believe that under some *circumstances* some limited forms of violence *may* be justified. Pacifists and just war theorists actually share a common moral vision and sometimes agree in their evaluations of specific conflicts. Both can be considered legitimate Christian responses to violence and conflict.

3. The Ethics of the Crusade

This commitment to love, justice, and peace is not shared by our last approach to the violence and war in the Christian tradition: the ethics of the crusade, or the idea of holy war. This last approach has these defining features:

(1) A *henotheistic* conception of God, meaning that God participates directly in the conflict as a partisan for one's own people

(2) An absolutistic division of opponents into one side that is deemed wholly good and another that is deemed wholly evil

(3) Utopian and unlimited goals, such as the eradication of evil or the extermination of the opponent

(4) An absence of a sense of moral community with moral responsibility for one's enemies, leading to an absence of restraint on the means employed in warfare

Of course, this description is simply a typology, and any particular approach to violence and war only more or less illustrates each attribute.

The conquest of Israel against the Canaanite people as described in the Deuteronomic history of the Hebrew Scriptures fits generally into the ethics of the crusade. This approach is especially well-illustrated by the rhetoric surrounding the large-scale crusades against the Muslims and Jews in the Middle Ages. The term "crusade" emerged from the practice by Christian participants in these wars of wearing a cloth cross on their garments. Crusades were wars under the cross. A letter of an otherwise saintly figure, Bernard of Clairvaux, is included in the readings for this chapter. The ethics of the crusade are not simply an artifact of ancient history, however. President Abraham Lincoln once remarked that both the Union and Confederate sides firmly believed that God was on their side during the Civil War (1861–1865). In recent times we have experienced wars of ethnic cleansing and genocidal massacre in the Balkans and Africa. Indeed, many critics of the just war tradition maintain that even justified wars eventually devolve into a crusade mentality as the conflict endures. The population bombing in World War II and, in particular, the atomic bombings of Hiroshima and Nagasaki, certainly suggest that a crusade mentality infected even this "good war." One observes that many voices in the recent "war on terrorism" have degenerated into the demonization of the enemies of the United States. While a crusade mentality seems to be an enduring feature of the church's life in the world, however, most Christian ethicists regard it as an illegitimate expression of Christian ethics that ultimately rejects the fundamental norms of love, justice, and peace.

3. Tertullian (155–240), *Apology*

Tertullian of Carthage was the first Christian writer to write in Latin and provided the first intellectually astute defense of the Christian faith. Tertullian was trained as a lawyer and became a convert to Christianity after witnessing the courage with which Christian martyrs faced hideous deaths in the arena. Tertullian's conception of Christian faithfulness was greatly influenced by the experience of persecution and martyrdom. He took an unflinching stand against compromise and worldliness that he saw creeping into the church. His most famous work is the Apology. *The literary genre of an "apology" is a reasoned defense against critics. Like Paul in Romans 13, Tertullian believed that all government is under the authority of God. Tertullian also argues quite firmly that all Christians must be nonviolent. In Tertullian's view, Christians have a higher duty than to bear the sword—to remain faithful and to pray that all of human life, including the government, comes under the sway of God's reign. Although Tertullian's later works were declared heretical by the church in the sixth century, he continued to exert a powerful influence on Christian theologians throughout Christian history.*

9. That[7] I may refute more thoroughly these charges, I will show that in part openly, in part secretly, practices prevail among you which have led you perhaps to credit similar things about us . . . How many, think you, of those crowding around and gaping for Christian blood—how many even of your rulers, notable for their justice to you and for their severe measures against us, may I charge in their own consciences with the sin of putting their offspring to death? As to any difference in the kind of murder, it is certainly the more cruel way to kill by drowning, or by exposure to cold and hunger and dogs. A maturer age [that is, adults] has always preferred death by the sword. In our case, murder being once for all forbidden, we may not destroy even the fetus in the womb, while as yet the human being derives blood from other parts of the body for its sustenance. To hinder a birth is merely a speedier homocide; nor does it matter whether you take away a life that is born, or destroy one that is coming to the birth. That is a human being which is going to be one; you have the fruit already in its seed . . .

30. For we offer prayer for the safety of our princes to the eternal, the true, the living God, whose favor, beyond all others, they must themselves desire. They know from whom they have obtained their power; they know, as they are mortals, from whom they have received life itself; they are convinced that He is God alone, on whose power alone they are entirely dependent, to whom they are second, after whom they occupy the highest places, before and above all the gods. Why not, since they are above all living creatures, and the living, as living, are superior to the dead? They reflect upon the extent of their power, and so they come to understand the highest; they acknowledge that they have all their might from God against whom their might is naught. Let the emperor make war on heaven; let him lead heaven captive in his triumph; let him put guards on heaven; let him impose taxes on heaven! He cannot. Just because he is less than heaven, he is great. For he himself is God's to whom heaven and every creature appertains. He gets his scepter where he first got his humanity; his power where he got the breath of life. Thither we lift our eyes, with hands outstretched, because free from sin; with head uncovered, for we have nothing whereof to be ashamed; finally, without a monitor, because it is from the heart we supplicate. Without ceasing, for all our emperors we offer prayer. We pray for life prolonged; for security to the empire; for protection to the imperial house; for brave armies, a faithful senate, a virtuous people, the world at rest, whatever, as [human] or Caesar, an emperor would wish . . .

33. There is also another and a greater necessity for our offering prayer in behalf of the emperors, nay, for the complete stability of the empire, and for

---

[7] Tertullian, *Apology* under the title *Apologetic* in *Latin Christianity: Its Founder, Tertullian,* The Ante-Nicene Fathers: Translations of the Writings of the Fathers down to A.D. 325, ed. Alexander Roberts and James Donaldson (Buffalo, N.Y.: Christian Literature Publishing, 1885) 25–26, 42–43, 45–46.

Roman interests in general. For we know that a mighty shock impending over the whole earth—in fact, the very end of all things threatening dreadful woes—is only retarded by the continued existence of the Roman Empire. We have no desire, then, to be overtaken by these dire events; and in praying that their coming may be delayed, we are lending our aid to Rome's duration . . .

37.   If we are enjoined, then, to love our enemies, as I have remarked above, whom have we to hate? If injured, we are forbidden to retaliate, lest we become as bad ourselves: who can suffer injury at our hands? In regard to this, recall your own experiences. How often you inflict gross cruelties on Christians, partly because it is your own inclination, and partly in obedience to the laws! How often, too, the hostile mob, paying no regard to you, takes the law into its own hand, and assails us with stones and flames! With the very frenzy of the Bacchanals, they do not even spare the Christian dead, but tear them, now sadly changed, no longer entire, from the rest of the tomb, from the asylum we might say of death, cutting them in pieces, rending them asunder. Yet, banded together as we are, ever so ready to sacrifice our lives, what single case of revenge for injury are you able to point to, though, if it were held right among us to repay evil by evil, a single night with a torch or two could achieve an ample vengeance?

But away with the idea of a sect divine avenging itself by human fires, or shrinking from the sufferings in which it is tried. If we desired, indeed, to act the part of open enemies, not merely of secret avengers, would there be any lacking in strength, whether of numbers or resources? . . . We are but of yesterday, and we have filled every place among you—cities, islands, fortresses, towns, market-places, the very camp, tribes, companies, palace, senate, forum—we have left nothing to you but the temples of your gods. For what wars should we not be fit, not eager, even with unequal forces, we who so willingly yield ourselves to the sword, if in our religion it were not counted better to be slain than to slay? Without arms even, and raising no insurrectionary banner, but simply in enmity to you, we could carry on the contest with you by an ill-willed severance alone. For if such multitudes of [people] were to break away from you, and betake themselves to some remote corner of the world, why, the very loss of so many citizens, whatever sort they were, would cover the empire with shame; nay, in the very forsaking, vengeance would be inflicted. Why, you would be horror-struck at the solitude in which you would find yourselves, at such an all-prevailing silence, and that stupor as of a dead world. You would have to seek subjects to govern. You would have more enemies than citizens remaining. For now it is the immense number of Christians which makes your enemies so few—almost all the inhabitants of your various cities being followers of Christ . . .

38.   Ought not Christians, therefore, to receive not merely a somewhat milder treatment, but to have a place among the law-tolerated societies, see-

ing they are not chargeable with any such crimes as are commonly dreaded from societies of the illicit class? For, unless I mistake the matter, the prevention of such associations is based on a prudential regard to public order, that the state may not be divided into parties, which would naturally lead to disturbance in the electoral assemblies, the councils, the curiae, the special conventions, even in the public shows by the hostile collisions of rival parties; especially when now, in pursuit of gain, people have begun to consider their violence an article to be bought and sold. But as those in whom all ardor in the pursuit of glory and honor is dead, we have no pressing inducement to take part in your public meetings; nor is there aught more entirely foreign to us than affairs of state. We acknowledge one all-embracing commonwealth—the world. We renounce all your spectacles, as strongly as we renounce the matters originating them, which we know were conceived of superstition, when we give up the very things which are the basis of their representations. Among us nothing is ever said, or seen, or heard, which has anything in common with the madness of the circus, the immodesty of the theatre, the atrocities of the arena, the useless exercises of the wrestling-ground. Why do you take offence at us because we differ from you in regard to your pleasures? If we will not partake of your enjoyments, the loss is ours, if there be loss in the case, not yours . . .

39.   I shall at once go on, then, to exhibit the peculiarities of the Christian society, that, as I have refuted the evil charged against it, I may point out its positive good. We are a body knit together as such by a common religious profession, by unity of discipline, and by the bond of a common hope. We meet together as an assembly and congregation, that, offering up prayer to God as with united force, we may wrestle with God in our supplications. This violence God delights in. We pray, too, for the emperors, for their ministers and for all in authority, for the welfare of the world, for the prevalence of peace, for the delay of the final consummation. We assemble to read our sacred writings, if any peculiarity of the times makes either forewarning or reminiscence needful. However it be in that respect, with the sacred words we nourish our faith, we animate our hope, we make our confidence more steadfast; and no less by inculcations of God's precepts we confirm good habits . . .

There is no buying and selling of any sort in the things of God. Though we have our treasure-chest, it is not made up of purchase-money, as of a religion that has its price. On the monthly day, if one likes, can put in a small donation; but only if it be his or her pleasure, and only if he or she be able: for there is no compulsion; all is voluntary. These gifts are, as it were, piety's deposit fund. For they are not taken thence and spent on feasts, and drinking-bouts, and eating-houses, but to support and bury poor people, to supply the wants of boys and girls destitute of means and parents, and of old persons confined now to the house; such, too, as have suffered shipwreck; and if there happen to be any in the mines, or banished to the islands, or shut up in the prisons, for nothing but their fidelity to the cause of God's church, they become the nurslings of their confession.

But it is mainly the deeds of a love so noble that lead many to put a brand upon us. "See," they say, "how they love one another," for themselves are animated by mutual hatred; "how they are ready even to die for one another," for they themselves will sooner put to death. And they are wroth [that is, angry] with us, too, because we call each other brothers and sisters; for no other reason, as I think, than because among themselves names of consanguinity are assumed in mere pretence of affection. But we are your kin, by the law of our common mother nature, though you are hardly humans, because kin so unkind. At the same time, how much more fittingly they are called and counted kin who have been led to the knowledge of God as their common Parent, who have drunk in one spirit of holiness, who from the same womb of a common ignorance have agonized into the same light of truth! . . . One in mind and soul, we do not hesitate to share our earthly goods with one another. All things are common among us but our wives . . .

Our feast explains itself by its name. The Greeks call it *agape,* that is, affection. Whatever it costs, our outlay in the name of piety is gain, since with the good things of the feast we benefit the needy; not as it is with you, do parasites aspire to the glory of satisfying their licentious propensities, selling themselves for a belly-feast to all disgraceful treatment—but as it is with God himself, a peculiar respect is shown to the lowly.

4. Augustine of Hippo (354–430), *The City of God;* Letter to Marcellinus

Augustine began his work on The City of God *in 413, three years after Alaric's Goths sacked the city of Rome. Many traditional Romans blamed the disintegration of the empire on this new religion that forsook the Roman virtues of honor and civic virtue for the weaker virtues of love and forgiveness. Augustine's response is a complex one: the church dwells in and makes use of the "City of this World" as it awaits a final consummation in the "City of God." The soul can rest only when it finds the true peace of the eternal city. In the meantime, we can only experience the more limited peace of the earthly city, which always is won by struggle against the destructiveness of human pride and greed.*

Augustine thus believes that resort to coercion and even violence is both inevitable and even at times a positive duty for Christians. Augustine develops the implications of this insight in the letter to Marcellinus. Augustine considers Jesus' apparent rejection of violence in the New Testament. Augustine instructs Marcellinus to focus on the intentions and inner motivations of the actor rather than simply the outward fruits of the action. For Augustine, Jesus commands selfless love and obedience to God, which may be compatible with the soldier who fights in the public interest.

From *The City of God:*

14.28. Of the Nature of the Two Cities, the Earthly and the Heavenly

Accordingly,[8] two cities have been formed by two loves: the earthly by the love of self, even to the contempt of God; the heavenly by the love of God, even to the contempt of self. The former, in a word, glories in itself, the latter in the Lord. For the one seeks glory from humans; but the greatest glory of the other is God, the witness of conscience. The one lifts up its head in its own glory; the other says to its God, "Thou art my glory, and the lifter up of mine head" (Ps 3:3). In the one, the prince and the nations it subdues are ruled by the love of ruling; in the other, the princes and the subjects serve one another in love, the latter obeying, while the former take thought for all. The one delights in its own strength, represented in the persons of its rulers; the other says to its God, "I will love Thee, O Lord, my strength" (Ps 18:1). And therefore the wise of the one city, living according to human standards, have sought for profit to their own bodies or souls, or both, and those who have known God "glorified God not as the Divine, neither were thankful, but became vain in their imaginations, and their foolish heart was darkened; professing themselves to be wise," that is, glorying in their own wisdom, and being possessed by pride, "they became fools, and changed the glory of the incorruptible God into an image made like to corruptible human beings, and to birds, and four-footed beasts, and creeping things." For they were either leaders or followers of the people in adoring images, "and worshipped and served the creature more than the Creator, who is blessed for ever" (Rom 1:21-25). But in the other city there is no human wisdom, but only godliness, which offers due worship to the true God, and looks for its reward in the society of the saints, of holy angels as well as holy people, "that God may be all in all" (1 Cor 15:28).

15.4. Of the Conflict and Peace of the Earthly City

But the earthly city, which shall not be everlasting (for it will no longer be a city when it has been committed to the extreme penalty), has its good in this world, and rejoices in it with such joy as such things can afford. But as this is not a good which can discharge its devotees of all distresses, this city is often divided against itself by litigations, wars, quarrels, and such victories as are either life-destroying or short-lived. For each part of it that arms against

---

[8] From Augustine of Hippo, *The City of God,* in Philip Schaff, ed., *St. Augustin: City of God; Christian Doctrine,* A Select Library of the Nicene and Post-Nicene Fathers of the Christian Church, first series, vol. 2 (Edinburgh: T&T Clark, 1887) revised.

another part of it seeks to triumph over the nations through itself . . . in bondage to vice. If, when it has conquered, it is inflated with pride, its victory is life-destroying; but if it turns its thoughts upon the common casualties of our mortal condition, and is rather anxious concerning the disasters that may befall it than elated with the successes already achieved, this victory, though of a higher kind, is still only short-lived; for it cannot abidingly rule over those whom it has victoriously subjugated. But the things which this city desires cannot justly be said to be evil, for it is itself, in its own kind, better than all other human good. For it desires earthly peace for the sake of enjoying earthly goods, and it makes war in order to attain to this peace; since, if it has conquered, and there remains no one to resist it, it enjoys a peace which it had not while there were opposing parties who contested for the enjoyment of those things which were too small to satisfy both. This peace is purchased by toil-some wars; it is obtained by what they style a glorious victory. Now, when victory remains with the party which had the more just cause, who hesitates to congratulate the victor, and style it a desirable peace? These things, then, are good things, and without doubt the gifts of God. But if they neglect the better things of the heavenly city, which are secured by eternal victory and peace never-ending, and so inordinately covet these present good things that they believe them to be the only desirable things, or love them better than those things which are believed to be better—if this be so, then it is necessary that misery follow and ever increase.

19.12. That Even the Fierceness of War and All the Disquietude of Human Beings Make towards This One End of Peace, Which Every Nature Desires

Whoever gives even moderate attention to human affairs and to our common nature, will recognize that if there is no one who does not wish to be joy-ful, neither is there anyone who does not wish to have peace. For even they who make war desire nothing but victory, desire, that is to say, to attain to peace with glory. For what else is victory than the conquest of those who resist us? And when this is done there is peace. It is therefore with the desire for peace that wars are waged, even by those who take pleasure in exercising their warlike nature in command and battle. And hence it is obvious that peace is the end sought for by war. For everyone seeks peace by waging war, but no one seeks war by making peace. For even they who intentionally interrupt the peace in which they are living have no hatred of peace, but only wish it changed into a peace that suits them better. They do not, therefore, wish to have no peace, but only one more to their mind. And in the case of sedition, when they have separated themselves from the community, they yet do not effect what they wish, unless they maintain some kind of peace with their co-conspirators. And therefore even robbers take care to maintain peace with their comrades, that they may with greater effect and greater safety invade the peace of others. And if any individuals happen to be of such unrivalled strength, and to be so jealous of partnership, that they trust no comrades, but make their own plots, and commit depredations and murders on their own account, yet maintain some shadow of peace with such persons as they are unable to kill, and from whom they wish to conceal their deeds. In their own homes, too, they make it their aim to be at peace with their families, and any other members of their households; for unquestionably prompt obedience to their every look is a source of pleasure to them. And if this be not rendered, they are angry, they chide and punish; and even by this storm they secure the calm peace of their own homes, as occasion demands. For they see that peace cannot be maintained unless all the members of the same domestic circle be subject to one head, such as they themselves are in their own houses . . . And thus all people desire to have peace with their own circle whom they wish to govern as suits themselves. For even those whom they make war against they wish to make their own, and impose on them the laws of their own peace . . .

Anyone, then, who prefers what is right to what is wrong, and what is well-ordered to what is perverted, sees that the peace of unjust persons is not worthy to be called peace in comparison with the peace of the just. And yet even what is perverted must of necessity be in harmony with, and in dependence on, and in some part of the order of things, for otherwise it would have no existence at all.

19.17 What Produces Peace, and What Discord, Between the Heavenly and Earthly Cities

But the families which do not live by faith seek their peace in the earthly advantages of this life; while the families which live by faith look for those eternal blessings which are promised, and use as pilgrims such advantages of time and of earth as do not fascinate and divert them from God, but rather aid them to endure with greater ease, and to keep down the number of those burdens of the corruptible body which weigh upon the soul. Thus the things necessary for this mortal life are used by both kinds of individuals and families alike, but each has its own peculiar and widely different aim in using them. The earthly city, which does not live by faith, seeks an earthly peace, and the end it proposes, in the well-ordered concord of civic obedience and rule, is the combination of human wills to attain the things which are helpful to this life. The heavenly city, or rather the part of it which sojourns on earth and lives by faith, makes use of this peace only because it must, until this mortal condition which necessitates it shall pass away. Consequently, so long as it lives like a captive and a stranger in the earthly city, though it has already received the promise of redemption, and the gift of the Spirit as the earnest of it, it makes no scruple to obey the laws of the earthly city, whereby the things necessary for the maintenance of this mortal life are administered; and thus, as this life is common to both cities, so there is a harmony between them in regard to what belongs to it . . . This heavenly city, then, while it sojourns on earth, calls citizens out of all nations, and gathers together a society of pilgrims of all languages, not scrupling about diversities in the manners, laws, and institutions whereby earthly peace is secured and maintained, but recognizing that, however various these are, they all tend to one and the same end of earthly peace. It therefore is so far from rescinding and abolishing these diversities, that it even preserves and adopts them, so long only as no hindrance to the worship of the one supreme and true God is thus introduced. Even the heavenly city, therefore, while in its state of pilgrimage, avails itself of the peace of earth, and, so far as it can without injuring faith and godliness, desires and maintains a common agreement among all persons regarding the acquisition of the necessaries of life, and makes this earthly peace bear upon the peace of heaven; for this alone can be truly called and esteemed the peace of the reasonable creatures, consisting as it does in the perfectly ordered and harmonious enjoyment of God and of one another in God. When we shall have reached that peace, this mortal life shall give place to one that is eternal, and our body shall be no more this animal body which by its corruption weighs down the soul, but a spiritual body feeling no want, and in all its members subjected to the will. In its pilgrim state the heavenly city possesses this peace by faith; and by this faith it lives righteously when it refers to the attainment of that peace every good action towards God and humans; for the life of the city is a social life.

From the Letter to Marcellinus:

To Marcellinus, My Noble and Justly Famous Lord, My Son Most Beloved and Longed For, Augustin Sends Greeting in the Lord . . .

2.9.   Let[9] us now observe in the second place, what follows in your letter.[10] You have added that they said that the Christian doctrine and preaching were in no way consistent with the duties and rights of citizens, because among its precepts we find: "Recompense to no one evil for evil," (Rom 12:17) and, "Whosoever shall smite thee on one cheek, turn to that person the other also; and if any one take away thy coat, let go thy cloak also; and whosoever will

---

[9] Written in the year 412. These excerpts are from *St. Augustin: Confessions; Letters,* ed. Philip Schaf, Nicene and Post-Nicene Fathers, first series, vol. 1. Originally published by the Christian Literature Publishing Company, 1886, and subsequently made available by a number of publishers: T&T Clark (Edinburgh), Wm. B. Eerdmanns (Grand Rapids, Mich.), and Hendrickson Publishers (Peabody, Mass.). This series is available online at http: // http://www.ccel.org/fathers2/ (accessed September 17, 2004). These excerpts have been adapted; where necessary, the editors have made the original translation more inclusive, independently of consulting modern translations.

[10] Letter 136.2.

compel thee to go a mile with that person twain (Matt 5:39-41)—all which are affirmed to be contrary to the duties and rights of citizens; for who would submit to have anything taken away by an enemy, or forbear from retaliating the evils of war upon an invader who ravaged a Roman province? . . .

2.11.   But who, even though a stranger to our religion, is so deaf as not to know how many precepts enjoining concord, not invented by human discussions but written with the authority of God, are continually read in the churches of Christ? For this is the tendency even of those precepts which they are much more willing to debate than to follow: "That to the one who smites us on one cheek we should offer the other to be smitten; to the one who would take away our coat we should give our cloak also; and that with the one who compels us to go one mile we should go twain." For these things are done only that a wicked person may be overcome by kindness, or rather that the evil which is in the wicked person may be overcome by good, and that the person may be delivered from the evil—not from any evil that is external and foreign to the person, but from that which is within and is personal, under which one suffers loss more severe and fatal than could be inflicted by the cruelty of any enemy from without. The one who, therefore, is overcoming evil by good, submits patiently to the loss of temporal advantages, so that it may be shown how those things, through excessive love of which the other is made wicked, deserve to be despised when compared with faith and righteousness; in order that the injurious person may learn from the one who was wronged what is the true nature of the things for the sake of which the wrong was committed, and may be won back with sorrow for personal sin to that concord, than which nothing is more serviceable to the state, being overcome not by the strength of one passionately resenting, but by the good-nature of one patiently bearing wrong. For then it is rightly done when it seems that it will benefit the one for whose sake it is done, by producing in that person an amendment of ways and concord with others. At all events, it is to be done with this intention, even though the result may be different from what was expected, and the person, with a view to whose correction and conciliation this healing and salutary medicine, so to speak, was employed, refuses to be corrected and reconciled.

2.13.   In fine, that these precepts pertain rather to the inward disposition of the heart than to the actions which are done in the sight of others, requiring us, in the inmost heart, to cherish patience along with benevolence, but in the outward action to do that which seems most likely to benefit those whose good we ought to seek, is manifest from the fact that our Lord Jesus Himself, our perfect example of patience, when He was smitten on the face, answered: "If I have spoken evil, bear witness of the evil, but if not, why smitest thou me?" (John 18:23). If we look only to the words, he did not in this obey his own precept, for He did not present the other side of his face to him who had smitten him but, on the contrary, prevented him who had done the wrong from adding thereto; and yet he had come prepared not only to be smitten on the face, but even to be slain upon the cross for those at whose hands He suffered crucifixion, and for whom, when hanging on the cross, he prayed, "Father, forgive them, they know not what they do!" (Luke 23:34) . . .

2.14.   These precepts concerning patience ought to be always retained in the habitual discipline of the heart, and the benevolence which prevents the recompensing of evil for evil must be always fully cherished in the disposition. At the same time, many things must be done in correcting with a certain benevolent severity, even against their own wishes, persons whose welfare rather than their wishes it is our duty to consult and the Christian Scriptures have most unambiguously commended this virtue in a magistrate. For in the correction of a son, even with some sternness, there is assuredly no diminution of a father's love; yet, in the correction, that is done which is received with reluctance and pain by one whom it seems necessary to heal by pain. And on this principle, if the commonwealth observe the precepts of the Christian religion, even its wars themselves will not be carried on without the benevolent design that, after the resisting nations have been conquered, provision may be more easily made for enjoying in peace the mutual bond of piety and justice. For the person from whom is taken away the freedom which is abused in doing wrong is vanquished with benefit to self; since nothing is more truly a misfortune than that good fortune of offenders, by which pernicious impunity is maintained, and the evil disposition, like an enemy within a person, is strengthened. But the perverse and froward [that is, obstinate] hearts of people think human affairs are prosperous when persons are concerned about magnificent mansions, and indifferent to the ruin of souls; when mighty theatres are built up, and the foundations of virtue are undermined; when the madness of extravagance is highly esteemed, and works of mercy are scorned; when, out of the wealth and affluence of the rich, luxurious provision is made for actors, and the poor are grudged the necessaries of life; when that God who, by the public declarations of His doctrine, protests against public vice, is blasphemed by impious communities, which demand gods of such character that even those theatrical representations which bring disgrace to both body and soul are fitly performed in honor of them. If God permit these things to prevail, God is in that permission showing more grievous displeasure: if God leave these crimes unpunished, such impunity is a more terrible judgment. When, on the other hand, God overthrows the props of vice, and reduces to poverty those lusts which were nursed by plenty, God afflicts in mercy. And in mercy, also, if such a thing were possible, even wars might be waged by the good, in order that, by bringing under the yoke the unbridled lusts of human beings, those vices might be abolished which ought, under a just government, to be either extirpated or suppressed.

2.15.   For if the Christian religion condemned wars of every kind, the command given in the gospel to soldiers asking counsel as to salvation would rather be to cast away their arms, and withdraw themselves wholly from military service; whereas the word spoken to such was, "Do violence to no one, neither accuse any falsely, and be content with your wages," (Luke 3:14)—the command to be content with their wages manifestly implying no prohibition to continue in the service. Wherefore, let those who say that the doctrine of Christ is incompatible with the state's well-being, give us an army composed of soldiers such as the doctrine of Christ requires them to be; let them give us such subjects, such husbands and wives, such parents and children, such masters and servants, such kings, such judges—in fine, even such taxpayers and tax-gatherers, as the Christian religion has taught that people should be, and then let them dare to say that it is adverse to the state's well-being; yea, rather, let them no longer hesitate to confess that this doctrine, if it were obeyed, would be the salvation of the commonwealth.

5. Bernard of Clairvaux (ca. 1090–1153), *In Praise of the New Knighthood*

Bernard of Clairvaux was the founder of the Cistercian monastic order, which already numbered 163 monasteries by the time of his death. Bernard's great reputation propelled him to the center of the great ecclesiastical and political affairs of his age. He was asked to judge the claims of the rival popes during the Great Schism and was able to rally the major part of the church behind his choice, Innocent III. He also succeeded in brokering a treaty between warring England and France. Bernard also was the leading mystical writer of the twelfth century, mapping out the stages by which the faithful move from love of self for one's own sake, to love to God for one's own sake, to love of God for God's sake, and finally to love of self for the sake of God.

It is difficult to reconcile this Bernard, the great practitioner of love and reconciliation, with the Bernard who rallied Europe to the Second Crusade. Pope Eugene III, a son of the Cistercian order, became alarmed when Edessa fell to the Turks in 1134 and feared that Christendom would lose the Holy Land. At his request Bernard preached widely and enthusiastically throughout Europe. He also played a direct role in reorganizing the Knights Templar, a monastic order of knights pledged to defend the Holy Land from infidel invaders. The reading below is Bernard's exhortation to the Knights, written at the request of their leader, Hugh of Payens. Under Bernard's guidance, the Knights wedded their ferocious military zeal to monastic devotion. While Bernard warns that he is not calling for the wholesale slaughter of their enemies if conflict could be avoided, he regarded the Muslims as God's enemies who deserve destruction. In practice, the Knights Templar abandoned the careful boundaries established for war by Augustine, accepting no surrender from defeated enemies and ignoring the distinction between combatant and civilian. One final historical note: the Second Crusade was an unmitigated disaster, and the leadership of Europe was quick to place the entire blame on Bernard himself.

1. A Word of Exhortation for the Knights of the Temple

1. It[11] seems that a new knighthood has recently appeared on the earth, and precisely in that part of it which the Orient from on high visited in the flesh. As God then troubled the princes of darkness in the strength of God's mighty hand, so there God now wipes out their followers, the children of disbelief, scattering them by the hands of God's mighty ones. Even now God brings about the redemption of God's people raising up again a horn of salvation for us in the house of God's servant David.

This is, I say, a new kind of knighthood and one unknown to the ages gone by. It ceaselessly wages a twofold war both against flesh and blood and against a spiritual army of evil in the heavens. When someone strongly resists a foe in the flesh, relying solely on the strength of the flesh, I would hardly remark it, since this is common enough. And when war is waged by spiritual strength against vices or demons, this, too, is nothing remarkable, praiseworthy as it is, for the world is full of monks. But when the one sees a soldier powerfully girding himself with both swords[12] and nobly marking his belt, who would not consider it worthy of all wonder, the more so since it has been hitherto unknown? He is truly a fearless knight and secure on every side, for his soul is protected by the armor of faith just as his body is protected by armor of steel. He is thus doubly armed and need fear neither demons nor mortals. Not that he fears death—no, he desires it. Why should he fear to live or fear to die when for him to live is Christ, and to die is gain? Gladly and faithfully he stands for Christ, but he would prefer to be dissolved and to be with Christ, by far the better thing.

Go forth confidently then, you knights, and repel the foes of the cross of Christ with a stalwart heart. Know that neither death nor life can separate you from the love of God which is in Jesus Christ, and in every peril repeat, "Whether we live or whether we die, we are the Lord's" (see Phil 1:20). What a glory to return in victory from such a battle! How blessed to die there as a martyr! Rejoice, brave athlete, if you live and conquer in the Lord; but glory and exult even more if you die and join your Lord. Life indeed is a fruitful thing and victory is glorious, but a holy death is more important than either.

---

[11] Bernard of Clairvaux, "In Praise of the New Knighthood," trans. Conrad Greenia in *Bernard of Clairvaux: Treatises,* Cistercian Fathers Series, no. 19 (Kalamazoo, Mich.: Cistercian Publications, 1977) 129–31, 134–36, 140–41; revised. Now available, revised, also as, *In Praise of the New Knighthood: A Treatise on the Knights Templar and the Holy Places of Jerusalem.,* Cistercian Fathers Series, no. 19B (Kalamazoo, Mich.: Cistercian Publications, 2000). All rights reserved.

[12] Editors' note: In the medieval era, the "two swords" referred to two realms—one political and one spiritual. Sometimes reference was made to Mark 12:17.

If they are blessed who die in the Lord, how much more are they who die for the Lord!

2. To be sure, precious in the eyes of the Lord is the death of his holy ones [see Ps 116:15], whether they die in battle or in bed, but death in battle is more precious as it is the more glorious. How secure is life when the conscience is unsullied! How secure, I say, is life when death is anticipated without fear; or rather when it is desired with feeling and embraced with reverence! How holy and secure this knighthood and how entirely free of the double risk run by those men who fight not for Christ! Whenever you go forth, O worldly warrior, you must fear lest the bodily death of your foe should mean your own spiritual death, or lest perhaps your body and soul together should be slain by him.

Indeed, danger or victory for a Christian depends on the dispositions of his heart and not on the fortunes of war. If he fights for a good reason, the issue of his fight can never be evil; and likewise the results can never be considered good if the reason were evil and the intentions perverse. If you happen to be killed while you are seeking only to kill another, you die a murderer. If you succeed, and by your will to overcome and to conquer you perchance kill someone, you live a murderer. Now it will not do to be a murderer, living or dead, victorious or vanquished. What an unhappy victory—to have conquered another while yielding to vice, and to indulge in an empty glory at an enemy's fail when wrath and pride have gotten the better of you!

But what of those who kill neither in the heat of revenge nor in the swelling of pride, but simply in order to save themselves? Even this sort of victory I would not call good, since bodily death is really a lesser evil than spiritual death. The soul need not die when the body does. No, it is the soul which sins that shall die.

2. On the New Knighthood

1. But the knights of Christ may safely fight the battles of their Lord, fearing neither sin if they smite the enemy, nor danger at their own death; since to inflict death or to die for Christ is no sin, but rather, an abundant claim to glory. In the first case one gains for Christ, and in the second one gains Christ himself. The Lord freely accepts the death of the foe who has offended him, and yet more freely gives himself for the consolation of his fallen knight.

2. The knight of Christ, I say, may strike with confidence and die yet more confidently, for he serves Christ when he strikes, and serves himself when he falls. Neither does he bear the sword in vain, for he is God's minister, for the punishment of evildoers and for the praise of the good. If he kills an evildoer, he is not a killer of persons, but, if I may so put it, a killer of evil. He is evidently the avenger of Christ towards evildoers and he is rightly considered a defender of Christians. Should he be killed himself, we know that he has not perished, but has come safely into port. When he inflicts death it is to Christ's

profit, and when he suffers death, it is for his own gain. The Christian glories in the death of the pagan, because Christ is glorified; while the death of the Christian gives occasion for the King to show his liberality in the rewarding of his knight. In the one case the just shall rejoice when he sees justice done, and in the foe the just shall say, truly there is a reward for the just; truly it is God who judges the earth.

I do not mean to say that the pagans are to be slaughtered when there is any other way to prevent them from harassing and persecuting the faithful, but only that it now seems better to destroy them than that the rod of sinners be lifted over the lot of the just, and the righteous perhaps put forth their hands unto iniquity.

3. On the Lifestyle of the Knights of the Temple

8.   . . . Once he finds himself in the thick of battle, this knight sets aside his previous gentleness, as if to say, "Do I not hate those who hate you, O Lord; am I not disgusted with your enemies?" [see Ps 139:21]. These knights at once fall violently upon the foe, regarding them as so many sheep. No matter how outnumbered they are, they never regard these as fierce barbarians or as awe-inspiring hordes. Nor do they presume on their own strength, but trust in the Lord of Armies to grant them the victory. They are mindful of the words of Maccabees, "It is simple enough for a multitude to be vanquished by a handful. It makes no difference to the God of heaven whether he grants deliverance by the hands of few or many; for victory in war is not dependent on a big army, and bravery is the gift of heaven" (1 Macc 3:18-19). On numerous occasions they had seen one fighter pursue a thousand, and two put ten thousand to flight.

Thus in a wondrous and unique manner they appear gentler than lambs, yet fiercer than lions. I do not know if it would be more appropriate to refer to them as monks or as soldiers, unless perhaps it would be better to recognize them as being both. Indeed they lack neither monastic meekness nor military might. What can we say of this, except that this has been done by the Lord, and it is marvelous in our eyes. These are the picked troops of God, whom God has recruited from the ends of the earth; the valiant people of Israel chosen to guard well and faithfully that tomb which is the bed of the true Solomon, each one sword in hand, and superbly trained to war.

6. Paul Ramsey (1913–1988): "Justice in War"

Paul Ramsey can be credited with reinvigorating the just war tradition in the modern era and introducing the concept to a Protestant audience. Ramsey anchors his ethical system in God's covenant love modeled in the life and teaching of Jesus Christ. Following the example of Jesus means that for the Christian "everything is permitted that love permits, but everything is re-

quired that love requires." For Ramsey, justice is not a norm separate from love but is the prudential application of Christian love to the social and political dilemmas that we face. In the following reading, Ramsey begins with the assumption that in political life Christians continually encounter weaker victims who are threatened unjustly by the strong. Ramsey asks what is required of Christians who seek to embody Christian love in such situations. His response is not simply that limited war is permitted, but it is commanded for those who endeavor to be faithful to the example of Jesus.

. . . I[13] want to deal with the *origin* and the *meaning* of another criterion for the morality of war's conduct. It is a more intrinsic one, having to do with the justice or injustice of an *act* of war, considered apart from its consequences. In the course of tracing its origin, the systematic meaning of "just conduct" in war will be exhibited. This is the distinction between *legitimate* and *illegitimate* military actions. This distinction cuts across all distinctions among weapons systems and applies to them all, even though it is nuclear weapons that have decisively raised the question whether there are just and unjust acts of war by raising the question whether these particular weapons can possibly be used in a just manner. To learn the meaning of "justice in war" (and its origin out of love-informed-reason) will be to learn what it means to say, in connection with military policy, that the end does not justify the means and that it can never be right to do wrong for the sake of some real or supposed good.

The western theory of the just war originated, not primarily from considerations of abstract or "natural" justice, but from the interior of the ethics of Christian love, or what John XXIII termed "social charity." It was a work of charity for the Good Samaritan to give help to the man who fell among thieves [see Luke 10:25-37]. But one step more, it may have been a work of charity for the inn-keeper to hold himself ready to receive beaten wounded men, and for him to have conducted his business so that he was solvent enough to extend credit to the Good Samaritan. By another step it would have been a work of charity, and not of justice alone, to maintain and serve in a police patrol on the Jericho road to prevent such things from happening. By yet another step, it might well be a work of charity to resist, by force of arms, any external aggression against social order that maintains the police patrol along the road to Jericho. This means that, where the enforcement of an ordered community is not effectively present, it may be a work of justice and a work of social charity to resort to other available and effective means of resist injustice: what do you think Jesus would have made the Samaritan do if he had come upon the scene while the robbers were still at their fell work?

Now, I am aware that this is no proper way to interpret a parable of Jesus. Yet, these several ways of retelling the parable of the Good Samaritan quickly

[13] Paul Ramsey, *The Just War: Force and Political Responsibility* (New York: Charles Scribner's Sons, 1968) 141–47; adapted. Used by permission of The Estate of Paul Ramsey.

exhibit something that is generally true about the teachings of Jesus—namely, that by deed and word he showed the individual the meaning of being perfectly ready to have the will of God reign and God's mercy shed abroad by his life and actions. These versions quickly exhibit how a social ethic emerged from Christian conscience formed by this revelation, and what the early Christians carried with them when they went out into the world to borrow, and subsequently to elevate and refine, Stoic concepts of natural justice.

While Jesus taught that disciples in their own cases should turn the other cheek [see Matt 5:39; Luke 6:29], he did not enjoin that his disciples should lift up the face of other oppressed persons for *them* to be struck against on *their* other cheeks. It is no part of the work of charity to allow this to continue to happen. Instead, it is the work of love and mercy to deliver as many as possible of God's children from tyranny, and to protect from oppression if as many of those for whom Christ died as it may be possible to save. When choice *must* be made between the perpetrator of injustice and the many victims of it, the latter may and should be preferred—even if effectively to do so would require the use of armed force against some evil power. This is what I mean by saying that the justice of sometimes resorting to armed conflict originated in the interior of the ethics of Christian love.

Thus Christian conscience shaped itself for effective action. It allowed even the enemy to be killed only because military personnel and targets stood objectively there at the point where intersect the needs and claims of many more of the human community. For their sakes the bearer of hostile force may and should be repressed. Thus, participation in war (and before that, the use of any form of force or resistance) was justified as, in this world to date, an unavoidable necessity if we are not to omit to serve the needs of others in the only concrete way possible, and maintain a just endurable order in which they may live.

There was another side to this coin. The justification of participation in conflict at the same time severely limited war's conduct. What is justified is also limited! Since it was for the sake of the innocent and the helpless of earth that Christians first thought themselves obliged to make war against an enemy whose objective deeds had to be stopped, since for their sakes do Christians justify themselves in resisting by any means even an enemy-neighbor, they could never proceed to kill equally innocent people as a means of getting at the enemy's forces. Thus was twin-born the justification of war and the limitation which surrounded noncombatants with moral immunity from direct attack. Thus was twin-born the distinction between combatant and noncombatant in all Christian reflection about the morality of warfare. This is the distinction between *legitimate* and *illegitimate* military objectives. The same considerations which justify killing the bearer of hostile force—by the same stroke—prohibit noncombatants from ever being directly attacked with deliberate intent.

This understanding of the moral economy in the just use of political violence contains, then, two elements: (1) a specific justification for sometimes killing another human being and (2) severe and specific restrictions upon anyone who is under the hard necessity of doing so. Both are exhibited in the use of force proper to the domestic police power. It is never just for a police officer to forget the distinction between the bearer of hostile force who must be stopped and the "innocent" bystanders (no matter how mixed-up they are). The officer may hit some innocent party accidentally, but it would never be right for the officer to "enlarge the target" and deliberately and directly kill any number in the crowd on Times Square *as a means of* preventing some criminal from injurious action. Nor do we allow the police the right to get a criminal's children into their power as hostages and threaten to kill them in order to "deter" the criminal. Yet the source of the justification of such limited use of force is evidently to be found in "social charity." This is clear from the fact that a person, who in one situation could legitimately be killed if that were the only way to save other lives, would in another situation be saved at grave risk to the lives of the very same policemen—that is, if that person alone is in need of rescue because he (or she) has gone off his rocker and is threatening to jump from the ledge of a building twenty stories up.

This is the moral economy which regulates the use of force *within* political communities, where it is both *morally* and legally binding. This same moral economy is *morally* if not *legally* binding upon the use of force between nations. It will become *both* legally and morally binding if ever there is world law and order abolishing the nation-state system. War may *in fact* be more than an extension of politics in another form, but the *laws* of war are only an extension, where war is the only available means, of the rules governing any use of political power. We are not apt ever to "abolish war" if we keep on denying that there is a morality *of* war, which is only a concise summary of right and charitable reason in the simultaneous *justification* and the *limitation* of the use of power necessary to the political life of humankind.

To summarize the theory of just or civilized conduct in war as this was developed within Christendom: love for neighbors threatened by violence, by aggression, or tyranny, provided the grounds for admitting the legitimacy of the use of military force. Love for neighbors[14] at the same time required that such force should be limited. Christians are commanded to do anything a realistic love commands (and so sometimes they must fight). But this also prohibits them from doing anything for which such love can find no justification (and so it can never approve of unlimited attack upon any human life not closely cooperating in or directly engaged in the force that ought to be repelled).

This means that nuclear war against the civil centers of an enemy population, the A-Bomb on Hiroshima, or obliteration bombing perpetrated by both sides in World War II were all alike immoral acts of war; and that Christians can support

---

[14] Editors' note: "Love for neighbor," of course, has several references in Scripture, in both Testaments (see Lev 19:18; Mark 12:31 and parallels, with Jesus quoting Leviticus).

such actions only by dismissing the entire western tradition of civilized warfare that was originally born in the interior of that supreme compassion which always seeks if possible to wound none whom by his wounds Christ died to save. This theory of just and severely limited conflict has guided action and served as the regulative norm for military conduct for nineteen centuries. If one cannot irresponsibly forsake those who need to be saved from an oppressor, neither can one directly and indiscriminately attack innocent people in order to restrain that same oppressor. If to protect one's own children one should resist aggressors, that gives one no leave directly to intend and directly to do the death of the aggressors' children as a means of dissuading them from his evil deeds.

If the just war theory did not already exist, Christians would have to invent it. If in the fullness of God's time[15] and the emptiness of ours, Christ came into our present world (instead of when he did), then would the just war theory still have to be produced. Then would Christian thought bring together the notions of justice lying around in the Renaissance and the Enlightenment (if you can imagine these periods without their Christian background) as St. Augustine and other great Christian thinkers brought together the notions of justice lying around in the Greco-Roman world, galvanized them into action, elevated and firmed them up, illumined and sensitized human justice to produce severer restrictions upon the forms of human conflict which the Christian or any truly just person can ever believe justified. Had I the space I could derive the same moral restrictions upon the use of force from the ethical perspectives of the Old Testament. These would have been productive of a remarkably similar just war theory, had Judaism been the predominant influence in Western civilization.

I can only briefly indicate that this distinction between combatant and noncombatant never supposed that the latter were to be roped off ladies at a medieval tournament. The fact of twilight, as Dr. Johnson said, does not mean you cannot tell day from night—so with noncombatant status, and the difference between discriminant and indiscriminant acts of war.[16] Moreover, it was never supposed that noncombatants were immune from all damage but only from direct, intended attack. The range of indirect, unintended, collateral damage might be quite large. Moreover, closeness of civilian cooperation, in contrast to some degree of remoteness from the force used, was sufficient to bring the civilian under the category of "combatant." But these qualifications were never the same as "enlarging the target" to include the whole of civil society as a legitimate military objective, directly damaging whole peoples in order to get at their leaders and fighters. Translated into modern terminology, this means that just or limited warfare must be *forces*-counter-*forces* warfare, and that *people*-counter-*people* warfare is wholly unjust.

[15] Editors' note: This is an allusion to Eph 1:10.
[16] Editors' note: Samuel Johnson was an eighteenth-century author and is often quoted for his pithy sayings.

At stake in preserving this distinction is not only whether warfare can be kept barely civilized, but whether civilization can be kept from barbarism. Can civilization survive in the sense that we can continue in political and military affairs to *act civilized,* or must we accept total war on grounds that clearly indicate that we have already become *totalitarian*—by reducing everyone without discrimination and everyone to the whole extent of his being to a mere means of achieving political and military goals? Even if an enemy government says that is all its people are, a Christian or any truly just person cannot agree to this.

Now pacifism teaches people what massive deterrence is built on. It "teaches people to make no distinction between the shedding of innocent blood and the shedding of any human blood. And in this way pacifism has corrupted enormous numbers of people who will not act according to its tenets. They become convinced that a number of things are wicked which are not; hence, seeing no way of avoiding 'wickedness,' they set no limits to it."[17] That is to say, pacifism teaches people to believe that there is no *significant moral* difference, except in the *ends* sought, between murder and killing in war. It seems incredible to accept that anyone really seriously believes that soldiers are only "licensed murderers" and that murderers are only unlicensed soldiers. Yet, at the operational level where the thoughts of a multitude of human hearts shall today be revealed, this seems to be what it comes down to. The desperate attempt to maintain the current state of non-war by indiscriminately aiming weapons at people, and a fervent attempt to abolish war by declaring it in any shape to be a wickedness to which no moral limits can or should be applied, lie down peaceably together in the declaration by both parties that there is no moral economy that should or can govern the use of armed violence.

It has certainly to be admitted that all the wars of the past have been conducted more or less justly, more or less unjustly; but attacks on civilian life have been *peripheral* even if often carried out. In former ages it simply took too much muscle to fight war unlimitedly. You will understand the point on which present-day politics squirms, and military strategy squirms, if you see that in the nuclear age the nations are trying to make *unjust war* the *central war* and to *base* strategy on the deliberate aim of attacking cities. They will never succeed in basing politics or purposive military strategy on such an inherently irrational and immoral plan of war . . .

The traditional teaching about the conduct of war taught us that it is never right to intend or do wrong that good may come of it. Nuclear weapons have only added to this perennial truth a morally insignificant footnote: it can never do *any good* to intend or do wrong that good may come of it.

---

[17] Walter Stein, ed.: *Nuclear Weapons and Christian Conscience* (London: Merlin Press 1961) 56.

7. Martin Luuther King Jr., "Letter from Birmingham City Jail"

Martin Luther King wrote this treatise imprisoned in the Birmingham, Al-abama, city jail, charged with leading a public demonstration without a per-mit. King, the leader of the Southern Christian Leadership Conference, came to Birmingham to direct a bus boycott protesting segregation on public trans-portation. King's treatise is a response to an open letter written by eight white religious leaders from Alabama. While not attacking the cause of integration it-self, these leaders criticized King as an "outside agitator" and cautioned that the pace of social change must be slow and deliberate. Their letter hurt King profoundly, for he had hoped that the moderate churches eventually would support the cause of civil rights. The erudite tone of the public letter—in stark contrast to the vulgar racism he normally encountered—also provoked King to compose a learned response of his own. By the time he set down his pen, King had crafted a systematic theological defense of the civil rights movement. King's letter is instructive on many levels. It is a careful reflective use of all four sources of Christian ethics, it is a profound statement on the relationship of love and justice, and it is a classic statement on non-violent social change.

April 16, 1963

MY DEAR FELLOW CLERGYMEN:

While[18] confined here in the Birmingham city jail, I came across your re-cent statement calling my present activities "unwise and untimely." Seldom do I pause to answer criticism of my work and ideas. If I sought to answer all the criticisms that cross my desk, my secretaries would have little time for any-thing other than such correspondence in the course of the day, and I would have no time for constructive work. But since I feel that you are men of genu-ine good will and that your criticisms are sincerely set forth, I want to try to answer your statements in what I hope will be patient and reasonable terms.

I think I should indicate why I am here In Birmingham, since you have been influenced by the view which argues against "outsiders coming in." I

---

[18] Reprinted by arrangement with the Estate of Martin Luther King Jr., c/o Writers House as agent for the proprietor, New York, NY. Copyright 1963 Martin Luther King, Jr., copyright re-newed 1991 Coretta Scott King.* Annotation of Martin Luther King Jr.: "This response to a pub-lished statement by eight fellow clergymen from Alabama (Bishop C. C. J. Carpenter, Bishop Joseph A. Durick, Rabbi Hilton L. Grafman, Bishop Paul Hardin, Bishop Nolan B. Harmon, the Reverend George M. Murray. the Reverend Edward V. Ramage and the Reverend Earl Stallings) was composed under somewhat constricting circumstance. Begun on the margins of the newspaper in which the statement appeared while I was in jail, the letter was continued on scraps of writing paper supplied by a friendly Negro trusty, and concluded on a pad my attorneys were eventually permitted to leave me. Although the text remains in substance unaltered, I have indulged in the au-thor's prerogative of polishing it for publication." *It is not adapted for inclusive language.

have the honor of serving as president of the Southern Christian Leadership Conference, an organization operating in every southern state, with headquarters in Atlanta, Georgia. We have some eighty-five affiliated organizations across the South, and one of them is the Alabama Christian Movement for Human Rights. Frequently we share staff, educational and financial resources with our affiliates. Several months ago the affiliate here in Birmingham asked us to be on call to engage in a nonviolent direct-action program if such were deemed necessary. We readily consented, and when the hour came we lived up to our promise. So I, along with several members of my staff, am here because I was invited here. I am here because I have organizational ties here.

But more basically, I am in Birmingham because injustice is here. Just as the prophets of the eighth century B.C. left their villages and carried their "thus saith the Lord" far beyond the boundaries of their home towns, and just as the Apostle Paul left his village of Tarsus and carried the gospel of Jesus Christ to the far corners of the Greco-Roman world, so am I compelled to carry the gospel of freedom beyond my own home town. Like Paul, I must constantly respond to the Macedonian call for aid.

Moreover, I am cognizant of the interrelatedness of all communities and states. I cannot sit idly by in Atlanta and not be concerned about what happens in Birmingham. Injustice anywhere is a threat to justice everywhere. We are caught in an inescapable network of mutuality, tied in a single garment of destiny. Whatever affects one directly, affects all indirectly. Never again can we afford to live with the narrow, provincial "outside agitator" idea. Anyone who lives inside the United States can never be considered an outsider anywhere within its bounds.

You deplore the demonstrations taking place in Birmingham. But your statement, I am sorry to say, fails to express a similar concern for the conditions that brought about the demonstrations. I am sure that none of you would want to rest content with the superficial kind of social analysis that deals merely with effects and does not grapple with underlying causes. It is unfortunate that demonstrations are taking place in Birmingham, but it is even more unfortunate that the city's white power structure left the Negro community with no alternative.

In any nonviolent campaign there are four basic steps: collection of the facts to determine whether injustices exist; negotiation; self-purification; and direct action. We have gone through all these steps in Birmingham. There can be no gainsaying the fact that racial injustice engulfs this community. Birmingham is probably the most thoroughly segregated city in the United States. Its ugly record of brutality is widely known. Negroes have experienced grossly unjust treatment in the courts. There have been more unsolved bombings of Negro homes and churches in Birmingham than in any other city in the nation. These are the hard, brutal facts of the case. On the basis of these conditions, Negro leaders sought to negotiate with the city fathers. But the latter consistently refused to engage in good-faith negotiation.

Then, last September, came the opportunity to talk with leaders of Birmingham's economic community. In the course of the negotiations, certain promises were made by the merchants—for example, to remove the stores humiliating racial signs. On the basis of these promises, the Reverend Fred Shuttlesworth and the leaders of the Alabama Christian Movement for Human Rights agreed to a moratorium on all demonstrations. As the weeks and months went by, we realized that we were the victims of a broken promise. A few signs, briefly removed, returned; the others remained.

As in so many past experiences, our hopes had been blasted, and the shadow of deep disappointment settled upon us. We had no alternative except to prepare for direct action, whereby we would present our very bodies as a means of laying our case before the conscience of the local and the national community. Mindful of the difficulties involved, we decided to undertake a process of self-purification. We began a series of workshops on nonviolence, and we repeatedly asked ourselves: "Are you able to accept blows without retaliating?" "Are you able to endure the ordeal of jail?" We decided to schedule our direct-action program for the Easter season, realizing that except for Christmas, this is the main shopping period of the year. Knowing that a strong economic withdrawal program would be the by-product of direct action, we felt that this would be the best time to bring pressure to bear on the merchants for the needed change.

Then it occurred to us that Birmingham's mayoralty election was coming up in March, and we speedily decided to postpone action until after election day. When we discovered that the Commissioner of Public Safety, Eugene "Bull" Connor, had piled up enough votes to be in the run-off we decided again to postpone action until the day after the run-off so that the demonstrations could not be used to cloud the issues. Like many others, we waited to see Mr. Connor defeated, and to this end we endured postponement after postponement. Having aided in this community need, we felt that our direct-action program could be delayed no longer.

You may well ask: "Why direct action? Why sit-ins, marches and so forth? Isn't negotiation a better path?" You are quite right in calling for negotiation. Indeed, this is the very purpose of direct action. Nonviolent direct action seeks to create such a crisis and foster such a tension that a community which has constantly refused to negotiate is forced to confront the issue. It seeks so to dramatize the issue that it can no longer be ignored. My citing the creation of tension as part of the work of the nonviolent-resister may sound rather shocking. But I must confess that I am not afraid of the word "tension." I have earnestly opposed violent tension, but there is a type of constructive, nonviolent tension which is necessary for growth. Just as Socrates felt that it was necessary to create a tension in the mind so that individuals could rise from the bondage of myths and half-truths to the unfettered realm of creative analysis and objective appraisal, we must see the need for nonviolent gadflies to create the kind of tension in society that will help men rise from the dark depths of prejudice and racism to the majestic heights of understanding and brotherhood.

The purpose of our direct-action program is to create a situation so crisis-packed that it will inevitably open the door to negotiation. I therefore concur with you in your call for negotiation. Too long has our beloved Southland been bogged down in a tragic effort to live in monologue rather than dialogue.

One of the basic points in your statement is that the action that I and my associates have taken in Birmingham is untimely. Some have asked: "Why didn't you give the new city administration time to act?" The only answer that I can give to this query is that the new Birmingham administration must be prodded about as much as the outgoing one, before it will act. We are sadly mistaken if we feel that the election of Albert Boutwell as mayor will bring the millennium to Birmingham. While Mr. Boutwell is a much more gentle person than Mr. Connor, they are both segregationists, dedicated to maintenance of the status quo. I have hope that Mr. Boutwell will be reasonable enough to see the futility of massive resistance to desegregation. But he will not see this without pressure from devotees of civil rights. My friends, I must say to you that we have not made a single gain in civil rights without determined legal and non-violent pressure. Lamentably, it is an historical fact that privileged groups seldom give up their privileges voluntarily. Individuals may see the moral light and voluntarily give up their unjust posture; but, as Reinhold Niebuhr has reminded us, groups tend to be more immoral than individuals.

We know through painful experience that freedom is never voluntarily given by the oppressor; it must be demanded by the oppressed. Frankly, I have yet to engage in a direct-action campaign that was "well timed" in the view of those who have not suffered unduly from the disease of segregation. For years now I have heard the word "Wait!" It rings in the ear of every Negro with piercing familiarity. This "Wait" has almost always meant 'Never." We must come to see, with one of our distinguished jurists, that "justice too long delayed is justice denied."

We have waited for more than 340 years for our constitutional and God-given rights. The nations of Asia and Africa are moving with jetlike speed toward gaining political independence, but we still creep at horse-and-buggy pace toward gaining a cup of coffee at a lunch counter. Perhaps it is easy for those who have never felt the stinging dart of segregation to say, "Wait." But when you have seen vicious mobs lynch your mothers and fathers at will and drown your sisters and brothers at whim; when you have seen hate-filled policemen curse, kick and even kill your black brothers and sisters; when you see the vast majority of your twenty million Negro brothers smothering in an airtight cage of poverty in the midst of an affluent society; when you suddenly find your tongue twisted and your speech stammering as you seek to explain to your six-year-old daughter why she can't go to the public amusement park that has just been advertised on television, and see tears welling up in her eyes when she is told that Funtown is closed to colored children, and see ominous clouds of inferiority beginning to form in her little mental sky, and see her beginning to distort her personality by developing an unconscious bitterness toward white people; when you have to concoct an answer for a five-year-old son who is asking: "Daddy, why do white people treat colored people so mean?"; when you take a cross-county drive and find it necessary to sleep night after night in the uncomfortable corners of your automobile because no motel will accept you; when you are humiliated day in and day out by nagging signs reading "white" and "colored"; when your first name becomes "nigger," your middle name becomes "boy" (however old you are) and your last name becomes "John," and your wife and mother are never given the respected title "Mrs."; when you are harried by day and haunted by night by the fact that you are a Negro, living constantly at tiptoe stance, never quite knowing what to expect next, and are plagued with inner fears and outer resentments; when you know forever fighting a degenerating sense of "nobodiness," then you will understand why we find it difficult to wait. There comes a time when the cup of endurance runs over, and men are no longer willing to be plunged into the abyss of despair. I hope, sirs, you can understand our legitimate and unavoidable impatience.

You express a great deal of anxiety over our willingness to break laws. This is certainly a legitimate concern. Since we so diligently urge people to obey the Supreme Court's decision of 1954 outlawing segregation in the public schools, at first glance it may seem rather paradoxical for us consciously to break laws. One may well ask: "How can you advocate breaking some laws and obeying others?" The answer lies in the fact that there are two types of laws: just and unjust. I would be the last to advocate disobeying just laws. One has not only a legal but a moral responsibility to obey just laws. Conversely, one has a moral responsibility to disobey unjust laws. I would agree with St. Augustine that "an unjust law is no law at all" [*De lib. arb.* On Free Will 1.5].

Now, what is the difference between the two? How does one determine whether a law is just or unjust? A just law is a human-made code that squares with the moral law or the law of God. An unjust law is a code that is out of harmony with the moral law. To put it in the terms of St. Thomas Aquinas: An unjust law is a human law that is not rooted in eternal law and natural law.[19] Any law that uplifts human personality is just. Any law that degrades human personality is unjust. All segregation statutes are unjust because segregation distorts the soul and damages the personality. It gives the segregator a false sense of superiority and the segregated a false sense of inferiority. Segrega-

---

[19] Thomas Aquinas, Summa Theologiae, translated by the Fathers of the English Dominican Province under the title *Summa Theologica* (New York: Benzinger Brothers, 1948) I-II 95.2 See page 52 of this text.

tion, to use the terminology of the Jewish philosopher Martin Buber,[20] substitutes an "I-it" relationship for an "I-thou" relationship and ends up relegating persons to the status of things. Hence segregation is not only politically, economically and sociologically unsound, it is morally wrong and awful. Paul Tillich said that sin is separation. Is not segregation an existential expression of humankind's tragic separation, our awful estrangement, our terrible sinfulness? Thus it is that I can urge men to obey the 1954 decision of the Supreme Court, for it is morally right; and I can urge them to disobey segregation ordinances, for they are morally wrong.

Let us consider a more concrete example of just and unjust laws. An unjust law is a code that a numerical or power majority group compels a minority group to obey but does not make binding on itself. This is difference made legal. By the same token, a just law is a code that a majority compels a minority to follow and that it is willing to follow itself. This is sameness made legal.

Let me give another explanation. A law is unjust if it is inflicted on a minority that, as a result of being denied the right to vote, had no part in enacting or devising the law. Who can say that the legislature of Alabama which set up that state's segregation laws was democratically elected? Throughout Alabama all sorts of devious methods are used to prevent Negroes from becoming registered voters, and there are some counties in which, even though Negroes constitute a majority of the population, not a single Negro is registered. Can any law enacted under such circumstances be considered democratically structured?

Sometimes a law is just on its face and unjust in its application. For instance, I have been arrested on a charge of parading without a permit. Now, there is nothing wrong in having an ordinance which requires a permit for a parade. But such an ordinance becomes unjust when it is used to maintain segregation and to deny citizens the First Amendment privilege of peaceful assembly and protest.

I hope you are able to see the distinction I am trying to point out. In no sense do I advocate evading or defying the law, as would the rabid segregationist. That would lead to anarchy. One who breaks an unjust law must do so openly, lovingly, and with a willingness to accept the penalty. I submit that an individual who breaks a law that conscience tells him is unjust and who willingly accepts the penalty of imprisonment in order to arouse the conscience of the community over its injustice, is in reality expressing the highest respect for law.

Of course, there is nothing new about this kind of civil disobedience. It was evidenced sublimely in the refusal of Shadrach, Meshach and Abednego to obey the laws of Nebuchadnezzar, on the ground that a higher moral law was at

---

[20] Editors' note: Buber was famous for the book: *I and Thou*. One (second) edition is: Trans. Ronald Gregor Smith (New York: Scribner, 1958).

stake.[21] It was practiced superbly by the early Christians, who were willing to face hungry lions and the excruciating pain of chopping blocks rather than submit to certain unjust laws of the Roman Empire. To a degree, academic freedom is a reality today because Socrates practiced civil disobedience. In our own nation, the Boston Tea Party represented a massive act of civil disobedience.

We should never forget that everything Adolf Hitler did in Germany was "legal" and everything the Hungarian freedom fighters did in Hungary was "illegal." It was "illegal" to aid and comfort a Jew in Hitler's Germany. Even so, I am sure that, had I lived in Germany at the time, I would have aided and comforted my Jewish brothers. If today I lived in a Communist country where certain principles dear to the Christian faith are suppressed, I would openly advocate disobeying that country's antireligious laws.

I must make two honest confessions to you, my Christian and Jewish brothers and sisters. First, I must confess that over the past few years I have been gravely disappointed with the white moderate. I have almost reached the regrettable conclusion that the Negro's great stumbling block in his stride toward freedom is not the White Citizen's Counciler or the Ku Klux Klanner, but the white moderate, who is more devoted to "order" than to justice; who prefers a negative peace which is the absence of tension to a positive peace which is the presence of justice; who constantly says: "I agree with you in the goal you seek, but I cannot agree with your methods of direct action"; who paternalistically believes he can set the timetable for another man's freedom; who lives by a mythical concept of time and who constantly advises the Negro to wait for a "more convenient season." Shallow understanding from people of good will is more frustrating than absolute misunderstanding from people of ill will. Lukewarm acceptance is much more bewildering than outright rejection . . .

In your statement you assert that our actions, even though peaceful, must be condemned because they precipitate violence. But is this a logical assertion? Isn't this like condemning a robbed person because his or her possession of money precipitated the evil act of robbery? Isn't this like condemning Socrates because his unswerving commitment to truth and his philosophical inquiries precipitated the act by the misguided populace in which they made him drink hemlock? Isn't this like condemning Jesus because his unique God-consciousness and never-ceasing devotion to God's will precipitated the evil act of crucifixion? We must come to see that, as the federal courts have consistently affirmed, it is wrong to urge an individual to cease his efforts to gain his basic constitutional rights because the quest may precipitate violence. Society must protect the robbed and punish the robber.

I had also hoped that the white moderate would reject the myth concerning time in relation to the struggle for freedom. I have just received a letter from a

---

[21] Editors' note: See Dan 3.

white brother in Texas. He writes: "All Christians know that the colored people will receive equal rights eventually, but it is possible that you are in too great a religious hurry. It has taken Christianity almost two thousand years to accomplish what it has. The teachings of Christ take time to come to earth." Such an attitude stems from a tragic misconception of time, from the strangely rational notion that there is something in the very flow of time that will inevitably cure all ills. Actually, time itself is neutral; it can be used either destructively or constructively. More and more I feel that the people of ill will have used time much more effectively than have the people of good will. We will have to repent in this generation not merely for the hateful words and actions of the bad people but for the appalling silence of the good people. Human progress never rolls in on wheels of inevitability; it comes through the tireless efforts of men willing to be co-workers with God, and without this hard work, time itself becomes an ally of the forces of social stagnation. We must use time creatively, in the knowledge that the time is always ripe to do right. Now is the time to make real the promise of democracy and transform our pending national elegy into a creative psalm of brotherhood. Now is the time to lift our national policy from the quicksand of racial injustice to the solid rock of human dignity.

You speak of our activity in Birmingham as extreme. At fist I was rather disappointed that fellow clergymen would see my nonviolent efforts as those of an extremist. I began thinking about the facts that stand in the middle of two opposing forces in the Negro community. One is a force of complacency, made up in part of Negroes who, as a result of long years of oppression, are so drained of self-respect and a sense of "somebodiness" that they have adjusted to segregation; and in part of a few middle class Negroes who, because of a degree of academic and economic security and because in some ways they profit by segregation, have become insensitive to the problems of the masses. The other force is one of bitterness and hatred, and it comes perilously close to advocating violence. It is expressed in the various black nationalist groups that are springing up across the nation, the largest and best-known being Elijah Muhammad's Muslim movement. Nourished by the Negro's frustration over the continued existence of racial discrimination, this movement is made up of people who have lost faith in America, who have absolutely repudiated Christianity, and who have concluded that the white man is an incorrigible "devil."

I have tried to stand between these two forces, saying that we need emulate neither the "do-nothingism" of the complacent nor the hatred and despair of the black nationalist. For there is the more excellent way of love and nonviolent protest. I am grateful to God that, through the influence of the Negro church, the way of nonviolence became an integral part of our struggle.

If this philosophy had not emerged, by now many streets of the South would, I am convinced, be flowing with blood. And I am further convinced that if our white brothers dismiss as "rabble-rousers" and "outside agitators" those of us who employ nonviolent direct action, and if they refuse to support our nonviolent efforts, millions of Negroes will, out of frustration and despair, seek solace and security in black-nationalist ideologies a development that would inevitably lead to a frightening racial nightmare.

Oppressed people cannot remain oppressed forever. The yearning for freedom eventually manifests itself, and that is what has happened to the American Negro. Something within has reminded him of his birthright of freedom, and something without has reminded him that it can be gained. Consciously or unconsciously, he has been caught up by the Zeitgeist (spirit of the times), and with his black brothers and sisters of Africa and his brown and yellow brothers and sisters of Asia, South America and the Caribbean, the United States Negro is moving with a sense of great urgency toward the promised land of racial justice. If one recognizes this vital urge that has engulfed the Negro community, one should readily understand why public demonstrations are taking place. The Negro has many pent-up resentments and latent frustrations, and he must release them. So let them march; let them make prayer pilgrimages to the city hall; let them go on freedom rides—and try to understand why they must do so. If their repressed emotions are not released in nonviolent ways, they will seek expression through violence; this is not a threat but a fact of history. So I have not said to my people: "Get rid of your discontent." Rather, I have tried to say that this normal and healthy discontent can be channeled into the creative outlet of nonviolent direct action. And now this approach is being termed extremist.

But though I was initially disappointed at being categorized as an extremist, as I continued to think about the matter I gradually gained a measure of satisfaction from the label. Was not Jesus an extremist for love: "Love your enemies, bless them that curse you, do good to them that hate you, and pray for them which despitefully use you, and persecute you" [Matt 5:44] Was not Amos an extremist for justice: "Let justice roll down like waters and righteousness like an ever-flowing stream" [Amos 5:24].[22] Was not Paul an extremist for the Christian gospel: "I bear in my body the marks of the Lord Jesus" [Gal 6:17].[23] Was not Martin Luther an extremist: "Here I stand; I cannot do otherwise, so help me God." And John Bunyan: "I will stay in jail to the end of my days before I make a butchery of my conscience." And Abraham Lincoln: "This nation cannot survive half slave and half free." And Thomas Jefferson: "We hold these truths to be self-evident, that all men are created equal . . . " [Declaration of Independence]. So the question is not whether we will be extremists, but what kind of extremists we will be. Will we be extremists for hate or for love? Will we be extremists for the preservation of injustice or for the extension of justice? In that dramatic scene on Cal-

---

[22] Editors' note: Corresponds with the New American Standard Bible translation, available at http://www.biblegateway.com (accessed September 18. 2004).

[23] Editors' note: Corresponds with the King James Version of the Bible translation, available at http://www.biblegateway.com (accessed September 18. 2004).

vary's hill three men were crucified. We must never forget that all three were crucified for the same crime—the crime of extremism. Two were extremists for immorality, and thus fell below their environment. The other, Jesus Christ, was an extremist for love, truth and goodness, and thereby rose above his environment. Perhaps the South, the nation and the world are in dire need of creative extremists . . .

Let me take note of my other major disappointment. I have been so greatly disappointed with the white church and its leadership. Of course, there are some notable exceptions. I am not unmindful of the fact that each of you has taken some significant stands on this issue. I commend you, Reverend Stallings, for your Christian stand on this past Sunday, in welcoming Negroes to your worship service on a non-segregated basis. I commend the Catholic leaders of this state for integrating Spring Hill College several years ago.

But despite these notable exceptions, I must honestly reiterate that I have been disappointed with the church. I do not say this as one of those negative critics who can always find something wrong with the church. I say this as a minister of the gospel, who loves the church; who was nurtured in its bosom; who has been sustained by its spiritual blessings and who will remain true to it as long as the cord of life shall lengthen.

When I was suddenly catapulted into the leadership of the bus protest in Montgomery, Alabama, a few years ago, I felt we would be supported by the white church. I felt that the white ministers, priests and rabbis of the South would be among our strongest allies. Instead, some have been outright opponents, refusing to understand the freedom movement and misrepresenting its leadership; all too many others have been more cautious than courageous and have remained silent behind the anesthetizing security of stained-glass windows. . .

I have heard numerous southern religious leaders admonish their worshipers to comply with a desegregation decision because it is the law, but I have longed to hear white ministers declare: "Follow this decree because integration is morally right and because Negroes are your brothers and sisters." In the midst of blatant injustices inflicted upon the Negro, I have watched white church people stand on the sideline and mouth pious irrelevancies and sanctimonious trivialities. In the midst of a mighty struggle to rid our nation of racial and economic injustice, I have heard many ministers say: "Those are social issues, with which the gospel has no real concern." And I have watched many churches commit themselves to a completely other worldly religion which makes a stranger, unbiblical distinction between body and soul, between the sacred and the secular.

I have traveled the length and breadth of Alabama, Mississippi and all the other southern states. On sweltering summer days and crisp autumn mornings I have looked at the South's beautiful churches with their lofty spires pointing heavenward. I have beheld the impressive outlines of her massive religious-education buildings. Over and over I have found myself asking: "What kind of people worship here? Who is their God? Where were their voices when the lips of Governor Barnett dripped with words of interposition and nullification? Where were they when Governor Wallace gave a clarion call for defiance and hatred? Where were their voices of support when bruised and weary Negro men and women decided to rise from the dark dungeons of complacency to the bright hills of creative protest?"

Yes, these questions are still in my mind. In deep disappointment I have wept over the laxity of the church. But be assured that my tears have been tears of love. There can be no deep disappointment where there is not deep love. Yes, I love the church. How could I do otherwise? I am in the rather unique position of being the son, the grandson and the great-grandson of preachers. Yes, I see the church as the body of Christ [1 Cor 12:27]. But, oh! How we have blemished and scarred that body through social neglect and through fear of being nonconformists.

There was a time when the church was very powerful. It was during that period when the early Christians rejoiced at being deemed worthy to suffer for what they believed. In those days the church was not merely a thermometer that recorded the ideas and principles of popular opinion; it was a thermostat that transformed the mores of society. Whenever the early Christians entered a town, the people in power became disturbed and immediately sought to convict the Christians for being "disturbers of the peace" and "outside agitators"' But the Christians pressed on, in the conviction that they were "a colony of heaven," [see Phil 3:20] called to obey God rather than humans [see Acts 5:29]. Small in number, they were big in commitment. They were too God intoxicated to be "astronomically intimidated." By their effort and example they brought an end to such ancient evils as infanticide and gladiatorial contests.

Things are different now. So often the contemporary church is a weak, ineffectual voice with an uncertain sound. So often it is an archdefender of the status quo. Far from being disturbed by the presence of the church, the power structure of the average community is consoled by the church's silent and often even vocal sanction of things as they are.

But the judgment of God is upon the church as never before. If today's church does not recapture the sacrificial spirit of the early church, it will lose its authenticity, forfeit the loyalty of millions, and be dismissed as an irrelevant social club with no meaning for the twentieth century. Every day I meet young people whose disappointment with the church has turned into outright disgust.

Perhaps I have once again been too optimistic. Is organized religion too inextricably bound to the status quo to save our nation and the world? Perhaps I must turn my faith to the inner spiritual church, the church within the church, as the true *ekklesia* and the hope of the world. But again I am thankful to God that some noble souls from the ranks of organized religion have broken loose from the paralyzing chains of conformity and joined us as active partners in the struggle for freedom. They have left their secure congregations and walked the streets of Albany, Georgia, with us. They have gone down the highways of the South on tortuous rides for freedom. Yes, they have gone to jail with us. Some have been dismissed from their churches, have lost the support of their bishops and fellow ministers. But they have acted in the faith that right defeated is stronger than evil triumphant. Their witness has been the spiritual salt [see Matt 5:13; Luke 14:34] that has preserved the true meaning of the gospel in these troubled times. They have carved a tunnel of hope through the dark mountain of disappointment.

I hope the church as a whole will meet the challenge of this decisive hour. But even if the church does not come to the aid of justice, I have no despair about the future. I have no fear about the outcome of our struggle in Birmingham, even if our motives are at present misunderstood. We will reach the goal of freedom in Birmingham, and all over the nation, because the goal of America is freedom. Abused and scorned though we may be, our destiny is tied up with America's destiny. Before the pilgrims landed at Plymouth, we were here. Before the pen of Jefferson etched the majestic words of the Declaration of Independence across the pages of history, we were here. For more than two centuries our forebears labored in this country without wages; they made cotton king; they built the homes of their masters while suffering gross injustice and shameful humiliation—and yet out of a bottomless vitality they continued to thrive and develop. If the inexpressible cruelties of slavery could not stop us, the opposition we now face will surely fail. We will win our freedom because the sacred heritage of our nation and the eternal will of God are embodied in our echoing demands.

Before closing I feel impelled to mention one other point in your statement that has troubled me profoundly. You warmly commended the Birmingham police force for keeping "order" and "preventing violence." I doubt that you would have so warmly commended the police force if you had seen its dogs sinking their teeth into unarmed, nonviolent Negroes. I doubt that you would so quickly commend the police if you were to observe their ugly and inhumane treatment of Negroes here in the city jail; if you were to watch them push and curse old Negro women and young Negro girls; if you were to see them slap and kick old Negro men and young boys; if you were to observe them, as they did on two occasions, refuse to give us food because we wanted to sing our grace together. I cannot join you in your praise of the Birmingham police department.

It is true that the police have exercised a degree of discipline in handling the demonstrators. In this sense they have conducted themselves rather "nonviolently" in public. But for what purpose? To preserve the evil system of segregation. Over the past few years I have consistently preached that nonviolence demands that the means we use must be as pure as the ends we seek. I have tried to make clear that it is wrong to use immoral means to attain moral ends. But now I must affirm that it is just as wrong, or perhaps even more so, to use moral means to preserve immoral ends. Perhaps Mr. Connor and his policemen have been rather nonviolent in public, as was Chief Pritchett in Albany, Georgia but they have used the moral means of nonviolence to maintain the immoral end of racial injustice. As T. S. Eliot has said: "The last temptation is the greatest treason: To do the right deed for the wrong reason."

I wish you had commended the Negro sit-inners and demonstrators of Birmingham for their sublime courage, their willingness to suffer and their amazing discipline in the midst of great provocation. One day the South will recognize its real heroes. They will be the James Merediths, with the noble sense of purpose that enables them to face jeering, and hostile mobs, and with the agonizing loneliness that characterizes the life of the pioneer. They will be old, oppressed, battered Negro women, symbolized in a seventy-two-year-old woman in Montgomery, Alabama, who rose up with a sense of dignity and with her people decided not to ride segregated buses, and who responded with ungrammatical profundity to one who inquired about her weariness: "My feets is tired, but my soul is at rest." They will be the young high school and college students, the young ministers of the gospel and a host of their elders, courageously and nonviolently sitting in at lunch counters and willingly going to jail for conscience's sake. One day the South will know that when these disinherited children of God sat down at lunch counters, they were in reality standing up for what is best in the American dream and for the most sacred values in our Judaeo-Christian heritage, thereby bringing our nation back to those great wells of democracy which were dug deep by the founders in their formulation of the Constitution and the Declaration of Independence.

Never before have I written so long a letter. I'm afraid it is much too long to take your precious time. I can assure you that it would have been much shorter if I had been writing from a comfortable desk, but what else can one do when he is alone in a narrow jail cell, other than write long letters, think long thoughts and pray long prayers?

If I have said anything in this letter that overstates the truth and indicates an unreasonable impatience, I beg you to forgive me. If I have said anything that understates the truth and indicates my having a patience that allows me to settle for anything less than brotherhood, I beg God to forgive me.

I hope this letter finds you strong in the faith. I also hope that circumstances will soon make it possible for me to meet each of you, not as an integrationist or a civil rights leader but as a fellow clergyman and a Christian brother. Let us all hope that the dark clouds of racial prejudice will soon pass away and the deep fog of misunderstanding will be lifted from our fear-drenched communities, and in some not too distant tomorrow the radiant stars of love and brotherhood will shine over our great nation with all their scintillating beauty.

Yours for the cause of Peace and Brotherhood,
MARTIN LUTHER KING, JR.

Chapter Six

Stewardship:
Work, Property, and the Environment

This chapter addresses the issues of economic justice and the environment in Christian ethics. These two areas, often treated separately in ethical analysis, are connected through the Judeo-Christian understanding of stewardship. Etymologically, both "economy" and "ecology" originate in the Greek noun, *oikos,* which means "household." Thus, the term "economics" connotes the laws or rules for household management, while the term "ecology" connotes a study of the greater common "household" of the biosphere. Both sciences are concerned with proper use of the world's resources so that we create a life that is good for human beings and sustainable for the natural world. In the biblical world, a manager of household resources was called a steward. In most cases, he was a servant who was charged with the duty to administer the estate of his master. True stewardship, then, begins with the awareness that human beings are not simply creatures like all other beings on the earth, but are called to a role of active, purposeful activity. On the other hand, the concept of stewardship also reminds us that the world is not ours to dispose of as we wish; rather, in all our actions, we are responsible to the world's maker, God, whose purposes are larger than our own.

In our treatment of justice in chapter 3, we found that economic justice is one of the great themes of the Bible. (Readers are encouraged to review this section now.) We found that biblical justice is rooted in covenant. The great prophets never let Israel forget that it had a special obligation to care especially for the weak and vulnerable. This vision continued in the New Testament: in Jesus' special ministry to the sick and outcast, in the communal sharing of property in the first church in Jerusalem, and in the dream of a future kingdom of God characterized by justice and peace. This central biblical vision shapes the contours of a broad Christian approach to economic life and ecology. In the remainder of this essay, we will indicate some implications for these narrower issues: work and vocation, property, economic systems, distributive justice and the problem of poverty, and ecological ethics.

Work and Vocation

The biblical creation stories picture an exalted role for human beings in the created order. In Genesis 1, the first story, human beings reveal that they are stamped with the "image of God" (v. 27) as they fulfill their creative governance of the earth that God has made. The second creation story in Genesis 2–3 pictures the original paradise not as an ethereal land above the clouds where disembodied souls flit about plucking harps, but as a garden that requires constant labor. The garden is idyllic because the work is productive and life-giving, and the first man and woman are satisfied with its produce. Paradise does not last, however. As the story continues, human beings usurp the authority of God and take what is not theirs. The story suggests that human sinfulness distorts the world of work, creating the chronic problems of shortage, oppression, and alienating work. Together these two creation stories suggest that human beings need creative, productive work to be fulfilled, but also that we rarely create for ourselves a social world that lives up to that vision.

The Christian moral tradition recognizes the fulfilling possibilities of work in the concept of *vocation*. Originally the term applied only to the "calling" to a life of religious service. Martin Luther broadened vocation to embrace all walks of life. In his mind, Christians are called to fulfill their callings not by separating ourselves from society but by serving God and neighbor in and through the social roles in which we find ourselves. Luther lived at the end of the Medieval Era, when most persons inherited roles but could not choose them. The concept of vocation was considerably advanced by the Puritans in the seventeenth century, who were the first to believe that a fulfilling vocation must be sought out rather than simply inherited. Any career or social role might serve as a vocation, provided that this "special calling" is consistent with the "general calling" to live out the Christian life. John Wesley's sermon *On the Use of Money* (reading 3) reflects this understanding of vocation. He urges his followers to "gain all you can" through honest industry, provided that they do nothing to harm the bodies or souls of themselves or their neighbors.

The centrality of meaningful work to human life also is affirmed in Catholic social teachings. Consistent themes in this tradition are calls for full employment, the eradication of degrading work, and the payment of a fair wage. Consequently, Catholic social teachings tend to lend stalwart support to the labor movement.

Property

John Locke defined the essential rights in a just society as life, liberty, and property. Liberal societies have seen these freedoms as linked, so that citizens cannot guarantee their lives and basic liberties without securing a right to private property. Property rights include the authority to use property as one sees fit, profit through a property's purchase and resale, and pass property along to one's heirs. While liberal theorists recognize that property rights are not absolute, they tend to look with deep suspicion on any scheme to curtail rights to one's property or to redistribute property to achieve some sort of egalitarian "end state."[1]

The Judeo-Christian tradition affirms private property but rejects some of liberalism's maximalist interpretations of property rights. The Hebrew Scriptures often see wealth as a blessing and as a reward for faithfulness. The Decalogue also protects personal property in its admonitions not to steal and not to covert the neighbor's house, wife, servants, or livestock (Exod 20:17). Nevertheless, the Bible also is clear that God alone is the Maker and Owner of all things: "The earth is the LORD'S and all that is in it / the world and those who live in it" (Ps 24:1). Because human beings only hold property in trust, we are obligated to give freely when our neighbor is in need. Concerns about the corrupting influence of wealth predominate in the teachings of Jesus: Jesus himself rejects settled family life and calls on his followers to do the same (for example, Mark 10:23-31; Luke 9:57-62). He confronts his disciples with a stark choice: "You cannot serve God and wealth" (Matt 6:24; Luke 16:13). To summarize, the Bible sees wealth not only as blessing, but also as "peril and obligation."[2]

The ambiguity of wealth and property in the Christian tradition is clearly visible in the readings in this chapter from Thomas Aquinas (reading 2) and John Wesley (reading 3). Aquinas' position on property reflects his medieval milieu. He roots his social thought in the belief that human beings are naturally social animals and that the central aim of social life is the common good. He concludes, then, that in the *use* of property, individuals must share freely with those in need. However, Aquinas also believes that procurement and management of private property is consistent with reason, for we tend to take better care of responsibilities that are dear to us than those that are distant. John Wesley's ministry in eighteenth-century England coincided with the beginnings of the Industrial Revolution and the rise of economic liberalism. His sermon *On the Use of Money* sets forth a rigorous scrutiny of personal economic life, though his admonitions reflect a concern for personal piety more than Aquinas' concern for the common good.

Christian Ethics and Economic Systems

The writers of the Bible assume an agrarian economy and trade based on barter and personal exchange. Its vision for economic life predates the rise of modern economic systems and even the development of economics as a social

---

[1] For a classic exposition of this argument, see Robert Nozick, *Anarchy, State, and Utopia* (New York: Basic Books, 1974).

[2] This memorable phrase is from Sondra Ely Wheeler, *Wealth as Peril and Obligation: The New Testament on Possessions* (Grand Rapids, Mich.: Wm. B. Eerdmans, 1995).

science. Thus, while the Bible has a great deal to say about property, justice, and wealth, modern Christians must find ways to apply these convictions to a world that is very different. One consequence of the Bible's cultural distance is that Christians are free to critique *all* economic structures and systems from the standpoint of faith. There is *no* Christian economic system but only systems that more or less reflect core biblical values.

The modern world has produced two major economic systems, capitalism and socialism, which were locked in a bitter struggle for much of the twentieth century. Capitalism is built on a few key institutions: the ownership of private property, competition in the marketplace for the production and sale of goods and services, and free enterprise with a minimum of government intrusions in the market. The state is to intervene only to protect property, enforce contracts, and break up monopolies that stifle competition. Capitalism also presupposes a particular moral vision. It assumes that human beings are rational creatures who will pursue their self-interest. It values individual autonomy and the commensurate virtues of personal responsibility, thrift, and honesty. Socialism, on the other hand, sees a more activist state that sets an overall vision for the community, builds consensus, and ensures that this vision is carried out.[3] In its moral vision, socialism values equality over liberty and affirms the virtues of community, corporate responsibility, and the common good. As Douglas Sturm notes in his *On Meanings of Justice* included in chapter 3 of this work, the moral visions of capitalism and socialism extend deeply into the foundations of Western civilization—indeed to the Bible itself—and thus continue to have wide currency in moral debate.

As we move into the twenty-first century, the epochal struggle between capitalism and socialism seems to be resolving itself in various forms of "mixed" economies. Today most of the world's economies are built on the foundation of private property and the free market but also allow some measure of government intervention to establish minimum wages, demand public accountability of corporations, distribute wealth more equitably, and place some controls on environmental degradation.[4] These mixed economies offer some sort of balance between freedom and dynamism, on the one hand, and equality and security, on the other. Nevertheless, some deep problems remain that are endemic to capitalism itself. The market is an amoral, impersonal mechanism that blindly rewards efficiency and correct judgments about consumer demands. It seems to render irrelevant personal loyalties, acts of service and love, and a yearning for a common good.

---

[3] See George C. Lodge, *Perestroika for America: Restructuring Business-Government Relations for World Competitiveness* (Boston: Harvard Business School Press, 1990) 15–17.

[4] Particular economies vary a great deal in how much weight is given to each side of the mixture. The U.S. economy, for example, slants more heavily in a capitalist direction than most European economies.

The pastoral letter, *Economic Justice for All* (reading 4), written by the U.S. bishops, is one clear example of an attempt to both affirm the good features of capitalism and address its serious shortcomings. This document is representative of a broad quest in the tradition of the Catholic social teachings to set forth some guidelines for economic life without simply baptizing one of the two modern economic systems. An especially clear example of this quest is The One-hundreth Year *(Centesimus Annus)*, written under the auspices of Pope John Paul II in 1991 to celebrate and reaffirm the one-hundreth-year anniversary of the landmark document Of New Things *(Rerum Novarum)*. The document envisions a society that promotes human dignity through free work, enterprise, and participation. It expresses some faith that the free market is the most efficient means to produce and distribute goods, though it warns that the market must be "appropriately controlled by forces of society and the state, to guarantee that the basic needs of the whole of society are satisfied." The document criticizes the materialism of capitalist societies that defines the good life in terms of "having" instead of "being." The document calls for some sort of moral calculus in the market. "It is therefore necessary," the document concludes, "to create lifestyles in which the quest for truth, beauty, goodness, and communion with others for the sake of common growth are the factors which determine consumer choices, savings, and investments."[5]

The Problem of Poverty and Liberation Theology

Concern for the poor is a constant theme in Scripture. At a minimum, Scripture proclaims an obligation to alleviate some of the worst suffering of the poor through acts of charity. Acts of beneficence only deal with the symptoms of poverty, however, and not its causes. In recent decades, the theological movement of liberation theology has endeavored to analyze the root causes of poverty from a theological perspective. The reading by Gustavo Gutierrez included in this chapter is representative of this movement. As preparation for this reading, a review of liberation theology's main themes is in order.

First, liberation theology developed the concept of *structural sin*. Sin certainly has an inner, individual dimension. We often make bad choices even when we have freedom to do otherwise. But if we think carefully about our lives, we realize that many of our choices are profoundly shaped by culture and institutional structures. These forces can mask evil and render it invisible to us. The late Bishop Oscar Romero defined structural evil this way: "The Church has denounced sin for centuries. It has certainly denounced the sin of

---

[5] Pope John Paul II, *Centesimus Annus*, §§35–36. A full text of the encyclical can be found at http://www.vatican.va/holy_father/john_paul_ii/encyclicals/documents/hf_jp-ii_enc_01051991_centesimus-annus_en.html (accessed September 18, 2004).

the individual, and it has also denounced the sin which perverts relationships between human beings, particularly at the family level. But now it has again reminded us of what has been fundamental from its beginning: of social sin, that is to say, the crystallization of individual egoisms in permanent structures which maintain this sin and exert its power over the great majorities."[6]

An example of a "permanent structure" of sin is the system of slavery that was wholeheartedly supported by most white Southern churches until the Civil War. They regarded slavery not simply as an unavoidable evil but as right and just. Slave owners participated in an ideology that slaves were misguided children who needed tutelage and control to save them from their worst impulses. Even if individual southern Christians were able to break free from this fiction, they faced an entire legal system that made it illegal to free slaves, to educate them, or to associate socially with them. We can see, then, that structural sin and personal sin reinforce each other in a circular relationship: individual sins create structures of sin, which in turn engender and render invisible individual sin.

Second, liberation theology developed a new theological method based in *praxis*. Traditional theology tended to establish theological first principles and then apply them to the current situation through a process of deduction. Liberation theology, in contrast, begins with a moral solidarity with the poor and commitment to look at the world through their eyes. It seeks to unmask the legitimations for oppression by critical readings of the culture's ideologies. This "ideological suspicion" is matched by an "exegetical suspicion" that uncovers the faulty biblical interpretations that support the oppressive ideologies. The next step is a new theological interpretation that puts forth a more adequate theology. Finally, it repeats the process by subjecting this new interpretation to the same critique. The liberation theologian Juan Louis Segundo called this new method a "hermeneutical circle."[7]

Third, if sin is structural as well as personal, then salvation requires *social and political liberation* as well as personal liberation. Liberation theologians see the hopes for peace and justice in the kingdom of God as a positive program for change in this world. In liberation theology, traditional theological categories like sin, guilt, redemption, and reconciliation take on a decidedly political cast.

Our last theme of liberation theology is *"the preferential option for the poor."* Liberation theologians reject the passive, distant God of traditional theology for a God that works actively for the oppressed. They direct us back to the Gospels.

---

[6] Quoted in José Ignacio González Faus, "Sin" in *Mysterium Liberationis: Fundamental Concepts of Liberation Theology*, ed. Ignacio Ellacuría and Jon Sobrino (Maryknoll, N.Y.: Orbis Books, 1993) 537.

[7] See chapter one of Juan Louis Segundo, *The Liberation of Theology* (Maryknoll, N.Y.: Orbis Books, 1976). Note that this method also is employed by Rosemary Radford Ruether in the selection from her book *Sexism and God-Talk* that is included in chapter 2 of this book.

Peppered throughout the Gospel of Luke, for example, is the promise of a great reversal of fortunes between the rich and the poor, the powerful and the powerless. When Mary learns of her pregnancy, she sings that God

> has brought down the powerful from their thrones,
>   and lifted up the lowly;
> he has filled the hungry with good things,
>   and sent the rich away empty. (Luke 1:52-53)

Jesus preaches blessings to the poor, the hungry, the weeping and woe to the rich, the full, and the laughing (6:20-27).

Throughout the Gospels we read that Jesus had a special love for the poor and promises them that their reward will be great. In Matthew 25, the identification between Jesus and the poor is complete. Jesus tells the surprised faithful during the last judgment that "as you did it to one of the least of these members of my family, you did it to me" (Matt 25:40).

Ecology

Decades of pollution, ecosystem destruction, species extinction, and global warning have moved environmental issues to center stage in Christian ethics. We are beginning to understand that true stewardship is not simply about proper distribution of the earth's riches to human beings but must include care for creation as well. We must acknowledge that Christianity does not have a particularly good track record in this area. The industrialized world is both the source of the greatest threat to the environment and the portion of the world's cultures that has been most shaped by Christianity. Nearly forty years ago, the biologist Lynn White argued that this overlap is not coincidental. Our environmental crisis is the bitter fruit born out of modern technology's "ruthlessness toward nature." White argued that this attitude is rooted deeply in Western versions of Christianity. When Christianity spread to pagan lands, it supplanted the old animisms and nature religions with a transcendent God, separate from and aloof from the natural world. Deprived of its sacredness, the natural order became a "thing" to be exploited by human beings.[8]

Recent decades have seen efforts to recover a Christian heritage that can support a robust ecological ethic. One of the most creative of these efforts is ecofeminism, represented in this chapter by an article by Rosemary Radford Ruether (reading 6). Ecofeminists link the oppression of women and the degradation of the environment. Both, they argue, are rooted in a rejection of the nature and the body in favor of a disembodied realm of mind and spirit. As a corrective, Ruether draws from the Hebrew covenantal tradition, which

[8] Lynn White Jr., "The Historical Roots of our Ecological Crisis," *Science* 155 (1967) 1203–7. White does not see this tendency in the Eastern churches, which have seen nature as a symbolic system through which God is revealed to human beings.

included the land as a partner in the people's covenant with God. She supplements this largely Protestant focus with the Catholic tradition's sacramental cosmology, which sees the natural world as imbued with the divine Spirit.

READINGS

1. Biblical Foundations

Readers may wish to review the passages related to justice from chapter 3. In addition, these passages are foundational for the biblical understanding of stewardship:

GENESIS 1–3

Compared to other creation stories of the ancient Near East, these two creation stories give an exalted role to human beings. In the first story (1:1–2:4a), human beings are created "in the image of God" and given the task to govern the world. In the second story (2:4b–3:24), the first man and woman are given a productive garden to fulfill their physical needs. These passages have played a central role in Christianity's understanding both of work and of their place in the natural world.

LEVITICUS 25:1-34; DEUTERONOMY 15

Together these passages set forth the legal requirements for "The Sabbatical Year" and the "Year of Jubilee." Every seven years Israel is commanded to remit all debts, set free Hebrew slaves, allow the soil to rest, and renew their covenant with God. Every fifty years (the Sabbath of Sabbaths, or Year of Jubilee) all land must be returned to its original family of ownership. These provisions were a way to restore equality among all children of Israel. We have no evidence that Israel actually practiced these provisions, though Jeremiah 34:8ff. records a half-hearted attempt to fulfill these obligations during a siege of Jerusalem as a way to curry favor with God. Nevertheless, the Sabbath and Jubilee Years became a central hope of the prophetic movement. During the time of Jesus, the Jubilee Year became almost synonymous for the kingdom of God.

MATTHEW 25:31-48

This parable is the last told by Jesus in Matthew and thus stands as the capstone of his ministry. The scene is the judging of "[a]ll the nations" at the end of time. Jesus describes a complete identification between the "Son of Man" and "the least of these who are members of my family" *(adelphoi)*. Our interpretation of this parable is in part dependent on who we understand the *adelphoi* to be. Matthew uses the term both in a general sense to refer to anyone who is in need (5:22-24, 47; 7:3-5) and in a more restrictive sense to refer to the disciples who are sent out two by two to proclaim their faith (10:40-42). If the former meaning is intended in this parable, then Jesus is identified with the "socio-economically poor" and the nations are judged by how they meet the physical needs of the poor. If the latter meaning is intended, then Jesus is identified with the "evangelically poor" and the nations are judged by how it receives the evangelically poor and their message.

LUKE 1:39-56, 4:16-22, 6:17-26

These passages are only a few of the many references in the Gospel of Luke to the sudden reversal of fortunes between the rich and the poor in the kingdom of God. Compare Luke's version of the Beatitudes with Matthew's (5:1-12), which is less confrontational and more spiritualized.

2. Thomas Aquinas, Selections from the *Summa Theologiae*

The selections from the Summa *in this chapter explore the virtue of justice. Aquinas saw justice as the cardinal virtue most directly concerned with external actions and other persons. Its central concern is to establish right relations with others within the context of the common good. These particular passages explore the dictates of justice concerning property. Before addressing the questions of theft and trade, he first must take a position on private property. Aquinas adds nuance to the longstanding tradition of the church that private ownership is contrary to natural law. He answers that private property is a reasonable addition to natural law to further the common good. Property rights are not absolute, however, but must be set aside in times of need.*[9]

WHETHER IT IS NATURAL FOR A PERSON TO POSSESS EXTERNAL THINGS

External[10] things can be considered in two ways. First, as regards their nature, and this is not subject to the power of human beings, but only to the power of God, whose mere will all things obey. Secondly, as regards their use, and in this way, human beings have a natural dominion over external things,

---

[9] See Jean Porter, "The Virtue of Justice (IIa IIae, qq. 58–122)" in *The Ethics of Aquinas,* ed. Stephen J. Pope (Washington, D.C.: Georgetown University Press, 2002) 272–86.

[10] Thomas Aquinas, *Summa Theologiae,* translated by the Fathers of the English Dominican Province under the title *Summa Theologica,* 5 vols. (Westminster, Maryland: Christian Classics, 1981). Reprinted under a license agreement granted by Benziger Brothers (New York, 1948); adapted. See note 1 in chapter 1 of this book; these selections are from II-II.66.1; 66.2; 66.7; 77.1; 77.4.

because, by their reason and will, they are able to use them for their own profit, as these things were made on their account: for the imperfect is always for the sake of the perfect, as stated above. It is by this argument that the Philosopher proves that the possession of external things is natural to human beings. Moreover, this natural dominion of humanity over other creatures, which is competent to them in respect of their reason wherein God's image resides, is shown forth in their creation (Gen 1:26) by the words: "Let us make humanity to our image and likeness: and let them have dominion over the fishes of the sea," etc.

WHETHER IT IS LAWFUL
FOR A PERSON TO HAVE PERSONAL OWNERSHIP OF A THING

Two things are competent to human beings in respect of exterior things. One is the power to procure and dispense them, and in this regard it is lawful for human beings to possess property. Moreover this is necessary to human life for three reasons. First because each person is more careful to procure what is for himself or herself alone than that which is common to many or to all: since each one would shirk the labor and leave to another that which concerns the community, as happens where there is a great number of servants. Secondly, because human affairs are conducted in more orderly fashion if each person is charged with taking care of some particular thing himself or herself, whereas there would be confusion if everyone had to look after any one thing indeterminately. Thirdly, because a more peaceful state is ensured to humanity if each one is contented with his or her own. Hence it is to be observed that quarrels arise more frequently where there is no division of the things possessed.

The second thing that is competent to human beings with regard to external things is their use. On this respect human beings ought to possess external things, not as their own, but as common, so that, to wit, they are ready to communicate them to others in their need. Hence the Apostle says (1 Tim 6:17-18): "Charge the rich of this world . . . to give easily, to communicate to others," etc.

Community of goods is ascribed to the natural law, not that the natural law dictates that all things should be possessed in common and that nothing should be possessed as one's own: but because the division of possessions is not according to the natural law, but rather arose from human agreement which belongs to positive law, as stated above. Hence the ownership of possessions is not contrary to the natural law, but an addition thereto devised by human reason.

WHETHER IT IS LAWFUL TO STEAL THROUGH STRESS OF NEED

In cases of need all things are common property, so that there would seem to be no sin in taking another's property, for need has made it common . . .

Things which are of human right cannot derogate from natural right or Divine right. Now according to the natural order established by Divine Providence, inferior things are ordained for the purpose of succoring human needs by their means. Wherefore the division and appropriation of things which are based on human law, do not preclude the fact that human needs have to be remedied by means of these very things. Hence whatever certain people have in super-abundance is due, by natural law, to the purpose of succoring the poor . . .

Since, however, there are many who are in need, while it is impossible for all to be succored by means of the same thing, all persons are entrusted with the stewardship of their own things, so that out of them they may come to the aid of those who are in need. Nevertheless, if the need be so manifest and urgent, that it is evident that the present need must be remedied by whatever means be at hand (for instance when a person is in some imminent danger, and there is no other possible remedy), then it is lawful to succor one's own need by means of another's property, by taking it either openly or secretly: nor is this properly speaking theft or robbery . . .

It is not theft, properly speaking, to take secretly and use another's property in a case of extreme need: because that which one takes for the support of one life becomes one's own property by reason of that need.

WHETHER IT IS LAWFUL TO SELL A THING FOR MORE THAN ITS WORTH

It is altogether sinful to have recourse to deceit in order to sell a thing for more than its just price, because this is to deceive one's neighbor so as to in-jure the neighbor . . . But, apart from fraud, we may speak of buying and sell-ing in two ways. First, as considered in themselves, and from this point of view, buying and selling seem to be established for the common advantage of both parties, one of whom requires that which belongs to the other, and vice versa, as the Philosopher states. Now whatever is established for the common advantage, should not be more of a burden to one party than to another, and consequently all contracts between them should observe equality of thing and thing. Again, the quality of a thing that comes into human use is measured by the price given for it, for which purpose money was invented, as stated in *Ethic*. Therefore if either the price exceed the quantity of the thing's worth, or, conversely, the thing exceed the price, there is no longer the equality of jus-tice: and consequently, to sell a thing for more than its worth, or to buy it for less than its worth, is in itself unjust and unlawful.

Secondly we may speak of buying and selling, considered as accidentally tending to the advantage of one party, and to the disadvantage of the other: for instance, when someone has great need of a certain thing, while another will suffer if he or she be without it. On such a case the just price will depend not only on the thing sold, but on the loss which the sale brings on the seller. And thus it will be lawful to sell a thing for more than it is worth in itself, though the price paid be not more than it is worth to the owner. Yet if the one person derives a great advantage by becoming possessed of the other's property, and the seller be not at a loss through being without that thing, the latter ought not to raise the price, because the advantage accruing to the buyer, is not due to the seller, but to a circumstance affecting the buyer. Now people should not sell what is not theirs, though they may charge for the loss they suffer.

On the other hand if people find that they derive great advantage from something they have bought, one may, of one's own accord, pay the seller something over and above: and this pertains to their honesty.

Whether, in trading, it is lawful to sell a thing at a higher price than what was paid for it

A trader is one whose business consists in the exchange of things. According to the Philosopher, exchange of things is twofold; one, natural as it were, and necessary, whereby one commodity is exchanged for another, or money taken in exchange for a commodity, in order to satisfy the needs of life. Such like trading, properly speaking, does not belong to traders, but rather to housekeepers or civil servants who have to provide the household or the state with the necessaries of life. The other kind of exchange is either that of money for money, or of any commodity for money, not on account of the necessities of life, but for profit, and this kind of exchange, properly speaking, regards traders, according to the Philosopher. The former kind of exchange is commendable because it supplies a natural need: but the latter is justly deserving of blame, because, considered in itself, it satisfies the greed for gain, which knows no limit and tends to infinity. Hence trading, considered in itself, has a certain debasement attaching thereto, in so far as, by its very nature, it does not imply a virtuous or necessary end. Nevertheless gain which is the end of trading, though not implying, by its nature, anything virtuous or necessary, does not, in itself, connote anything sinful or contrary to virtue: wherefore nothing prevents gain from being directed to some necessary or even virtuous end, and thus trading becomes lawful. Thus, for instance, people may intend the moderate gain which they seek to acquire by trading for the upkeep of their households, or for the assistance of the needy: or again, people may take to trade for some public advantage, for instance, lest their country lack the necessaries of life, and seek gain, not as an end, but as payment for their labor.

3. John Wesley, "The Use of Money"

The following reading is a sermon by John Wesley (1703–1791), who founded the Methodist movement. Wesley organized the movement into tightly organized local societies that were, in turn, composed of small neighborhood cell groups. The name "Methodist" originated as a derisive jeer from critics, who believed that Wesley's followers were too fixated on structure and order. This attention to organization made the Methodist the most successful of the eighteenth-century pietist movements, however. By the end of the eighteenth century, the Methodist movement boasted approximately 1.5 million members in England and America—nearly one fourth of the population in these lands. Participation in the Methodist movement required a complete transformation of life. Methodists were required not only to reform their conduct but to care for the health and livelihood of others. Wesley himself gave away most of his earnings and he urged the Methodists to follow his example. "The Use of Money" was first delivered in 1744, a period of rapid growth for the movement. Early Methodists came largely from the lower classes. One ironic result of Methodism's emphasis on reformed character and financial assistance, however, is that the membership increasingly became more comfortable as the decades progressed. Tellingly, one of Wesley's last sermons was "On the Danger of Increasing Riches."

> "I[11] say unto you, Make unto yourselves friends of the mammon of unright-eousness; that, when ye fail, they may receive you into the everlasting habita-tions." (Luke 16:9)

2.   An excellent branch of Christian wisdom is here inculcated by our Lord on all his followers, namely, the right use of money — a subject largely spo-ken of, after their manner, by people of the world; but not sufficiently consid-ered by those whom God hath chosen out of the world . . . "The love of money," we know, "is the root of all evil;" [1 Tim 6:10] but not the thing it-self. The fault does not lie in the money, but in them that use it. . . It is true, were human beings in a state of innocence, or were all people "filled with the Holy Ghost," so that, like the infant church at Jerusalem, "none counted any-thing they had their own," but "distribution was made to everyone as they had need," [Acts 4:31-35], the use of it would be superseded; as we cannot con-ceive there is anything of the kind among the inhabitants of heaven. But, in the present state of humankind, it is an excellent gift of God, answering the noblest ends. In the hands of God's children, it is food for the hungry, drink for the thirsty, raiment for the naked. It gives to travelers and strangers where to lay their heads [see Matt 25:31-46]. By it we may supply the place of a hus-band to the widow, and of a father to the fatherless. It may be a defense for the oppressed, a means of health to the sick, of ease to them that are in pain; it may be as eyes to the blind, as feet to the lame; yea, a lifter up from the gates of death!

3.   It is therefore of the highest concern that all who fear God know how to employ this valuable talent [see Matt 25:14-30]; that they be instructed how it may answer these glorious ends, and in the highest degree. And, perhaps, all the instructions which are necessary for this may be reduced to three plain

---

[11] From John Wesley, "The Use of Money" in *Sermons on Several Occasions*, ed. Thomas O. Summers, rev. ed., vol. 2 (Nashville, Tenn.: Southern Methodist Publishing House, 1878) 338–52; revised. Scriptures are quoted as in original.

rules, by the exact observance whereof we may approve ourselves faithful stewards of "the mammon of unrighteousness" [see Luke 16:1-13].

I.1. The first of these is (those that heareth, let them understand! [see Rev 1:3]): *Gain all you can.* Here we may speak like the children of the world [see Luke 16:8]: We meet them on their own ground. And it is our bounden duty to do this: We ought to gain all we can gain, without buying gold too dear, without paying more for it than it is worth. But this it is certain we ought not to do; we ought not to gain money at the expense of life, nor (which is in effect the same thing) at the expense of our health. Therefore, no gain whatsoever should induce us to enter into, or to continue in, any employ, which is of such a kind, or is attended with so hard or so long labor, as to impair our constitution. Neither should we begin or continue in any business which necessarily deprives us of proper seasons for food and sleep, in such a proportion as our nature requires. Indeed, there is a great difference here. Some employments are absolutely and totally unhealthy; as those which imply the dealing much with arsenic, or other equally hurtful minerals, or the breathing an air tainted with steams of melting lead, which must at length destroy the firmest constitution. Others may not be absolutely unhealthy, but only to persons of a weak constitution. Such are those which require many hours to be spent in writing; especially if a person write sitting, and lean upon his stomach, or remain long in an uneasy posture. But whatever it is which reason or experience shows to be destructive of health or strength, that we may not submit to; seeing "the life is more" valuable "than meat, and the body than raiment" [Matt 6:25]. And if we are already engaged in such an employ, we should exchange it as soon as possible for some which, if it lessen our gain, will, however not lessen our health.

2. We are, secondly, to gain all we can without hurting our mind any more than our body. For neither may we hurt this. We must preserve, at all events, the spirit of a healthful mind. Therefore we may not engage or continue in any sinful trade, any that is contrary to the law of God or of our country. Such are all that necessarily imply our robbing or defrauding the king of his lawful customs. For it is at least as sinful to defraud the king of his right, as to rob our fellow subjects. And the king has full as much right, to his customs as we have to our houses and apparel. Other businesses there are, which however innocent in themselves, cannot be followed with innocence now at least, not in England; such, for instance, as will not afford a competent maintenance without cheating or lying, or conformity to some custom which is not consistent with a good conscience. These, likewise, are sacredly to be avoided, whatever gain they may be attended with, provided we follow the custom of the trade; for to gain money we must not lose our souls. There are yet others which many pursue with perfect innocence, without hurting either their body or mind; And yet perhaps you cannot: Either they may entangle you in that com-

pany which would destroy your soul; and by repeated experiments it may appear that you cannot separate the one from the other; or there may be an idiosyncrasy—a peculiarity in your constitution of soul, (as there is in the bodily constitution of many), by reason whereof that employment is deadly to you, which another may safely follow. So I am convinced, from many experiments, I could not study, to any degree of perfection, either mathematics, arithmetic, or algebra, without being a Deist, if not an Atheist. And yet others may study them all their lives without sustaining any inconvenience. None therefore can here determine for another, but everyone must judge for themselves and abstain from whatever they in particular find to be hurtful to their souls.

3.   We are, thirdly, to gain all we can without hurting our neighbor. But this we may not, cannot do, if we love our neighbor as ourselves [see Lev 19:18; Mark 12:31 and parallels]. We cannot, if we love everyone as ourselves, hurt anyone *in their substance*. We cannot devour the increase of their lands, and perhaps the lands and houses themselves, by gaming, by overgrown bills (whether on account of physic, or law, or anything else), or by requiring or taking such interest as even the laws of our country forbid. Hereby all pawnbroking is excluded: seeing, whatever good we might do thereby, all who are unprejudiced see with grief to be abundantly overbalanced by the evil. And if it were otherwise, yet we are not allowed to "do evil that good may come" [see Rom 3:8]. We cannot, consistent with Christian love, sell our goods below the market price; we cannot study to ruin our neighbors' trades, in order to advance our own; much less can we entice away or receive any of their servants or workers whom they have need of. No one can gain by swallowing up the neighbor's substance, without gaining the damnation of hell!

4.   Neither may we gain by hurting our neighbors *in their bodies*. Therefore we may not sell anything which tends to impair health. Such is, eminently, all that liquid fire, commonly called drams or spirituous liquors. It is true, these may have a place in medicine; they may be of use in some bodily disorders; although there would rarely be occasion for them were it not for the unskillfulness of the practitioner. Therefore, such as prepare and sell them *only for this end* may keep their conscience clear. But who are they? Who prepare and sell them only for this end? Do you know ten such distillers in England? Then excuse these. But all who sell them in the common way, to any that will buy, are poisoners general. They murder His Majesty's subjects by wholesale, neither does their eye pity or spare. They drive them to hell like sheep. And what is their gain? Is it not the blood of these people? Who then would envy their large estates and sumptuous palaces? A curse is in the midst of them: the curse of God cleaves to the stones, the timber, the furniture of them . . .

6.   This is dear-bought gain. And so is whatever is procured by hurting our neighbors *in their souls,* by ministering, suppose, either directly or indirectly, to their unchastity, or intemperance, which certainly none can do, who has any

fear of God, or any real desire of pleasing God. It nearly concerns all those to consider this, who have anything to do with taverns, eating-houses, opera-houses, play-houses, or any other places of public, fashionable diversion. If these profit the souls of others, you are clear; your employment is good, and your gain innocent; but if they are either sinful in themselves, or natural inlets to sin of various kinds, then, it is to be feared, you have a sad account to make. O beware, lest God say in that day, "These have perished in their iniquity, but their blood do I require at thy hands!"

7.   These cautions and restrictions being observed, it is the bounden duty of all who are engaged in worldly business to observe that first and great rule of Christian wisdom with respect to money, "Gain all you can." Gain all you can by honest industry. Use all possible diligence in your calling. Lose no time. If you understand yourself and your relation to God and humanity, you know you have none to spare. If you understand your particular calling as you ought, you will have no time that hangs upon your hands. Every business will afford some employment sufficient for every day and every hour. That wherein you are placed, if you follow it in earnest, will leave you no leisure for silly, un-profitable diversions. You have always something better to do, something that will profit you, more or less. And "whatsoever thy hand findeth to do, do it with thy might" [see Deut 6:5; Mark 12:30]. Do it as soon as possible: No delay! No putting off from day to day, or from hour to hour! Never leave any-thing till to-morrow, which you can do to-day [see Luke 12:35-40]. And do it as well as possible. Do not sleep or yawn over it: Put your whole strength to the work. Spare no pains. Let nothing be done by halves, or in a slight and careless manner. Let nothing in your business be left undone if it can be done by labor or patience . . .

II.1.   Having gained all you can, by honest wisdom and unwearied diligence, the second rule of Christian prudence is: *Save all you can.* Do not throw the precious talent into the sea: Leave that folly to heathen philosophers. Do not throw it away in idle expenses, which is just the same as throwing it into the sea. Expend no part of it merely to gratify "the desire of the flesh, the desire of the eye, or the pride of life" [1 John 2:16].

2.   Do not waste any part of so precious a talent merely in gratifying the de-sires of the flesh; in procuring the pleasures of sense of whatever kind; par-ticularly, in enlarging the pleasure of tasting. I do not mean, avoid gluttony and drunkenness only: an honest heathen would condemn these. But there is a regular, reputable kind of sensuality, an elegant Epicureanism, which does not immediately disorder the stomach, nor (sensibly, at least) impair the understanding. And yet (to mention no other effects of it now) it cannot be maintained without considerable expense. Cut off all this expense! Despise delicacy and variety, and be content with what plain nature requires.

3.   Do not waste any part of so precious a talent merely in gratifying the desire of the eye by superfluous or expensive apparel or by needless ornaments [see 1 Tim 2:9-10, for example]. Waste no part of it in curiously adorning your houses; in superfluous or expensive furniture; in costly pictures, painting, gilding, books; in elegant rather than useful gardens. Let your neighbors, who know nothing better, do this: "Let the dead bury their dead." But "what is that to thee?" says our Lord: "Follow thou me." Are you willing? [see Luke 9: 57-62 and John 21:22]. Then you are able so to do.

4.   Lay out nothing to gratify the pride of life, to gain the admiration or praise of others [see Matt 6]. This motive of expense is frequently interwoven with one or both of the former. Human beings are expensive in diet, or apparel, or furniture, not barely to please their appetite, or to gratify their eye, their imagination, but their vanity too. "So long as thou dost well unto thyself, others will speak good of thee" [see Prv 14:20]. So long as thou art "clothed in purple and fine linen, and farest sumptuously every day," [see Luke 16:19-31] no doubt many will applaud thy elegance of taste, thy generosity and hospitality. But do not buy their applause so dear. Rather be content with the honor that cometh from God.

5.   Who would expend anything in gratifying these desires if one considered that to gratify them is to increase them? Nothing can be more certain than this: daily experience shows, the more they are indulged, they increase the more. Whenever, therefore, you expend anything to please your taste or other senses, you pay so much for sensuality. When you lay out money to please your eye, you give so much for an increase of curiosity—for a stronger attachment to these pleasures which perish in the using. While you are purchasing anything which others use to applaud, you are purchasing more vanity. Had you not then enough of vanity, sensuality, curiosity before? Was there need of any addition? And would you pay for it, too? What manner of wisdom is this? Would not literally throwing your money into the sea be a less mischievous folly?

7.   Do not leave it to your children to throw away. If you have good reason to believe that they would waste what is now in your possession in gratifying and thereby increasing the desire of the flesh, the desire of the eye, or the pride of life [see 1 John 2:16] at the peril of theirs and your own soul, do not set these traps in their way. Do not offer your sons or your daughters unto Belial [see 2 Cor 6:15], any more than unto Moloch [see Act 7:43].[12] Have pity upon them, and remove out of their way what you may easily foresee would increase their sins, and consequently plunge them deeper into everlasting perdition! How amazing then is the infatuation of those parents who think they can never leave their children enough! What! Cannot you leave them enough of arrows,

---

[12] Editors' note: From the passage in Acts, *The New American Bible* references Amos 5:27-27 and Jeremiah 7:18; 8:2; 19:13.

firebrands, and death? Not enough of foolish and hurtful desires? Not enough of pride, lust, ambition vanity? Not enough of everlasting burnings? . . .

III.1.   But let not anyone imagine that they have done anything, barely by going thus far, by "gaining and saving all they can," if they were to stop here. All this is nothing, if we go not forward, if we do not point all this at a farther end. Nor, indeed, can we properly be said to save anything, if we only lay it up. You may as well throw your money into the sea, as bury it in the earth. And you may as well bury it in the earth, as in your chest, or in the Bank of England. Not to use, is effectually to throw it away. If, therefore, you would indeed "make yourselves friends of the mammon of unrighteousness" [see Luke 16:1-13], add the third rule to the two preceding. Having, first, gained all you can, and, secondly saved all you can, then: *Give all you can.*

2.   In order to see the ground and reason of this, consider, when the Possessor of heaven and earth brought you into being, and placed you in this world, placed you here not as a proprietor, but a steward. As such God entrusted you, for a season, with goods of various kinds; but the sole property of these still rests in God, nor can be alienated from God. As you yourself are not your own [see 1 Cor 6:19], but God's, such is, likewise, all that you enjoy. Such is your soul and your body, not your own, but God's. And so is your substance in particular. And God has told you, in the most clear and express terms, how you are to employ it for him, in such a manner, that it may be all a holy sacrifice, acceptable through Christ Jesus. And this light, easy service [see Matt 11:30], God has promised to reward with an eternal weight of glory.

3.   The directions which God has given us, touching the use of our worldly substance, may be comprised in the following particulars. If you desire to be a faithful and a wise steward [see Luke 12:41-48], out of that portion of your Lord's goods which God has for the present lodged in your hands, but with the right of resuming whenever it pleases God [see Matt 25:14-30 and Luke 12:35-40], first, provide things needful for yourself; food to eat, raiment to put on, whatever nature moderately requires for preserving the body in health and strength. Secondly, provide these for your wife, your children, your servants, or any others who pertain to your household. If when this is done there be an overplus left, then "do good to them that are of the household of faith" [Gal 6:10]. If there be an overplus still, "as you have opportunity, do good unto all people" [Gal 6:10]. In so doing, you give all you can; nay, in a sound sense, all you have: for all that is laid out in this manner is really given to God. You "render unto God the things that are God's" [Mark 12:17 and parallels], not only by what you give to the poor, but also by that which you expend in providing things needful for yourself and your household.

4.   If, then, a doubt should at any time arise in your mind concerning what you are going to expend, either on yourself or any part of your family, you have an easy way to remove it. Calmly and seriously inquire: "(1) In expending this, am I acting according to my character? Am I acting herein, not as a proprietor, but as a steward of my Lord's goods? (2) Am I doing this in obedience to his Word? In what Scripture does he require me so to do? (3) Can I offer up this action, this expense, as a sacrifice to God through Jesus Christ? (4) Have I reason to believe that for this very work I shall have a reward at the resurrection of the just?" [see Luke 14:14]. You will seldom need anything more to remove any doubt which arises on this head; but by this fourfold consideration you will receive clear light as to the way wherein you should go.

5.   If any doubt still remain, you may further examine yourself by prayer according to those heads of inquiry. Try whether you can say to the Searcher of Hearts, your conscience not condemning you, "Lord, thou seest I am going to expend this sum on that food, apparel, furniture. And thou knowest, I act herein with a single eye as a steward of thy goods, expending this portion of them thus in pursuance of the design thou hadst in entrusting me with them. Thou knowest I do this in obedience to the Lord, as thou commandest, and because thou commandest it. Let this, I beseech thee, be a holy sacrifice, acceptable through Jesus Christ! And give me a witness in myself that for this labor of love I shall have a recompense when thou rewardest all people according to their works." Now if your conscience bear you witness in the Holy Ghost that this prayer is well-pleasing to God, then have you no reason to doubt but that expense is right and good, and such as will never make you ashamed.

4. U.S. Catholic Bishops, *Economic Justice for All: Pastoral Letter on Catholic Social Teaching and the U.S. Economy*

In this pastoral letter the U.S. Catholic bishops endeavor to flesh out the implications of Catholic social teachings for the particularities of the U.S. economy. The basic theme of the letter is the promotion of human dignity by full participation in the economic life of society. The bishops remind the Catholic Church in the U.S. of its special obligation to the poor and vulnerable. The section of the document included here sets forth a Christian vision for economic life, grounded in an extensive treatment of money and poverty in the Scriptures. The bishops caution, "We speak as moral leaders, not economic technicians" (§7). Their intention is not to define a national economic policy, but to establish a basic moral direction for Christians in the economic sphere.

B. Ethical Norms for Economic Life

1. The Responsibilities of Social Living

63.   Human[13] life is life in community. Catholic social teaching proposes several complementary perspectives that show how moral responsibilities and duties in the economic sphere are rooted in this call to community.

a. Love and Solidarity

64.   *The commandments to love God with all one's heart and to love one's neighbor as oneself are the heart and soul of Christian morality* [see Mark 12:29-31, for example]. Jesus offers himself as the model of this all-inclusive love: ". . . love one another as I have loved you" (John 15:12). These commands point out the path toward true human fulfillment and happiness. They are not arbitrary restrictions on human freedom. Only active love of God and neighbor makes the fullness of community happen. Christians look forward in hope to a true communion among all persons with each other and with God. The Spirit of Christ labors in history to build up the bonds of solidarity among all persons until that day on which their union is brought to perfection in the Kingdom of God.[14] Indeed Christian theological reflection on the very reality of God as a trinitarian unity of persons—Father, Son, and Holy Spirit—shows that being a person means being united to other persons in mutual love.[15]

65.   What the Bible and Christian tradition teach, human wisdom confirms. Centuries before Christ, the Greeks and Romans spoke of the human person as a "social animal" made for friendship, community, and public life. These insights show that human beings achieve self-realization not in isolation, but in interaction with others.[16]

67.   The Christian tradition recognizes, of course, that the fullness of love and community will be achieved only when God's work in Christ comes to completion in the kingdom of God. This kingdom has been inaugurated among us, but God's redeeming and transforming work is not yet complete. Within history, knowledge of how to achieve the goal of social unity is limited. Human sin continues to wound the lives of both individuals and larger social bodies and places obstacles in the path toward greater social solidarity. If efforts to protect human dignity are to be effective, they must take these lim-

---

[13] United States [formerly, National] Conference of Catholic Bishops, *Economic Justice for All: Pastoral Letter on Catholic Social Teaching and the U.S. Economy* (Washington, D.C.: United States Catholic Conference, 1986). A full text copy of the letter can be found at http://www.osjspm.org/cst/eja.htm (accessed September 20, 2004).

[14] Pope Paul VI, On Evangelization in the Modern World *(Evangelii Nuntiandi)* §24.

[15] Pastoral Constitution on the Church in the Modern World *(Gaudium et Spes)* §32.

[16] Ibid., §25.

its on knowledge and love into account. Nevertheless, sober realism should not be confused with resigned or cynical pessimism. It is a challenge to develop a courageous hope that can sustain efforts that will sometimes be arduous and protracted.

b. Justice and Participation

68.   Biblical justice is the goal we strive for. This rich biblical understanding portrays a just society as one marked by the fullness of love, compassion, holiness, and peace. On their path through history, however, sinful human beings need more specific guidance on how to move toward the realization of this great vision of God's [k]ingdom. This guidance is contained in the norms of basic or minimal justice. These norms state the *minimum* levels of mutual care and respect that all persons owe to each other in an imperfect world.[17] Catholic social teaching, like much philosophical reflection, distinguishes three dimensions of basic justice: commutative justice, distributive justice, and social justice.[18]

69.   *Commutative justice calls for fundamental fairness in all agreements and exchanges between individuals or private social groups.* It demands respect for the equal human dignity of all persons in economic transactions, contracts, or promises. For example, workers owe their employers diligent work in exchange for their wages. Employers are obligated to treat their employees as persons, paying them fair wages in exchange for the work done and establishing conditions and patterns of work that are truly human.[19]

70.   *Distributive justice requires that the allocation of income, wealth, and power in society be evaluated in light of its effects on persons whose basic material needs are unmet.* The Second Vatican Council stated: "The right to have a share of earthly goods sufficient for oneself and one's family belongs to everyone. The fathers and doctors of the Church held this view, teaching that we are obliged to come to the relief of the poor and to do so not merely out of our superfluous goods."[20] Minimum material resources are an absolute necessity for human life. If persons are to be recognized as members of the human community, then the community has an obligation to help fulfill these basic needs unless an absolute scarcity of resources makes this strictly impossible. No such scarcity exists in the United States today.

---

[17] See §9 of this work.

[18] Josef Pieper, *The Four Cardinal Virtues* (Notre Dame, Ind.: University of Notre Dame Press, 1966) 43–116; David Hollenbach, "Modern Catholic Teachings concerning Justice," *The Faith That Does Justice,* ed. John C. Haughey (New York: Paulist Press, 1977) 207–31.

[19] Jon P. Gunnemann, "Capitalism and Commutative Justice," presented at the 1985 meeting of the Society of Christian Ethics, in the *Annual of the Society of Christian Ethics.*

[20] Pastoral Constitution *(Gaudium et Spes),* §69.

71.   Justice also has implications for the way the larger social, economic, and political institutions of society are organized. *Social justice implies that persons have an obligation to be active and productive participants in the life of society and that society has a duty to enable them to participate in this way.* This form of justice can also be called "contributive," for it stresses the duty of all who are able to help create the goods, services, and other nonmaterial or spiritual values necessary for the welfare of the whole community. In the words of Pius XI, "It is of the very essence of social justice to demand from each individual all that is necessary for the common good."[21] Productivity is essential if the community is to have the resources to serve the well-being of all. Productivity, however, cannot be measured solely by its output in goods and services. Patterns of production must also be measured in light of their impact on the fulfillment of basic needs, employment levels, patterns of discrimination, environmental quality, and sense of community.

72.   The meaning of social justice also includes a duty to organize economic and social institutions so that people can contribute to society in ways that respect their freedom and the dignity of their labor. Work should enable the working person to become "more a human being," more capable of acting intelligently, freely, and in ways that lead to self-realization.[22]

73.   Economic conditions that leave large numbers of able people unemployed, underemployed, or employed in dehumanizing conditions fail to meet the converging demands of these three forms of basic justice. Work with adequate pay for all who seek it is the primary means of achieving basic justice in our society. Discrimination in job opportunities or income levels on the basis of race, sex, or other arbitrary standards can never be justified.[23] It is a scandal that such discrimination continues in the United States today. Where the effects of past discrimination persist, society has an obligation to take positive steps to overcome the legacy of injustice. Judiciously administered affirmative action programs in education and employment can be important expressions of the drive for solidarity and participation that is at the heart of true justice. Social harm calls for social relief.

74.   Basic justice also calls for the establishment of a floor of material well-being on which all can stand. This is a duty of the whole of society and it creates particular obligations for those with greater resources. This duty calls into question extreme inequalities of income and consumption when so many lack

---

[21] Pope Pius XI, Of a Divine Redeemer *(Divini Redemptoris)* §51. See John A. Ryan, *Distributive Justice,* 3rd ed. (New York: Macmillan, 1942) 188. The term "social justice" has been used in several different but related ways in the Catholic ethical tradition. See William Ferree, "The Act of Social Justice," *Philosophical Studies,* 72 (Washington, D.C.: The Catholic University of America Press, 1943).

[22] Pope John Paul II, On Human Work *(Laborem Exercens)* §§6, 9.

[23] Pastoral Constitution *(Gaudium et Spes),* §29.

basic necessities. Catholic social teaching does not maintain that a flat, arithmetical equality of income and wealth is a demand of justice, but it does challenge economic arrangements that leave large numbers of people impoverished. Further, it sees extreme inequality as a threat to the solidarity of the human community, for great disparities lead to deep social divisions and conflict.[24]

75.   This means that all of us must examine our way of living in the light of the needs of the poor. Christian faith and the norms of justice impose distinct limits on what we consume and how we view material goods. The great wealth of the United States can easily blind us to the poverty that exists in this nation and the destitution of hundreds of millions of people in other parts of the world. Americans are challenged today as never before to develop the inner freedom to resist the temptation constantly to seek more. Only in this way will the nation avoid what Paul VI called "the most evident form of moral underdevelopment," namely greed.[25]

76.   These duties call not only for individual charitable giving but also for a more systematic approach by businesses, labor unions, and the many other groups that shape economic life—as well as government. The concentration of privilege that exists today results far more from institutional relationships that distribute power and wealth inequitably than from differences in talent or lack of desire to work. These institutional patterns must be examined and revised if we are to meet the demands of basic justice. For example, a system of taxation based on assessment according to ability to pay[26] is a prime necessity for the fulfillment of these social obligations.

c. Overcoming Marginalization and Powerlessness

77.   These fundamental duties can be summarized this way: *basic justice demands the establishment of minimum levels of participation in the life of the human community for all persons.* The ultimate injustice is for a person or group to be treated actively or abandoned passively as if they were nonmembers of the human race. To treat people this way is effectively to say they simply do not count as human beings. This can take many forms, all of which can be described as varieties of marginalization, or exclusion from social life.[27] This exclusion can occur in the political sphere: restriction of free speech, concentration of power in the hands of a few, or outright repression by the state. It can also take economic forms that are equally harmful. Within the United States, individuals, families, and local communities fall victim to a

---

[24] Ibid. See §§180–82 of this document.
[25] Pope Paul VI, On the Development of Peoples *(Populorum Progressio)* §19.
[26] Pope John XXIII, Mother and Master *(Mater et Magistra)* §132.
[27] Synod of Bishops (1971), Justice in the World" *(Justicia in Mundo)* §§10, 16; and Pope Paul VI, On the Occasion of the Eightieth Anniversary of *Rerum Novarum (Octogesima Adveniens)* §15.

downward cycle of poverty generated by economic forces they are powerless to influence. The poor, the disabled, and the unemployed too often are simply left behind. This pattern is even more severe beyond our borders in the least-developed countries. Whole nations are prevented from fully participating in the international economic order because they lack the power to change their disadvantaged position. Many people within the less-developed countries are excluded from sharing in the meager resources available in their homelands by unjust elites and unjust governments. These patterns of exclusion are created by free human beings. In this sense they can be called forms of social sin.[28] Acquiescence in them or the failure to correct them when it is possible to do so is a sinful dereliction of Christian duty.

78.   Recent Catholic social thought regards the task of overcoming these patterns of exclusion and powerlessness as a most basic demand of justice. Stated positively, justice demands that social institutions be ordered in a way that guarantees all persons the ability to participate actively in the economic, political, and cultural life of society.[29] The level of participation may be legitimately greater for some persons than for others, but there is a basic level of access that must be made available for all. Such participation is an essential expression of the social nature of human beings and of their communitarian vocation.

2. Human Rights: The Minimum Conditions for Life in Community

79.   Catholic social teaching spells out the basic demands of justice in greater detail in the human rights of every person. These fundamental rights are prerequisites for a dignified life in community. The Bible vigorously affirms the sacredness of every person as a creature formed in the image and likeness of God. The biblical emphasis on covenant and community also shows that human dignity can only be realized and protected in solidarity with others. In Catholic social thought, therefore, respect for human rights and a strong sense of both personal and community responsibility are linked, not opposed. Vatican II described the *common good* as "the sum of those conditions of social life which allow social groups and their individual members relatively thorough and ready access to their own fulfillment."[30] These conditions include the right to fulfillment of material needs, a guarantee of fundamental freedoms, and the protection of relationships that are essential to participation in the life of so-

---

[28] Pastoral Constitution, §25; Justice in the World, §51; Pope John Paul II, The Gift of the Redemption: Apostolic Exhortation on Reconciliation and Penance (Washington D.C.: U.S. Catholic Conference, 1984) §16; Congregation for the Doctrine of the Faith, Instruction on Christian Freedom and Liberation, §§42, 74.

[29] In the words of the 1971 Synod of Bishops: "Participation constitutes a right which is to be applied in the economic and in the social and political field"; Justice in the World, §18.

[30] Pastoral Constitution *(Gaudium et Spes)*, §26.

ciety.[31] These rights are bestowed on human beings by God and grounded in the nature and dignity of human persons. They are not created by society. Indeed society has a duty to secure and protect them.[32]

80.   The full range of human rights has been systematically outlined by John XXIII in his encyclical Peace on Earth *(Pacem in Terris)*. His discussion echoes the United Nations Universal Declaration of Human Rights and implies that internationally accepted human rights standards are strongly supported by Catholic teaching. These rights include the civil and political rights to freedom of speech, worship, and assembly. A number of human rights also concern human welfare and are of a specifically economic nature. First among these are the rights to life, food, clothing, shelter, rest, medical care, and basic education. These are indispensable to the protection of human dignity. In order to ensure these necessities, all persons have a right to earn a living, which for most people in our economy is through remunerative employment. All persons also have a right to security in the event of sickness, unemployment, and old age. Participation in the life of the community calls for the protection of this same right to employment, as well as the right to healthful working conditions, to wages, and other benefits sufficient to provide individuals and their families with a standard of living in keeping with human dignity, and to the possibility of property ownership.[33] These fundamental personal rights—civil and political as well as social and economic—state the minimum conditions for social institutions that respect human dignity, social solidarity, and justice. They are all essential to human dignity and to the integral development of both individuals and society, and are thus moral issues.[34] Any denial of these rights harms persons and wounds the human community. Their serious and sustained denial violates individuals and destroys solidarity among persons.

81.   Social and economic rights call for a mode of implementation different from that required to secure civil and political rights. Freedom of worship and

---

[31] Pope John Paul II, Address at the General Assembly of the United Nations (October 2, 1979) §§13, 14.

[32] See Pope Pius XII, 1941 Pentecost Address, in Vincent Yzermans, *The Major Addresses of Pope Pius XII*, vol. 1 (St. Paul: North Central Publishing, 1961) §§32–33.

[33] Peace on Earth *(Pacem in Terris)* §§8–27. See On Human Work *(Laborem Exercens)*, §§18–19. Peace on Earth and other modern papal statements refer explicitly to the "right to work" as one of the fundamental economic rights. Because of the ambiguous meaning of the phrase in the United States, and also because the ordinary way people earn their living in our society is through paid employment, the NCCB [National Conference of Catholic Bishops] has affirmed previously that the protection of human dignity demands the right to useful employment be secured for all who are able and willing to work. See NCCB, "The Economy: Human Dimensions" (November 20, 1975) 5, in NCCB, Justice in the Marketplace, §470. See also Congregation for the Doctrine of the Faith, Instruction on Christian Freedom and Liberation, §85.

[34] On the Development of Peoples *(Populorum Progressio)*, §14.

of speech imply immunity from interference on the part of both other persons and the government. The rights to education, employment, and social security, for example, are empowerments that call for positive action by individuals and society at large.

82.   However, both kinds of rights call for positive action to create social and political institutions that enable all persons to become active members of society. Civil and political rights allow persons to participate freely in the public life of the community, for example, through free speech, assembly, and the vote. In democratic countries these rights have been secured through a long and vigorous history of creating the institutions of constitutional government. In seeking to secure the full range of social and economic rights today, a similar effort to shape new economic arrangements will be necessary.

83.   The first step in such an effort is the development of a new cultural consensus that the basic economic conditions of human welfare are essential to human dignity and are due persons by right. Second, the securing of these rights will make demands on <u>all</u> members of society, on all private sector institutions, and on government. A concerted effort on all levels in our society is needed to meet these basic demands of justice and solidarity. Indeed political democracy and a commitment to secure economic rights are mutually reinforcing.

3. Moral Priorities for the Nation

85.   *The common good demands justice for all, the protection of the human rights for all.*[35] Making cultural and economic institutions more supportive of the freedom, power, and security of individuals and families must be a central, long-range objective for the nation. Every person has a duty to contribute to building up the commonweal. All have a responsibility to develop their talents through education. Adults must contribute to society through their individual vocations and talents. Parents are called to guide their children to the maturity of Christian adulthood and responsible citizenship. Everyone has special duties toward the poor and marginalized. Living up to these responsibilities, however, is often made difficult by the social and economic patterns of society. Schools and educational policies both public and private often serve the privileged exceedingly well, while the children of the poor are effectively abandoned as second-class citizens. Great stresses are created in family life by the way work is organized and scheduled, and by the social and cultural values communicated on TV. Many in the lower middle class are barely getting by and fear becoming victims of economic forces over which they have no control.

86.   *The obligation to provide justice for all means that the poor have the single most urgent economic claim on the conscience of the nation.* Poverty

---

[35] Mother and Teacher *(Mater et Magistra)* §65.

can take many forms, spiritual as well as material. All people face struggles of the spirit as they ask deep questions about their purpose in life. Many have serious problems in marriage and family life at some time in their lives, and all of us face the certain reality of sickness and death. The Gospel of Christ proclaims that God's love is stronger than all these forms of diminishment. Material deprivation, however, seriously compounds such sufferings of the spirit and heart. To see a loved one sick is bad enough, but to have no possibility of obtaining health care is worse. To face family problems, such as death of a spouse or a divorce, can be devastating, but to have these lead to the loss of one's home and end with living on the streets is something no one should have to endure in a country as rich as ours. In developing countries these human problems are even more greatly intensified by extreme material deprivation. This form of human suffering can be reduced if our own country, so rich in resources, chooses to increase its assistance.

87. As individuals and as a nation, therefore, we are called to make a fundamental "option for the poor."[36] The obligation to evaluate social and economic activity from the viewpoint of the poor and the powerless arises from the radical command to love one's neighbor as one's self [Mark 12:31, for example]. Those who are marginalized and whose rights are denied have privileged claims if society is to provide justice for *all*. This obligation is deeply rooted in Christian belief. As Paul VI stated: "In teaching us charity, the Gospel instructs us in the preferential respect due the poor and the special situation they have in society: the more fortunate should renounce some of their rights so as to place their goods more generously at the service of others."[37] John Paul II has described this special obligation to the poor as "a call to have a special openness with the small and the weak, those that suffer and weep, those that are humiliated and left on the margin of society, so as to help them win their dignity as human persons and children of God."[38]

88. The prime purpose of this special commitment to the poor is to enable them to become active participants in the life of society. It is to enable *all* persons to share in and contribute to the common good.[39] The "option for the poor," therefore, is not an adversarial slogan that pits one group or class against

[36] On the recent use of this term see: Congregation for the Doctrine of the Faith, Instruction on Christian Freedom and Liberation, §§46–50, 66–68; Evangelization in Latin America's Present and Future, Final Document of the Third General Conference of the Latin American Episcopate (Puebla, Mexico, January 27–February 13, 1979), esp. 4.1, "A Preferential Option for the Poor," in J. Eagleson and P. Scharper, eds, *Puebla and Beyond* (Maryknoll, N.Y.: Orbis Books, 1979) 264–67; Donald Dorr, *Option for the Poor: A Hundred Years of Vatican Social Teaching* (Maryknoll, N.Y.: Orbis Books, 1983).

[37] On the Occasion of the Eightieth Anniversary of *Rerum Novarum (Octogesima Adveniens)* §23.

[38] Address to Bishops of Brazil, §§6, 9, in *Origins* 10 (1980) 135.

[39] Pope John Paul II, Address to Workers at Sao Paulo, §4, in *Origins,* 10 (1980) 138; Instruction on Christian Freedom and Liberation, §§66–68.

another. Rather it states that the deprivation and powerlessness of the poor wounds the whole community. The extent of their suffering is a measure of how far we are from being a true community of persons. These wounds will be healed only by greater solidarity with the poor and among the poor themselves.

89. In summary, the norms of love, basic justice, and human rights imply that personal decisions, social policies, and economic institutions should be governed by several key priorities. These priorities do not specify everything that must be considered in economic decision making. They do indicate the most fundamental and urgent objectives.

90. a.   *The fulfillment of the basic needs of the poor is of the highest priority.* Personal decisions, policies of private and public bodies, and power relationships must be all evaluated by their effects on those who lack the minimum necessities of nutrition, housing, education, and health care. In particular, this principle recognizes that meeting fundamental human needs must come before the fulfillment of desires for luxury consumer goods, for profits not conducive to the common good, and for unnecessary military hardware.

91. b.   *Increasing active participation in economic life by those who are presently excluded or vulnerable is a high social priority.* The human dignity of all is realized when people gain the power to work together to improve their lives, strengthen their families, and contribute to society. Basic justice calls for more than providing help to the poor and other vulnerable members of society. It recognizes the priority of policies and programs that support family life and enhance economic participation through employment and widespread ownership of property. It challenges privileged economic power in favor of the well-being of all. It points to the need to improve the present situation of those unjustly discriminated against in the past. And it has very important implications for both the domestic and the international distribution of power.

92. c.   *The investment of wealth, talent, and human energy should be specially directed to benefit those who are poor or economically insecure.* Achieving a more just economy in the United States and the world depends in part on increasing economic resources and productivity. In addition, the ways these resources are invested and managed must be scrutinized in light of their effects on non-monetary values. Investment and management decisions have crucial moral dimensions: they create jobs or eliminate them; they can push vulnerable families over the edge into poverty or give them new hope for the future; they help or hinder the building of a more equitable society. They can have either positive or negative influence on the fairness of the global economy. Therefore, this priority presents a strong moral challenge to policies that put large amounts of talent and capital into the production of luxury consumer goods and military technology while failing to invest sufficiently in education,

health, the basic infrastructure of our society and economic sectors that produce urgently needed jobs, goods, and services.

93. d.   *Economic and social policies as well as organization of the work world should be continually evaluated in light of their impact on the strength and stability of family life.* The long-range future of this nation is intimately linked with the well-being of families, for the family is the most basic form of human community.[40] Efficiency and competition in the marketplace must be moderated by greater concern for the way work schedules and compensation support or threaten the bonds between spouses and between parents and children. Health, education, and social service programs should be scrutinized in light of how well they ensure both individual dignity and family integrity.

94.   These priorities are not policies. They are norms that should guide the economic choices of all and shape economic institutions. They can help the United States move forward to fulfill the duties of justice and protect economic rights . . . There will undoubtedly be disputes about the concrete applications of these priorities in our complex world. We do not seek to foreclose discussion about them. However, we believe that an effort to move in the direction they indicate is urgently needed.

5. Gustavo Gutierrez, "The Biblical Meaning of Poverty"

Gustavo Gutierrez is considered one of the most influential founders of liberation theology. His book, A Theology of Liberation: History, Politics, Salvation *(originally published in 1971) was truly groundbreaking and remains a classic in the field. Gutierrez is a priest in the Dominican Order and was profoundly shaped by his early experiences working among the poor in Lima. He has been invited to fill visiting professorships around the world, but his principal position remains at the Pontifical Institute in Peru, his native land. In this essay, Gutierrez explores the meaning of poverty in the Bible. He works through the apparent paradox that poverty is regarded as a "scandal" by Scripture, but also, the poor are especially loved by God.*

Poverty[41] is a central theme both in the Old and the New Testaments. It is treated both briefly and profoundly; it describes social situations and expresses spiritual experiences communicated only with difficulty; it defines personal attitudes, a whole people's attitude before God, and the relationships of people with each other. It is possible, nevertheless, to try to unravel the knots and to clear the horizon by following the two major lines of thought

[40] Pastoral Constitution *(Gaudium et Spes)*, §47.
[41] Gustavo Gutierrez, *A Theology of Liberation*, translated and edited by Sister Caridad Inda and John Eagleson, anniversary ed. with new introduction (Maryknoll, N.Y.: Orbis Books, 1988) 165–73, 252–55; revised.

which seem to stand out: poverty as a scandalous condition and poverty as spiritual childhood. The notion of evangelical poverty will be illuminated by a comparison of these two perspectives.

Poverty: A Scandalous Condition

In the Bible poverty is a scandalous condition inimical to human dignity and therefore contrary to the will of God.

This rejection of poverty is seen very clearly in the vocabulary used. In the Old Testament the term which is used least to speak of the poor is *rash,* which has a rather neutral meaning. As Gelin says, the prophets preferred terms which are "photographic" of real, living people. The poor person is, therefore, *èbyon,* the one who desires, the beggar, the one who is lacking something and who awaits it from another. The poor person is also *dal,* the weak one, the frail one; the expression the poor of the land (the rural proletariat) is found very frequently. The poor person is also *ani,* the bent over one, the one laboring under a weight, the one not in possession of his [or her] whole strength and vigor, the humiliated one. And finally the poor person is *anaw,* from the same root as the previous term but having a more religious connotation—"humble before God." In the New Testament the Greek term *ptokos* is used to speak of the poor person. *Ptokos* means one who does not have what is necessary to subsist, the wretched one driven into begging.

Indigent, weak, bent over, wretched are terms which well express a degrading human situation. These terms already insinuate a protest. They are not limited to description; they take a stand. This stand is made explicit in the vigorous rejection of poverty. The climate in which poverty is described is one of indignation. And it is with the same indignation that the cause of the poverty is indicated: the injustice of the oppressors. The cause is well expressed in a text from Job. [See Job 24:2-14.]

Poverty is not caused by fate; it is caused by the actions of those whom the prophet condemns:

> These are the words of the Lord:
> For crime after crime of Israel
> I will grant them no reprieve
> because they sell the innocent for silver
> and the destitute for a pair of shoes.
> They grind the heads of the poor into the earth
> and thrust the humble out of their way . . . (Amos 2:6-7).

There are poor because some people are victims of others. "Shame on you," it says in Isaiah:

> you who make unjust laws
> and publish burdensome decrees,

depriving the poor of justice,
robbing the weakest of my people of their rights,
despoiling the widow and plundering the orphan. (10:1-2)

The prophets condemn every kind of abuse, every form of keeping the poor in poverty or of creating new poor people. They are not merely allusions to situations; the finger is pointed at those who are to blame. Fraudulent commerce and exploitation are condemned (Hos 12:8; Amos 8:5; Mic 6:10-11; Isa 3:14; Jer 5:27; 6:12), as well as the hoarding of lands (Mic 2:13; Ezek 22:29; Hab 2:5-6), dishonest courts (Amos 5:7; Jer 22:13-17; Mic 3:9-11; Isa 5:23; 10:1-2), the violence of the ruling classes (2 Kgs 23:30,3 5; Amos 4:1; Mic 3:1-2; 6:12; Jer 22:13-17), slavery (Neh 5:1-5; Amos 2:6; 8:6), unjust taxes (Amos 4:1; 5:11-12), and unjust functionaries (Amos 5:7; Jer 5:28). In the New Testament oppression by the rich is also condemned, especially in Luke (6:24-25; 12:13-21; 16:19-31; 18:18-26) and in the Letter of James (2:5-9; 4:13-17; 5:16).

But it is not simply a matter of denouncing poverty. The Bible speaks of positive and concrete measures to prevent poverty from becoming established among the People of God. In Leviticus and Deuteronomy there is very detailed legislation designed to prevent the accumulation of wealth and the consequent exploitation. It is said, for example, that what remains in the fields after the harvest and the gathering of olives and grapes should not be collected; it is for the alien, the orphan, and the widow (Deut 24:19-21; Lev 19:9-10). Even more, the fields should not be harvested to the very edge so that something remains for the poor and the aliens (Lev 23:22). The Sabbath, the day of the Lord, has a social significance; it is a day of rest for the slave and the alien (Exod 23:12; Deut. 5:14). The triennial tithe is not to be carried to the temple; rather it is for the alien, the orphan, and the widow (Deut 14:28-29; 26:12). Interest on loans is forbidden (Exod 22:25; Lev 25:35-37; Deut 23:20). Other important measures include the Sabbath year and the jubilee year. Every seven years the fields will be left to lie fallow "to provide food for the poor of your people" (Exod 23:11; Lev 25:27), although it is recognized that this duty is not always fulfilled (Lev 26:34-35). After seven years the slaves were to regain their freedom (Exod 21:26) and debts were to be pardoned (Deut. 15:1-18). This is also the meaning of the jubilee year of Leviticus 25:10ff. "It was," writes de Vaux, "a general emancipation . . . of all the inhabitants of the land. The fields lay fallow: all persons reentered their ancestral properties, i.e. the fields and houses which had been alienated returned to their original owners."

Behind these texts we can see three principal reasons for this vigorous repudiation of poverty. In the first place, poverty contradicts the very meaning of the Mosaic religion. Moses led his people out of the slavery, exploitation, and alienation of Egypt so that they might inhabit a land where they could live with human dignity. In Moses' mission of liberation there was a close relationship between the religion of [YHWH] and the elimination of servitude: "Moses and Aaron then said to all the Israelites, 'In the evening you will know that it was the Lord who brought you out of Egypt, and in the morning you will see the glory of the Lord, because he has heeded your complaints against him; it is not against us that you bring your complaints; we are nothing.' 'You shall know this,' Moses said, "when the Lord, in answer to your complaints, gives you flesh to eat in the evening, and in the morning bread in plenty. What are we? It is against the Lord that you bring your complaints, and not against us'" (Exod 16:6-8).

The worship of [YHWH] and the possession of the land are both included in the same promise. The rejection of the exploitation of some people by others is found in the very roots of the people of Israel. God is the only owner of the land given to his people (Lev 25:23, 38); God is the one Lord who saves his people from servitude and will not allow them to be subjected to it again (Deut 5:15; 16:22; Lev 25:42; 26:13). And thus Deuteronomy speaks of "the ideal of a brotherhood where there was no poverty." In their rejection of poverty, the prophets, who were heirs to the Mosaic ideal, referred to the past, to the origins of the people; there they sought the inspiration for the construction of a just society. To accept poverty and injustice is to fall back into the conditions of servitude which existed before the liberation from Egypt. It is to retrogress.

The second reason for the repudiation of the state of slavery and exploitation of the Jewish people in Egypt is that it goes against the *mandate of Genesis* (1:26; 2:15). Humanity is created in the image and likeness of God and is destined to dominate the earth. Human beings fulfill themselves only by transforming nature and thus entering into relationships with other persons. Only in this way do they come to a full consciousness of themselves as the subjects of creative freedom which is realized through work. The exploitation and injustice implicit in poverty make work into something servile and dehumanizing. Alienated work, instead of liberating humanity, enslaves it even more. And so it is that when just treatment is asked for the poor, the slaves, and the aliens, it is recalled that Israel also was alien and enslaved in Egypt (Exod 22:21-23; 23:9; Deut 10:19; Lev 19:34).

And finally, humanity not only has been made in the image and likeness of God. It is also the *sacrament of God*. We have already recalled this profound and challenging Biblical theme. The other reasons for the Biblical rejection of poverty have their roots here: to oppress the poor is to offend God; to know God is to work justice among humanity. We meet God in our encounter with humans; what is done for others is done for the Lord.

In a word, the existence of poverty represents a sundering both of human solidarity and also of communion with God. Poverty is an expression of a sin, that is, of a negation of love. It is therefore incompatible with the coming of the Kingdom of God, a Kingdom of love and justice.

Poverty is an evil, a scandalous condition, which in our times has taken on enormous proportions. To eliminate it is to bring closer the moment of seeing God face to face, in union with other human beings.

Poverty: Spiritual Childhood

There is a second line of thinking concerning poverty in the Bible. The poor person is the "client" of [YHWH]; poverty is "the ability to welcome God, an openness to God, a willingness to be used by God, a, humility before God."

The vocabulary which is used here is the same as that used to speak of poverty as an evil. But the terms used to designate the poor person receive an ever more demanding and precise religious meaning. This is the case especially with the term *anaw,* which in the plural *(anawim)* is the privileged designation of the spiritually poor.

The repeated infidelity to the Covenant of the people of Israel led the prophets to elaborate the theme of the "tiny remnant" (Isa 4:3; 6:13). Made up of those who remained faithful to [YHWH], the remnant would be the Israel of the future. From its midst there would emerge the Messiah and consequently the first fruits of the New Covenant (Jer 31:31-34; Ezek 36:26-28). From the time of Zephaniah (seventh century B.C.[E.]), those who waited the liberating work of the Messiah were called "poor": "But I will leave in you a people afflicted and poor, the survivors in Israel shall find refuge in the name of the Lord" (Zeph 3:12-13). In this way the term acquired a spiritual meaning. From then on poverty was presented as an ideal: "Seek the Lord, all in the land who live humbly by his laws, seek righteousness, seek a humble heart" (Zeph 2:3). Understood in this way poverty is opposed to pride, to an attitude of self-sufficiency; on the other hand, it is synonymous with faith, with abandonment and trust in the Lord. This spiritual meaning will be accentuated during the historical experiences of Israel after the time of Zephaniah. Jeremiah calls himself poor *(èbyon)* when he sings his thanksgiving to God (20:13). Spiritual poverty is a precondition for approaching God: "All these are of my own making and all these are mine. This is the very word of the Lord. The one I look to is a person downtrodden and distressed, one who reveres my words" (Isa 66:2).

The Psalms can help us to understand more precisely this religious attitude. To know [YHWH] is to seek God (9:11; 34:11), to abandon and entrust oneself to God (10:14; 34:9; 37:40), to hope in God (25:3-5, 21; 37:9), to fear the Lord (25:12, 14; 34:8, 10), to observe God's commandments (25:10); the poor are the just ones, the whole ones (34:20,22; 37:17-18), the faithful ones (37:28; 149:1). The opposite of the poor are the proud, who are the enemy of [YHWH] and the helpless (10:2; 18:28; 37:10; 86:14).

Spiritual poverty finds its highest expression in the Beatitudes of the New Testament. The version in Matthew—thanks to solid exegetical studies—no longer seems to present any great difficulties in interpretation. The poverty which is called "blessed" in Matt. 5:1 ("Blessed are the poor in spirit") is spiritual poverty as understood since the time of Zephaniah: to be totally at the disposition of the Lord. This is the precondition for being able to receive the Word of God. It has, therefore, the same meaning as the Gospel theme of spiritual childhood. God's communication with us is a gift of love; to receive this gift it is necessary to be poor, a spiritual child. This poverty has no direct relationship to wealth; in the first instance it is not a question of indifference to the goods of this world. It goes deeper than that; it means to have no other sustenance than the will of God. This is the attitude of Christ. Indeed, it is to him that all the Beatitudes fundamentally refer.

In Luke's version ("Blessed are you poor" [6:20]) we are faced with greater problems of interpretation. Attempts to resolve these difficulties follow two different lines of thinking. Luke is the evangelist who is most sensitive to social realities. In his Gospel, as well as in Acts, the themes of material poverty, of goods held in common, and of the condemnation of the rich are frequently treated. This has naturally led to thinking that the poor whom he blesses are the opposite of the rich whom he condemns; the poor would be those who lack what they need. In this case the poverty that he speaks of in the first Beatitude would be material poverty.

But this interpretation presents a twofold difficulty. It would lead to the canonization of a social class. The poor would be the privileged of the Kingdom, even to the point of having their access to it assured, not by any choice on their part but by a socioeconomic situation which had been imposed on them. Some commentators insist that this would not be evangelical and would be contrary to the intentions of Luke. On the opposite extreme within this interpretation are those who claim to avoid this difficulty and yet preserve the concrete sociological meaning of poverty in Luke. Situating themselves in the perspective of [W]isdom literature, they say that the first Beatitude opposes the present world to the world beyond; the sufferings of today will be compensated for in the future life. Extraterrestrial salvation is the absolute value which makes the present life insignificant. But this point of view implies purely and simply that Luke is sacralizing misery and injustice and is therefore preaching resignation to it.

Because of these impasses, an explanation is sought from another perspective: Matthew's. Like him Luke would be referring to *spiritual poverty,* or to openness to God. As a concession to the social context of Luke there is in this interpretation an emphasis on real poverty insofar as it is "a privileged path towards poverty of soul."

This second line of interpretation seems to us to minimize the sense of Luke's text. Indeed, it is impossible to avoid the concrete and "material" meaning which the term *poor* has for this evangelist. It refers first of all to those who live in a social situation characterized by a lack of the goods of this world and even by misery and indigence. Even further, it refers to a marginated[42] social group, with connotations of oppression and lack of liberty.

All this leads us to retrace our steps and to reconsider the difficulties— which we have recalled above—in explaining the text of Luke as referring to the materially poor.

[42] Editors' note: The translator's term for "marginalized."

"Blessed are you poor for yours is the Kingdom of God" does not mean, it seems to us: "Accept your poverty because later this injustice will be compensated for in the Kingdom of God." If we believe that the Kingdom of God is a gift which is received in history, and if we believe, as the eschatological promises—so charged with human and historical content—indicate to us, that the Kingdom of God necessarily implies the reestablishment of justice in this world, then we must believe that Christ says that the poor are blessed because the Kingdom of God has begun: "The time has come; the Kingdom of God is upon you" (Mark 1:15). In other words, the elimination of the exploitation and poverty that prevent the poor from being fully human has begun; a Kingdom of justice which goes even beyond what they could have hoped for has begun. They are blessed *because* the coming of the Kingdom will put an end to their poverty by creating a world of brotherhood. They are blessed because the Messiah will open the eyes of the blind [see Isa 35:5] and will give bread to the hungry. Situated in a prophetic perspective, the text in Luke uses the term poor in the tradition of the first major line of thought we have studied: poverty is an evil and therefore incompatible with the Kingdom of God, which has come in its fullness into history and embraces the totality of human existence.

An Attempt at Synthesis: Solidarity and Protest

Material poverty is a scandalous condition. Spiritual poverty is an attitude of openness to God and spiritual childhood. Having clarified these two meanings of the term poverty we have cleared the path and can now move forward towards a better understanding of the Christian witness of poverty. We turn now to a third meaning of the term: poverty as a commitment of solidarity and protest.

We have laid aside the first two meanings. The first is subtly deceptive; the second partial and insufficient. In the first place, if material poverty is something to be rejected, as the Bible vigorously insists, then a witness of poverty cannot make of it a Christian ideal. This would be to aspire to a condition which is recognized as degrading to [human beings]. It would be, moreover, to move against the current of history. It would be to oppose any idea of the domination of nature by human beings and the consequent and progressive creation of better conditions of life. And finally, but not least seriously, it would be to justify, even if involuntarily, the injustice and exploitation which is the cause of poverty.

On the other hand, our analysis of the Biblical texts concerning spiritual poverty has helped us to see that it is not directly or in the first instance an interior detachment from the goods of this world, a spiritual attitude which becomes authentic by incarnating itself in material poverty. Spiritual poverty is something more complete and profound. It is above all total availability to the Lord. Its relationship to the use or ownership of economic goods is inescapable, but secondary and partial. Spiritual childhood—an ability to receive, not a passive acceptance—defines the total posture of human existence before God, humanity, and things.

How are we therefore to understand the evangelical meaning of the witness of a real, material, concrete poverty? *Lumen Gentium* [Dogmatic Constitution on the Church] invites us to look for the deepest meaning of Christian poverty *in Christ:* "Just as Christ carried out the work of redemption in poverty and under oppression, so the Church is called to follow the same path in communicating to humanity the fruits of salvation. Christ Jesus, though He was by nature God . . . emptied himself, taking the nature of a slave (Phil 2:6), arid being rich, he became poor (2 Cor 8:9) for our sakes. Thus, although the Church needs human resources to carry out her mission, she is not set up to seek earthly glory, but to proclaim humility and self-sacrifice, even by her own example." The Incarnation is an act of love. Christ became human, died, and rose from the dead to set us free so that we might enjoy freedom (Gal 5:1). To die and to rise again with Christ is to vanquish death and to enter into a new life (cf. Rom 6:111). The cross and the resurrection are the seal of our liberty.

The taking on of the servile and sinful condition of humanity, as foretold in Second Isaiah, is presented by Paul as an act of voluntary impoverishment: "For you know how generous our Lord Jesus Christ has been: He was rich, yet for your sake he became poor, so that through his poverty you might become rich" (2 Cor. 8:9). This is the humiliation of Christ, his *kenosis* (Phil. 2:6-11). But he does not take on [humanity's] sinful condition and its consequences to idealize it. It is rather because of love for and solidarity with [people] who suffer in it. It is to redeem them from their sin and to enrich them with his poverty. It is to struggle against human selfishness and everything that divides [humanity] and enables there to be rich and poor, possessors and dispossessed, oppressors and oppressed.

Poverty is an act of love and liberation. It has a redemptive value. If the ultimate cause of [humanity's] exploitation and alienation is selfishness, the deepest reason for voluntary poverty is love of neighbor [see Lev 19:18; Mark 12:31, for example]. Christian poverty has meaning only as a commitment of solidarity with the poor, with those who suffer misery and injustice. The commitment is to witness to the evil which has resulted from sin and is a breach of communion. It is not a question of idealizing poverty, but rather of taking it on as it is—an evil—to protest against it and to struggle to abolish it. As [Paul] Ricoeur says, you cannot really be with the poor unless you are struggling against poverty. Because of this solidarity—which must manifest itself in specific action, a style of life, a break with one's social class—one can also help the poor and exploited to become aware of their exploitation and seek liberation from it. Christian poverty, an expression of love, is solidarity *with the poor* and is a protest *against poverty.* This is the concrete, contemporary meaning of the witness of poverty. It is a poverty lived not for its own sake, but rather as an authentic imitation of Christ; it is a poverty which means taking on the sinful condition of humanity to liberate them from sin and all its consequences.

Luke presents the community of goods in the early Church as an ideal. "All whose faith had drawn them together held everything in common" (Acts 2:44); "none of them claimed any of their possessions as their own, but everything was held in common" (Acts 4:33). They did this with a profound unity, one "in heart and soul" (ibid.). But as J. Dupont correctly points out, this was not a question of erecting poverty as an ideal, but rather of seeing to it that there were no poor: "They had never a needy person among them, because all who had property in land or houses sold it, brought the proceeds of the sale, and laid the money at the feet of the apostles; it was then distributed to any who stood in need" (Acts 4:34-35). The meaning of the community of goods is clear: to eliminate poverty because of love of the poor person. Dupont rightly concludes, "If goods are held in common, it is not therefore in order to become poor for love of an ideal of poverty; rather it is so that there will be no poor. The ideal pursued is, once again, charity, a true love for the poor."

We must pay special attention to the words we use. The term poor might seem not only vague and churchy, but also somewhat sentimental and aseptic. The "poor" persons today are the oppressed ones, the ones marginated from society, the members of the proletariat struggling for their most basic rights; they are the exploited and plundered social class, the country struggling for its liberation. In today's world the solidarity and protest of which we are speaking have an evident and inevitable "political" character insofar as they imply liberation. To be with the oppressed is to be against the oppressor. In our times and on our continent to be in solidarity with the "poor," understood in this way, means to run personal risks—even to put one's life in danger. Many Christians—and non-Christians—who are committed to the Latin American revolutionary process are running these risks. And so there are emerging new ways of living poverty which are different from the classic "renunciation of the goods of this world."

Only by rejecting poverty and by making itself poor in order to protest against it can the Church preach something that is uniquely its own: "spiritual poverty," that is, the openness of [humanity] and history to the future promised by God. Only in this way will the Church be able to fulfill authentically—and with any possibility of being listened to—its prophetic function of denouncing every injustice to humanity. And only in this way will it be able to preach the word which liberates, the word of genuine brotherhood.

Only authentic solidarity with the poor and a real protest against the poverty of our time can provide the concrete, vital context necessary for a theological discussion of poverty. The absence of a sufficient commitment to the poor, the marginated, and the exploited is perhaps the fundamental reason why we have no solid contemporary reflection on the witness of poverty.

For the Latin American Church especially, this witness is an inescapable and much-needed sign of the authenticity of its mission.

6. Rosemary Radford Ruether,
"Ecofeminism and Healing Ourselves, Healing the Earth"

Rosemary Radford Ruether is a leading voice in feminist theology and ecofeminism and is a contributor to chapter 2 of this work, deals with sources of Christian ethics. The following selection is one of two lectures given by the author at a 1994 conference organized by the Britain and Ireland School of Feminist Theology. Ruether's first lecture traced the connections between the domination of women and the domination of nature in Western civilization. This second lecture, suggests some latent resources in the Judeo-Christian moral tradition that offer some hope for healing.

Ecological[43] crisis in its myriad phenomena is a well-documented litany. There is toxic pollution of air, water and soil, soil erosion and desertification, the thinning of the ozone layer, allowing cancerous radiation, exhaustion of supplies of fossil fuels, destruction of rain forests, causing climate changes as well as accelerated extinction of species. All these phenomena are expressions of the threat to the basis of planetary life wrought by the rapid expansion of modern technological methods of production, transportation, heating and waste disposal, the effects of which are multiplied by rapidly expanding human populations.

Deep ecologists and ecofeminists see a need to slow industrial development and population growth and changes in the kind of technology and waste disposal that are immediate causes of such crises, but point to the deeper cultural and spiritual problem underlying patterns of social and ecological domination, rooted in the splitting of mind from body, the alienation of the human concept of the self from the physical world. Ecofeminists stress the psychosocial roots of this alienation of mind from body, "man" from nature, in sexism, in the subjugation of women and the way the subjugation of women has formed both the symbolic-cultural and the practical-economic basis for the subjugation of nature.

In my first lecture, I reviewed the long history in Western thought, going back to the rise of patriarchy in the ancient Near East in the 4th or 5th millennia B.C., and continuing in modern Western thought in its scientific worldview and colonial system of world domination, of the interlocking relation of domination of women and domination of nature.[44] The question I wish to explore in this lecture is prospects for healing, healing the human community from sexism and from its alienation from the rest of nature, who are both

---

[43] Rosemary Radford Ruether, "Ecofeminism and Healing Ourselves, Healing the Earth," *Feminist Theology* 9 (May 1995) 51–62. This journal also contains Ruether's first lecture, "Ecofeminism: Symbolic and Social Connections of the Oppression of Women and the Domination of Nature."

[44] See my [Ruether's] *Gaia and God: An Ecofeminist Theology of Earth-Healing* (San Francisco: HarperSanFrancisco, 1992).

earth-kin and the sustaining matrix of our own lives. I will mainly explore some of the symbolic or theological changes to express and sustain a healing culture and only point briefly to the needed social changes, particularly in sexist domination of men over women.

Where can we find resources for a healing culture? I don't believe there is a ready-made feminist ecological culture that can be recovered from past cultures or at least accessible past cultures. I leave to the side the question of whether there were lost feminist ecological cultures suppressed by the rise of patriarchy back in some early gardener societies of early village and agricultural life. I question the assumption of any original paradise often implied in these constructions. Even if we could effectively recover the thought world behind such preliterate lost societies, I suspect they would be dealing with issues different from our own. The efforts to recover such pre-patriarchal ecofeminist cultures I see basically as imaginative efforts of people in advanced industrial societies driven by new crises of our times. I like many of the ideas in such imaginative efforts, but believe we need to own these as our own imaginative efforts springing from our context, rather than claiming that we have literally deciphered lost thought worlds of 8000 years ago from hints on fragments of sculpture.

Catherine Keller has suggested that feminists are the great recyclers of culture. In constructing a feminist or ecofeminist culture and spirituality, we are like Filipino orphans sifting through the great mountains of trash abandoned by destructive social systems and trying to recover useable bits and pieces from which to construct a new habitation.[45] While this is a grim image of our relation to the past, it does highlight two important aspects of our task: first, that there is much from the past that is useable, but it is useable only by being reconstructed in new forms, as material for new visions, as compost for new growth; and secondly that it is we who must be the artisans of this new culture. It will not be given to us ready made, either from the Jewish and Christian traditions, or from religious of other cultures.

We are facing a new situation which humans never faced before: namely, that human species power could grow so great that it could destroy its own planetary life basis. Past cultures saw humans as much less powerful, either struggling to subdue a powerful adversarial nature or else as being sustained within a much greater nature that might be bountiful or violent, but was not ours to control. Virtually all accessible cultures, including indigenous ones, had patterns of more or less severe subjugation of women, and many also tied this to subjugation of serf, slave or worker populations. Their cosmologies and religious mandates reflect and justify these patterns of domination.

---

[45] Oral remarks by Catherine Keller in a workshop in the conference on Buddhist-Christian Dialogue, Berkeley, August 1991; See also her article, "Talk about the Weather: The Greening of Eschatology" in *Ecofeminism and the Sacred,* ed. Carol J. Adams (New York: Continuum, 1993) 43.

But religious cultures do not only mandate the domination on which their societies are built. They also in various ways seek harmony and justice, overcoming enmity and alienation, finding reconciliation between humans, between humans and the world of nature and with the ultimate Source of Life, however that is understood. It is in these quests for harmony, reconciliation and justice that we may find the "shiny bits" in our trash heap to reconstruct a new house. Our legacy doubtless will have to be reconstructed by our children and children's children as well. The best we can do is to shape a house that is more sustainable as the base for their rebuilding.

I believe there are many cultures that can provide us with clues to a healing culture. The great Asian spiritualities of Taoism and Buddhism and, more problematically, Hinduism and Confucianism, have possibilities to be explored, particularly in the vision of letting go of overweening egoistic individualism, of compassion for all sentient beings and harmonization of the dynamic forces at work in the cosmos and society.

The many local cultures of indigenous peoples of the Americas, Africa, Asia and the Pacific islands, scorned by monotheists as "paganism," have gained new respect as we recognize how each of these peoples created their own bioregional culture that sustained the human community as a part of the community of animals and plants, earth and sky, past ancestors and future descendents. But we Western people, who have so deeply despised and destroyed the peoples of these cultures, cannot readily look to them for salvation. We must support their struggles to survive as distinct local cultures, and in the process learn some helpful hints for our work of culture-rebuilding by respectfully aiding their survival. As Europeans we can also turn to hints from our own pre-Christian pasts in the Celtic, Germanic and Slavic worlds, careful to free ourselves from fascist, racial misuse of such quests for European roots.

As a Euro-North American I find myself in a different place from Europeans. These Celtic or other Old European roots are not part of my landscape. The indigenous peoples of North America have been so alienated and destroyed that I have little right to claim use of their culture. Native American peoples have grown deeply suspicious and hostile to counter-cultural exploitation of their traditions from 'New Age people'. My first responsibility is to support their own separate survival in this land. Only if I really put in my dues over many years supporting their land and fishing rights, might I also earn the right to enter and learn from their culture.

This leaves me with the necessity of facing my own cultural heritage as my first task as an ecofeminist, the culture of the Jewish and Christian heritages with its roots in the Greek and Ancient Near Eastern worlds and its reshaping in modern Western cultures as the primary cultural base of my work. This does not mean that this is the only or even the best cultural base for such work. It simply means that I need to start from where I am, from my roots and their potential for new healthy growth.

We need to see ourselves in a process of converging dialogues, as ecofeminists of many regions make their own cultural syntheses: Zimbabwean ecofeminists like Tumani Nyjeka integrate Shona and Christian traditions; Indian ecofeminists like Vandana Shiva examine useable elements from pre-Hindu and Western scientific ideas;[46] Korean ecofeminists like Chung Hyun Khung integrate Christian, Buddhist, Confucian and Shamanist elements of their cultures.[47] Out of both an encouragement of these many distinct syntheses and dialogue between them we can perhaps begin to glimpse the flowering of many healing cultures in mutually supportive relations.

The first thing we as Western Christians need to give up is the illusion that there is one right way to create one world culture and we can and should do it all. Once we give up the Christian (and U.S. American) imperial universalist demand, we can be freed to play with the insightful aspects of our Christian-Jewish-Greek and Near Eastern heritage, as well as critically appraising its problems, letting go of both the need to inflate its significance as the one true way or the opposite impulse to repudiate it as a total toxic waste. In my book *Gaia and God,* I suggest two patterns of Biblical thought that can be important resources for ecological theology, spirituality and ethics: covenantal ethics and sacramental cosmology.

Covenantal ethics, as one finds it particularly in the sabbatical legislation of Hebrew Scripture, gives us a vision of the local land and household, with its rooted community of humans, the farmer-householder, wife, children and attached workers, domestic animals and wild animals, land, all living in one covenantal relation with a caretaking God. Although the patriarchal and slaveholding construction of this local covenantal unit must be rejected, what is insightful is the sense that humans, even the householder, do not own this land and cannot do with it what they will.

Humans are caretakers of a land that ultimately comes from and belongs to God and are accountable to God for the wellbeing of all beings in it, humans, animals, the soil itself. This wellbeing demands limited use of human and animal labor and the soil, and periodic rest and restoration. Every seven days, all beings must rest and be restored [see Exod 20:8-19, for example]. There is no mandate here for a workaholic ethic. To work and produce ad infinitum, without regular time for rest, restoration and celebration is a sin, not a virtue. Not only must there be regular rest, restoration and celebration, but on a periodic basis, every seven years, there must be a great rest and restoration, in which all lies fallow for a whole year.[48]

---

[46] Vandana Shiva, *Staying Alive: Women, Ecology and Development in India* (New Delhi: Kali for Women, 1989).

[47] C. Hyun Khung, "Come Holy Spirit: Renew the Whole Creation," address at the World Council of Churches, February 1991, published in the journal *In God's Image* (Autumn 1992).

[48] Editors' note: the Sabbath Year and Year of Jubillee are also noted in other selections, above.

Then after seven times seven years in the Great Jubilee there must be the great restoration, which includes the revolutionary dismantling of the systems of unjust accumulation of land and exploitation of labor that have occurred over the past two generations. Debts must be cancelled, slaves must be freed, land alienated from peasants through debt and enslavement must be restored. There must be a land reform that recreates a society where each household has the land for its own maintenance. Unjust social and economic relations are cancelled, as well as animals and land given rest so all can be restored to a just and sustainable balance.[49]

As nations today through the United Nations enter into environmental covenants to limit toxic wastes dumped into the sea, or blown into the air, how can we deepen the fuller sense of the meaning of being in a covenantal relation as humans together on the one planet earth? How can we begin to recognize that covenantal relations means, not only limiting destructive use of the land, air and water, but also periodic restoration; returning land stolen from Mayan Indians in Chiapas by the *ladifundistas,* replanting devastated forests and mandating indigenous people and not lumber companies as their caretakers?

Covenantal ethics is complemented in the Biblical heritage with sacramental cosmology found in the Jewish Wisdom tradition and New Testament cosmic Christology rooted in it. Here we have a sense, not only of the whole cosmic community of nature as alive, but as grounded in and bodying forth the divine Spirit which is its source of life and renewal of life. Here we find a deep respect for the body as the sacramental bodying forth of the creative Spirit, not simply as human body, but as the whole body of the cosmos that surrounds us and sustains our life.[50]

The God in whom we live and move and have our being is not some detached spiritual being in heaven, but the one who is in and through and under the whole life process. The whole cosmos is God's body. For Christians it is the Body of Christ [1 Cor 12:27] as the overcoming of our alienation and separation from God's sacramental presence in creation. We are called to commune with God, not by turning away from body, but in and through the mystery of bodies who are sacramental presences of the divine.

While Protestant ecological theologians, such as Presbyterian Richard Austin, have been strong on the covenantal type of ecological theology and ethics,[51] Catholics have particularly contributed to the recovery of the sense of the sacramentality of the cosmos, an understanding of God grounded in Wisdom theology and cosmological Christology. Elizabeth Johnson's book, *She Who Is,* transforms the whole of Trinitarian thought into a sophiological terms, while Matthew Fox's *The Cosmic Christ* reclaims the understanding of Christ as the renewal of the cosmic ground of being. Ecologians, such as

---

[49] Lev 25; see Ruether, *Gaia and God,* 207–15.

[50] Wis 6–8; see Ruether, *Gaia and God,* 229–27.

[51] Richard Cartwright Austin, *Hope for the Land: Nature in the Bible* (Atlanta: John Knox, 1988).

Matthew Fox and Thomas Berry, have reached out in expanded ecumenical dialogue with Asian and Indigenous spiritualities and have explored the spiritual possibilities of post-Newtonian physics. In a collaboration between Thomas Berry and physicist Brian Swimme, a new cosmic story is emerging which they believe might provide the world view for ecological consciousness and culture.[52]

What are some of the symbolic shifts that might go into an ecological culture? One important element is the reshaping of our dualistic concept of reality as split between soulless matter and transcendent male-identified consciousness. We need to discover our actual reality as latecomers to the planet. The world of nature, plants and animals existed billions of years before we came on the scene. Nature does not need us to rule over it, but ran itself very well and better without humans. We are the parasites that feed on the top of the food chain, consuming more and more, and tossing off our wastes in a way that poisons the channels of renewal.

We need to recognize our utter dependency on the life-producing matrix of the planet in order to learn to reintegrate our human system of production, consumption and waste into the ecological feedback patterns by which nature sustains and renews life. This might begin by revisualizing the relation of mind or human intelligence to nature. Mind or consciousness does not originate in the stars, as Plato thought, nor is it infused into bodies by a transcendent God outside the world. Rather, human consciousness is an intensification of interactive awareness that exists to some degree on every level of reality, from subatomic physics, to organic molecules, to photosynthesizing plants to increasingly self-aware and communicating animals. We might think of our particular gift of symbol-making consciousness as the point at which all nature becomes conscious of itself in a new self-reflective way, not in the sense of separating us from other species, but in the sense of celebrating the whole cosmic creative process, as well as learning to harmonize our needs with those of the rest of the earth-community.

Such a reintegration of mind into body, consciousness into nature, will also reshape our concept of God. God in patriarchal thought has been modeled after alienated male-identified mind or soul that has been thought of as prior to body, existing in an unoriginated, unembodied mental realm outside of and ruling over the physical cosmos. Ecofeminist theology embodies God in and through and under the whole cosmic process. God in this sense can be imagined neither as exclusively male nor as anthropomorphic, but rather as the font from which the variety of plants and animals well up in each generation, the matrix that sustains and renews their life-giving interdependency.

---

[52] Elizabeth A. Johnson, *She Who Is: The Mystery of God in Feminist Theological Perspective* (New York: Crossroad, 1992); Matthew Fox, *The Coming of the Cosmic Christ* (San Francisco: Harper and Row, 1988); T. M. Berry, *The Dream of the Earth* (San Francisco: Sierra Club Books, 1988); B. Swimme and Thomas Mary Berry, *The Universe Story* (San Francisco: HarperSanFrancisco, 1992).

Patriarchal theologians will immediately accuse ecofeminist theologians of immanentism, of a concept of God that lacks transcendence. But here we need to rethink the whole concept of transcendence, freeing it from its captivity in the dualistic mind-body, male-female split that aligns God with split-off male rationality and females with mindless matter. We need transcendence in ecofeminist theology, not as a concept of a God who is male disembodied mind outside the universe, but as a renewing divine Spirit radically free from our systems of domination and distortion.

The male God who rules from outside the universe is not transcendent in this sense, but is the ultimate captive justification of patriarchal domination and delusion. The true spirit of renewing life is both truly free of all such rationalizations of injustice, but also closer to us than we are to ourselves. Ecofeminist Wisdom both sustains daily life processes and also grounds the creative transformations by which we free ourselves from such distortions to rediscover the real nexus of just relations.[53]

Perhaps the most difficult theoretical task for ecofeminist theology is to bring together in one framework the God who underlies the evolutionary life process and the God of compassion who defends the poor and the weak [see Ps 146:9, for example]. To put it another way, how does ecofeminism deal with the relation between God and nature in terms of good and evil? If evil is seen as distorted relationships, ontologically and socially, that falsely names mind as alienated from body, and uses this split to model hierarchical relations between men and women, ruling and subjugated races and classes, then perhaps we can name evil as unnatural, as a falsification of the biophilic relations that sustain mind-body unity and human-human mutuality. In this sense to overcome evil as distorted relationality is to restore justice to human relations and harmony to earth.

But nature is nevertheless not paradise. There is mortality, finitude, competition between species for food and space, the feeding of every species on the bodies of other species in one form or another, violent upheavals of land and sea and air which are painful, tragic and at times very destructive of particular lives, although having a place in the sustaining of the whole. If God is this life-sustaining process of nature, then God seems very distant, if not contrary, to the God of liberation theology, the God of preferential option for the poor and the most vulnerable. Is this kind of God of the ethics of compassion unnatural, lacking roots in nature and contrary to the life process of evolutionary survival?

Since it is humans who have generated this concept of a God of compassion for the poor and weak as our best ethic, and humans ourselves are the product of natural evolution, we cannot say that such as ethic is unnatural, but

---

[53] I owe the inspiration for this analysis of transcendence to the article by Dorothy Soelle, "Godlanguage and Patriarchy," in *COELI International* (Summer, 1992) 1ff.

perhaps that it is paradoxically related to the ethic of mutual limitation of life for the sake of the whole that causes the weakest members of each species to die or be killed so the strongest survive. Human spirit produces the ethic of compassion for the weak to temper the ethic of survival of the fittest, but ultimately we can do so only through a complex synthesis of the two ethics that is never stable or complete and always replete with tragedy.

To allow endless human fertility to populate the earth is no more compassionate than to allow so many plants to jostle one another in a garden that none has space to grow. A good gardener weeds out many plants to create the space for few to grow optimally. We need to limit our numbers as well while at the same time creating conditions for those who live to grow optimally. This is integral to the work of both justice and compassion. But we need also to seek the most compassionate ways to limit our numbers, starting with limiting the affluence of those groups who consume the most and empowering all women throughout the world to be the decision makers on their own reproduction, rather than cutting down the lives of the born through disease and violence, as is presently the case.

This sense of mutual self-limitation for the sake of the welfare of the whole also must reshape the human sense of self in relation to the life cycle. The sustaining of organic community of plant and animal life is a continual cycle of growth and decay. The Western flight from mortality has been a flight from the disintegration side of the life cycle, from accepting ourselves as part of that process. By pretending that we can immortalize ourselves, our souls, and perhaps even our bodies for some future resurrection, we are immortalizing our garbage and polluting the earth. If we are really to learn to recycle our garbage as fertilizer for new growth, our waste as matter for new artifacts, we need a spirituality of recycling that accepts ourselves as part of that process of growth, decay, reintegration into the earth and new growth.

Human bodies are finite organisms, centers of experience, which also decay, fall into organic waste and are to be composted back into the nexus of matter to rise again as new organic forms. And what of our consciousness, what we have called our souls? I think this is not separable from this same process of disintegration, extinguished with our distinct mortal organisms and entering again into the well of dependent origination. Perhaps we might think of God as the great consciousness underlying the whole life process that carries and expands with the remembering of each of our many mortal embodiments.

These tentative conversions of the dualistic ways we have symbolized the relation of mind and body, God and nature, good and evil, mortal and immortal are for the sake of freeing us from the cultural rationalizations and justifications of alienation and domination. But in order for such symbolic transformation to bear fruit they must be incarnated into new social systems that relate men and women, races and ethnic groups, in a global community where all enjoy adequate means of life and where the land, air, soil, forests, oceans and rivers can be freed of toxic poisons and provide the sustaining basis for all earth creatures. This will also involve new sustainable technologies that draw on sustainable energy sources rather than fossil fuels, and which recycle all waste or no longer produce what cannot be recycled. But the technological aspect of environmental sustainability must be integrated into the struggle for justice, justice between humans, justice between humans and the rest of earth creatures.

The gap between our small efforts on the local level and the global system that perpetuates injustice and violence between humans and the rest of nature is so huge it is easy to be paralyzed and despair. We have no guarantee that optimal justice or goodness will win. Nature's inherent tendency to survive does not guarantee that humans will survive or that the kinds of earth creatures we particularly love will survive. Nor is God outside the whole system to sweep in to rescue us from our folly. The God of life process and also compassion for the weak is in the process, suffering and struggling for life in it and with it.

Our faith does not lie in assurance of victory, but in commitment to keep up the struggle for an earth community in just and sustainable balances, even as we lose many individuals and even whole species along the way. We need to shape new households that model just and sustainable relations between humans, beginning with relations between men and women, and between human and natural ecology. These household communities need to be attractive models of sustainable technology, harmonized social relations and celebrative culture. We need to shape such households, not to withdraw into them, but as the base for an alternative earth culture and a struggle to reshape the larger systems into a sustainable earth community as a whole. This struggle to reshape the death systems of our world cannot flow only from anger, fear and guilt. It must be deeply grounded in joy in the goodness of life and reverence for its gracious vitality. To create glimpses of health and joy is our task as ecofeminist practical theologians.

Chapter Seven

Christian Love at the Margins of Life

Christian love demands the utmost respect for life. As we learned in chapter 5, the tradition of pacifism forbids the intentional killing of human life, while the tradition of the just war allows it only to protect innocent life. While by no means easy to fulfill, these requirements were at least straightforward for most of Christian history. In recent decades, however, many Christians have become less sure about their obligations to those at the margins of life—those emerging into life and those departing from it. This perplexity has myriad sources: more complex understandings of conception and fetal development, the relative safety of abortion procedures, the development of advanced life support techniques, advances in neurology, and perhaps most of all the increasing desire to exercise personal autonomy over choices in both reproduction and death.

This chapter will thus focus on these two issues from the margins of life: abortion and euthanasia.[1] The positions we take on these issues ought to be consistent with one another and with other ethical commitments we have made. The "consistent life ethic" is one such attempt to develop a coherent moral system based on the basic moral duty to further human dignity in all areas of life. It links pro-life and anti-euthanasia positions to commitments to work for greater economic justice, improved race relations, peace, and alternatives to capital punishment. While many Christians may disagree with these positions, the consistent life ethic has attracted a broad range of support from both Catholics and Protestant Evangelicals. A representative article by David Gushee is in this chapter because it illustrates the ecumenical dialogue that we have hoped to further through this book.

---

[1] What we learn here is directly applicable to a broader range of issues. Clarity about abortion will shed some light on stem cell research, cloning, and new reproductive technologies. Clarity about euthanasia will shed some light on medically futile treatments, harvesting of organs for transplant, and obligations to patients in persistent vegetative states.

Fetal Personhood and Abortion

Abortion is a surprisingly common occurrence in contemporary life. The Alan Guttmacher Institute estimates that 1.31 million abortions took place in the United States in 2000, terminating about one-quarter of all pregnancies. Each year in the United States about two percent of all women between 15 and 44 years of age have an abortion. While the legality and safety of abortion contributes to its frequency, the institute also estimates that 20 million of the 46 million abortions worldwide in 2000 were obtained illegally.[2] Abortion is by no means confined to the contemporary world. Some historians estimate that as many as twenty percent of all pregnancies were terminated by abortion in the United States already in 1840, when abortion was both unsafe and considered a social taboo.[3]

The frequency of abortion in modern life is matched only by the rancor of the debate between disputants. At the heart of the issue are perplexing questions about the nature of humanity itself. What does it mean to be a human being? The issue is not simply about "when life begins," for we do not grant most living things the fundamental respect that we give human beings. The issue also cannot be resolved simply by an appeal to human DNA or a human physical structure, for these criteria also apply to cadavers and human tissue. The issue—rightly put—is, "Who do we consider a *living, human person?* To use slightly different terminology, we are asking, "Who is a *full member of the human community?*" or "Who is *"one of us?"*

Christians have answered this question in various ways throughout history when they have considered fetal life. A brief review of this history is in order as preparation for the normative debate over abortion that is taken up by the readings in this chapter.

The Bible does not address abortion directly. There are no references to abortion in the New Testament and only one indirect statement about fetal life in the Hebrew Bible. The law code of the Book of Exodus (21:22) prescribes the death penalty as punishment for causing the death of a pregnant woman but only a fine for causing a fatal miscarriage. One can infer, then, that the Mosaic law values fetal life but does not grant it full legal personhood. Without any clear directive for abortion in the Bible, Christians have had to work through the implications of broader biblical themes, such as love, justice, respect for human limits, and responsibilities for all members of the covenant community. Some ethicists also point to the tremendous importance on biological procreation in the Hebrew culture. Some others find meaning in the

---

[2] The Alan Guttmacher Institute, "Facts in Brief: Inducted Abortion." http://www.agi-usa.org/pubs/fb_induced_abortion.html (accessed September 20, 2004).

[3] Raymond J. Devettere, *Practical Decision Making in Health Care Ethics: Cases and Concepts* (Washington, D.C.: Georgetown University Press, 1995) 292–93. Chapter 11 of Devettere's text is an excellent introduction to the moral history of abortion and is the source for many of the facts in this introduction.

poetic references in the Hebrew Bible to God's knowledge of human beings that extends even to prenatal life (for example, Ps 139:13-16).

In an effort to gain additional clarity, early Christian moralists turned for guidance to classical philosophy. Plato, whose philosophy was esteemed by the early and medieval church, believed that the crude material substance of the human body is animated by an eternal soul, which enters the body sometime before birth and departs from it at death. Plato believed that fetal movement, which can be felt by the mother sometime around the midpoint of pregnancy, indicated the infusion of the life-giving soul into the fetus. Aristotle agreed with Plato that the developing fetus is not "one of us" until it is vivified by the soul, though he disagreed with Plato about the timing of this momentous event. Aristotle believed that humans have not one soul, but three. He regarded a soul as less a substance than a capacity for a certain type of action. All living things have a "vegetative soul," which engenders them with the power to grow and develop. All animals have an "animal soul," which provides the capacity to exercise the will. Human beings alone, however, also have a "rational soul," which is the capacity to reason. When does the human fetus become fully human? Aristotle believed that the development of the three souls is sequential, so that the rational soul could not appear until the animal soul is in place. Since gender differentiation is a common trait in all animals, its appearance may signal the development of the animal soul. Aristotle believed that male embryos develop male genitalia as early as forty days, while female embryos do not develop a vaginal opening until the ninetieth day.[4] Since we could not know whether the fetus is male or female, Aristotle reasoned that the developing fetus could be regarded as a human person as early as the fortieth day.

The Christian church largely adopted the teachings of Plato and Aristotle as it formulated its positions on abortion. The early church emphatically rejected infanticide and exposure of infants, which were widely practiced in the Roman world.[5] Officially, the church discouraged abortion at any time, but it regarded only abortions after vivification as tantamount to homicide. This position was formalized in Gracian's *Decretum*, the body of canon law that governed the church from 1227 until 1917. The determination of vivification largely followed Plato's teachings until the thirteenth century, when they were set aside in favor of Aristotle's theory.

---

[4] Aristotle's curious position is based on the faulty understanding of embryology in the ancient world. Early scientists probably mistook the residual tail present in early fetuses as male genitalia. Today we know that all fetuses begin as females, though an infusion of hormones differentiates males at the end of the first trimester.

[5] See, for example, our selection from Tertullian's *Apology* in chapter 5. Tertullian also considers abortion a "speedier form of child murder." However, it is not clear whether Tertullian has in mind all abortions or only those that occur after the time of vivification.

During the twentieth century, the new science of embryology has largely supplanted the authority formerly given to classical philosophers. Many Christian moralists point to the development of certain biological structures in the embryo that indicate that the embryo has passed a critical threshold of personhood. As we learned in the first chapter, however, bare scientific "fact" is not a sufficient basis for ethics. These biological markers make sense only within a particular value system. The following list indicates some of the major positions in Christian ethics of what constitutes a human person and the biological markers in fetal development that are associated with them:

- A living being with a human genetic code → fertilization (the first 24 hours after intercourse)
- Stable existence as an individual organism → the implantation of the zygote in the uterus (a few days after conception)
- Psychic awareness → the connection of neurons to the cerebral cortex (around the 20th week),
- Capacity for independent life → fetal viability (now the 26th–28th week)

The timing of the threshold event is critical for moral reasoning. Those ethicists who regard fertilization as the critical event, for example, might allow barrier methods of contraception but not those that block implantation. Those ethicists who regard psychic awareness as critical may allow early abortions under some conditions but not later ones.

Some Christian ethicists distinguish *actual* and *potential* personhood. They may conclude, for example, that an early fetus does not yet have a capacity for psychic awareness that is necessary for personhood, but nevertheless argue that the fetus should be protected in anticipation of its potential to develop into a true person at a later time.

Christian moral reasoning also takes place in the context of abortion law. In the United States, this law is shaped by the landmark *Roe v. Wade* (1973) decision. "Jane Roe" (a pseudonym) challenged a new restrictive Texas statute that forbade abortions unless the expectant mother's life was directly threatened. In response, the U.S. Supreme Court ruled that women have a constitution right to privacy in the area of family planning.[6] Its ruling instructed states that they could not restrict abortion during the first trimester of pregnancy. They are allowed to regulate abortion procedures during the second trimester, but only to ensure their safety for the mother. The court recognized a growing claim of the fetus on the state as it approaches viability. It thus permitted states to regulate or even forbid abortions in the last trimester of pregnancy, provided they are not necessary to protect the life or health of the mother.

---

[6] Because the Supreme Court treated abortion as a privacy issue, the United States has much less regulation of abortion—and much less public support for pregnant women—than almost any other developed nation. See Mary Ann Glendon, *Abortion and Divorce in Western Law* (Cambridge, Mass.: Harvard University Press, 1987).

One of the most important follow-up cases to Roe was *Planned Parenthood Association of Southeastern Pennsylvania v. Casey* (1992). President Reagan managed to fill the court with conservative justices, and most court watchers were shocked that it did not simply overturn *Roe*. The court ruled that the personhood of the fetus is fundamentally a matter of religious faith, and thus not a matter for the justices to decide. However, the court also recognized that the fetus is at least a potential child and thus a legitimate subject of the state's interest. The court fundamentally reaffirmed the right to abortion, but it allowed states to regulate abortion before viability, provided those regulations do not create an "undue burden" on the woman.

Two readings included in this chapter add another dimension that we have not yet explored. The authors, Beverly Harrison and Sidney Callahan, are aligned on different sides of the issue though both argue their positions on feminist grounds. These essays reveal that the abortion debate is so acrimonious because it is a lightning rod for a host of cultural issues: the meaning and purpose of sexuality, the changing concept of "motherhood," gender roles and social power, and the relative weight given to autonomy and responsibility in human community. The issue cuts to the very heart of what it means to be a person in society. Feminists especially have a vital stake in the outcome of this debate.

Assisted Suicide and Euthanasia

Euthanasia means "good death." The term conjures up hopes for a quick and easy death that is free of suffering and indignity. End-of-life care is a pressing issue today because modern medical technology now allows us to maintain cardio-vascular functions in a dying body almost indefinitely. However, not many people believe that we *should* do all that medical technology *can* do.

Before we begin our analysis of this issue, some definitions are in order. First, we need to distinguish *active euthanasia,* a direct intervention that causes the patient's death, and *passive euthanasia,* the withdrawal or withholding of medical treatments so that a disease can run its course. A second set of distinctions are between *voluntary euthanasia,* in which the patient expresses a clear desire to die, *involuntary euthanasia,* in which a patient is euthanized against his or her wishes, and *non-voluntary euthanasia,* in which the patient does not express clear wishes about end of life treatment. A consensus has emerged in recent decades that voluntary, passive euthanasia is morally acceptable. In these cases, patients may refuse medical interventions like tube feedings, antibiotics, and respiration so that they are allowed to die. Involuntary euthanasia, of course, is tantamount to murder and non-voluntary euthanasia normally is forbidden. Thus, the real moral debate concerns voluntary, active euthanasia.

Both federal and state laws now support voluntary passive euthanasia. Most states have developed "living-will" and "durable-power-of-attorney" statutes that ensure that these decisions are truly voluntary and communicate end-of-life wishes to the medical staff. Only the State of Oregon and the Netherlands have developed a legal framework that allows physician-assisted suicide. Oregon has survived several legal challenges to its law by the Bush administration. It is anticipated that the Supreme Court ultimately will have to settle the dispute.

Does the Christian moral tradition allow a dying patient to take pills or receive an injection that actively ends his or her life? Could a Christian physician or nurse assist a patient who wants to do so? As we work through these issues, we should keep in mind both its similarities and important differences from the issue of abortion. Both concern our responsibilities to one another and ourselves when we are most vulnerable at the margins of life. Both issues also draw from our understandings of what it means to be a human being. But there are crucial differences as well. First, abortion often deals with direct conflicts or interests between parties in a way that euthanasia normally does not. Second, a decision for euthanasia is made by an autonomous person about her or his own life, while one of the parties in the abortion is entirely dependent on the decisions of others. Third, abortion will end a life that has only begun to live into its potential, while euthanasia ends a life that has largely run its course.

Christians can find only indirect guidance from Scripture as they work through the issue of euthanasia. The Hebrew Bible is full of stories that mention suicide. The most notable of stories concerns Samson, whose death by his own hand is pictured as the redeeming moment of his life (Judges 16:18-31). The writer of the New Testament Letter to the Hebrews considers Samson an exemplary figure, keeping good company with David, Samuel, and the prophets (Hebrews 11:32). The New Testament does not mention suicide, but it has to come to terms with the example of Jesus, who gave himself up to death. One may draw different conclusions from Jesus' martyrdom. On the one hand, Christians regard his death as a great travesty of justice and affirm his deep respect for all human life. On the other hand, Jesus' example also teaches us that human life is not ultimate and that death itself can be redeemed when it serves a higher cause.

In the end, Jesus' deep respect for life and aversion to killing shaped the Christian tradition most profoundly. Until this century, all branches of the Christian church unequivocally rejected suicide. This rejection is all the more striking when we consider the affirmation of some forms of suicide in much of classical philosophy. Plato, Aristotle, the Epicureans, and the Stoics all supported suicide when life became so burdensome that it could no longer be lived virtuously. By implication, it may even be a virtue to assist another to commit suicide in order to end his or her suffering. These classical sources have gained a wider following today among those who seek greater control over their deaths. Gilbert Meilaender argues against this perspective in the last reading of this chapter. He responds that from a Christian perspective, our lives are not our own. As children of God, our true aim is not to "minimize suffering" but to "maximize love and care."

READINGS

---

1. Biblical Foundations

EXODUS 21:22

The case listed in this passage belongs to the "covenant code," the statutes that establish the basic rules of justice in early Israel. There are differences in the translation of the phrase "so that no harm follows." The original Hebrew specifies only a fine for causing a fatal miscarriage. The verse was translated differently in the Septuagint, the Greek translation of the Hebrew Scriptures completed in the third century B.C.E. This translation prescribed the death penalty both for the accidental homicide and the miscarriage. The Septuagint's wording may reflect the teachings of Aristotle, whose works were well-regarded in Alexandria, Egypt, at that time. The mistranslation took on great importance for patristic and medieval theologians, who typically had no capacity to read the Hebrew bible in its original language.

PSALM 139:13-16

Psalm 139 is best understood as a poetic expression of wonder at God's knowledge and grace. This particular stanza of the Psalm answers the question "Whither shall I go from thy spirit?" (v. 7).[7] The psalmist expresses wonder at the presence of God, which extends from heaven to the depths of the sea, from the darkest places even to his mother's womb.

PHILIPPIANS 2:5-11

In these verses Paul probably is quoting an early Christian hymn that celebrates the humility and obedience of Jesus. The hymn praises Jesus' willingness to "empty" himself (v. 7) in death to achieve a larger purpose, but also affirms that death does not have the last word.

---

[7] Editors' note: As translated in the King James Version (KJV) of the Bible, available at http://www.biblegateaway.com (accessed September 20, 2004).

2. David Gushee, "The Consistent Ethic of Life"

David Gushee is the Graves Professor of Moral Philosophy at Union University, an institution affiliated with the Tennessee Baptist Convention. Gushee addresses what Spencer Perkins called the "pro-life credibility gap," that is, the tendency of some conservative Protestants to take fervent anti-abortion stands but ignore other issues that affirm human life and further the quest for social justice. His response, the "consistent life ethic" or "seamless garment approach" illustrates a point of contact between many Catholics and socially engaged conservative Protestants. Gushee himself is now a Protestant but has Catholic roots.

Paths to the Consistent Life Ethic

What[8] moral vision shall Christians bring into our nation's public square? Is there a way to sort through the rich but multifaceted moral witness of the Scripture and of later Christian tradition and end up with a coherent moral vision? Can Christians get beyond our current moral divisions and offer at least a core moral witness to church and society upon which most or all can agree?

I want to propose today that what has been called the consistent life ethic (or consistent ethic of life, or seamless garment approach) is the best single statement of Christian moral vision currently available on the landscape of Christian thought. It is a perspective that emerges from Scripture, has strong roots in Christian tradition, and is quite relevant to contemporary experience. It is a moral vision that speaks effectively to at least those open to hearing the Christian voice in the public square. And, while it is not a recipe for ending the scandalous divisions that afflict the church's moral teaching and public proclamation, it is an approach that does extract the best moral commitments of the "left" and the "right" in American church life . . .

Consider the following striking comments from the late Spencer Perkins, a black Christian leader who died suddenly just a few years ago. In 1989, Perkins wrote:

> Abortion—and the pro-life movement—present black evangelicals with a dilemma. It is not that we question the evil of abortion; Jesus clearly would have condemned it. But for me, a black man, to join your demonstrations against abortion, I would need to know that you understand God's concern for justice everywhere . . .
>
> It is not a simple, glib response, then, when I must counsel an unwed black teenager against an abortion, even though I believe with all my heart that abor-

---

[8] ©2000–2003 by The Christian Ethics Today Foundation (www.ChristianEthicsToday.com) and is available online at www.christianethicstoday.com/Issue/032/Issue_032_February_2001.htm. The article was originally delivered for the Staley Lectures at Cumberland College in April, 2000; revised (for inclusivity).

tion is morally wrong. I feel that if the love of Christ compels me to save the lives of children, that same love should compel me to take more responsibility for them once they are born.[9]

Perkins was struck by what he called a "pro-life credibility gap." Those Christians who led the pro-life movement and were most visible in it were, in his view, not at all interested in issues of justice for African-Americans. Instead, as he put it, "Ever since I can remember, it has been almost axiomatic that if we blacks took a stand on an issue, conservative [white] evangelical Christians would line up on the opposite side of the street, blocking our way." What is the meaningfulness of the term "pro-life" if those who use it are not interested in advancing the well being (the "life") of a suffering black population here and now? That is Perkins' question, and it's a good one . . .

The larger pattern has been named by Pope John Paul II, as a "culture of death." He elaborates as follows: "It is possible to speak in a certain sense of a war of the powerful against the weak: a life that would require greater acceptance, love and care is considered useless . . . and is therefore rejected in one way or another. A person who, because of illness, handicap or, more simply, just by existing, compromises the well-being or life-style of those more favoured tends to be looked upon as an enemy to be resisted or eliminated. In this way a kind of conspiracy against life is unleashed."[10]

The demand for a consistent ethic of life, then, has emerged as an outcry, not always fully coherent, from those who have noted—or experienced—gaps in the church's moral vision and practice or who have paid attention to dangerous trends in the culture. Women notice a concern for babies but not for their mothers or for abused or exploited women in general. Blacks notice a concern for abortion but not racial justice. Those who work with the poor notice overall complacency toward that field of misery and degradation, while those concerned for the ill and elderly watch with shock as the acceptance of euthanasia grows. What is needed is a moral vision big enough to encompass the full range of moral problems that Christians face both in their own lives and in a confused culture. The consistent ethic of life is the best answer I have yet seen.

Fundamentals of the Consistent Life Ethic

A definition of the consistent life ethic could be crafted as follows: a moral commitment to respecting, protecting, and enhancing human life at every stage and in every context. This moral commitment is grounded in a particular reading of Scripture and a particular understanding of Christian theology

---

[9] Quoted in David K. Clark and Robert V. Rakestraw, eds., *Readings in Christian Ethics,* vol. 2, *Issues and Applications* (Grand Rapids, Mich.: Baker Books, 1996) 268, 270.

[10] Pope John Paul II, *The Gospel of Life,* trans. of *Evangelium vitae* (New York: Random House Publishers) 22.

that goes back deep into the history of the church. Michael Gorman describes the roots of a consistent life ethic this way: "The earliest Christian ethic, from Jesus to Constantine, can be described as a consistent pro-life ethic . . . It pleaded for the poor, the weak, women, children and the unborn. This pro-life ethic discarded hate in favor of love, war in favor of peace, oppression in favor of justice, bloodshed in favor of life. The Christian's response to abortion was one important aspect of this consistent pro-life ethic."[11]

Let us consider for a few moments the biblical underpinnings of this historically important perspective.

1. GOD IS THE AUTHOR OF HUMAN LIFE

Genesis 2:7 reads as follows: "The LORD God formed the man from the dust of the ground and breathed into his nostrils the breath of life, and the man became a living being."[12]

The Bible tells us that God was directly and personally responsible for making the first man, Adam, and the first woman, Eve. The Scripture repeatedly harkens back to God's role as originator of the human race. As the potter shapes the clay, so God shaped us [see Jer 18:6]. This is a fact not only to be respected, but also to be celebrated, as the psalmist does:

> For you created my inmost being;
> you knit me together in my mother's womb.
> I praise you because I am fearfully and wonderfully made;
> your works are wonderful,
> I know that full well.
> My frame was not hidden from you
> when I was made in the secret place.
> When I was woven together in the depths of the earth,
> your eyes saw my unformed body.
> All the days ordained for me
> were written in your book
> before one of them came to be.
>
> (Ps 139:13-16)

The Bible affirms that we exist by God's will, that we are the creatures of a loving creator God. The consistent life ethic is grounded here. It is impos-

---

[11] Michael J. Gorman, *Abortion and the Early Church: Christian, Jewish and Pagan Attitudes in the Greco-Roman World,* reprint ed. (Eugene, Ore.: Wipf and Stock, 1988) 90.

[12] Editors' note as found in the New International Version (NIV) of the Bible, available at http://www.gateway.com (accessed September 20, 2004). This is almost exactly the same as the most recent version of the New American Bible. Unless otherwise noted, other passages in this selection are also from the NIV translation: © Copyright 1973, 1978, 1984 by International Bible Society (http://www.gospelcom.net/ibs/, accessed September 20, 2004). All rights reserved worldwide.

sible to sustain it with full vigor outside of a theistic worldview that includes a belief in God as Creator.

2. GOD MADE US "IN GOD'S IMAGE" AND "LIKENESS"

Genesis 1:26-27 reads:

> Then God said, 'Let us make humankind in our image, according to our likeness; and let them have dominion over the fish of the sea, and over the birds of the air, and over the cattle, and over all the wild animals of the earth, and over every creeping thing that creeps upon the earth.'
> So God created humankind in his image,
>   in the image of God he created them;
>   male and female he created them."[13]

While God created all forms of life, only humans are described as being made in God's image *(selem)* and likeness *(demut)*. To be made in the image of God probably means two things. One has to do with the attributes that we share in common with God. Our capacities reflect his in a small way—our ability to think, to love, to create, to relate to others, to make choices. To explain "image," various central God-like attributes have been proposed at different stages of Christian thought. It used to be that our reasoning capacity was lifted up for emphasis. These days it is relationality that is often described as most God-like or God-resembling. But whatever is emphasized, in various ways God made humans and only humans to be like himself. How remarkable that we were designed to share certain attributes of God our Maker.

The other dimension of meaning here has to do not with human attributes but instead human responsibilities. Bruce Birch has argued that this is actually the right way to understand the meaning of the *imago dei*—"adam is God's own special representative, not simply by designation . . . but by design."[14] To be made in the image of God is to share in the tasks of God, the work of God on this earth. We will "image" God—represent God—to the rest of creation. We see the theme already in this passage, where God commands us to take responsibility and represent his rule over the fish and the birds, the livestock, and all the creatures.

Whichever aspect of the *imago dei* is lifted up for emphasis, it is a designation that confers awesome responsibilities on all who relate to human life—that is, all of us.

---

[13] Editors' note: Scripture passage adapted to NRSV for inclusivity.
[14] Bruce Birch, *Let Justice Roll Down: The Old Testament, Ethics, and Christian Life* (Louisville, Ky.: Westminster/ John Knox, 1991) 87.

3. GOD HAS DECLARED HUMAN LIFE WORTHY OF HONOR, GLORY, AND RESPECT

Ponder the majestic language of Psalm 8:

When I look at your heavens, the work of your fingers,
 the moon and the stars that you have established;
what are human beings that you are mindful of them,
 mortals that you care for them?

Yet you have made them a little lower than God,
 and crowned them with glory and honor.[15]

(Ps 8:3-5)

Despite our many obvious faults—our deeply embedded sinful nature—Scripture tells us that God has crowned humanity as a whole, and each human life in particular, with glory and honor. We are declared to be just "a little lower than the heavenly beings" (v. 5; NIV)—some translations say, "than God" [as above]. Thus that is what we are, by God's decree—even when we don't look like it, even when our unworthiness of such a designation seems all too clear.

Thus far we have seen that God is the author of each and every human life. God made us in his image, his likeness. God has declared human life worthy of honor, glory, and respect. These are the theological truths that undergird the concept of the "sanctity of human life," which itself lies at the heart of the consistent life ethic.

To speak of the sanctity of human life is to claim that God has declared both by action and by his word that every human life is of immense value to him. Sanctity comes from the Latin *sanctus,* which means holy. Christians believe that God has declared every human life sacred, even holy, not because of our own moral goodness but because of the value that God has placed upon it. God sees each human life however humble or flawed as special, set apart; not to be trifled with, dishonored, or disrespected.

In addition, the immense value that God places on our lives has tremendous moral implications. Let's consider three of these moral implications:

1. We must value human lives according to God's standard,
 not our own

Listen to James 2:1-4: "My brothers and sisters, do you with your acts of favoritism really believe in our glorious Lord Jesus Christ? For if a person with gold rings and in fine clothes comes into your assembly, and if a poor person in dirty clothes also comes in, and if you take notice of the one wearing the fine clothes and say, 'Have a seat here, please,' while to the one who

---

[15] Scripture passage adapted to NRSV for inclusivity.

is poor you say, 'Stand there,' or, 'Sit at my feet,' have you not made distinctions among yourselves, and become judges with evil thoughts?"[16]

If God sees human beings as of extraordinary importance, we must as well. If God loves people, we must too. Many have noted the way in which human beings establish varying rings or boundaries of moral obligation. This is an issue I discuss in *The Righteous Gentiles of the Holocaust*.[17] We draw invisible but very momentous circles of moral concern, including those within while excluding those without from the range of our care, protection, and sometimes even respect.

Yet a large part of the burden of Jesus' teaching, not to mention key elements of the rest of the Scripture, is to teach us to shatter those boundaries. With stories like the Good Samaritan [Luke 10:25-37], or Lazarus and the Rich Man [Luke 16:19-31], or the Sheep and Goats Judgment (Matt 25[:31-46]), for example, Jesus makes it impossible for Christians in good conscience to confine the boundaries of moral obligation to a narrow few. Whatsoever we did to the least of these, we did to him [Matt 25: 40, 45].

The consistent life ethic is rooted in this moral claim: that human beings are to be valued according to God's standards rather than our own. This eliminates the possibility of embracing any mere instrumentalism in Christian ethics. We cannot value lives according to their perceived usefulness or attractiveness or "value added" to us. God bestows value on each life and that value remains constant from conception until death. We are to treat each other accordingly. Indeed, we must treat our own selves in this way—which is the reason why suicide has always been ruled out in the Christian tradition. Even the individual is not free to assign value to his [or her] own life. God makes that call, not us.

2. A second moral implication: we must work to prevent murder, violence, and other direct assaults on the sanctity of life

Exodus 20:13 reads: "You shall not murder." This text, the Sixth Commandment, is a critical cornerstone of the consistent life ethic. The sacredness of human life implies reverence for life at every stage from conception to death. It implies that the right to life is the first and fundamental human right. It requires that believing Christians be on the front lines of efforts to prevent or end the shedding of human blood wherever this occurs.

Christians, especially in our own violent society, often forget or fail to notice early biblical statements of God's revulsion at the violence we do to one another. It is no coincidence that the primordial sin of murder is lifted up for

---

[16] Editors' note: Scripture passage adapted to NRSV for inclusivity.

[17] *The Righteous Gentiles of the Holocaust: A Christian Interpretation* (Minneapolis: Fortress Press, 1994).

such emphasis: "What have you done? Listen! Your brother's blood cries out to me from the ground. Now you are under a curse and driven from the ground, which opened its mouth to receive your brother's blood from your hand" (Gen 4:10-11). These words from God to Cain are fully consistent with God's later decision to send a flood upon the earth and start over with Noah and his family. Listen—"So God said to Noah, I am going to put an end to all people, for the earth is filled with violence because of them. I am surely going to destroy both them and the earth" (Gen 6:13).

Cardinal Bernardin, and the Catholic moral tradition generally, grounds the moral piece of the consistent life ethic right here at this point: the "prohibition against direct attacks on innocent life." Such direct attacks—in abortion, murder, genocide, bombing of noncombatants in war, and so on—are ruled out by the prohibition of murder, which itself is grounded in the sacredness God has attributed to human life.[18]

3. Finally, we must seek the flourishing of each other's lives

Matthew 22:39 reads, "Love your neighbor as yourself." The sacredness of human life means not only that we refrain from killing each other (a negative prohibition), but also that we take positive steps to see others flourish. We have not exhausted the moral demands placed upon us as human beings by merely avoiding direct harm. We must also, at times, render direct aid. And we must support various institutions and initiatives in various spheres of life that contribute to the flourishing of human life. I think that this is fundamentally what is meant when we are called to "love one another" [John 13:34] or to "love your neighbor as yourself."

Nuances, Criticisms, and Applications

I believe that the consistent life ethic does apply, as its name indicates, from womb to tomb. In a longer presentation of this material I walk through such issues as personal relationships, sexuality, race, poverty, genocide, divorce, war, suicide, capital punishment, euthanasia, genetic engineering and other biotech issues, and abortion, all as issues to which a consistent life ethic is directly applicable. Here, by way of conclusion, let me identify several nuances that must be built into the consistent life ethic for it to stand up to critical scrutiny. Addressing these concerns will give me a chance to offer a few issue-oriented examples.

Our responsibility to defend innocent life is more easily grasped and undertaken than the broader task of enhancing life. If a murderer is about to kill someone on the street, and I protect his intended victim, I have done my duty on the

---

[18] Joseph Cardinal Bernardin, *Consistent Ethic of Life* (Lanham, Md.: Sheed and Ward, 1988) 16.

"defending innocent life" side. It would be a more difficult and open-ended commitment to work for the full flourishing of the intended victim's life in all its complexity. Yet this is supposed to be a basic moral commitment of Christian people under the consistent life ethic. It shows that the moral work of the Christian is never exhausted, though sometimes we Christians get exhausted!

Not every moral issue undermines or threatens life in the same way. Abortion is the direct taking of human life (in my view) right now; nuclear, biological, or chemical war may happen and must be prevented, but is not happening now. That makes it a threat to life at this stage. Generally, the more direct and immediate is the life-taking, the more direct and immediate is our moral obligation to address it.

In war, a distinction is drawn between the taking of innocent life and combatant life. Unless one is a pacifist, it is assumed that combatants will die in war and that this is morally permissible (though tragic) if the war is just. A consistent life ethic may lead one to pacifism; for me, it leads to a very strict application of just war theory and the desire for a culture and an international order that cherishes peace and life rather than reveling in death. But under no legitimate Christian approach to war is genocide or other intentional taking of noncombatant life morally permissible.

Some threats to life are subtle, long-term, and chronic rather than obvious, direct, and immediate. Poverty, for example, slowly "grinds the face of the poor into the dust," as the Bible puts it,[19] rather than immediately ending life in most cases. Racism is the same way. Environmental degradation frequently poisons the planet in ways we don't even notice at the time. These subtle and chronic issues are all relevant to a consistent life ethic and must not drop off the radarscope.

Capital punishment poses a serious test case to the consistent life ethic because when rightly applied it is inflicted on the guilty rather than the innocent. This does make it a different species of issue than most other life issues. However, I think the Catholics have it right these days as they make this argument—while the State has the right to take life in defense of the innocent, it may do better in a violent culture to communicate its respect for human life by refraining from executing criminals at this time.

It may be argued that God takes plenty of lives in the Bible, especially in the Old Testament. To this we must answer that first, there are dimensions of God's activity that Christians are not called to imitate, God being God and humans being humans. Second, all theological and ethical work involves a sorting through of biblical texts and themes and an arranging of them into a pattern that must then be defended. That is what I am trying to do here. Finally, Christian ethics, if it is to be truly Christian, assesses all Scripture in terms of Jesus Christ. His character, person, and work are the final court of appeal.

---

[19] Editors' note: See Isa 3:15; the quoted words are very similar to the The Message translation of the Bible, the KJV, and the New International Reader's Version. All these versions of the Bible are available at http://www.biblegateway.com (accessed September 20, 2004).

Finally, there is the question of the church's public witness especially as it relates to politics. The consistent life ethic offers a coherent Christian framework for thinking about party platforms, candidate perspectives, public policy agendas, and so on. It can help save Christians from unthinking partisanship or candidate loyalty. It helps us be proactive rather than reactive, and gives us something to stand for rather than against. My next lecture will take up the whole issue of the place of politics in the church's public witness. Let me end this one by saying that any public moral witness we offer will have about as much impact as the integrity of our living right now.

That is, it is only if we live out a consistent life ethic or something close to it that we will be able to speak it to the world. If in the church—let's just begin there—we treat each other as sacred, made in the image of God, fully worthy of value and respect, from womb to tomb—then we might have something to say to politicians about what they should do. As Ron Sider put it: "It is a farce for the church to ask Washington to legislate what Christians refuse to live."[20] So let us live it.

3. Beverly Wildung Harrison, "A Theology of Pro-Choice: A Feminist Perspective on Abortion"

Beverly Wildung Harrison is professor emerita of Christian ethics, Union Theological Seminary, New York, New York. She is a prolific writer in Christian feminist ethics. Her best known books are Our Right to Choose *and* Making the Connections: Essays in Feminist Social Ethics, *both from Beacon Press. This 1981 article sets forth the foundations for a Christian feminist prolife position and remains influential to this day.*

Much[21] discussion of abortion betrays the heavy hand of misogyny, or the hatred of women. We all have a responsibility to recognize this bias, sometimes subtle, when ancient negative attitudes toward women intrude into the abortion debate. It is morally incumbent upon us to convert the Christian position to a teaching more respectful of women's history and experience.

My professional peers who are my opponents on this question feel that they own the Christian tradition in this matter and recognize no need to rethink their positions in the light of this claim. As a feminist, I cannot sit in silence when women's right to determine how procreative power is to be used is under challenge. That right is being withdrawn by the State even before its moral basis has been fully elaborated. Those who deny that women deserve to control procreative power claim the right to do so out of "moral sensibility,"

---

[20] Ronald J. Sider, *Completely Pro-Life: Building a Consistent Stance* (Downers Grove, Ill.: Intervarsity Press, 1987) 25.

[21] Beverly Wildung Harrison, "A Theology of Pro-Choice," *The Witness* 64, no. 7 (July 1981) 14–18. Reprinted with permission from *The Witness:* www.thewitness.org.

in the name of the "sanctity of human life." We have a long way to go before the sanctity of human life will include genuine regard and concern for every female already born, and no social policy which obscures that fact deserves to be called "moral."

I believe the human wisdom which informs our ethics about abortion comes from what earlier Catholic moral theologians meant by "natural law" more than from quoting the Bible alone. Unfortunately, however, natural law reflection in a Roman Catholic context has been every bit as awful as Protestant biblicism on any subject that involves human sexuality, including discussion of women's "nature" and women's "divine vocation" in relation to procreative power.

Protestants who oppose procreative choice either tend to follow Roman Catholic moral theology or ground their positions in Biblicist anti-intellectualism, claiming that "God's word" requires no justification other than their claim that it (God's word) says what it says. Against such irrationalism, no rational objections have a chance. If Protestant fundamentalists do give reasons why they believe that abortion is evil, they too revert to traditional natural law assumptions about women, sex and procreation. Therefore, it is against the claims of traditional Catholic natural law thinking on the subject of sexuality, procreation, and women's power of rational choice that objection must be registered.

Any treatment of a moral problem is inadequate if it fails to question the morality of the act in a way which represents the concrete experience of the agent who faces a decision with respect to that act. Misogyny in Christian discussions of abortion is evidenced in that the decision is never treated as an integral part of the female agent's life process. Abortion is treated as an abstractable act, rather than as what it always is—a possible way to deal with a pregnancy.

Those who uphold the immorality of abortion are wise to obscure the fact that it is a fully living human female who is the moral agent in the decision. In the case of pregnancy, the woman's life is deeply, irrevocably affected.

Where the question of abortion might arise, a woman finds herself facing an *unwanted* pregnancy. Consider the actual circumstances which may precipitate this. One is the situation in which a woman did not intend to be sexually active or did not enter into the act voluntarily. Since women are frequently victims of sexual violence, numerous cases of this type arise because of rape, incest, or forced marital coitus. Many morally sensitive opponents of abortion will concede that in such cases it may be morally justifiable. I would insist that in such cases it is a moral good, because it is not rational to treat a newly fertilized ovum as though it had the same value as the existent, pregnant, female person, and because it is morally wrong to make the victim of sexual violence suffer the further agonies of unwanted pregnancy.

Another, more frequent case results when a woman—or usually a young girl—participates in heterosexual activity without clear knowledge of how pregnancy occurs and without intention to conceive. A girl who became pregnant in this manner would, by traditional natural law morality, be held to be in a state of "invincible ignorance" and therefore not morally culpable. I once met a scholarly Roman Catholic nun who argued, quite seriously, that her church should not consider the abortions of young Catholic girls as morally culpable since the church was "overprotective" of them, which prevented them from understanding procreation and the sexual pressures which contemporary society puts on girls.

A related type of pregnancy occurs when a woman runs risks by not using contraceptives, perhaps because taking precautions is not "ladylike" or requires her to be "unspontaneous" about sex. However, when pregnancies occur because women are skirting the edges of knowledge and running risks, is enforced motherhood a desirable solution? Such pregnancies could be minimized by eradicating childish myths, embedded in natural law teaching, about female sexuality.

In likelihood, the largest number of abortions arise because mature women who are sexually active with men and who understand the consequences experience contraceptive failure. Schizophrenia in this area is exhibited in that many who believe that women have more responsibility than men to practice contraception, and that family planning is a moral good, rule out abortion altogether. Such a split consciousness ignores the fact that there is no inexorable biological line between prevention of conception and abortion. More important, this ignores genuine risks involved in female contraceptive methods. The reason we do not have more concern for finding safer contraceptive methods for men and women is that matters relating to women's health and well-being are never urgent in this society. Moreover, many failures are due to the irresponsibility of the producers of contraceptives rather than to "bad luck." Given these facts, should a woman who actively attempts to avoid pregnancy be punished for contraceptive failure when it occurs?

Theological Context

In the history of Christian theology, the central metaphor for understanding life, including human life, is as a gift of God. Creation itself is seen primarily under this metaphor. In this context, it follows that procreation itself takes on special meaning when expressed within a patriarchal society in which it is the male's power which is enhanced by this "divine gift."

Throughout history, women's power of procreation stands in definite tension with male control. In fact, ancient historical evidence suggests that what we call patriarchy derives from the need of men, and later of male-dominated political institutions such as tribes and states, to control women's procreative power. We must assume, then, that many of the efforts at social control—including church teaching on contraception and abortion—were part of an overall system. The perpetuation of patriarchal control itself depended on wresting the power of procreation from women. Another critical point is that in the last four centuries the entire Christian story has had to undergo dramatic accommodations to new and emergent world conditions grounded in the scientific revolution. As the older theological metaphors for creation encountered a new human self-understanding, Christian theology had either to incorporate this new reality in its story or to become obscurantist.

The range of human freedom to shape and enhance creation is now celebrated theologically up to the point of changes in sexuality or ways of seeing women's nature. Around these issues a barrier has been drawn which declares: *No Freedom Here!* The only difference between mainline Protestant and Catholic theologians is on the question of contraception. That Protestant male clergy are usually married does have a positive experiential effect on their dealing with this issue; generally they have accepted the moral appropriateness of contraception. Most Protestants and nearly all Catholics, however, draw back from recognizing abortion as a defensible exercise of human freedom or self-determination.

The problem, then, is that Christian theology everywhere else celebrates the power of human freedom to shape and determine the quality of human life, except when the issue of abortion arises. The power of man to shape creation radically is never rejected. When one stops to consider the awesome power over nature which males take for granted and celebrate, including the power to alter the conditions of human life in myriad ways, the suspicion dawns that the near hysteria that prevails about the immorality of women's right to choose abortion derives its force from misogyny rather than from any passion for the sacredness of human life. The refusal of male theologians to incorporate the full range of human power to shape creation into their theological worldview when that power relates to the quality of women's lives and women's freedom and women's role as full moral agents is an index of the continuing misogyny in Christian tradition.

By contrast, a feminist theological approach recognizes that nothing is more urgent, in light of the changing circumstances of human beings on Planet Earth, than to recognize that the entire natural-historical context of human procreative power has shifted. We desperately need a "desacralization" of our biological power to reproduce, and at the same time, a real concern for human dignity and the social conditions for personhood and the values of human relationship. And note that "desacralization" does not mean complete devaluation of the worth of procreation. It means that we must shift away from the notion that the central metaphors for divine blessing are expressed at the biological level to the recognition that social values bear the image of what is most holy. The best statement I know on this point comes from a Roman Catholic feminist who is also a distinguished sociologist of religion, Marie Augusta Neal:

As long as the central human need called for was continued motivation to propagate the race, it was essential that religious symbols idealize that process above all others. Given the vicissitudes of life in a hostile environment, women had to be encouraged to bear children and men to support them; child-bearing was central to the struggle for existence. Today, however, the size of the base population, together with knowledge already accumulated about artificial insemination, sperm banking, cloning, make more certain a peopled world. The more serious human problems now are who will live, who will die and who will decide.[22]

Alternative Reading of History

Between persons who oppose all abortions on moral grounds and those who believe that abortion is sometimes or frequently morally justifiable, *there is no difference of moral principle.* Pro-choice advocates and anti-abortion advocates share the ethical principle of respect for human life, which is probably why the debate is so acrimonious. I have already indicated that one major source of disagreement is the way in which the theological story is appropriated in relation to the changing circumstances of history. In addition, we should recognize that whenever strong moral disagreement is encountered, we simultaneously confront a different reading of history. The way we interpret the past is already laden with a sense of what the "moral problem" is.

For example, professional male Christian ethicists tend to assume that the history of the morality of abortion can best be traced by studying the teaching of the now best-remembered theologians. Looking at the matter this way, one can find plenty of proof-texts to show that *some* of the "church fathers" (as we call them) condemned abortion and some even equated abortion with either homicide or murder. However, when a "leading" churchman equated abortion with homicide or murder, he also *and simultaneously* equated *contraception* with homicide or murder as well. This reflects the then almost hysterical anti-sexual bias of the Christian tradition.

However, this anti-sexual tradition is not universal, even among theologians and canon lawyers. On the subject of sexuality and its abuse, many well-known theologians had nothing to say and abortion was not even mentioned. An important, untold chapter in Christian history is the great struggle that took place in what we call the medieval period, when clerical celibacy came to be *imposed,* and the rules of sexual behavior rigidified.

By contrast, my thesis is that there is a relative disinterest in the question of abortion overall in Christian history. Occasionally, Christian theologians picked up the issue, *especially when those theologians were "state-related theologians,"* i.e., articulating policy not only for the church but for the po-

---

[22] Marie Augusta Neal, "Sociology and Sexuality: A Feminist," *Christianity and Crisis,* 39, May 14, 1979, 118–22.

litical authority. Demographer Jean Meyer, himself a Catholic, insists that the Christian tradition took over "expansion by population growth" from the Roman Empire. Christians only opposed abortion strongly when Christianity was closely identified with the state or when the theologians repudiated sexuality except in the reluctant service of procreation.

The "Holy Crusade" quality of present teaching on abortion is quite new and related to cultural shifts which are requiring the Christian tradition to choose sides in ideological struggle and to rethink its entire attitude to women and sexuality. No Protestant clergy gave early support for proposed 19th-century laws banning abortion in the United States. It is my impression that Protestant clergy, usually married and often poor, were aware that romanticizing "nature's bounty" with respect to procreation resulted in a great deal of human suffering. The Protestant clergy who finally did join the anti-abortion crusade in the 19th century were racist, classist, white clergy, who feared that America's strength was being threatened because white, middle-class, "respectable" women had a lower birthrate than black and ethnic women. Sound familiar?

One other point must be stressed. Until the late 19th century, the natural law tradition, and biblicism following it, always tended to define the act of abortion as interruption of pregnancy after ensoulment, or the coming of the breath of God to the fetus. The point at which ensoulment was said to take place varied, but most typically it was at quickening. Quickening was important because knowledge about embryology was terribly primitive until the last half century. As a result, where abortion was condemned, it was understood to refer to the termination of pregnancy well into the process of that pregnancy after ensoulment. Until the late 19th century, then, abortion in ecclesiastical teaching applied only to termination of prenatal life in more advanced stages of pregnancy.

Another distortion in the male-generated history of this issue derives from failure to note that, until the development of safe, surgical, elective abortion, the "act of abortion" frequently referred to something done to the woman, with or without her consent (see Exodus 22), as an act of violence. Now, in recent discussion, it is the woman who does the "wrongful" act. When "to do an abortion" meant terminating a pregnancy against the woman's wishes, grounds for moral objections were clear.

Furthermore, whether the act was done with or without the woman's consent, until recent decades abortion always endangered the woman as much as it did the prenatal life in her womb. No one has a right to discuss the morality of abortion today without recognizing that one of the traditional moral reasons for objection to abortion was concern for women's well-being.

Beyond all this, however, the deepest moral flaw in the pro-life position's historical view is that none of its proponents have attempted to reconstruct the all but desperate struggle by sexually active women to gain some proximate control over nature's profligacy in conception. Under the most adverse conditions, women have had to try to control their fertility—everywhere, always. Even when women are infertile, their relationship to procreation irrevocably marks and shapes their lives. Those who have sought to avoid sexual contacts with males, through celibacy or through lesbian love, have been potential, even probable, victims of male sexual violence or have had to bear heavy social stigma for refusing the centrality of dependence on men and of procreation in their lives. Women's lack of social power, in all recorded history, has made this struggle to control procreation a life-bending, often life-destroying one.

So women have had to do whatever they could to avoid too numerous pregnancies. In most societies and cultures, procreation has been in the hands of women's culture. Some primitive birth control techniques have proven rather effective. Increasingly, anthropologists are gaining hints of how procreative control occurred in some pre-modern societies. A woman often has chosen to risk her life in order not to have that extra child that would destroy the family's ability to cope or that would bring about a crisis unmanageable within her life.

We have to concede that modern medicine, for all its misogyny, has replaced some rather ghastly practices still widely used where surgical abortion is unavailable. In the light of these gains, more privileged western women must not lose the ability to imagine the real-life pressures which lead women in other cultures to submit to ground-glass douches, reeds inserted in the uterus, etc., to induce labor. The radical nature of methods women resort to bespeaks the desperation involved in unwanted pregnancy.

Nor should we suppress the fact that a major means of birth control now is, as it was in earlier times, *infanticide.* And let no one imagine that women made decisions to expose or kill new-born infants casually. Women understand what many men cannot seem to grasp—that the birth of a child requires that some person must be prepared to care, without interruption, for that infant, to provide material resources and energy-draining amounts of time and attention. It seems to me that men, especially celibate men, romanticize the total and uncompromising dependency of the newly born infant upon the already existing human community. This dependency is even greater in a fragmented, centralized urban-industrial modern culture than in a rural culture, where another pair of hands often increased an extended family unit's productive power. No historical interpretation of abortion as a moral issue which ignores these matters deserves moral standing in the present debate.

In drawing this section to a close, I want to stress that if present efforts to criminalize abortion succeed we will need a state apparatus of massive proportions to enforce compulsory childbearing. In addition, withdrawal of legal abortion will create one more massively profitable underworld economy in which the Mafia and other sections of quasi-legal capitalism may and will profitably invest. The radical right promises to get the state out of regulation of people's lives, but what they really mean is that they will let economic activity go unrestrained. What their agenda signifies for the personal lives of women is quite another matter.

An adequate historical perspective on abortion recognizes the long struggle women have waged for some degree of control over fertility and of their efforts to regain control of procreative power from patriarchal and state-imperial culture and institutions. Such a perspective also takes into account that more nearly adequate contraceptive methods and the existence of safe, surgical, elective abortion represent positive historic steps toward full human freedom and dignity for women. While the same gains in medical knowledge also open the way to sterilization abuse and to social pressures against some women's use of their power of procreation, I know of no woman who would choose to return to a state of lesser knowledge about these matters.

There has been an objective gain in the quality of women's lives for those fortunate enough to possess procreative choice. That millions of women do not possess even the rudimentary conditions for such a choice is obvious. Our moral goal should be to struggle against those real barriers—poverty, racism and cultural oppression—which prevent authentic choice from being a reality for every woman.

4. Sidney Callahan, "Abortion and the Sexual Agenda"

Sidney Callahan holds the McKeever Chair in Moral Theology at St. John's University, Jamaica, New York. She is a prominent voice in contemporary Catholic ethics: a frequent columnist for Commonweal Magazine, a board member of many Catholic organizations that address faith and public life, and the author of many publications in the area of sexual and family ethics. In this oft-reprinted article, Callahan first summarizes the argument of her pro-choice opponents and then offers a response. Readers will want to compare her understanding of Christian feminism with that of Beverly Harrison in the previous selection.

The[23] abortion debate continues. In the latest and perhaps most crucial development, pro-life feminists are contesting pro-choice feminist claims that abortion rights are prerequisites for women's full development and social equality. The outcome of this debate may be decisive for the culture as a whole. Pro-life feminists, like myself, argue on good feminist principles that women can never achieve the fulfillment of feminist goals in a society permissive toward abortion.

These new arguments over abortion take place within liberal political circles. This round of intense intra-feminist conflict has spiraled beyond earlier right-versus-left abortion debates, which focused on "tragic choices," medical judgments, and legal compromises. Feminist theorists of the pro-choice position now put forth the demand for unrestricted abortion rights as a

---

[23] Sidney Callahan, "Abortion and the Sexual Agenda: A Case for Pro-Life Feminism" *Commonweal* 113 (April 25, 1996) 232–38.

moral imperative and insist upon women's right to complete reproductive freedom. They morally justify the present situation and current abortion practices. Thus it is all the more important that pro-life feminists articulate their different feminist perspective.

These opposing arguments can best be seen when presented in turn. Perhaps the most highly developed feminist arguments for the morality and legality of abortion can be found in Beverly Wildung Harrison's *Our Right to Choose*[24] and Rosalind Pollack Petchesky's *Abortion and Woman's Choice.*[25] Obviously it is difficult to do justice to these complex arguments, which draw on diverse strands of philosophy and social theory and are often interwoven in pro-choice feminists' own version of a "seamless garment." Yet the fundamental feminist case for the morality of abortion, encompassing the views of Harrison and Petchesky, can be analyzed in terms of four central moral claims: (1) the moral right to control one's own body; (2) the moral necessity of autonomy and choice in personal responsibility; (3) the moral claim for the contingent value of fetal life; (4) the moral right of women to true social equality.

THE MORAL RIGHT TO CONTROL ONE'S OWN BODY

Pro-choice feminism argues that a woman choosing an abortion is exercising a basic right of bodily integrity granted in our common law tradition. If she does not choose to be physically involved in the demands of a pregnancy and birth, she should not be compelled to be so against her will. Just because it is her body which is involved, a woman should have the right to terminate any pregnancy, which at this point in medical history is tantamount to terminating fetal life. No one can be forced to donate an organ or submit to other invasive physical procedures for however good a cause. Thus no woman should be subjected to "compulsory pregnancy." And it should be noted that in pregnancy much more than a passive biological process is at stake.

From one perspective, the fetus is, as Petchesky says, a "biological parasite" taking resources from the woman's body. During pregnancy, a woman's whole life and energies will be actively involved in the nine-month process. Gestation and childbirth involve physical and psychological risks. After childbirth a woman will either be a mother who must undertake a twenty-year responsibility for childrearing, or face giving up her child for adoption or institutionalization. Since hers is the body, hers the risk, hers the burden, it is only just that she alone should be free to decide on pregnancy or abortion.

This moral claim to abortion, according to the pro-choice feminists, is especially valid in an individualistic society in which women cannot count on

---

[24] *Our Right to Choose: Toward a New Ethic of Abortion* (Boston Beacon Press, 1983).

[25] *Abortion and Woman's Choice: The State, Sexuality, and Reproductive Freedom* (New York: Longman, 1984).

medical care or social support in pregnancy, childbirth, or childrearing. A moral abortion decision is never made in a social vacuum, but in the real life society which exists here and now.

THE MORAL NECESSITY OF AUTONOMY AND CHOICE IN PERSONAL RESPONSIBILITY

Beyond the claim for individual bodily integrity, the pro-choice feminists claim that to be a full adult morally, a woman must be able to make responsible life commitments. To plan, choose, and exercise personal responsibility, one must have control of reproduction. A woman must be able to make yes or no decisions about a specific pregnancy, according to her present situation, resources, prior commitments, and life plan. Only with such reproductive freedom can a woman have the moral autonomy necessary to make mature commitments, in the area of family, work, or education.

Contraception provides a measure of personal control, but contraceptive failure or other chance events can too easily result in involuntary pregnancy. Only free access to abortion can provide the necessary guarantee. The chance biological process of an involuntary pregnancy should not be allowed to override all the other personal commitments and responsibilities a woman has: to others, to family, to work, to education, to her future development, health, or well-being. Without reproductive freedom, women's personal moral agency and human consciousness are subjected to biology and chance.

THE MORAL CLAIM FOR THE CONTINGENT VALUE OF FETAL LIFE

Pro-choice feminist exponents like Harrison and Petchesky claim that the value of fetal life is contingent upon the woman's free consent and subjective acceptance. The fetus must be invested with maternal valuing in order to become human. This process of "humanization" through personal consciousness and "sociality" can only be bestowed by the woman in whose body and psychosocial system a new life must mature. The meaning and value of fetal life are constructed by the woman; without this personal conferral there only exists a biological, physiological process. Thus fetal interests or fetal rights can never outweigh the woman's prior interest and rights. If a woman does not consent to invest her pregnancy with meaning or value, then the merely biological process can be freely terminated. Prior to her own free choice and conscious investment, a woman cannot be described as a "mother" nor can a "child" be said to exist.

Moreover, in cases of voluntary pregnancy, a woman can withdraw consent if fetal genetic defects or some other problem emerges at any time before birth. Late abortion should thus be granted without legal restrictions. Even the minimal qualifications and limitations on women embedded in *Roe v. Wade* are unacceptable—repressive remnants of patriarchal unwillingness to give power to women.

THE MORAL RIGHT OF WOMEN TO FULL SOCIAL EQUALITY

Women have a moral right to full social equality. They should not be restricted or subordinated because of their sex. But this morally required equality cannot be realized without abortion's certain control of reproduction. Female social equality depends upon being able to compete and participate as freely as males can in the structures of educational and economic life. If a woman cannot control when and how she will be pregnant or rear children, she is at a distinct disadvantage, especially in our male-dominated world.

Psychological equality and well-being is also at stake. Women must enjoy the basic right of a person to the free exercise of heterosexual intercourse and full sexual expression, separated from procreation. No less than males, women should be able to be sexually active without the constantly inhibiting fear of pregnancy. Abortion is necessary for women's sexual fulfillment and the growth of uninhibited feminine self-confidence and ownership of their sexual powers.

But true sexual and reproductive freedom means freedom to procreate as well as to inhibit fertility. Pro-choice feminists are also worried that women's freedom to reproduce will be curtailed through the abuse of sterilization and needless hysterectomies. Besides the punitive tendencies of a male-dominated healthcare system, especially in response to repeated abortions or welfare pregnancies, there are other economic and social pressures inhibiting reproduction. Genuine reproductive freedom implies that day care, medical care, and financial support would be provided mothers, while fathers would take their full share in the burdens and delights of raising children.

Many pro-choice feminists identify feminist ideals with communitarian, ecologically sensitive approaches to reshaping society. Following theorists like Sara Ruddick and Carol Gilligan, they link abortion rights with the growth of "maternal thinking" in our heretofore patriarchal society. Maternal thinking is loosely defined as a responsible commitment to the loving nurture of specific human beings as they actually exist in socially embedded interpersonal contexts. It is a moral perspective very different from the abstract, competitive, isolated, and principled rigidity so characteristic of patriarchy.

How does a pro-life feminist respond to these arguments? Pro-life feminists grant the good intentions of their pro-choice counterparts but protest that the pro-choice position is flawed, morally inadequate, and inconsistent with feminism's basic demands for justice. Pro-life feminists champion a more encompassing moral ideal. They recognize the claims of fetal life and offer a different perspective on what is good for women. The feminist vision is expanded and refocused.

FROM THE MORAL RIGHT TO CONTROL ONE'S OWN BODY
TO A MORE INCLUSIVE IDEAL OF JUSTICE

The moral right to control one's own body does apply to cases of organ transplants, mastectomies, contraception, and sterilization; but it is not a conceptualization adequate for abortion. The abortion dilemma is caused by the fact that 266 days following a conception in one body, another body will emerge. One's own body no longer exists as a single unit but is engendering another organism's life. This dynamic passage from conception to birth is genetically ordered and universally found in the human species. Pregnancy is not like the growth of cancer or infestation by a biological parasite; it is the way every human being enters the world. Strained philosophical analogies fail to apply: having a baby is not like rescuing a drowning person, being hooked up to a famous violinists's artificial life-support system, donating organs for transplant—or anything else.

As embryology and fetology advance, it becomes clear that human development is a continuum. Just as astronomers are studying the first three minutes in the genesis of the universe, so the first moments, days, and weeks at the beginning of human life are the subject of increasing scientific attention. While neonatology pushes the definition of viability ever earlier, ultrasound and fetology expand the concept of the patient *in utero*. Within such a continuous growth process, it is hard to defend logically any demarcation point after conception as the point at which an immature form of human life is so different from the day before or the day after, that it can be morally or legally discounted as a non-person. Even the moment of birth can hardly differentiate a nine-month fetus from a newborn. It is not surprising that those who countenance late abortions are logically led to endorse selective infanticide.

The same legal tradition which in our society guarantees the right to control one's own body firmly recognizes the wrongfulness of harming other bodies, however immature, dependent, different looking, or powerless. The handicapped, the retarded, and newborns are legally protected from deliberate harm. Pro-life feminists reject the suppositions that would except the unborn from this protection.

After all, debates similar to those about the fetus were once conducted about feminine personhood. Just as women, or blacks, were considered too different, too underdeveloped, too "biological," to have souls or to possess legal rights, so the fetus is now seen as "merely" biological life, subsidiary to a person. A woman was once viewed as incorporated into the "one flesh" [see Mark 10:8; Matt 19:6; NRSV] of her husband's person; she too was a form of bodily property. In all patriarchal unjust systems, lesser orders of human life are granted rights only when wanted, chosen, or invested with value by the powerful.

Fortunately, in the course of civilization there has been a gradual realization that justice demands the powerless and dependent be protected against the uses of power wielded unilaterally No human can be treated as a means to an end without consent. The fetus is an immature, dependent form of human life which only needs time and protection to develop. Surely, immaturity and dependence are not crimes . . .

It also seems a travesty of just procedures that a pregnant woman now, in effect, acts as sole judge of her own case, under the most stressful conditions. Yes, one can acknowledge that the pregnant woman will be subject to the potential burdens arising from a pregnancy, but it has never been thought right to have an interested party, especially the more powerful party, decide his or her own case when there may be a conflict of interest. If one considers the matter as a case of a powerful versus a powerless, silenced claimant, the pro-choice feminist argument can rightly be inverted: since hers is the body, hers the risk, and hers the greater burden, then how in fairness can a woman be the sole judge of the fetal right to life?

Human ambivalence, a bias toward self-interest, and emotional stress have always been recognized as endangering judgment. Freud declared that love and hate are so entwined that if instant thoughts could kill, we would all be dead in the bosom of our families. In the case of a woman's involuntary pregnancy, a complex, long-term solution requiring effort and energy has to compete with the immediate solution offered by a morning's visit to an abortion clinic. On the simple, perceptual plane, with imagination and thinking curtailed, the speed, ease, and privacy of abortion, combined with the small size of the embryo, tend to make early abortions seem less morally serious—even though speed, size, technical ease, and the private nature of an act have no moral standing.

As the most recent immigrants from non-personhood, feminists have traditionally fought for justice for themselves and the world. Women rally to feminism as a new and better way to live. Rejecting male aggression and destruction, feminists seek alternative, peaceful, ecologically sensitive means to resolve conflicts while respecting human potentiality. It is a chilling inconsistency to see pro-choice feminists demanding continued access to assembly-line, technological methods of fetal killing—the vacuum aspirator, prostaglandins, and dilation and evacuation. It is a betrayal of feminism, which has built the struggle for justice on the bedrock of women's empathy. After all, "maternal thinking" receives its name from a mother's unconditional acceptance and nurture of dependent, immature life. It is difficult to develop concern for women, children, the poor and the dispossessed—and to care about peace—and at the same time ignore fetal life.

FROM THE NECESSITY OF AUTONOMY AND CHOICE
IN PERSONAL RESPONSIBILITY TO AN EXPANDED SENSE OF RESPONSIBILITY

A distorted idea of morality overemphasizes individual autonomy and active choice. Morality has often been viewed too exclusively as a matter of human agency and decisive action. In moral behavior persons must explicitly choose and aggressively exert their wills to intervene in the natural and social environments. The human will dominates the body, overcomes the given, breaks out of the material limits of nature. Thus if one does not choose to be pregnant or cannot rear a child, who must be given up for adoption, then better to abort the pregnancy. Willing, planning, choosing one's moral commitments through the contracting of one's individual resources becomes the premier model of moral responsibility.

But morality also consists of the good and worthy acceptance of the unexpected events that life presents. Responsiveness and responsibility to things unchosen are also instances of the highest human moral capacity. Morality is not confined to contracted agreements of isolated individuals. Yes, one is obligated by explicit contracts freely initiated, but human beings are also obligated by implicit compacts and involuntary relationships in which persons simply find themselves. To be embedded in a family, a neighborhood, a social system, brings moral obligations which were never entered into with informed consent.

Parent-child relationships are one instance of implicit moral obligations arising by virtue of our being part of the interdependent human community. A woman, involuntarily pregnant, has a moral obligation to the now-existing dependent fetus whether she explicitly consented to its existence or not. No pro-life feminist would dispute the forceful observations of pro-choice feminists about the extreme difficulties that bearing an unwanted child in our society can entail. But the stronger force of the fetal claim presses a woman to accept these burdens; the fetus possesses rights arising from its extreme need and the interdependency and unity of humankind. The woman's moral obligation arises both from her status as a human being embedded in the interdependent human community and her unique life-giving female reproductive power. To follow the pro-choice feminist ideology of insistent individualistic autonomy and control is to betray a fundamental basis of the moral life.

FROM THE MORAL CLAIM OF THE CONTINGENT VALUE OF FETAL LIFE TO THE MORAL CLAIM FOR THE INTRINSIC VALUE OF HUMAN LIFE

The feminist pro-choice position which claims that the value of the fetus is contingent upon the pregnant woman's bestowal—or willed, conscious "construction"—of humanhood is seriously flawed. The inadequacies of this position flow from the erroneous premises (1) that human value and rights can be granted by individual will; (2) that the individual woman's consciousness can exist and operate in an *a priori* isolated fashion; and (3) that "mere" biological, genetic human life has little meaning. Pro-life feminism takes a very different stance to life and nature.

Human life from the beginning to the end of development has intrinsic value; which does not depend on meeting the selective criteria or tests set up by powerful others. A fundamental humanist assumption is at stake here. Either we are going to value embodied human life and humanity as a good thing or take some variant of the nihilist position that assumes human life is just one more random occurrence in the universe such that each instance of human life must explicitly be justified to the universe to prove itself worthy to continue. When faced with a new life, or an involuntary pregnancy, there is a world of difference in whether one first asks, "Why continue?" or "Why not?" Where is the burden of proof going to rest? The concept of "compulsory pregnancy" is as distorted as labeling life "compulsory aging."

In a sound moral tradition, human rights arise from human needs and it is the very nature of a right, or valid claim upon another, that it cannot be denied, conditionally delayed, or rescinded by more powerful others at their behest. It seems fallacious to hold that in the case of the fetus it is the pregnant woman alone who gives or removes its right to life and human status solely through her subjective conscious investment or "humanization." Surely no pregnant woman (or any other individual member of the species) has created her own human nature by an individually willed act of consciousness, nor for that matter been able to guarantee her own human rights. An individual woman and the unique individual embryonic life within her can only exist because of their participation in the genetic inheritance of the human species as a whole. Biological life should never be discounted. Membership in the species, or collective human family is the basis for human solidarity, equality, and natural human rights.

THE MORAL RIGHT OF WOMEN TO FULL SOCIAL EQUALITY FROM A PRO-LIFE FEMINIST PERSPECTIVE

Pro-life feminists and pro-choice feminists are totally agreed on the moral right of women to the full social equality so far denied them. The disagreement between them concerns the definition of the desired goal and the best means to get there. Permissive abortion laws do not bring women reproductive freedom, social equality, sexual fulfillment, or full personal development.

Pragmatic failures of a pro-choice feminist position combined with a lack of moral vision are, in fact, causing disaffection among young women. Middle-aged pro-choice feminists blamed the "big chill" on the general conservative backlash. But they should look rather to their own elitist acceptance of male models of sex and to the sad picture they present of women's lives. Pitting women against their own offspring is not only morally offensive, it is psychologically and politically destructive. Women will never climb to equality and social empowerment over mounds of dead fetuses, numbering now in the millions. As long as most women choose to bear children, they stand to gain from the same constellation of attitudes and institutions that will also protect the fetus in the woman's womb—and they stand to lose from the cultural assumptions that support permissive abortion. Despite temporary conflicts of interest, feminine and fetal liberation are ultimately one and the same cause.

Women's rights and liberation are pragmatically linked to fetal right because to obtain true equality, women need (1) more social support and changes in the structure of society, and (2) increased self-confidence, self-expectations, and self-esteem. Society in general, and men in particular, have to provide women more support in rearing the next generation, or our devastating feminization of poverty will continue. But if a woman claims the right to decide by herself whether the fetus becomes a child or not, what does this do to paternal and communal responsibility? Why should men share responsibility for child support or childrearing if they cannot share in what is asserted to be the woman's sole decision? Furthermore, if explicit intentions and consciously accepted contracts are necessary for moral obligations, why should men be held responsible for what they do not voluntarily choose to happen? By pro-choice reasoning, a man who does not want to have a child, or whose contraceptive fails, can be exempted from the responsibilities of fatherhood and child support. Traditionally, many men have been laggards in assuming parental responsibility and support for their children; ironically, ready abortion, often advocated as a response to male dereliction, legitimizes male irresponsibility and paves the way for even more male detachment and lack of commitment.

For that matter, why should the state provide a system of day-care or child support, or require workplaces to accommodate women's maternity and the needs of childrearing? Permissive abortion, granted in the name of women's privacy and reproductive freedom, ratifies the view that pregnancies and children are a woman's private individual responsibility. More and more frequently, we hear some version of this old rationalization: if she refuses to get rid of it, it's her problem. A child becomes a product of the individual woman's freely chosen investment, a form of private property resulting from her own cost-benefit calculation. The larger community is relieved of moral responsibility.

With legal abortion freely available, a clear cultural message is given: conception and pregnancy are no longer serious moral matters. With abortion as an acceptable alternative, contraception is not as responsibly used; women take risks, often at the urging of male sexual partners. Repeat abortions increase, with all their psychological and medical repercussions. With more abortion there is more abortion. Behavior shapes thought as well as the other way round. One tends to justify morally what one has done; what becomes commonplace and institutionalized seems harmless. Habituation is a powerful psychological force. Psychologically it is also true that whatever is avoided becomes more threatening; in phobias it is the retreat from anxiety-producing events which reinforces future avoidance. Women begin to see themselves as too weak to cope with involuntary pregnancies. Finally, through the potency of social pressure and force of inertia, it becomes more and more difficult, in fact almost unthinkable, *not* to use abortion to solve problem pregnancies. Abortion becomes no longer a choice but a "necessity."

But "necessity," beyond the organic failure and death of the body, is a dynamic social construction open to interpretation. The thrust of present feminist pro-choice arguments can only increase the justifiable indications for "necessary" abortion; every unwanted fetal handicap becomes more and more unacceptable. Repeatedly assured that in the name of reproductive freedom, women have a right to specify which pregnancies and which children they will accept, women justify sex selection, and abort unwanted females. Female infanticide, after all, is probably as old a custom as the human species possesses. Indeed, all kinds of selection of the fit and the favored for the good of the family and the tribe have always existed. Selective extinction is no new program.

THE NEED TO FEMINIZE SEXUALITY

There are far better goals for feminists to pursue. Pro-life feminists seek to expand and deepen the more communitarian, maternal elements of feminism—and move society from its male-dominated course. First and foremost, women have to insist upon a different, woman-centered approach to sex and reproduction. While Margaret Mead stressed the "womb envy" of males in other societies, it has been more or less repressed in our own. In our male-dominated world, what men don't do, doesn't count. Pregnancy, childbirth, and nursing have been characterized as passive, debilitating, animal-like. The disease model of pregnancy and birth has been entrenched. The female disease or impairment, with its attendant "female troubles," naturally handicaps women in the "real" world of hunting, war, and the corporate fast track. Many pro-choice feminists, deliberately childless, adopt the male perspective when they cite the "basic injustice that women have to bear the babies," instead of seeing the injustice in the fact that men cannot. Women's biologically unique capacity and privilege has been denied, despised, and suppressed under male dominations; unfortunately, many women have fallen for the phallic fallacy.

Childbirth often appears in pro-choice literature as a painful, traumatic, life-threatening experience. Yet giving birth is accurately seen as an arduous but normal exercise of life-giving power, a violent and ecstatic peak experience, which men can never know. Ironically, some pro-choice men and women think and talk of pregnancy and childbirth with the same repugnance that ancient ascetics displayed toward orgasms and sexual intercourse. The similarity may not be accidental. The obstetrician Niles Newton, herself a mother, has written of the extended threefold sexuality of women, who can experience orgasm, birth, and nursing as passionate pleasure-giving experiences. All of these are involuntary processes of the female body. Only orgasm, which males share, has been glorified as an involuntary function that is nature's great gift; the involuntary feminine process of childbirth and nursing have been seen as bondage to biology.

Fully accepting our bodies as ourselves, what should women want? I think women will only flourish when there is a feminization of sexuality, very different from the current cultural trend toward masculinizing female sexuality. Women can never have the self-confidence and self-esteem they need to achieve feminist goals in society until a more holistic, feminine model of sexuality becomes the dominant cultural ethos. To say this affirms the view that men and women differ in the domain of sexual functioning, although they are more alike than different in other personality characteristics and competencies. For those of us committed to achieving sexual equality in the culture, it may be hard to accept the fact that sexual differences make it imperative to talk of distinct male and female models of sexuality. But if one wants to change sexual roles, one has to recognize pre-existing conditions. A great deal of evidence is accumulating which points to biological pressures for different male and female sexual functioning.

Males always and everywhere have been more physically aggressive and more likely to fuse sexuality with aggression and dominance. Females may be more variable in their sexuality, but since Masters and Johnson, we know that women have a greater capacity than men for repeated orgasm and a more tenuous path to arousal and orgasmic release. Most obviously, women also have a far greater socio-biological investment in the act of human reproduction. On the whole, women as compared to men possess a sexuality which is more complex, more intense, more extended in time, involving higher investment, risks, and psychosocial involvement.

In pro-choice feminism, a permissive, erotic view of sexuality is assumed to be the only option. Sexual intercourse with a variety of partners is seen as "inevitable" from a young age and as a positive growth experience to be managed by access to contraception and abortion. Unfortunately, the pervasive cultural conviction that adolescents, or their elders, cannot exercise sexual self-control, undermines the responsible use of contraception. When a pregnancy occurs, the first abortion is viewed in some pro-choice circles as a *rite de passage*. Responsibly choosing an abortion supposedly ensures that a young woman will take charge of her own life, make her own decisions, and carefully practice contraception. But the social dynamics of a permissive, erotic model of sexuality, coupled with permissive laws, work toward repeat abortions. Instead of being empowered by their abortion choices, young women having abortions are confronting the debilitating reality of *not* bringing a baby into the world; *not* being able to count on a committed male partner; *not* accounting oneself strong enough, or the master of enough resources, to avoid killing the fetus. Young women are hardly going to develop the self-esteem, self-discipline, and self-confidence necessary to confront a male-dominated society through abortion.

The male-oriented sexual orientation has been harmful to women and children. It has helped bring us epidemics of venereal disease, infertility, pornography, sexual abuse, adolescent pregnancy, divorce, displaced older women, and abortion. Will these signals of something amiss stimulate pro-choice feminists to rethink what kind of sex ideal really serves women's best interests? While the erotic model cannot encompass commitment, the committed model can—happily—encompass and encourage romance, passion, and playfulness. In fact, within the security of long-term commitments, women may be more likely to experience sexual pleasure and fulfillment . . .

The pro-life feminist position is not a return to the old feminine mystique. That espousal of "the eternal feminine" erred by viewing sexuality as so sacred that it cannot be humanly shaped at all. Woman's *whole* nature was supposed to be opposite to man's, necessitating complementary and radically different social roles. Followed to its logical conclusion, such a view presumes that reproductive and sexual experience is necessary for human fulfillment. But as the early feminists insisted, no woman has to marry or engage in sexual intercourse to be fulfilled, nor does a woman have to give birth and raise children to be complete, nor must she stay home and function as an earth mother. But female sexuality does need to be deeply respected as a unique potential and trust. Since most contraceptives and sterilization procedures really do involve only the woman's body rather than destroying new life, they can be an acceptable and responsible moral option . . .

New feminist efforts to rethink the meaning of sexuality, femininity, and reproduction are all the more vital as new techniques for artificial reproduction, surrogate motherhood, and the like present a whole new set of dilemmas. In the long run, the very long run, the abortion debate may be merely the opening round in a series of far-reaching struggles over the role of human sexuality and the ethics of reproduction. Significant changes in the culture, both positive and negative in outcome, may begin as local storms of controversy. We may be at one of those vaguely realized thresholds when we had best come to full attention. What kind of people are we going to be? Pro-life feminists pursue a vision for their sisters, daughters, and granddaughters. Will their great-granddaughters be grateful?

5. Gilbert Meilaender, "Euthanasia and Christian Vision"

Gilbert Meilaender is the Richard and Phyllis Duesenberg Professor of Christian Ethics at Valparaiso University in Indiana. His areas of specialization include theological ethics (working especially with the Lutheran tradition) and bioethics. He serves as a member of the President's Council of Bioethics and is a fellow of the Hastings Center. Meilaender's books on bioethics include Body, Soul, and Bioethics (1995) and Bioethics: A Primer for Christians (1997).

Every[26] teacher has probably experienced, along with countless frustrations, moments in the classroom when something was said with perfect lucidity. I still recall one such moment three years ago when I was teaching a seminar dealing with ethical issues in death and dying. Knowing how difficult it can be to get students to consider these problems from within religious perspectives, I decided to force the issue at the outset by assigning as the first reading parts of those magnificent sections from Volume III/4 of Karl Barth's

---

[26] First published as "Euthanasia and Christian Vision," *Thought* [Fordham University] 57 (1982) 465–75. Copyright © 1982; reprinted by permission of Gilbert Meilaender.

Church Dogmatics in which he discusses "Respect for Life" and "The Protection of Life." I gave the students little warning in advance, preferring to let the vigor and bombast of Barth's style have whatever effect it might . . .

One young woman in the class, seeking to explain why Barth puzzled her so, put it quite simply: "What I really don't like about him is that he seems to think our lives are not our own." To which, after a moment of awed silence, I could only respond: "If you begin to see that about Barth, even if it gets under your skin and offends you deeply, then indeed you have begun to understand what he is saying."

In his discussion of "The Protection of Life," and, in fact, within his specific discussion of euthanasia, Barth notes many of the difficult questions we might raise which seem to nudge us in the direction of approving euthanasia in certain tormenting cases. And then, rejecting these "tempting questions," he responds with his own typical flair. "All honour to the well-meaning humanitarianism of underlying motive! The derivation is obviously from another book that which we have thus far consulted."[27] In this essay I want to think about euthanasia not from the perspective of any "well-meaning humanitarianism" but from within the parameters of Christian belief—though, as we will see, one of the most important things to note is that, within those parameters, only what is consonant with Christian belief can be truly humane.

The Paradigm Case

Determining what really qualifies as euthanasia is easy no matter. Need the person "euthanatized" be suffering terribly? Or, at least, be near death? Suppose the person simply feels life is no longer worth living in a particular condition which may be deeply dissatisfying though not filled with suffering? Suppose the person's life is filled with suffering or seemingly devoid of meaning but he [or she] is unable to request euthanasia (because of a comatose condition, senility, etc,)? Or suppose the person is suffering greatly but steadfastly says [she or] he does not want to die? Suppose the euthanatizer's motive is not mercy but despair at the continued burden of caring for the person—will that qualify?

The list of questions needing clarification is endless once we start down this path. But I intend to get off the path at once by taking as our focus of attention a kind of paradigm case of what must surely count as euthanasia. If we can understand why *this* is morally wrong, much else will fall into place. James Rachels has suggested that "the clearest possible case euthanasia" would be one having the following features:[28]

---

[27] Karl Barth, *Church Dogmatics,* vol. 3.4, ed. G. W. Bromiley and T. F. Torrance (Edinburgh: T&T Clark, 1961) 425.

[28] James Rachels, "Euthanasia," *Matters of Life and Death: New Introductory Essays in Moral Philosophy,* ed. Tom Regan (New York: Random House, 1980) 29.

(1) The person is deliberately killed.
(2) The person would have died soon anyway.
(3) The person was suffering terrible pain.
(4) The person asked to be killed.
(5) The motive of the killing was mercy—to provide the person with as good a death as possible the circumstances.

Such a case is not simply "assisted suicide," since the case requires the presence of great suffering, imminence of death in any case, and a motive of mercy. Furthermore, considering this sort of case sets aside arguments about nonvoluntary and involuntary euthanasia and gives focus to our discussion.[29] If this case of voluntary euthanasia is permissible, other cases may also be (or may not). If this case itself morally wrong, we are less likely to be able to argue for euthanasia in nonvoluntary and involuntary circumstances.

Aim and Result

One way of arguing that the paradigm case of euthanasia is morally permissible (perhaps even obligatory) is to claim that it does not differ in morally relevant ways from other acts which most of us approve. Consider a patient whose death is imminent, who is suffering terribly, and who may suddenly stop breathing and require resuscitation. We may think it best not to resuscitate such a person but simply to let [that person] die. What could be the morally significant difference between such a "letting die" and simply giving this person a lethal injection which would have ended his [or her] life (and suffering) just as quickly? If it is morally right not to prolong [her or] his dying when [she or] he ceases breathing for a few moments, why is it morally wrong to kill him [or her] quickly and painlessly? Each act responds to the fact that death is imminent and recognizes that terrible suffering calls for relief. And the result in each case is the same: death.

In order to appreciate the important difference between these possibilities we must distinguish what we aim at in our action from the result of the action . . . This is a distinction which moral reflection can scarcely get along without. For example, if we fail to distinguish between aim and result we will be unable to see any difference between the self-sacrifice of a martyr and the suicide of a person weary of life. The result is the same for each: death. But the aim or purpose is quite different. Whereas the suicide aims at . . . death, the martyr aims at faithfulness to God (or loyalty of some other sort). Both martyr and suicide recognize in advance that the result of [the] choice and act will be death. But the martyr does not aim at death.

---

[29] Nonvoluntary euthanasia occurs when the person euthanatized is in a condition which makes it impossible for him [or her] to express a wish (e.g., senile, comatose). Involuntary euthanasia occurs when the person euthanatized expresses a desire *not* to be killed but is nevertheless euthanatized.

This distinction between aim and result is also helpful in explaining the moral difference between euthanatizing a suffering person near death and simply letting such a person die. Suppose this patient were to stop breathing, we were to reject the possibility of resuscitation, and then the person were suddenly to begin breathing again. Would we, simply because we had been willing to let this patient die, now proceed to smother [the person] so that [she or] he would indeed die? Hardly. And the fact that we would not indicates that we did not aim at his [or her] death (in rejecting resuscitation), though his [or her] death could have been one result of what we did aim at (namely, proper care for him [or her] in his dying). By contrast, if we euthanatized such a person by giving . . . a lethal injection, we would indeed aim at . . . death; we would invest the act of aiming at [the person's] death with the personal involvement of our purpose.

A rejoinder: It is possible to grant the distinction between aim and result while still claiming that euthanasia in our paradigm case would be permissible (or obligatory). It may be true that there is a difference between allowing a patient to die and aiming at someone's death. But if the suffering of the dying person is truly intense and the person requests death, on what grounds could we refuse to assist [the person]? If we refuse on the grounds that it would be wrong for us to aim at [her or] his death (which will certainly result soon anyway after more terrible suffering), are we not saying that we are unwilling to do [her or] him a great good if doing it requires that we dirty our hands in any way? To put the matter this way makes it seem that our real concern is with our own moral rectitude, not with the needs of the sufferer. It seems that we are so concerned about ourselves that in our eagerness to narrow the scope of our moral responsibility we have lost sight of the need and imperative to offer care.

This is, it should be obvious, what ethicists call a *consequentialist* rejoinder. It suggests that the good results (relieving the suffering) are sufficiently weighty to make the aim (of killing) morally permissible or obligatory. And, as far as I can tell, this rejoinder has become increasingly persuasive to large numbers of people.

Consequentialism may be described as that moral theory which holds that from the fact that some state of affairs *ought to be* it follows that we *ought to do* whatever is necessary to bring about that state of affairs. And, although teleological theories of morality are very ancient, consequentialism as a full-blown moral theory is traceable largely to Bentham and Mill[30] in the late 18th and early 19th centuries. To remember this is instructive, since it is not implausible to suggest that such a moral theory would be most persuasive when Christendom had, in large measure, ceased to be Christian. Those who know themselves

---

[30] Editors' note: Jeremy Bentham (1748–1832) and John Stuart Mill (1806–1873) founded the philosophical school called Utilitarianism. According to this theory, actions are considered right or wrong by their consequences, that is, the degree to which they produce the greatest happiness for the greatest number.

as creatures—not Creator—will recognize limits even upon their obligation to do good. As creatures we are to do all the good we can, but this means all the good we "morally can"—all the good we can within certain limits. It may be that the Creator *ought to do* whatever is necessary to bring about states of affairs which *ought to be,* but we stand under no such godlike imperative.

One of the best ways to understand the remarkable appeal today of consequentialism as a moral theory is to see it as an ethic for those who (a) remain morally serious, but (b) have ceased to believe in a God whose providential care will ultimately bring about whatever ought to be the case. If God is not there to accomplish what ought to be the case, we are the most likely candidates to shoulder the burden of that responsibility.[31] Conversely, it may be that we can make sense of distinguishing between two acts whose *result* is the same but whose *aim* is different only if we believe that our responsibilities (as creatures) are limited—that the responsibility for achieving certain results has been taken out of our hands (or, better, never given us in the first place). It ought to be the case that dying people not suffer terribly (indeed, that they not die). But, at least for Christians, it does not follow from that "ought to be" that we "ought to do" whatever is necessary—even euthanasia—to relieve them of that suffering.[32]

---

[31] Whether this enlargement of the scope of our responsibility really works is another matter. Being responsible for everything may, for human beings, come quite close to being responsible for nothing. Charles Fried comments: "If, as consequentialism holds, we were indeed equally morally responsible for an infinite radiation of concentric circles originating from the center point of some action, then while it might look as if we were enlarging the scope of human responsibility and thus the significance of personality, the enlargement would be greater than we could support . . . Total undifferentiated responsibility is the correlative of the morally overwhelming, undifferentiated plasma of happiness or pleasure." *Right and Wrong* (Cambridge, Mass.: Harvard University Press, 1978) 34f.

[32] It is a hard, perhaps unanswerable, question whether there might ever be exceptions to this general standard for Christian conduct which I have enunciated. There might be a circumstance in which the pain of the sufferer was so terrible and unconquerable that one would want to consider an exception. To grant this possibility is not really to undermine the principle since, as Charles Fried has noted, the catastrophic "is a distinct moral concept, identifying an extreme situation in which the usual rules of morality do not apply [Fried, *Right and Wrong,* 10]. We would be quite mistaken to build the whole of our morality on the basis of the catastrophic; in fact, it would then become the norm rather than the exception. One possible way to deal with such extreme circumstances without simply lapsing into consequentialism is to reason in a way analogous to Michael Walzer's reasoning about the rules of war in *Just and Unjust Wars* (New York: Basic Books, 1977). Walzer maintains that the rules of war are binding even when they put us at a disadvantage, even when they may cost us victory. But he grants that there might be "extreme emergencies" in which we could break the rules; namely, when doing so was (a) morally necessary (i.e., the opponent was so evil—a Hitler—that it was morally imperative to defeat him) and (b) strategically necessary (no other way than violating the rules of war was available for defeating this opponent). Reasoning in an analogous way we might wonder whether the rule prohibiting euthanasia could be violated if (a) the suffering was so unbearable that the sufferer lost all capacity to bear that suffering with any sense of moral purpose or faithfulness to God; and (b) the pain was truly unconquerable. Whether such extreme circumstances ever occur is a question whose answer I cannot give. And even if such circumstances are possible, I remain uncertain about the force of this "thought experiment," which is offered tentatively.

We are now in a position to see something important about the argument which claims that euthanasia (in the paradigm case) is permissible because it does not differ morally from cases of "letting die" which most of us approve. This argument often begins in a failure to distinguish aim and result; however, it is, as we have seen, difficult for moral theory to get along without this distinction. Seeing this, we recognize that the argument really becomes a claim that if the results are sufficiently good, any aim necessary to achieve them is permissible. And precisely at this turn in the argument it may be difficult to keep "religion" and "morality" in those neat and separate compartments we have fashioned for them. At this point one steeped in Christian thought and committed to Christian life may wish to say with Barth: All honor to the well-meaning humanitarianism—and it is well-meaning. But the derivation—fit only for those who would, even if reluctantly, be "like God"—is obviously "derived from another book" than that which Christians are wont to consult.

Aim and Motive

If the distinction between aim and result makes it difficult to justify euthanasia in the paradigm case, another distinction may be more useful. We might suggest that the act of euthanatizing be redescribed in terms of the motive of mercy. We could describe the act not as killing but as relieving suffering. Or, rather than engaging in such wholesale redescription of the act, we might simply argue that our moral evaluation of the act cannot depend solely on its aim but must also consider its motive.

Consider the following illustration.[33] A condemned prisoner is in his cell only minutes before his scheduled execution. As he sits in fear and anguish, certain of his doom, another man who has managed to sneak into the prison shoots and kills him. This man is either (a) the father of children murdered by the prisoner, or (b) a close friend of the prisoner. In case (a) he shoots because he will not be satisfied simply to have the man executed. He desires that his own hand should bring about the prisoner's death. In case (b) the friend shoots because he wishes to spare his friend the terror and anguish of those last minutes, to deliver him from the indignity of the sheer animal fright he is undergoing.

Would it be proper to describe the father's act in (a) as an act of killing and the friend's in (b) as an act of relieving suffering? Although many people may be tempted to do so, it muddies rather than clarifies our analysis. If anything is clear in these cases, it is that both the vengeful father and the compassionate friend *aim* to kill though their *motives* are very different. Only by refusing to redescribe the aim of the act in terms of its motive do we keep the moral issue clearly before us. That issue is whether our moral evaluation of the act

---

[33] This illustration is "inspired" by a different set of hypothetical cases offered by Paul Ramsey in "Some Rejoinders," *The Journal of Religious Ethics* 4 (1976) 204.

should depend solely on the agent's *aim* or whether that evaluation must also include the *motive*.

That the motive makes some difference almost everyone would agree. Few of us would be content to analyze the two cases simply as instances of "aiming to kill" without considering the quite different motives. The important question, however, is whether the praiseworthy motive of relieving suffering should so dominate our moral reflection that it leads us to term the act "right." I want to suggest that it should not, at least not within the parameters of Christian belief.

One might think that Christian emphasis on the overriding importance of love as a motive would suggest that whatever was done out of love was right. And, to be sure, Christians will often talk this way. Such talk, however, must be done against the background assumptions of Christian anthropology. Apart from that background of meaning we may doubt whether we have really understood the motive of love correctly. We need therefore to sketch in the background against which we can properly understand what loving care for a suffering person should be.[34]

Barth writes that human life "must always be regarded as a divine act of trust."[35] This means that all human life is "surrounded by a particular solemnity," which, if recognized, will lead us to "treat it with respect." At the same time, however, "life is no second God, and therefore the respect due to it cannot rival the reverence owed to God." One who knows this will seek to live life "within its appointed limits." Recognizing our life as a trust, we will be moved not by an "absolute will to live" but a will to live within these limits. Hence, when we understand ourselves as creatures, we will both value God's gift of life and recognize that the Giver himself constitutes the limit beyond which we ought not value the gift. "Temporal life is certainly not the highest of all goods. Just because it belongs to God, [humans] may be forbidden to will its continuation at all costs." And at the same time, "if life is not the highest possession, then it is at least the highest and all-inclusive price" which human beings can pay. In short, life is a great good, but not the greatest (which is fidelity to God).

Death, the final enemy of life, must also be understood dialectically. The human mind can take and has quite naturally taken two equally plausible attitudes toward death.[36] We can regard death as of no consequence, heeding the Epicurean maxim that while we are alive death is not yet here, and when death is here we are no more. Thus the human being, in a majestic transcendence of

---

[34] In what follows I draw upon my own formulations in previous articles: "The Distinction between Killing and Allowing to Die," *Theological Studies* 37 (1976), 467–70, and "Lutheran Theology and Bioethics: A Juxtaposition," *SPC Journal* 3 (1980) 25–30.

[35] The passages cited in this paragraph may be found scattered throughout pages 336–42 and pages 401–2 of vol. 3.4 of *Church Dogmatics*.

[36] For what follows cf. C. S. Lewis, *Miracles* (New York: Macmillan, 1947) 129ff., and Paul Ramsey, *The Patient as Person* (New Haven, Conn. and London: Yale University Press, 1970) 144ff.

the limits of earthly life, might seek to soar beyond the limits of finitude and find his [or her] good elsewhere. If death is of no consequence, we may seek it in exchange for some important good. Equally natural to the human mind is a seemingly opposite view that death is the *summum malum,* the greatest evil to be avoided at all costs. Such a view, finding good only in earthly life, can find none in suffering and death.

The Christian mind, however, transcending what is "natural" and correcting it in light of the book it is accustomed to consult, has refused to take either of these quite plausible directions. Understood within the biblical narrative, death is an ambivalent phenomenon—too ambivalent to be seen only as the greatest of all evils, or as indifferent. Since the world narrated by the Bible begins in God and moves toward God, earthly life is [one's] trust to be sustained faithfully and [one's] gift to be valued and cared for. When life is seen from this perspective, we cannot say that death and suffering are of no consequence; on the contrary, we can even say with Barth that the human task in the face of suffering and death is not to accept but to offer "final resistance."[37] It is just as true, however, that death could never be the greatest evil. That title must be reserved for disobedience to and disbelief in God—a refusal to live within our appointed limits. So we can also repeat with Barth that "life is no second God."[38] We remember, after all, that Jesus goes to the cross in the name of obedience to his Father. We need not glorify or seek suffering, but we must be struck by the fact that a human being who is a willing sufferer stands squarely in the center of Christian piety. Jesus bears his suffering not because it is desirable but because the Father allots it to him within the limits of his earthly life. Death is—there is no way to put the matter simply—a great evil which God can turn to [God's] good purposes. It is an evil which must ordinarily be resisted but which must also at some point be acknowledged. We can and ought to acknowledge what we do not and ought not seek . . .

This vision of the world, and of the meaning of life and death, has within Christendom given guidance to those reflecting on human suffering and dying. That moral guidance has amounted to the twofold proposition that, though we might properly cease to oppose death while aiming at other choiceworthy goods in life (hence, the possibility of martyrdom), we ought never aim at death as either our end or our means.

Against this background of belief we can better understand what *love* and *care* must be within a world construed in Christian terms. In this world no action which deliberately hastens death can be called "love." Not because the euthanatizer need have any evil motive. Indeed, as the case of the compassionate friend makes clear, the one who hastens death may seem to have a praiseworthy motive. Rather, such action cannot be loving because it cannot be part of the

[37] Barth, *Church Dogmatics,* 3.4, 368.
[38] Ibid., 342.

meaning of commitment to the well-being of another human being within the appointed limits of earthly life. The benevolence of the euthanatizer is enough like love to give us pause, to tempt us to call it love. And perhaps it may even be the closest those who feel themselves to bear full responsibility for relief of suffering and production of good in our world can come to love. But it is not the creaturely love which Christians praise, a love which can sometimes do no more than suffer as best we can with the sufferer.

Christian Love Enacted and Inculcated

Against this background—a background which pours meaning into words like "love" and "care"—we can contemplate the kind of case often considered in discussions of euthanasia. A person may be in severe pain, certain to die within only a few days. Most of us would agree that further "lifesaving" treatments were not in order for such a person, that they would do no more than prolong [her or] his dying. Why, one may ask, do we not subject such a patient to useless treatments? Because, we reply, [she or] he is in agony and it would be wrong to prolong that agony needlessly. But now, if we face the facts honestly, we will admit that it takes this patient longer to die—and prolongs [her or] his suffering— if we simply withhold treatment than if we euthanatize [the patient]. Hence, there seems to be a contradiction within our reasoning. The motive for withholding treatment was a humanitarian one: relief of suffering. But in refusing to take the next step and euthanatize the patient we prolong [her or] his suffering and, thereby, belie our original motive. Hence the conclusion follows, quite contrary to the moral guidance embedded in the Christian vision of the world: Either we should keep this person alive as long as possible (and not pretend that our motive is the relief of suffering), or we should be willing to euthanatize [her or] him.

The argument gets much of its force from the seeming simplicity of the dilemma, but that simplicity is misleading. For, at least for Christian vision, the fundamental imperative is not "minimize suffering" but "maximize love and care." In that Christian world, in which death and suffering are great evils but not the greatest evil, love can never include in its meaning hastening a fellow human being toward (the evil of) death, nor can it mean a refusal to acknowledge death when it comes (as an evil but not the greatest evil). We can only know what the imperative "maximize love" means if we understand it against the background assumptions which make intelligible for Christians words like "love" and "care." The Christian mind has certainly not recommended that we seek suffering or call it an unqualified good, but it is an evil which, when endured faithfully, can be redemptive . . .

I suggested above that we should not redescribe the *aim* of an act in terms of its *motive*. (We should not say that an act of killing a suffering person was simply an act of relieving suffering. We should say rather that we aimed at the death of the person in order to relieve [the] suffering. This keeps the moral issue more clearly before us.) But by now it will be evident that I have in fact gone some way toward redescribing the *motive* of the act in terms of its *aim*. (If the act is aimed at hastening the death of the suffering person, we should not see it as motivated by love.) Is this any better? The answer, I think, is "it depends."

It would not be better, it might even be worse, if my purpose were to deny any humanitarian motive to the person tempted to euthanatize a sufferer. Few people would find such a denial persuasive, and because we would not, we are tempted to turn in the opposite direction and describe the act's aim in terms of its motive. We do recognize a difference between the vengeful father and the compassionate friend even though both aim to kill the condemned prisoner, and we want our moral judgments to be sufficiently nuanced to take account of these differences. The simple truth is that our evaluation of the act (described in terms of aim) and our evaluation of the act (described in terms of motive) often fall apart. In a world broken by sin and its consequences this should perhaps come as no surprise. Christians believe that we sinners—all of us—are not whole, and many of the stubborn problems of systematic ethical reflection testify to the truth of that belief. It is our lack of wholeness which is displayed in our inability to arrive at one judgment (or even one description) "whole and entire" of a single act. We find ourselves in a world in which people may sometimes seem to aim at doing evil from the best of motives (and think they must do so). And then we are tempted to elide aim and motive and call that evil at which they aim "good."

No amount of ethical reflection can heal this rift in our nature. From that predicament we will have to look for a deliverance greater than ethics can offer. However, here and now, in our broken world, we do better to take the aim of an act as our guiding light in describing and evaluating the act—and then evaluate the motive in light of this aim. This is better because moral reflection is not primarily a tool for fixing guilt and responsibility (in which case motive comes to the fore). It is, first and foremost, one of the ways in which we train ourselves and others to see the world rightly. We would be wrong to assert that no euthanatizer has or can have a humanitarian motive. But if we want not so much to fix praise or blame but to teach the meaning of the word "love," we are not wrong to say that love could never euthanatize. In the Christian world this is true. And in that world we know the right name for our own tendency to call those other, seemingly humanitarian, motives "love." The name for that tendency is *temptation*. We are being tempted to be "like God" [see Gen 3:5] when we toy with the possibility of defining our love— and the meaning of humanity— apart from the appointed limits of human life.

To redescribe the motive in terms of the act's aim, to attempt to *inculcate* a vision of the world in which love could never euthanatize, is therefore not only a permissible but necessary for Christians. It is the only proper way to respond to the supposed dilemmas we are confronted with by reasoning which brackets Christian background assumptions from the outset. The Christian moral stance which emerges here is not a club with which to beat over the head those who disagree. It does not provide a superior vantage point from which to deny them any humanitarian motive in the ordinary sense. But it is a vision of what "humanity" and "humanitarian motives" should be. We may therefore say of those who disagree: "All honour to the well-meaning human-itarianism of underlying motive! But the derivation is obviously from another book than that which we have thus far consulted."

Scripture Index

Index of Persons and Subjects